Greenhill Books

On the Napoleonic Wars

UNIVERSITY OF OXFORD

THIS is to certify that it appears by the Register of the Ancient House of Congregation of Doctors and Regent Masters of the University of Oxford that

David Geoffrey Chandler

Keble College

after having satisfied all the conditions prescribed in that respect by the Statutes of the University, was on the **thirtieth** *day of* **November 1991** *duly admitted to the degree of*

Doctor of Letters

As witness my hand this **thirtieth** *day of* **November 1991.**

Assistant Registrar

On the Napoleonic Wars

COLLECTED ESSAYS

Dr David G. Chandler,
D.Litt

Greenhill Books, London
Stackpole Books, Pennsylvania

DEDICATED TO
MY FRIENDS AND COLLEAGUES
IN MILITARY HISTORY AND WAR STUDIES
AT R.M.A. SANDHURST 1960–1994:
THE 'OLD, MIDDLE AND YOUNG GUARDS'.

On The Napoleonic Wars
first published 1994 by Greenhill Books,
Lionel Leventhal Limited, Park House, 1 Russell Gardens,
London NW11 9NN
and
Stackpole Books, 5067 Ritter Road, Mechanicsburg, PA 17055, USA.

© David G. Chandler, 1994

British Library Cataloguing in Publication Data
Chandler, David
On the Napoleonic Wars: Collected Essays
by David Chandler
I. Title
940.2

ISBN 1–85367–158–4

Library of Congress Cataloging-in-Publication Data
On the napoleonic wars : collected essays / by David G. Chandler.
p.   cm
Includes bibliographical references.
ISBN 1–85367–158–4
1. Napoleon I, Emperor of the French, 1769–1821—Military
leadership.   2. France—History, Military—1789–1815.   3. Military
art and science—Europe—History.   4.Napoleonic Wars, 1800–1815—
Campaigns.   5. Wellington, Arthur Wellesley, Duke of, 1769–1852—
Military leadership.   I. Title.
DC203.9.C454   1994
944.05—dc20   93–32339
                                              CIP

Typeset by DP Photosetting, Aylesbury, Bucks
Printed in England by Clays Ltd, St Ives plc

CONTENTS

LIST OF MAPS AND DIAGRAMS

ACKNOWLEDGEMENTS

O ver more years than I care to recall I have become indebted to a large number of people – many still with us but others, alas, no longer so – for my development (for better or for worse) into a military historian. My late father, the Rev. G.E. Chandler, provided the initial spark, which was fanned into a flame by two teachers and one don, C. Tutton, H. Wylie, and C.T. Atkinson respectively; but possibly it was a fellow-undergraduate at Keble College, J.R. Selby, who, as a second year historian with his Finals ahead, persuaded me to take over the College magazine in 1953 (the now long-defunct *Clocktower*), and thus precipitated me into writing (if only for local consumption) in order to fill the gaps as printer's deadlines and unfulfilled contribution crises loomed. I must also mention another contemporary, James Martin, who inhabited the rooms across the corridor from mine, shared many a late-night cup of coffee and allowed himself to be cajoled into joining my editorial board. A mathematician, he went on to become a renowned author by writing the first *intelligible* computer manuals. At the Oxford *Encaenia* in 1993, a new chair bearing his name was announced.

I also received much encouragement while up at Oxford from Professor J.S. Bromley, late of Southampton University, not to forget the Keble College Dean of that early-1950s era, Dr. F.D. Price. But of course the influence of Brigadier Peter Young, my precedessor but one in the post I recently relinquished at the Royal Military Academy Sandhurst, was also of the greatest significance not only to myself but to a whole generation of 'young' military historians in the 1960s. Needless to say, I also owe much to all my Sandhurst friends over the past $33^1/_2$ years, and to such notable military historians as Sir Michael Howard, Professors Bob O'Neill and Brian Bond and all members past and present of the British Commission for Military History – not to forget my American friends too numerous to mention.

Brigadier Young's encouragement was fortunately matched by a number of editors and publishers who proved willing to take a risk on me. Alan Hodge of *History Today* accepted my first articles. My first publisher was Hugh Street of

7

Hugh Evelyn, who invited me in 1962 to contribute a volume (it turned out to be a pair) to his series of *Traveller's Guides*. My next patron was Peter Ritner of the Macmillan Company of New York, who commissioned the *Campaigns of Napoleon* in 1963. Then in 1965 Sam Carr of Batsford encouraged me to write in my other main field – the Marlburian era. Rather more recently my good friends Charlie Smith, president of Simon and Schuster's Academic Reference Division in New York, and nearer to home Rod Dymott of Arms and Armour Press (Cassell) and most especially Lionel Leventhal of Greenhill Books, have given me much time and practical advice that I have never regretted taking.

I would like to mention some of the usually unsung heroines of the type-writer and the word-processor who deserve my grateful thanks. My cousin Miss Pat Deans and Miss P.C. McGlinchy head the list, having provided me with an efficient service dating back to the 1960s. Many others later proved equally helpful – including most recently Mrs. Jenny Toyne Sewell (despite the many calls upon her time at Government House), Maureen Stanyard and Chris MacLennan, who have all three proved stalwarts in deciphering my not very easy handwriting which has, alas, deteriorated over the years. Others who have helped me include Denyse Marples, Myra Wright, Margaret Ward, Janet Donaldson and Jan Ingram. Then there have been the cartographers who have made fine maps and diagrams out of my rough designs – Colonel R.W.S. Norfolk, OBE, DL, Sheila Waters, Arthur Banks, Richard and Hazel Watson, Stephen Maison and Keith Chaffer. Publishers' editorial assistants too numerous to list have also given me much invaluable aid, and Kate Ryle (who has helped me with this present book) must here stand for them all. Lastly, I mention my loyal and forbearing wife Gill, for many years my part-time indexer and research assistant. To one and all I proffer my heartfelt thanks.

In conclusion I wish to acknowledge a number of people who have kindly given permission for the reproduction of the articles and chapters which have gone to make this book. Gordon Marsden of *History Today* must assuredly head the list, for giving me leave to reproduce no less than five articles (the first two of them, moreover, in two parts each) which have appeared in its pages: namely Chapters Three (1962), Four (1967), Eight (1974) and Eleven (1970), not to forget the Preface (December 1985). The Macmillan Publishing Company of New York agreed to my reproducing the Introduction to *Napoleon's Marshals* (1987), which now stands as Chapter Five. My friend, Robert Cowley, of the enterprising *Military History Quarterly*, granted leave for me to reuse 'Austerlitz' in Chapter Six. Maggie Calmels of Marshall Cavendish Partworks Limited permitted me to reproduce Chapters Twelve and Thirteen, first published in *History Makers* (1969 and 1970). Gérard Turbé of the new, superb French journal *Samothrace* kindly permitted me to use as Chapter Two the English version of my article for him (1993). For permission to reprint the Introduction and part of the Edward Healey Journal as Chapter Fourteen (first published in two parts in 1986) from the *Journal of the Society for Army Historical Research*, I thank Michael Cane, the retiring editor. Lastly Bob Snibbe, founder of the *Napoleonic Society of America* and its *Member's Bulletin*, released 'Napoleon the Man' for the Epilogue.

The remaining six subjects – namely Chapters One, Seven, Nine, Ten, Fifteen and Sixteen – were given as papers to various audiences over the years, but have never been publicly published. The dates and places are indicated in the chapter introductions concerned.

David G. Chandler
15 January 1994

AUTHOR'S NOTE

Textual references to quotations have been omitted. However, a Bibliography has been appended at the end of the volume, divided between the chapters, and in the Acknowledgements and individual chapter introductions information will be found giving details of where and when each chapter originally appeared or was given as a lecture. As the Bibliography is intended as a practical guide, references to documentary sources have been kept to a minimum.

The text has been arranged in chronological order, heedless of dates of original writing.

General Introduction

When I consider that almost thirty-four years have passed since I first began to lecture at the Royal Military Academy Sandhurst (4 July 1960), I find it very hard to believe. Now that it has become my time to retire – and launch myself into the new activities of a 'second career' – it has been a very pleasant gesture on the part of my friend of almost as long, the publisher Lionel Leventhal, to suggest that a volume might be made of sundry articles I have written on the Napoleonic period over the years. Such a 'salute' does not come at the end of every historian's career or mark all sixtieth birthdays, and it pleases me a great deal to think that some of my *incunabula* – 'random jottings' if you prefer – will in this way be made available to present and some future generations of the vast Napoleonic readership who will not have had the chance to read them.

I have often been asked when and how one becomes identifiable as a military historian, and as my publisher is encouraging me to employ this introduction as a kind of *apologia pro vita mea* – or Memoir – perhaps I may address that subject here. Doubtless everybody in the category of 'harmless drudge' (to borrow Dr Johnson's description of himself as a lexicographer) has his own tale to tell, but for what it is worth the following has been my experience. 'Mighty oaks from tiny acorns grow', as the old saying has it. Everything began, appropriately enough perhaps, in 1939, 'the year war broke out', to quote the signature-patter of a now long-dead radio comedian of the time, when I was all of five years old. My first interest was not, curiously enough, anything to do with the outbreak of the Second World War that September, at least not in any obvious way, but only in an indirect sense. My late father was a Church of England clergyman in the Holderness seaside town of Withernsea (East Yorkshire) at the time. One evening he had to make a call to see the rector of Patrington nearby. My mother being away at the time, and the maid having left us to do factory war-work (for the unheard of pay of £5 a week), my father decided he would have to take me along with him. To keep me quiet, he on a whim bought me at the local W.H. Woolworth's a paperbook book entitled *The History of Britain told in Pictures* costing all of one shilling (5p.) – which was a bit steep as Woolworth's still prided itself as the 'threepenny and sixpenny store'.

Arrived in Patrington, I was left in the old Armstrong Siddeley car parked in the driveway (the rector being a confirmed bachelor not too fond of having children in his drawing-room) while father proceeded to Mr Holt on his own. I must have been small, for I clearly recall kneeling down between the front and back seats using the leather banquette as a book-rest. One picture from the start simply enthralled me: a cut-away drawing of a medieval castle, showing the Great Hall, the upstairs dormitory, the tilt-yard, the guard-room near the drawbridge etc. I returned to this picture time and again. I suppose it should have made me into a potential military architect or (after a long time delay) into a 'Dungeons and Dragons' game addict, but instead it drew my attention to military history for the first time – not that I was in any way aware of what this might lead to in later life.

Most boys growing up during the Second World War could not but become fascinated by what was going on around them, however dimly understood. I can remember a Highland Regiment – the Camerons I think – attending morning service at St Matthew's Church, Owthorne, shortly after Dunkirk during that 'Invasion Summer of 1940', all with their rifles which were stacked along the aisles. Then there were the occasional army exercises – long lines of vehicles halting along Hull Road outside the vicarage before spreading their 'scrim' camouflage nets: I can still hear the whistle and chatter of radio sets, the crisp sending and acknowledgement of orders. Once, thrill of thrills, there was a whole regiment of self-propelled guns parked all the way down both Queen and Bannister Streets. There were guns on the promenade, barbed-wire barricades, tank-blocks and pill-boxes along the cliffs and beaches, a searchlight battery on England's Hill and anti-aircraft guns near Queen Street South and Hollym Road – and numbers of houses near the sea-front pressed into becoming billets for soldiers. We had 'Support the Soldier', 'Build a Spitfire' and 'Buy War Bonds' weeks. There were occasional military band concerts, and weekly 'socials' for the troops in our Parish Hall which I was occasionally allowed to visit for an hour or two of fascinated observation; although allegedly I caught scarlet fever at one.

A road barrier was established on Hull Road manned by soldiers who slept in a bell-tent in Mr Stevenson's farmyard, and for a whole year I 'adopted' a Scots soldier called Frank; and many were the – for me – happy afternoons I spent pestering him while sharing his stints on sentry-go. I swear that rather later, in 1944, I saw a V1 flying-bomb (or 'Doodlebug') fly past our house towards Hull – presumably Heinkel or U-boat launched off the mouth of the River Humber – but I could be kidding myself, for memory can play strange tricks, as every military historian who has interviewed 'old soldiers' will know only too well.

There was, from time to time, a reminder that it was not all just fun. My father was often called out to comfort the bereaved families as the dreaded telegrams began to arrive. Then there was the time when one midday the SS *Canada* struck a mine a mile offshore, and the local rowing boats went out to bring back the survivors to the line of waiting ambulances. For some years the masts and funnel could still be seen at low-tide. Then there were the train-loads of evacuees from Hull. Our guest at the vicarage was Mr Harvey, a school-master, who tried to dig us an outdoor air-raid shelter until water was struck only two feet down. He then helped strengthen our understairs cupboard with steel plates – and this became our refuge when the sirens wailed their warning. I used to scribble pencil graffiti on the whitewashed walls – nasty things happening to 'fatty' Goering and even worse ones to Adolf Hitler. They were still there fifteen years ago when I took one of my sons to visit the house. Not quite as impressive as cave-paintings of prehistoric times or the relics preserved at Pompeii under the lava dust, perhaps, but still proof that 'young Chandler' had spent long nights there lying on his bunk scribbling away on the wall until the torch battery (very hard to replace and strictly rationed) began to grow dim, or my parents told me to turn it off and go to sleep. 'Don't you know there's a war on, boy?' Well, yes I did – in my own way.

And then there were the air-raids themselves. The up-and-down wailing of sirens sounding the alarm became a frequent feature of life. The very first I remember was a daytime alert while I was at Norfolk House School doing gym in St Nicholas's Parish Hall. The teacher – Miss Le Gassie (inevitably dubbed 'gas-bags') – had us all lie on the floor away from the windows criss-crossed with anti-splinter sticky tape. Nothing happened, and soon my father arrived to take me home. I was very proud, I remember, of his special blue armband with a white cross upon it and, in red, 'A.R.P.', which permitted him to drive during air-raids. I have it by me as I write. The more serious night raids came a year or so later. I remember listening to the straining engines of bomb-laden Heinkels passing overhead towards Hull, or the more even note of their lightened return heading for Germany or Norway – and the occasional higher note of a fighter, one of 'ours' we hoped, and more rarely the tearing-calico sound of machine-gun fire or the *crump-crump-crump* as the local battery of Bofors anti-aircraft guns opened up against a raider, doubtless illuminated by the searchlight battery on England's Hill – or, later, by the closely kept secret of radar. 'Giving them what-for. Serve 'em right!' We were not very charitable to raiders.

There were often less comforting bangs and crashes. The whistle and rumble of the Hull *blitz* seemed to go on hour after hour; and one early morning after the 'all-clear' (that welcome, clear, single siren-note) had sounded, my father took me outside to see the whole western horizon glowing flickering-red: Hull suffering its agony. Then a fighter flew past quite low, dropping two flares – white and blue – to identify itself to the AA gunners; that seemed very reas-suring. On another morning we found a large piece of *ack-ack* shrapnel which had pitted our front doorstep, to my mother's great annoyance. We never were hit directly, even when Withernsea became a German 'conscience target' and received more than its fair share of HE and incendiary-bombs. In due course the defences of Hull improved – I recall seeing the barrels of large 4.2in AA guns sticking out of their camouflaged concrete positions near Hedon on the outskirts of Hull during our occasional forays to the city to spend our clothes-coupons or seek for near-vanished luxuries in the department stores there. One, Thornton Varley's, was totally destroyed, as was the Hull museum and other public buildings. But our vicarage twice had single windows blown out by the strange tricks played by the blast of mercifully distant land-mines – the real damage-causers.

Land-mines arrived by parachute, with instantaneous detonation or delayed action fuses. Either way they left a vast crater and could cause great damage. Hilston church – some eight miles from Withernsea – was totally destroyed by one such mine. Incredibly, owing to the vagaries of blast and detonation noise, a farmer and his wife living alongside the churchyard heard literally *nothing*, nor did their farmhouse sustain anything but superficial damage. Next morning, the story runs, the farmer got out of bed and drew back the blackout curtains to make the classic Yorkshire remark: 'Ee, lass! T'church be gorn!' St Matthew's church was more fortunate, but on one cold morning in 1942 I remember seeing the tail-fin of a large unexploded incendiary bomb sticking out of the roof. Withernsea sustained considerable damage and quite a few casualties as German bombers, especially of the tip-and-run daylight variety, used our supposedly camouflaged large lighthouse as a navigational mark, and often felt they could turn for home, honour vindicated, if they just crossed the British coastline and dumped their bombs there: hence little Withernsea's repeated baptisms of fire.

My parents were determined that my education now needed to progress beyond Miss B.A. Haynes's Norfolk House School, and as the war in 1943 had passed its most menacing stage for inhabitants of the British Isles, it was decided, on the advice of our family doctor, Dr Fouracre (who had a son there himself), that I, aged nine-and-a-half, should go to Terrington Hall Preparatory School near Malton and Castle Howard in the North Riding of Yorkshire.

This held about fifty boys and was run by a staff of seven or eight. Other than the bachelor headmaster, who had a proclivity for beating boys slow in mathematics or bad at games (two groups I soon qualified to join), only two masters stand out clearly in my memory. One, Mr Sargeant ('old Sagittus' to the disrespectful), taught Latin by the 'shriek-and-clobber' method: we all feared him, but he forced into me a basic sense of Latin syntax and style which has since stood me in good stead as a writer. The second, Mr Charles Tutton, was loved and respected by all boys, and certainly encouraged in me my early regard for history. He had a mannerism of expelling air through pursed lips which we vainly tried to emulate, and bowled a particularly cunning 'googly' in nets. He soon advised my father that I should be encouraged by way of holiday reading to tackle a serious history book, and father (a 'War Degree' – 1915 – Oxford history graduate himself) settled me down to read Rudyard Kipling's *History of England*. This was interspersed with his well-known historical poems, including:

> Legate, I heard the news last night, my cohort's ordered home;
> By sea to Portus Itius, from thence by road to Rome.
> I've marched the companies aboard; the arms are stowed below
> Now let another take my sword. Command me not to go!
> I've served in England forty years...

How it all comes back fifty years later. How strange that the memory recalls so much learnt in youth, yet forgets something learned only yesterday. To Mr Tutton's memory I owe a considerable debt.

The war barely impinged on our school life, although memories of food rationing recall such horrors as scrambled dried-egg and fomenting rhubarb jam which made quite a few of us a bit tiddly. Occasionally an army exercise had us all at the windows as the troops fought down the road and through the school grounds. On D-Day I was in the sanatorium during a chicken-pox epidemic; the passage on to German soil brought Chris Wansey an envied parcel from his padre-uncle containing a tobacco-tin of grey German soil and a battered *Wehrmacht* gas-mask. VE Day was celebrated in style with a school full-day holiday and a sumptuous tea on the lawn amidst flags of all descriptions. VJ Day came during the summer holidays when I was again in bed with some mysterious glandular disease. I must have been a spotty, plague-ridden youth.

Terrington Hall brought me two special friends – Frank Butler and Christopher Wansey (both, alas, long since dead) – with whom I roamed the neighbouring Yorkshire countryside playing 'Robin Hood', bicycled to Amplethorpe School to be taken in by an exhibit in the museum there which bore a card reading 'Oliver Cromwell's skull as a boy', or devised complex earthern fortifications *à la* Uncle Toby and Corporal Trim of *Tristram Shandy* fame, in which we manoeuvred our prized toy soldiers in many a bloody battle. In Art I also preferred drawing and painting historical scenes, and shared with David Harrison an ambitious project to reproduce *The Bayeux Tapestry* in pastel (I think we got half-way, but, of course, did the battle scenes first). These were happy days – periodic summonses to the headmaster's study apart. I read my first C.S. Forester 'Hornblower' books, which I found incomparably better than Marryat or W.G. Kingston, or even Henty. Before I knew it, the time had come for Common Entrance, and although I missed a Foundation Scholarship I duly secured a place at Marlborough College.

Translated to Wiltshire and the Marlborough Downs in September 1948, I spent four formative years, in the process of which I took the very last School Certificate (securing 'Matric.') and the very first of the new-fangled 'A-Levels'. After Junior House A1, (all too obviously designed, like much of Marlborough College, by a Victorian prison-architect), I had the good fortune to be moved to Senior House C3: good luck in two senses; first, because it was housed in half an eighteenth-century posting-inn serving the Old Bath Road, and where the Earl of Chatham died in 1778, and therefore retained a certain graciousness of style, including a fine view over the Master's Garden from the window desks in the (then) Adderley Library which I much frequented in the senior forms; and secondly because it brought me as my house-master and History VIth form-master that truly remarkable man, H.P. Wylie.

Badly gassed in the First World War, Mr Wylie, a firm exponent of the 'Whig Tradition' as a life-long disciple of Professor Butterfield's views, including his firm belief in the steady progress of mankind (western, anyway) towards some ultimate near-perfect state, understandably had scant regard for military history. All wars to him were, of course, regrettable lapses and even reverses in the March of Progress, but yet he somehow bravely put up with a precocious youth who, in a fit of adolescent rebellion, set out to work-up as many difficult *military* questions as possible with which to torment him during History VIth form discussion periods. Deservedly, perhaps, I soon found myself 'hoist with my own petard' and even more fascinated with Military History. Hubert Wylie was soon aware of this, and for a prize I'd won selected C.V. Wedgwood's *Thirty Years' War* and A.G. Macdonnel's *Napoleon and his Marshals*. The latter book in particular did it. It may be pretty questionable history – but as a good read it has few equals, and from that moment I believe I became a potential military historian. Even more importantly, Hubert Wylie provided me with a firm basis of mid-17th and early-19th century historical knowledge, taught me how to weigh evidence and present arguments, and with much red-ink and comments such as *'T'cha, boy – this is a hopelessly purple passage. Rewrite...!'*, set about improving my writing style in which he early detected some ability for narrative and literary form.

Two more particularly benign influences at Marlborough require mention. The first was R.A.U. ('Jumbo') Jennings, house-master of Littlecote and teacher of classics, who presented me with a much-thumbed set of Gibbons' *Decline and Fall of the Roman Empire* when I was ineligible for the re-award of the Common-room History Prize, and who introduced me to the pleasures of brass-rubbing, which took me and my new friend Michael Sackett on many a Saturday afternoon expedition to distant churches (and as often as not to tea on the vicarage lawn, our task completed). The second was W.H. ('Bill') Spray – later headmaster of Kingswood School – who taught me a great deal in the Vth Form, Butterworth-addict though he both was and (I think) still remains in retirement. He proved an invaluable humane and humanist foil to Hubert Wylie's decidedly austere (*'Aw! Stupid boy!'*) manner. Between them, these three notable schoolmasters fanned the spark of my nascent interest in history into a small but persistent flame.

Fortunately the Marlborough of the 1940s and early 1950s under the masterships of F.M. Heywood and later T.R.G. Garnett had almost dropped the old public-school image of 'God and Games before all' so distasteful to John Betjeman, and encouraged the development of individual interests. For me this meant many happy hours in the Art School producing ever more historical sketches, to the slight despair of Mr Barton ('Arty Barty'), and, as already mentioned, brass-rubbing. I was also a member of 'the Corps' (CCF), and greatly enjoyed the 'field-days' in Savernake Forest or along the valley of the River Kennett – and even the annual camps at Warminster and Aldershot. The thrill of being awarded one's first lance-corporal's stripe must rival that of first grasping one's field-marshal's baton. I duly became the junior sergeant platoon commander in D-Company (CCF training one afternoon a week was compulsory from age fifteen), and as such was the very last sub-unit to be inspected and to march past on the 1952 Corps Day annual inspection. I will always remember the trouble that Lt General Sir Brian Horrocks (the inspecting officer) took to find time for a short talk with me after inspecting at least 600 other cadets in the prized Marlburian dark-green berets drawn up in twenty more senior platoons. He had a kind face and a twinkle in his eye that made him the favourite of National Servicemen's mums in the early days of television.

I also recall in 1950 the greater part of an armoured division on manoeuvres roaring all night, it seemed, under Field-House Bridge straddling the A4, and then up Granham Hill overlooking the college towards Pewsey. There was also in 1952 a visit by General de Lattre de Tassigny, soon to die and be awarded the posthumous baton of a *Maréchal de France*.

There were the more peaceful October visits to the annual 'Mop Fair' in Marlborough's wide high street, and many, many visits to the town bookshops to browse and sometimes to buy treasured volumes for one shilling (5p.) or at most half-a-crown (25p.) a time, which still surround me as I write. Inside the College there were many tea parties (or 'brews' as we termed them) with John Metcalfe and (until he died) Chris Wansey who had come on to Marlborough with me from Terrington Hall. One memorable holiday my uncle took my cousins and myself to Paris – my first visit abroad. But all too soon it was 'A-Levels' time; and then goodbye to the strains of *The Old Bath Road* school-song.

In the bitterly cold winter of 1951, before taking my A-Levels in fact, I had sat the Group Scholarship examination for Keble College, Oxford, and had been delighted to emerge with a place as a 'Gentleman-Commoner'. Fate (the

College's choice) decided that I should go up straight from school (90 per cent did their two-year National Service first), so I moved into residence in my father's old college in autumn 1952. His old tutor, Dr Rice-Oxley, was still teaching, which provided a pleasant link. I am sure that I was fortunate to go up to Keble before 'doing my bit'. The continuity in terms of a habit of hard work outweighed the lesser maturity. I rowed with scant distinction but great enjoyment, edited the college magazine – *The Clocktower* – in coronation year, thrilled to the idea of *The New Elizabethan Age*, became president of the College Historical Society, *Tenmantale*, joined the Oxford Union Society (but never spoke there), served in the OUOTC (TA) rising to the giddy rank of full corporal, and survived my first adventures with friendly girls, two of them French (one a countess), another an English poetess, a fourth a fellow history-student, a fifth a colonel's daughter. 'Variety' was indeed 'the spice of life' (and there was also 'safety in numbers'!) until – wiser, widely travelled and certainly poorer – I fell for a Withernsea girl I had known off and on all my life, and has now been my wife for almost thirty-three years. By the mid-1950s it was now easier to travel abroad despite strict currency restrictions, and I spent three long vacations exploring parts of Italy, Spain and the Loire; the first two with David Morley-John (to die later after a motorcycle accident); the third (in 1956) with Michael Sackett, in a hired Renault '*Quatre chevaux*'. These were halcyon days indeed.

Of some significance for the future, I chose to study the History of the Art of War for my third-year elective. This involved the study of two set-texts; Clausewitz's *On War* and Corbett's *Principles of Maritime Strategy*. If the former – in the three red-bound volumes of the abysmal 1908 translation (far ahead were the days of the celebrated Princeton Howard and Paret edition) – did not put off a potential future military historian for life, then he was indeed a determined student of Mars and Minerva. Fortunately the second paper encompassed the study of the War of the Second Coalition in its political, naval and land-war aspects, studied mainly from contemporary documents. That was more to my liking, and I had the great good fortune to be tutored by the late C.T. Atkinson, already in 1955–6 long retired from Exeter College but still taking on the occasional student. I was thus privileged to sit at the feet of one of England's most notable military historians of the 1920s and 1930s, the author of *Marlborough and the Rise of the British Army* and other works of general and regimental history – besides a good hundred articles for the *Journal of the Society for Army Historical Research* and other learned publications. He fanned my flame into a blazing inferno of enthusiasm for military history, and I owe almost as much to him as to Hubert Wylie of Marlborough days.

My first degree safely awarded, I stayed on for a fourth year in the Oxford University Department of Education to secure the necessary teaching quali-fication, for I had now decided to join the teaching profession rather than the

Church (my first inclination). During this time I spent the Hilary Term as a student teacher at Bedford Modern School, and during this period both passed my driving test and secured the necessary recommendation for entrance to an Officer Cadet Training Unit by passing the War Office Selection Board – three cold early February days of searching practical, physical and intellectual testing which put me to bed for almost a week on return to my digs at Bedford with Daniel Dickey and his young family (overlooking the prison wall, I remember) but at least I was clutching the vital piece of paper on which my immediate future was to depend. I had already decided to go in for a Short Service Commission (at least three years commissioned service followed by four on the Reserve). This had the advantage of my receiving regular officer's pay and allowances, and permitted me to enter the corps of my choice – the Royal Army Educational Corps, officer service, which was tied to a regular or SSC engagement. Some friends thought me rather mad to 'throw away' an extra year of my life in this way, but I was never to regret it in the outcome.

I was duly called-up in August 1956 and told to report to the barracks of the East Surrey Regiment at Kingston-on-Thames to complete my ten weeks basic training before proceeding to OCTU at Eaton Hall near Chester. As I had already credited myself with six weeks-worth of training at Oxford with the OUOTC, I only had a month to complete. This made me something of an oddity, and accordingly I was not drafted to the Brigade Potential Officer Cadre at Canterbury as the other aspiring officer candidates were after the first week, but stayed on at Kingston with the rest of the intake. This proved an interesting experience for one of my privileged education and, to date, sheltered experience of life. I was at once dubbed scornfully 'a college-lad' by the rest of the squaddies, Cockneys to a man with never an 'O-Level' between them. I learnt the hard way the awe-inspiring power of an 'acting unpaid lance-corporal in charge of barrack room', and survived well enough by cunningly appointing myself scribe to an illiterate East-ender tough, who was the real power in our midst. I wrote his steaming love-letters for him; in return he afforded me 'protection' from our mates – and the arrangement worked famously, until the lady asked to be introduced to the 'nice writer'. Fortunately it was almost time for me to leave for OCTU.

It was the period of the mounting Suez Crisis, and one evening we were all taken without explanation by coach to the West End, where to our bewilderment we were marched into the Leicester Square Theatre to the thunderous applause of an invited (and paying) audience. Placed in the worst rows of front seats we watched the film première of *A Hill in Korea* – a war-drama about National Servicemen achieving wonders against hordes of Chinese earlier in the 1950s. We were charmed by our newly revealed national status, but the army authorities soon wiped the smiles off our pimply faces by announcing on our smug return to barracks at about 2300 hours a full barrack-room and kit inspection for early next morning. We came back to earth with a bump.

One late September day I was summoned into the orderly room and given a rail warrant for two weeks pre-OCTU leave. 'Mine not to reason why', so I packed my kit-bag and off I went home for fourteen days. A new set of orders with accompanying rail warrant reached me at Withernsea, and soon I was off in the local milk lorry to catch the early train to Chester from Hull. My early career as an officer-cadet was, however short-lived. The quartermaster at Kingston had decided to offload a 1940-type battledress on my unsuspecting frame, which did not exactly please the dapper Eaton Hall Guardsman adjutant on the first inspection. Soon a 'state of [administrative] war' existing between Chester and Kingston-on-Thames, during which the authorities had no recourse, it seemed, but to send my uncomplaining self back home again for a further three weeks paid leave. So far my military service had comprised four weeks duty and five weeks leave – but I feared this would be too good to last. And so, indeed, it proved. By October I was back at Eaton Hall with four months of pretty hard officer training ahead of me.

It was quite an experience. Office training is based on the premise that an officer-cadet should undergo everything that any Other Rank under his eventual command might be subjected to, and a little more so if possible. It was. Drill, change of kit, bawling platoon sergeants, despairing company sergeant majors, (especially CSM Barney Owen of our B Company whom I later met as WO1 at the Staff College, Camberley), a simply apoplectic Irish Guards regimental sergeant major (there was only one of those – Desmond Lynch, DCM, who came complete with large dog which we were convinced was his 'familiar'), who later most unexpectedly became a great friend of mine at Sandhurst, after his appointment as staff officer (Security) there; laid-back and pipe-smoking but rather sad-looking Captain John Bashall of the Wiltshire Regiment (No. 8 Platoon Commander), immensely respected Major John Shipster DSO, the Middlesex Regiment (DCO) (B Company Commander); and at yet more rarified levels the adjutant, Captain R. Mayfield, Scots Guards, the assistant adjutant (another Guardsman: 'Captain Edgerton-Warburton P.' as we irreverently dubbed him) and on top of all Colonel Sir Basil Eugster, DSO, OBE, MC, of the Irish Guards – whom I only met once for a half-hour supposedly relaxed pre-commissioning interview, and who later went on to become a general. These were the military stars in our firmament, the rulers of our every last minute.

Exercises, barrack-room inspections in our smoking coke-stove heated hut, assault-course sessions (I *loathed* these wholeheartedly until I discovered that if one shouted enough encouragement to one's perspiring peers, and looked particularly busy, one could often run round a particularly testing obstacle without actually going over or through it crying 'Well done, lads! On we go!' –

well, that was leadership of a 'Flashman' variety, wasn't it?), more drill, lessons on radios, the 2in mortar, the .303 rifle with spike bayonet, the good old LMG (or Bren gun), days on the ranges (fun), and route marches (not such fun), followed in remorseless succession. I 'lost my name' for 'filthy flesh' (a tiny gun-oil mark on the back of my neck) on one drill inspection, which earned me Major Shipster's sadly despairing remark on Company Orders '... Chandler, this is just *not* good enough, you know ...' and five nasty days on 'Restrictions' (the officer-cadets' up-market equivalent of other ranks' 'CB' ('confined to barracks' or 'jankers'). Somehow we all (but one) survived, having learned above all to act as a team. The less fortunate chap advertised a non-existent 'bring-and-buy sale' in Chester, and was put back an intake (dreaded fate) for his pains.

Everything culminated at the end of December with battle-camp at Trawsfynyd in Wales (now a nuclear power station) for a freezing week of final exercises including live-firing at night (most spectacular thanks to tracer-rounds of varied colours), individual command tasks (scaring, as we were using live ammunition and, even worse, these tests counted critically for everyone's final assessment), and the final forty-eight-hour exercise, which I thoroughly enjoyed as I had the good fortune to land the cushy job of Intelligence NCO at Company HQ – possessing a BA (Oxon), with speciality in Military History had its advantages, I now at last discovered. I spent most of this culminating 'hell' (for everybody else) in a warm tent liberally supplied with hot tea laced with rum *and* first choice of the 'compo' ration packs, occasionally making languid marks with coloured wax pencils on the talc-covered 'situation map' as exciting messages crackled in over the radio. Meanwhile my colleagues 500 yards away 'out there' in the freezing cold dug weapon slits, fought little engagements, advanced or retired to dig more weapon slits (jolly good practice for them too! I thought) – all this martial mayhem being relieved with the occasional 'grub-up' at aptly named 'Tin-Town' just outside the gates of the exercise area.

Then at last we were back at Eaton Hall, swaggering in the Cadets' Club like the (sort-of) veterans we now were in the eyes of the respectful Junior Intake. Much more drill – sessions with the regimental tailors – then the great day at last dawned. The Passing-out Parade was witnessed by proud girl-friends and parents (mine got stuck in a lift in Chester, I remember) and taken by a Brigadier H.A. Prince of a Territorial Army Brigade (a trifle down-market we felt, for *men* (average age nineteen years) of our vast experience. Then at last we came to the supreme moment – the march through the 'Golden Gates' past the statue of a Norman warlord on his steed (an ancestor of the Duke of Westminster, our absentee landlord); and after handing in all our kit and one last-minute inspection of our quarters to ensure they were spotlessly clean, there we were, off on commissioning leave glorying in our single 'pips', the latest batch of Short and National Service subalterns to grace the army of Her Majesty Queen Elizabeth II. In an earlier generation we would have been known as 'warts'.

A young officers' course at the Army School of Education at Wilton Park, Beaconsfield, prepared me professionally for my RAEC duties. There were only five subalterns involved on our course, although there were almost 200 RAEC National Service sergeants under training in a separate part of the estate, 'Camp 60'. A map-reading exercise in North Wales was one highlight of these three months; and a visit to beautiful Eltham Palace (until 1992 the RAEC Headquarters Mess) in south-east London, another. Military history only came into the picture when I was required to prepare and give a forty-five-minute lecture – and chose Marlborough's March to the Danube in 1704 as my subject. In many ways the early eighteenth century (probably due to C.T. Atkinson's influence at Oxford) has always been and indeed remains my favoured period for researching and writing to the present day. During this period I also completed my ship-model of a French frigate, *La Flore*. and was persuaded to enter it for the army arts and crafts exhibition, where to my gratified surprise it was placed first in its class, earning me £5. Phew! Even better, my seniority calculation based on my degree and certificate of education caught up with me, and overnight I became a lieutenant.

My first posting as a lieutenant was to Fulwood Barracks, Preston, where I was to serve as Garrison Education Officer to the (then) East and South Lancaster Regiments and No. 64 Company RASC. My small empire comprised a Victorian schoolhouse set behind the coal-heaps, manned by myself, two sergeant instructors RAEC, and a cleaner. Flush with prize-money and promotion pay, I soon took out my first insurance policy with the 'Pru' and bought my very first car (a grey Renault *Dauphine*). Almost every weekend I was off to Bangor University in North Wales, where I was hard a' courting a pretty zoology student from my home town whom I had known on and off for many years. I was soon teaching her to drive – and our flourishing relationship even survived this supreme test of mutual patience and discretion.

This was also the time of '*sputnik*', I recall, and all the excitement that caused. Two other events during my time at Preston stand out in my memory. The first was when 'higher authority' ordained the withdrawal of all 'Standard Unit Libraries' (some 320 selected books) that accompanied a major unit wheresoever it was ordered. Prior to withdrawal, each SUL was of course rigorously checked. Mine was three books deficient, and I was officially notified that the shortfall would be made good by a deduction from my pay. This riled the Yorkshireman in me, but my SO2 education officer, Major Leslie Elkington, kindly put me in touch with a friend of his at an address in Liverpool docks, suggesting I repair there. This I did, to find a large warehouse stacked to the ceiling with books of all types and many still uncrated SULs in literally mint condition. I was invited to help myself from the loose piles, and soon found my three titles. Over a cup of tea, I asked my benefactor what was going to be done with this book-mountain. He looked a trifle sheepish, but eventually informed me that they were all to be shovelled into special barges from which they were to be deposited into the River Mersey. I could hardly believe my ears; in those days, a hundred under-equipped Secondary Modern Schools would have welcomed one – now surplus to army requirement – Standard Unit Library. But it was not to be. Army regulations going back to the eighteenth century laid it down that surplus stores such as these were to be destroyed, and a certificate signed by a senior officer to that effect. Disillusion over this terrible waste was a major factor in my decision not to put in for a regular commission, as I was from time to time being asked to consider.

The second event was to prove happier in its outcome. One day in May 1958 I was summoned to Headquarters North-West District by my colonel. I was then informed that there was a vacancy for an instructor-officer in the Royal West African Frontier Force in Nigeria, and I had been 'volunteered' for the position. And, oh yes, regulations would make it necessary for me to extend my remaining period of active service by four months. I positively gobbled at this liberty – until I was informed that this extension was due to another rule that said that any officer proceeding to a tropical station was to receive three months mandatory home leave on full pay and allowances after eighteen months abroad. My attitude mellowed rapidly: who was I to query Her Majesty's wisdom if she wished me to go to the colonies upon her service etc., etc.? And so it was settled. Officer commanding No. 64 Company at once dubbed me 'Niger Ned'.

During posting leave my girlfriend became my fiancée, and with great aplomb took and passed her driving test the day before my departure. In the meantime with traditional 'left boot' efficiency, I was issued with 'jungle greens' of Asian pattern instead of khaki-drill as used in Africa. I was told my posting would be to Kaduna in the Northern Region of Nigeria, only to have it changed to Lagos on the coast at the last minute. The Crown Agents arranged for the collection of my baggage – and then in mid-August I was up, up and away to adventures new, on board a *Stratocruiser*.

The next eighteen months were to be most memorable. Nigeria was due to become independent in 1960, so I was privileged to live the life of a British officer in a colony in transition to independence – the very last of 'the African *Raj*' as it were. Within a month of landing at Ikeja Airport I was promoted temporary captain which was encouraging. Attached to RWAFF Headquarters at Apapa on the outskirts of Lagos, I had a *giddah* (or bungalow) to myself, with a full-time Yoruba servant called 'Sunday'. The humidity and wet-heat took some little getting used to – your khaki drill uniform would be soaking by mid-morning, necessitating as often as not a full change of clothing at coffee-break.

'Sunday' laundered my uniforms every day. 'Prickly-heat' around the midriff had to be powdered and borne stoically. Paludrin tablets against malaria had to be taken daily, 'mosquito boots' worn with trouser legs tucked into them and long-sleeved shirts donned from dusk. Mosquito nets over beds were *de rigueur* at night, making the atmosphere even stuffier, while ceiling fans rotated overhead keeping the air moving – these were days when the only air-conditioners were in the large food stores downtown, in the labour-ward at the military hospital, and in the general's office. The working day started at 7 am, but generally ended at 12.30. After a chilled light beer or two and lunch, a sticky siesta was often taken, and after 'tiffin' (tea) I often went down to the Lagos Army Sailing Club to spend a convivial and sporty couple of hours on or near the water before returning to the mess to bathe and change for dinner. One then tried to get to sleep against a background of chirping crickets and croaking frogs.

'Avoid and beware the Bight of Benin,' runs the old doggerel, 'Where few come out though many go in.' All in all it was in fact a pleasant-enough lifestyle. Working days would see me holding classes for Nigerian potential officers at Apapa, and making regular visits to supervise the military education proceeding at Abeokuta (some sixty miles away). Your average Ibo Nigerians (who made up most of the NCOs and clerks) had a hankering after western-style education that was sometimes hard to believe; it was a different matter with the mainly Hausa rank and file, who were Moslems from the Northern Region to a man, and looked to the regimental *mullah* for their Koranic instruction. Nearer by I would regularly visit the 'detachment' stationed at Ikoye, which held the duty-company performing ceremonial and security duties for Lagos itself. In its tiny officers' mess I got to know and like Captain Jakub Gowan, Sandhurst-trained ADC to the governor-general – an acquaintanceship that was to have an unexpected outcome in 1970 and 1976.

Most weekends would see groups of British soldiers and families sail off to Tarquah Bay aboard the RASC launch *Copperfield* to swim, sun and surf. There was a rest-house there where one could spend the odd night or two of local leave. One often found oneself surfing alongside the last governor-general, Sir William Robertson, who bore his high office lightly. There were occasional ceremonial parades on the racecourse to mark the Queen's Birthday or a visit by the Duke of Gloucester, visits to Government House along the marina for garden-parties and barbecues, to the Railway Club for dances and drinks, to private houses for formidable 'curry lunches' which started at ten in the morning and ended at about four pm, and occasional visits to the colourful but rather sleazy open-air nightclub, The Lido, or the rather better Ikeja Club. Married officers, their wives and families often invited bachelor officers for weekends, and I was practically adopted by Derek and Barbara Woodroffe and their three charming young daughters, Susan, Rosamund and Caroline, who made me feel like a favourite uncle. When they finally left for 'home', I inherited their much loved pie-dog, 'Mr Binks' (which I in turn eventually passed on to a medical officer and his young family when my turn to go arrived).

Progress towards Nigerian federal independence proceeded with occasional riots, a few border troubles with left-wing terrorists from neighbouring Cameroon, and, more surprisingly, several changes of officers' hats. These last were financially attractive events – for the military secretary ensured we all received special 'disturbance' allowances as we successively became the Nigerian Army and then the Nigerian Military Forces. It was like passing 'Go' and collecting £200 at 'Monopoly' – all for changing from a slouch-hat of Australian type with green-and-black hackle to service cap, and then back to slouch-hat (without hackle) again. With the proceeds of the first change I bought my second *Dauphine* – which I in due course brought home with me. It was all very enjoyable and memorable. The climate so near the equator was pretty unpleasant – but sun, sailing and surfing made all the difference.

Where Military History was concerned, I found myself thrown in at the deep end a few months after my arrival. Back in England, the MOD of the time decreed a new format for the staff/promotion examination – which officers needed to pass to become majors or, for the lucky few, enter the portals of the Staff College, Camberley – in peacetime the *sine qua non* for promotion to lieutenant-colonel and above. Included in this examination was a paper on *Military History*, requiring study of Marlborough's Campaigns, 1702–1710, the Italian Campaign of 1943–5, and the Burma Campaign of 1941–5. I soon found myself 'volunteered' to run courses for all aspiring regular captains in Nigeria. I eventually held two week-long courses at Apapa, and one each at Zaria and Enugu. My efforts were appreciated – with what justice I cannot say (I occasionally shudder when I find some old notes of mine dating back to 1959–60) – not only by the candidates but also by Major-General N.P. Foster (Commander NMF) and Brigadier John Goulson (Commander, Southern District). This must have helped me to secure the substantive rank of captain before I left Nigeria on completion of my eighteen-month tour. Both also kindly agreed to supply me with a reference.

It may also have helped in another way. I was still intending to teach in schools after completing the active part of my SSC, and my father was keeping a weather-eye open on my behalf for suitable post advertisements. By a happy chance his eyes lit upon a *very* small paragraph in *The Yorkshire Post* advertising faculty vacancies at the Royal Military Academy Sandhurst in the Departments of Mathematics and Modern Subjects. At that time there was no Department of Military History as such, although there was a Reader in Military History and English who employed (in-part) the company commanders to instil a little knowledge in this subject into the officer-cadets. But the very last line in the notice – which his eagle-eye fortunately espied – read: 'An ability to teach Military History might be an advantage.' My destiny was – unbeknown to me, of course – settled (bar accidents).

I had never even considered looking for such a post, but I decided to put in for it. My prospects did not appear very encouraging, for the Civil Service Commissioners (the Alençon Link) Basingstoke required the return of sundry application documents by dates that were passed before I even received the papers, as postal links between Basingstoke and the west coast of Africa could be somewhat intermittent, to say the least. However I persisted – and again unbeknown to me – a fairy godfather (or at least a benign influence) was at work on my behalf. The Director of Studies (or Dean) at Sandhurst, Steven Anderson, had been a wartime brigadier in the RAEC in West Africa, and noticing my tropical address, very fortunately for me kept a weather-eye open for my next overdue package of forms, birth certificates etc. Several times, I learned much later, he intervened with 'higher authority' to allow me a little more time – with results, as I shall note in due course, that shaped my future to a marked degree.

In the meantime, the pleasant-enough lifestyle of pre-Independence Nigeria continued to suit me very well. Highlights included a month-long visit by my fiancée, Gill, during which we drove to such places as Ibadan, to Benin (home of the famous bronze-heads), and along the coast through French Dahomey and Togoland to Ghana – where we visited Accra, the old slaving castles of the seventeenth century, and above all the fine if primitive rest-house at Winnebar, which was our furthest point west. We picnicked on surf-roaring beaches, watched a ceremonial meeting of Fanti and Ashanti chiefs with their retainers, twirling-umbrella-holding-attendants and beautiful kenti-cloth robes; ate a perfect *bifstek-à-poivre* at Cotonou Airport; luxuriated in juicy yellow 'oranges'; and arrived back at Lagos with just half-a-crown left in our collective pockets, having eaten the previous evening at Le Lac Hotel only by courtesy of the management who laid on a fine duck-and-all-the-trimmings for supper absolutely for free. Those were, indeed, the good old days.

Back in Lagos, with Gill as my (very brave) crew, I managed to win the coveted LASC silver-plated ashtray for GP13 sailing boats, and then it was time to send her back by Britannia airliner to Great Britain, Withernsea and Bangor University to complete her degree.

My remaining time in Lagos was not wholly uneventful. I had inherited the editing of the *NMF Magazine* which in turn led to occasional broadcasts on Radio Nigeria (television was as yet undreamt of on 'the Fever Coast'). I covered as NMF journalist a literally 'flying-visit' by Prime Minister Harold Macmillan to Ikeja Airport for a refuelling stop en route to South Africa – and heard his rehearsal of the famous 'winds of change' speech given to Sir Abubakar Talefwa Balewa (the federal Prime Minister) and a round half-dozen others (four being policemen besides myself and the inevitable pie-dog). I also learnt a hard lesson about 'historical tact' when I was tasked to work-up some short accounts of the famous battles in Burma which had earned the NMF's predecessors their battle-honours, and the whole Nigerian Federation an annual 'armed forces bank-holiday' called *Myohaung Day*. Working from regimental diaries and other official sources, it soon became devastatingly clear to me that the famous battle of Myohaung had been fought between less than a company of determined Japanese pitted against both the 61st and 62nd West African Divisions, who had, indeed, ultimately triumphed. Comforting myself with Wellington's order to his staff after narrowly-won Fuentes de Oñoro (1811) against the great Marshal Massena in the Peninsular War to '. . . write [him] a victory' for home consumption, I sailed as close to the wind as I dared and did my duty by the NMF. Then it was time to book my passage by Elder Dempster Line's flagship *Aureol*, close the garrison church accounts (not without a little difficulty as my good friends the Reverend Gerald and Betty Solomon may still remember), pack, prepare my car for export, survive a round of memorable parties given for me by my friends, hand over 'Mr Binks' – and then I was shipboard bound for Liverpool via Freetown and Madeira.

Returned by late March 1960 to a welcoming rainy 'England, Home and Beauty', I prepared for my return to civilian life. I attended several job interviews, but was delighted to be successful at the Civil Service Appointments Board held at Sandhurst, finding myself appointed a lecturer in the Department of Modern Subjects on the (then) not inconsiderable salary of £1080 per annum, with effect from 4 July 1960.

Reviewing my following thirty-three years closely associated with the Royal Military Academy Sandhurst, being 'of' the British army but not exactly 'in' it, I could – and one day may – write a book on the subject, although once having signed the Official Secrets Act it remains binding for life. Not that there are any great secrets of state that could be revealed by a 'grey job' (one of the army's more pejorative phrases for a Sandhurst lecturer) – but 'authority' remains strangely diffident about all kinds of matters not apparently in the least bearing on national security, but possibly 'twitchy' where individual reputations of still-serving very senior soldiers are concerned. But then, a country tends to get the army, as well as the government, that it deserves (or can afford), 'warts and all'. Here, therefore, I must restrain myself to a few observations pertinent to my development as a professional military historian, and above all as a writer of military history.

Sandhurst in the early 1960s was a very different place from the Sandhurst of today. The course was then two years long in duration, and far greater emphasis was laid on the education of our young men in the widest sense of the term than is feasible (or possibly necessary) today in the near-mid-1990s. However, matters have lately taken a small but distinct turn for the better in educational terms following the adoption of the one-year commissioning course from late 1992. This is common for all officer cadets, whether graduate (about 50 per cent at the present time) or school-recruited, whether from the ranks of the army or from overseas (fully seventy-six countries have been represented in varying combinations since 1948, the latest or imminent additions to the list being Hungary and Russia), whether men or (now) women.

My first year at Sandhurst was mainly taken up with finding my bearings and teaching British constitutional and other 'modern' subjects, including foreign political systems and the history of the British Commonwealth. My recent knowledge of the now newly independent state of Nigeria led to my being asked to give two central lectures on the subject. I was also hauled in to help train the RMAS boat club, and pulled off something of a coup by training the coxed-four that proceeded to defeat its Brittania Royal Naval College's equivalent crew on its own water – the River Dart – in my first autumn term.

More serious matters were developing over the year's end. First came my marriage to Gill, taken by my father in beautiful Beverley Minster in February 1961, which proved the start of a very happy and lasting relationship which, besides producing three sons of whom we are very proud (none of them going into the Services it is perhaps interesting to note despite, or possibly because of, the lures of growing up around Sandhurst – and none of them going on to teach history either – although the eldest took Modern History at Oxford and received a University Prize as well as the best First in History of his year, whilst the second emerged from Exeter and Saarbrucken Universities with the only First in Law in his, and the youngest is a mathematician who possibly 'peaked' a little too early and had to be content with a strong 2.1 from Cambridge, which at least means his father can talk on intellectually equal terms with him, despite his 'light blue' connotations), provided me with that greatest blessing of 'a happy and secure home base' which has made possible (or greatly eased) my considerable travels abroad, my belonging to such interesting societies as the Sealed Knot *ab origine* and the Napoleonic Association, my research in general and my writing and lecturing in particular.

Secondly, I was recruited by Brigadier Peter Young, DSO, MC (and two Bars), MA (Oxon.), FSA, FRHist.S, FRGS, Reader in Military History and English, into his newly created Department of Military History, alongside John Selby, John Keegan and John Adair – soon to be joined by Christopher Duffy and Antony Brett-James. Peter Young – a scholar of the English Civil War as well as a commando of the greatest distinction in the Second World War, became a great personal friend as well as an inspiring head of department, whose determination that his young men should research and publish in as many areas of military history and war studies as took their fancy has resulted in members of the department (today named War Studies) publishing something in excess of 150 books down to the present day. Peter Young was the third, and probably the most important, influence upon my professional life. A man of immense enterprise endowed with a full share of creature-cunning, who went on to found the Sealed Knot and publish almost fifty books bearing his name, Peter Young was in every way a larger-than-life character whom it was a pleasure to serve under – and who left his mark for the better, in personal and professional terms, on all who were privileged to know him.

Under his encouraging eye, my first article was accepted by *History Today* and was published in 1962. This was all the more amazing in that the very same article had been politely rejected by the same periodical in mid-1956, shortly before my call-up, and had only been adjusted to a small degree. Perhaps a 'Royal Military Academy' letter-heading had rather more clout with publishers than that of 'Owthorne Vicarage', but it would be pointless to speculate further! This started my association with an excellent historical journal that has survived to the present day.

This article proved 'the hinge of fate' for me as a serious author on Napoleonic topics. It gave rise to my receiving a telegram from Peter Ritner of the Macmillan Company of New York, asking me to consider writing a book on Napoleon's campaigns. I replied I would rather write one on the Duke of Marlborough. This elicited a second message from over the Atlantic which ran: 'Marlborough? Who's he? We want Napoleon!' And so in due course contracts were exchanged, and three years later my manuscript (albeit twice as long as contracted for!) was enthusiastically accepted, appeared in October 1966 and – as the saying goes – 'the rest is history'. I was launched as a military historian.

The Campaigns of Napoleon was in fact my second book to appear. Hugh Street of (the then) Evelyn Press, had taken a risk on me in 1962, and contracted me to edit and part-write *A Traveller's Guide to the Battlefields of Europe* in two volumes which first appeared by late 1965. When I look at the list of contributors I somehow suborned into participating in this work, I am amazed at the presumption I displayed in soliciting their co-operation at all. Besides half-a-dozen Sandhurst colleagues led by Peter Young, I had the cheek to approach Major-General J.F.C. Fuller, Major-General H. Essame, Professor Michael Roberts, Captain Cyril Falls, Mr (now Sir) Michael Howard, Professors Piero Pieri of Italy and Norman Gibbs, holder of the Chichele Chair in the History of War at Oxford, not to forget Brian Bond (now Professor at KCL) and Dr (now also professor) A.R. Birley. I feel even more embarrassed when I recall the financial reward on offer per thousand words. Over this delicate issue only one big name escaped my net. Captain (later Sir) Basil Liddell Hart most kindly had me over for tea at Medmenham and sounded enthusiastically willing to join the team. On leaving I cautiously brought up the subject of remuneration – and without a blink 'the captain who teaches generals' (as Guderian dubbed him) mentioned a rate per thousand words that was exactly forty times what I was empowered to offer (and everyone else, incidentally, had been prepared to accept). I gulped, mentioned the need to hurry home and help my wife bath the baby, and drove off assuring him that I would soon be back in touch and that he was not to bother himself by ringing me first.

Both volumes, and then *The Campaigns*, attracted mostly good reviews, and now, over a quarter-of-a-century and some twenty-five books later, I freely acknowledge the great debt I owe to my early sponsors who 'took a risk' on me in the early 1960s. Having to teach officer-cadets indubitably helped me to write in an acceptable manner, along the knife-edge between 'scholarly-but-dull' and 'readable-but-slight'.

The Campaigns of Napoleon has led a charmed life. It has never been out of print on either side of the Atlantic, and has appeared in Italian and Pakistani (but not French!) editions. Many good things stemmed from its success, not least invitations from various publishers to write further books, but also to give many lectures to university and other learned societies, and the offers of a number of visiting chairs or professorships in American universities. In 1970 I was able to secure leave from Sandhurst to accept the Mershon Chair for six months at Ohio State University (where I was a fascinated witness of student-troubles caused by the Vietnamese War). This was a great opportunity. In 1988 I was similarly permitted to take the Mary Ann Northen Chair in the Humanities involving four very happy months at the Virginia Military Institute, and in the summer of 1992 I similarly enjoyed the Seventh Chair in Military Affairs at the US Marine Corps University at Quantico, also in Virginia. The future holds the prospect of several more similar invitations. I have also served, or still serve, as a council member of the Society for Army Historical Research and the Army Record Society, and have been appointed a trustee of The Royal Tower of London Armouries.

Until January 1994 my duties at Sandhurst remained the focus of my real career, and the survival – and whenever possible the amelioration – of the, on average, five-yearly changes of direction in the organisation and contents of its courses and syllabuses naturally have taken up a great deal of my attention. One episode – linked with military history, RMAS, Ohio State University and Nigeria – perhaps merits description.

In the mid-1960s I had an Ibo Nigerian officer cadet – let us call him Tom Nwajei (not his name) – as a member of my Additional Military History class studying the American Civil War as a special subject. He was very keen, and I got to know him quite well. After returning to Nigeria he wrote me the occasional cheery letter at Christmas – but soon after the outbreak of the Biafran War I received a letter that impressed me so I kept it. Nwajei – now a major in the artillery – had joined Ojukwu's Biafra, but not without some travail of conscience. 'Here am I,' he wrote, 'faced by the dilemma of Robert E. Lee [in 1861]: whether to stay loyal to my soldier's oath, or to follow my people.' He had recognised the ethical dilemma. Clearly he had learned rather more from our classes years earlier than I had perhaps realised at the time.

Then his letters stopped – but not those from an American lady-friend of his working with Voluntary Services Overseas. As Biafra began to face defeat, she engaged my aid to get Tom awarded a place at an American university so that he could escape what was now inevitable defeat. Alas, in vain. A last letter arrived in which she sadly announced that Tom had been taken prisoner and was being held in a prison-camp near Enugu, the district commander being the ruthless Hausa commander known for good reason as 'the Scorpion'. Stories were reaching the European press about Hausa massacres of Ibos and other atrocities. So that might well have been the end for Major 'Tom Nwajei'.

This letter was forwarded to me in Columbus, Ohio, where I had just taken up my Mershon visiting professorship. To my surprise I found Nwajei's 'Robert E. Lee' letter behind my writing-case blotter. An idea started to form in my mind. Now that I was in 'neutral terrain' away from Sandhurst, why should I not write to my old friend of the Ikoye Detachment Officer's Mess – General Gowon, now president of a reunited Nigeria? He had been studying as a major at Camberley when the rebellion of the Eastern Province and the assassination of General Ironse, the preceding head of state, by a Hausa battalion during his inspection of them at Abeokuta, had caused him to be summoned home to take over control of a rudderless and disintegrating Federation – with notable military results as already indicated.

So I wrote to General Gowon, recalling our time together in 1958–60, and enclosing Nwajei's letter. I pointed out that I had no intention of interfering in Nigerian internal affairs, but I thought he might be interested in the feelings of a fellow Sandhurst-trained officer who was to the best of my belief now a prisoner-of-war near Enugu, who had clearly abandoned the Federal army as a matter of conscience to '... follow ... [his] ... people', and not, like so many others, as an adventurer. I must admit I almost did not post the letter. Postal links with Nigeria were poor, to say the least, and I sincerely doubted it would ever reach the president's desk. But sent off the letter was – to my future relief.

For six months I heard not a word, and supposed that my fears had proved correct. But on returning from the USA to Sandhurst with my family in August 1970 I found a recently date-stamped letter in my mail tray – from 'Thomas Nwajei'! It was almost eighteen sides long, and intended to bring me up to date since I had last heard from him some eighteen months before. Of course he did not know of my background information.

To cut a long story short, he had thought his time was come when summoned one morning five months previously to the prison-camp commandant's office to be signed over into the charge of several burly Hausa military police. Many other Biafran officers had never been heard of again after similar summonses. He was manacled hand and foot, driven to Enugu Airport, and thrown

31

into the back of a Dakota. He was vastly relieved to discover that this was not the prelude to a 'throw-him-out-over-the-bay' exercise when the plane flew north-westwards, as he could guess from the sun's movements through the windows. After dark they landed at a brightly lit airport, when his escort reappeared for the first time since take-off to open the cargo doors and drop him unceremoniously like a sack of potatoes to the tarmac ten feet below. This event was not to the liking of a smart young Nigerian captain waiting with an escort and Land-Rover near by. 'Tom' had his shackles removed and found himself whisked without a word to what proved to be Lagos prison. There he was shut in a cell and left to his thoughts.

Next morning an assistant-governor arrived with a little man who proceeded to measure him up – still without a word being spoken. Fears that this might be a prelude to a short walk and a long drop, and thence into a made-to-measure coffin, were slightly allayed when the man insisted on taking his inside-leg measurement. The party then withdrew, but soon 'Tom' was allowed the luxury of his first shower for four months. Twenty-four hours later, the same delegation returned to his cell, bearing a large cardboard box. Inside was a newly tailored uniform of a Biafran artillery major, correct in every detail. He was told to put it on and proceed to the governor's office. There he found the smart young captain and armed escort awaiting him, and with no explanation he was driven to Government House overlooking the Lagos Marina, and ushered, still under guard, into an anteroom.

President Gowon must be credited with full marks for what happened next – or rather did not happen. For two whole days 'Tom' was kept waiting in the anteroom, receiving meals at intervals but being taken back to Lagos prison each night. On the third day he was summoned into President Gowon's presence, who promptly dismissed the guard. There then followed what 'Tom Nwajei' described as the hardest grilling, man-to-man, of his life. Gowon needed convincing of *why* Nwajei, a fellow-Sandhurst-trained officer, had seen fit to desert from the Federal Army in the first place. After an hour General Gowan rang the bell, and 'Nwajei' was returned to prison. But not for long. The next morning a staff colonel entered his cell. He was informed that as an act of clemency designed to start the processes of reuniting Nigeria, the president had decided to pardon six captured Biafran officers. 'Nwajei' would lose all seniority and effectively be recommissioned as a second lieutenant from that date. His total and unquestioning loyalty to Federal Nigeria would be taken for granted. He would not be given another chance.

I was delighted to read of 'Tom's' adventures and their happy outcome – until I read the postscript in which he informed me that, making the most of his instruction under my tutelage years before, he intended to write an 'objective and accurate' history of the Biafran War. That earned him a congratulatory but curt telegram from me positively ordering him to do no such thing; fate was not to be tempted twice in such short order. His history could wait until his retirement.

Some years later, General Gowon paid a state visit to England. In his programme was an official visit to Sandhurst. All 'old Nigeria hands' including myself were summoned to meet the Great Man before lunch. When my turn came we chatted about old times in Lagos. As he moved on up the line he turned back for an instant to say: 'Thank you for your letter'. It is scaring to think that I almost never posted it. Two days later news came that he had been deposed from power in his absence abroad. Being the man he is, he spent the first years of imposed exile at Warwick University studying for a first degree in politics: imagine having a failed head of state of Black Africa's largest and potentially most economically sound country in your undergraduate seminar! He went on to take a master's degree and then a doctorate. Since then he has spent the long years mostly in the Ivory Coast with occasional visits to England, awaiting permission that may never come to return to the land of his birth. But a few years ago he was included in an embassy dinner in London by the current Nigerian head of state – so perhaps there is some hope as Nigeria cautiously moves from military government to civilian constitutional rule. In 1991, General Gowon attended the 250th Anniversary celebrations at RMA Sandhurst.

As for 'Tom Nwajei', in 1979 he came to London as a full colonel (!) charged with buying British arms and equipment for his country. I visited him at his suggestion one winter morning in his London hotel suite. The anteroom was crowded with anxious-looking British brigadiers and rival arms salesmen who could not understand why 'a grey-job academic' was ushered straight through them and into the presence. For half-an-hour the two of us reminisced about old times over a cup of coffee, while state business waited without. When I last heard, 'Tom Nwajei' had retired from the Nigerian Army, a brigadier. Perhaps we may one day read his *Unbiased History of the Biafran War*. Or perhaps not.

That cautionary tale must suffice for this present Introduction, although much else might be told. It has been a great honour to serve Sandhurst for the past thirty-three-and-a-half years, the last thirteen of them as head of the Department of War Studies which *The Times* went so far as to describe in an article on 5 November 1985 as '... the best of its kind in any Western military academy'. If that should be true – and I am not the one to judge – then the credit must largely go to the two dozen or so friends and colleagues who have taught, talked and written so much and so well during my time and those of my immediate predecessors in post. From first to last it has been very much of a team effort, and from my point of view a most worthwhile one. I shall certainly miss their daily companionship and friendly (usually, at least) assistance.

Sandhurst has opened so many doors to new experiences. I have spent nineteen years as President of the British Commission for Military History, and six more as President-Emeritus. Over that time I have attended, at the last count, twenty-four overseas academic conferences all round the world, from Washington to Moscow and Seoul, from Athens, Paris, Ottawa and Helsinki to Turin and Istanbul. In earlier times I conducted five lecture tours to BAOR, MELF and FARELF to aid officers prepare for the staff/promotion examinations. I have visited USMA West Point half-a-dozen times to lecture and St Cyr-Coëtiquidian three times, the Swedish Royal Military College and the Dutch Officer Academy at Breda once each. I have even visited the Frunze Higher Military Staff College in Moscow in 1970 at the height (or depth) of the Cold War, and in the process become the friend of the late Lieutenant-General Pavel Jiline, chief of military history in the (then) USSR, a fellow *aficionado* in Napoleonic history, albeit from rather different viewpoints. In 1974, at the height of *détente*, I was able to host him at a conference I held at Sandhurst. I have been able to conduct many overseas lecture tours to universities and other organisations, mostly in the USA and Canada, some of them in Sandhurst leave-times, but not a few (and even better) in mid-term time, when I could be spared.

Less officially, I have spent many happy hours war-gaming and then re-enacting the wars of the past, and since 1991 have held the position of Founder-President of the Union of European Re-enactment Societies (EURS) which has involved me so far in visits to Zurich, Boulogne, Villingen, Kiev and Ivrea in the interest of international amity through shared participation in hobbies and 'Living History'. At the last count, EURS could claim fifteen nations as membership with no less than 60,000 uniformed re-enactors between them (but, alas, very few from Great Britain despite its large and well-known 'Living History' and military re-enactment societies, for our islanders still prefer to look backwards to 'greater' times in our nation's past with nostalgia, rather than using that same interest in a shared past as one means of encouraging a greater participation in a shared united European Community future – but perhaps one day the tide will turn even here . . .).

I have also been able to participate in the making of films for TV – including BBC TV's 'War and Peace' (1971), and SSVC's 'Bridge at Remagen' (1982). I have become deeply involved in Cromwell Productions Ltd's first-rate and ongoing 'Campaign Series' for W.H. Smith & Son, and helped create the idea for Channel 4's 'Great Commanders' series (1993). Several broadcasting opportunities have come my way over the years from *NBS* in the late 1950s to BBC International Service and the Forces Broadcasting Service on many subjects from 'Officer recruitment in the Nigerian Military Forces' (1958) to a part in 'From Hoplite to Harrier' (1993). It has all been the most immense and worthwhile fun. In no way can I bemoan a dull or uneventful career to date. I also have plans for the future.

Most importantly of all, I have probably lectured to almost 20,000 British and overseas officer cadets and young officers (I would hesitate before claiming to have actually taught most of them anything!), helped in the running of almost a dozen residential conferences with the vital aid of my Sandhurst colleagues, and run or been involved in two dozen battlefield tours abroad for RMA Sandhurst, BAOR or specialist societies such as Major and Mrs Holt's Battlefield Tours and the Army Historical Society. And now I am about to publish, thanks to my good friend Lionel Leventhal's suggestion, my twenty-fifth book on Military History.

It has all been a very busy time, looking back, and one I would not have changed in any major particular. Only time will show if anything of lasting value has come of it all – but I trust the next third of a century (or such part of it as heaven vouchsafes) will be equally eventful, for we certainly live, in the words of the ancient Chinese curse, '. . . in interesting times'. May they also be benign rather than tumultuous war- and famine-filled times, and may military history continue to attract, inform and entertain future generations when they study the fascinating corridors of our shared military past. For, as Winston Spencer Churchill wrote many years ago, 'battles are the punctuation marks on the pages of secular history'. Should my puny but well-meaning efforts contribute anything to these fascinating areas, then I shall one day rest content. But not yet for a while, I hope.

David G. Chandler.

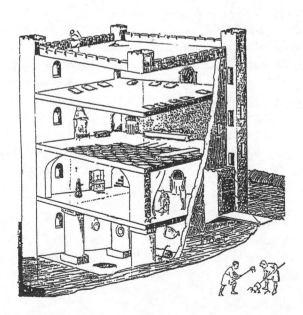

PREFACE:
WHAT IS MILITARY HISTORY?

To ask a military historian such a question is rather like asking Pontius Pilate to define 'truth'. In fact the enquiry involves two linked questions: not only 'What is military history?', but also 'What is it *for?*'. Of course there is no simple answer to either query, for there are many different shades of opinion as is perfectly right and proper if a subject is to remain dynamic. It must grow and develop and even explore what may turn out to be the occasional blind-alley. Each military historian must eventually reach his own position – without, it should be hoped, feeling impelled to denounce all that has gone before as irredentist nonsense or at best largely irrelevant *incunabula*.

'History,' according to Dionysius of Halicarnassus, 'is experience teaching through examples'. Military history – as part of the broad spectrum of historical study – is in the simplest terms the study of 'Man in War'. It connotes a broad range of subjects inextricably linked to the military affairs of the past, including the human, social, institutional, political and technological aspects as well as the specifically professional sides of 'the bless'd trade'. Knowledge of the wars of the past can assist the understanding of the problems of the present, and even (with the hope of avoiding the mistakes and misunderstandings that so tragically often give rise to recourse to armed struggles) aid us to make some educated guesses about what the future may hold. Man's combative instincts have dominated most periods of the past, and even in the supposedly peaceful years since 1945 there have been over 200 identifiable wars fought at various levels affecting many countries in the Second and Third Worlds in particular. Indeed, the first recorded histories, by such famous names as Homer and Thucydides, were largely devoted to accounts of human struggle, man against man, people against people. There has been little change.

Writing as a lecturer who for many years was responsible for sharing in the education of successive generations of officer-cadets and young officers at Sandhurst, it has long been clear that military history itself (as understood in the professional sense) is only one part of the study of the kaleidoscope of warfare. The various strata lead on one from another to develop a comprehensive awareness of the complexities of the whole subject. Thus military history (in the narrower sense of the study of campaigns, battles and leaders) is one foundation for war studies – the examination of the problems arising from the preparation for, and conduct of, war in the present century, particularly since 1945, together with the factors that have influenced those problems. Higher still up the scale come strategic studies – often the province of Staff Colleges – which have been described as:

> the study of modern military organisation, weapons and operations, and also the study of contemporary international and internal armed conflicts in their political, economic and military aspects; the role of alliances and other security systems; disarmament and arms control; strategic doctrines and national defence priorities.

Finally, at the level of the Royal Defence College, comes the consideration of grand strategy and national interest, of alliance policy, and the effective use of deterrence. Yet none of these several levels is mutually exclusive – but rather each draws as necessary from all that has preceded and indeed developed from it. We may hope that the senior planners of the South Atlantic Campaign of 1982 – once the political decision to act had been clearly communicated – took into account (or were at least aware of) the salient points that could be culled from the experiences of Suez, Normandy, Sicily, Gallipoli and even the Crimea (unopposed though the landing was, it was certainly on hostile soil) and Egypt (1801). Major-General Sir Jeremy Moore has mentioned that he found his knowledge of James Wolfe and Québec helpful in overcoming what Wavell called 'the loneliness of high command'. Thus military history has a part to play at all levels of a soldier's development – but above all at the foundation of his career when it is important to inculcate *esprit d'armée* in the aspiring officer. As Napoleon remarked, 'One must speak to the soul: it is the only way to electrify the man'.

I am also a military historian by inclination and interest in the fullest senses. Since sixth-form days at Marlborough, I have been fascinated by the military affairs of the past in general – and of the Marlburian and Napoleonic periods in particular. My particular focus is on the development of the military science and art, but I am also interested by the interplay of personality – the vital human element without which much else is, to me, somewhat meaningless. I am not a Tolstoian in that I am convinced that Napoleon made a lasting mark on the military aspects of his times – and on subsequent generations. For me, the subject does not at any level connote militarism any more than the study of medicine propagates disease. I do not hold with the view that a prime function of a military historian is to debunk legends and uncover misrepresentations. Certainly he must report his findings if they do run counter to accepted belief, but the subject deserves more than this, and there are still large areas even in the Napoleonic area which are virtually *terra incognita*, and even more in the late seventeenth and early eighteenth centuries.

It is also much in my mind that the study of military history is not solely for the academic élite – its study is also an ideal source of pleasure for the layman with a genuine interest in the 'passionate dramas' of the past. Indeed, military history can be all things to all men. Almost any approach, providing it observes scholarly rules concerning the testing of evidence and the drawing of sustainable conclusions, is welcome – and all have a valuable role to play providing they accord the same toleration to other views that they require themselves. Even the disagreements – reflecting the greatest attributes of the subject in its many forms – are intellectually stimulating. As Professor Geyl remarked, 'History is an argument without end'. Need one say more?

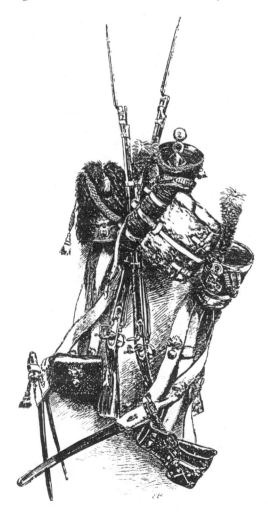

1

THE ORIGINS OF THE REVOLUTIONARY AND NAPOLEONIC WARS

A *number of years ago the famous Oxford historian, the late A.J.P. Taylor, gave a celebrated series of television lectures on how major wars had originated from 1789 to 1939. They were notable not only for their content – which was brilliant and often controversial – but also for their delivery. Alan Taylor not only foreswore any form of visual aid but also had no script or teleprompter. He simply talked to camera for precisely thirty minutes – developing an involved argument without ever once losing his train of thought or even repeating himself. As even his critics allowed, he was a master story-teller who could mesmerise his audience by sheer charisma or force of personality. His lectures were later published in book form as* Why Wars Begin *(London, 1979).*

Forty years ago, I well recall attending several of his lectures at Oxford. Hence I was interested, in 1986, to find myself invited by the Massachusetts Institute of Technology to present a paper on the above subject at MIT's New Windsor Conference Centre. My good friend Professor Gunther Rothenberg of Purdue University was also put up to give his views on the identical subject. But that was not all. The purpose of the conference was to bring together military historians and sociologists in the interest of seeking the inter-disciplinary middleground (the mid-1980s were much dominated by such 'intellectual crusades'). It was an interesting occasion, but only served to prove that the historian's and the sociologist's points of view were incompatible. Professor Rothenberg and I were at one in our individual approaches to the subject – although inevitably and perfectly properly we differed on points of detail. But at least we worked from historical evidence whilst the sociologists were determined to set up 'intellectual models' for the causation of wars, employing any evidence from any source that suited their preconceived notions and totally disregarding anything that challenged it. That is not the way any historian worth the name tackles any subject, and to the open dismay of the professorial organisers and coadjutators we all broke up after three days of papers and argument agreeing that it was a case of vive la différence *insofar as military history and sociological conceptualising were concerned.*

Here, published for the first time, is the basis of my paper. It forms a suitable starting-

point for this volume of my essays and occasional papers, as it is vital in studying any war to form one's own clear ideas as to why European events slid to international conflict by 1791, and what was seen to be at stake by the various contestants.

†

The causation of major wars between developed nations or groups of nations is necessarily a complex subject – a veritable kaleidoscope of variegated intentions, motives and interests that presents a very minefield of potential over-simplifications and misinterpretations to unwary historians – particularly those of the military variety.

It is, for instance, impossible to consider the origins of the Napoleonic wars without taking into account those of the French Revolution and Consulate – and even then many roots of conflict lie deep in the eighteenth century, if not in many cases still earlier, as will be seen as this paper develops.

The main part of this paper will be devoted to a consideration of the events leading up to the War of the First Coalition (1792–7) – the seminal struggle from which all else developed. The remaining space will be used to summarise the origins of the major wars that ensued between 1797 and 1815.

In the first instance it is necessary to obtain a grasp of the scale of these conflicts. Between the date in April 1792 when the Girondin government in Paris declared war in a fit of bravado against the King of Hungary and Bohemia (subordinate titles of the Emperor of Austria) and the signature of the Second Treaty of Paris on 21 November 1815 which formally brought hostilities between France and the Seventh Coalition to an end, there had been – with two brief interludes – varying states of war between varying groupings of nations for almost twenty-three-and-a-half years: virtually a complete generation of human life as these things are usually calculated. The first had been the short-lived Peace of Amiens – which lasted barely a year (25 March 1802 to 16 May 1803) where England and France were concerned, although perhaps it would be more accurate to date the pause from 1 October 1801, when the Preliminaries of Peace were signed by Lord Hawkesbury on behalf of Henry Addington's government with the First Consul's representatives in the Hôtel de Ville at Amiens. The second was the eleven-month peace of April 1814 to March 1815 (although the 'War of 1812' continued in North America). Only the dire experiences of the Thirty Years' War (1618–48) had been as protracted in modern European history – and probably only the Thirty Years' War in Indo-China and Vietnam (1945–75) – as interpreted by Communist Vietnamese – had been of greater length since.

This protracted struggle between France and her immediate neighbours soon spread from Europe to become a truly global struggle, although the epicentre – as in the two World Wars of the twentieth century – remained European. From the approaches to Paris (Valmy was fought within one hundred miles of the capital on 20 September 1792) the war spread to the Rhine, the Austrian Netherlands and Holland, thence into central Germany, Italy (both north and south) and Switzerland, not to forget Spain – all before 1800. From the entry of England into the war (January 1793) the maritime war spread to the West Indies, the Atlantic seaboard, and the Mediterranean, the Cape of Good Hope, the Indian Ocean and the Indian sub-continent, and before the decade's end there were armies locked in conflict in Egypt and Palestinian Syria. Intrigues involved the North African beys and Balkan princelings. Then, following the brief general pacification of 1802–3, came the explosion of the wars associated with Napoleon Bonaparte. Austria, the Tyrol, Prussia, the German principalities and powers (however minor), Poland and East Prussia were sucked into the vortex – several of them indeed to be fought over several times. Then, in late 1807, it was the turn of Portugal and soon the whole of the Iberian Peninsula to become involved in a seven-year struggle, and five years later much of western Russia as far as Moscow and Riga. Further afield there had been expeditions to Buenos Aires, more upheavals in the Balkans and the Two Sicilies and the Levant, and ultimately – in a separate but linked war – involving the youthful United States and Canada from 1812. The effects of war were thus felt, directly or indirectly, over much of the world's surface.

This far-flung struggle involved armies and fleets on a scale that had only rarely – if ever – been encountered in previous history. France mobilised an estimated 700,000 men (backed by possibly two million National Guards) to meet the great crisis of 1793–4; Prussia commanded all of 254,000 men in 1806; in 1812 Napoleon massed (to include allies) some 600,000 men against Russia, and that same year England had more than 230,000 men wearing a redcoat. In 1815 the Seventh Coalition was mobilising three-quarters of a million men against resurgent Napoleonic France when Waterloo brought the wars associated with the dynamic Corsican to an unmourned close. At the height of the struggle England maintained a navy of 113 ships-of-the-line (to the 155 that Napoleon might have had available – his allies and enforced satellites included – as late as 1808, that is three years after Trafalgar).

The casualties caused by this generation of warfare will never accurately be known. Insofar as actual armies are concerned, it is generally agreed that one million were killed in battle (all European armies taken together), with possibly twice as many more succumbing to disease, exhaustion, cold and hunger. Napoleon's army lost over half a million from all causes in Russia, 1812, alone, and almost as many again the next year in Germany – admittedly the worst two years from this point of view. The seven years of campaigns in the Peninsula cost France an estimated 220,000 casualties – or about 100 a day. Civilian deaths – Europe-wide – must have run into several millions more over the whole period. Details are known of French officer casualties between 1805 and 1815: the records reveal 15,000 killed and 35,000 wounded. Between 1792 and 1815, no less than 230 French general officers were killed in action (80 of these under the Republic). Another 66 were guillotined or shot (mostly during the Revolution), and when these totals are added to the twenty-four suicides, the thirty-two killed in duels, died in accidents, or assassinated, a grand total of 352 is obtained, representing almost a sixth of the 2248 officers who are known to have held general rank. Such statistics give some indication of the cost in human terms of the Revolutionary, Consular and Napoleonic Wars.

From these broad, generalised remarks intended to set the scene, we must pass to examine the origins – long-term, medium-term, immediate, pragmatic and ideological, realistic, misconceived and misunderstood – of a period which Professor A.J.P. Taylor (and many another to be sure) has dubbed 'the first modern war'. As one phase of the struggle led on to the next, it is necessary to pay most attention to the development – and spread – of the first bellicose situation. As already suggested, these wars were both individual and part of one all-embracing series, and the fact that France – the focal point, whether deservedly or not, of most of the trouble – moved from being (at the outset) a constitutional monarchy to a regicide republic, and thence by way of a Consulate and a life Consulate to an Empire, mattered very little; these political shifts changed the flavour of the struggle but not its essential shape or causation. There were occasional pauses to be sure – involving two or more combatants, and two short periods of general peace – and the reasons why these proved (or were intended to be) little more than truces or breathing spaces will also require some analysis.

It is a significant diplomatic and military fact that it required seven successive coalitions – of varying composition but all including Great Britain – to achieve a lasting peace and a return (however misguidedly and short-lived) to the *status quo ante bellum*. The involvement of various nations can be conveniently summarised in diagrammatic form (see page 43).

Details of the progressive growth and – in all but the last two instances – destruction or collapse of these seven coalitions will be found in summarised form in the Appendix to this chapter.

It is not the purpose of this paper either to discuss the detail of these conflicts or to set up theoretical models of causation. The approach adopted will be regarded as pragmatic – and probably decidedly old-fashioned to some – rather than abstract. This is deliberate as it is felt that Carl von Clausewitz decidedly had a point when he wrote: 'Just as some plants bear fruit only if they do not shoot up too high, so in the practical arts the leaves and flowers of theory must be pruned and the plant kept close to its proper soil – experience'.

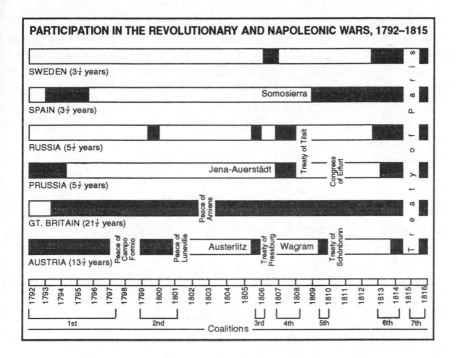

PARTICIPATION IN THE REVOLUTIONARY AND NAPOLEONIC WARS, 1792–1815

The outbreak of war in April 1792 was the culmination of many general and particular pressures, several of them having very deep roots indeed going back to the earliest years of the century – and some even further back. The eighteenth century had proved a very war-prone period. No less than sixteen wars were fought between 1700 and 1790. Four old empires suffered decline – Sweden, the Ottoman Turk, the Polish and the French; three new major powers arose – Great Britain, Russia and Prussia, and one old one – Austria – received a new (if short-lived) lease of life. During the nine decades leading to the French Revolution, only the United Provinces enjoyed relatively little involvement in wars after 1714. Britain, France and Austria took an active part in conflicts in no less than eight decades – and expansionist Russia in every one. Wars – fought according to the general rules of eighteenth-century limitation, whether deliberately or not, by more professional armies backed by better-organised national governments and economies – were deemed to be a satisfactory means of furthering a state's vital interests (at least by the successful powers). The leading powers enjoyed a high degree of internal stability: the losers tended to be not so fortunate, and foremost in the latter category must be placed France. Economically ruined in the reign of the Sun King, the French never recovered their old supremacy, and the appalling disasters of the Seven Years' War, in Europe, the colonies and at sea, inexorably fed the growing swell of discontent within the country. Well might Louis XV prophetically declare: 'Après moi la déluge!'

It was also a period when a group of strong rulers – who, if not causing the contentions of their generations, had at least intensified them – was being replaced in the 1780s by mortals of lesser clay in most instances. It is not altogether surprising that the heirs of Frederick the Great, Maria Theresa, or Gustavus III, let alone those of Louis XIV, tended to look back to earlier concepts of crisis management and problem resolution when faced by the great crises of the 1790s. An element of continuity with the struggles of the eighteenth century is therefore one strand in the causation of the vast wars of its last decade and the first fifteen years of the nineteenth. Emperor Leopold II, King Frederick William II of Prussia, George III of England and the Bourbon rulers of France, Spain and the Two Sicilites were not – individually or collectively – wholly *au fait* with the convoluted, introspective, troubled and complex time they were living through. As Fortescue percipiently remarked: 'The amazing abundance of half-witted sovereigns was one of the many fortunate accidents which allowed the French Revolution to gain so much headway.'

There were possibly three underlying trends that require mention here as potent sources of friction between states (although it is necessary to point out that reasons for hostility and reasons for actual war were by no means synonymous). First, there was the traditional rivalry and distrust – perhaps even hatred – between France and Austria. With roots going back to the Valois and early Bourbon feuds with the Austrian Habsburgs, this ancient rivalry had not by any means been laid to rest by the celebrated treaty of alliance of 1756 which was still formally in existence in early 1792. Indeed, France used its 'ally' Austria as the scapegoat for the disasters of the Seven Years' War. The popular vilification launched against 'the Austrian woman' (Queen Marie Antoinette) was one manifestation of this feeling. Another was the use of references to 'the deplorable treaty of 1756' by the Brissotins in the Legislative Assembly and the political Clubs of Paris in late 1791 and early 1792. Austria was denounced as a treaty-breaker and the heart of the (largely imagined) hostile Concert of Powers aiming to destroy the Revolution. Dislike of the French alliance was reciprocated by Vienna in full measure. France had obstructed all Austria's attempts to profit from the partition of Poland, the Bavarian Succession dispute or the River Scheldt issue – to mention but three. In the apt phrase of Blanning: 'With an ally like that, Austria had no need of enemies.'

The second source of potential hostility was the even older feud between England and France. Periodic attempts to produce commercial agreements between the two nations had done little to disguise deep underlying traditions of rivalry and hatred. Although the Treaty of Versailles (1783) seemed to avenge the French humiliations of the Peace of Paris two decades earlier, Great Britain's economic recovery from her North American disaster had been unexpectedly rapid, and had not borne out critical prognostications that the future land of John Bull would have '. . . declined to the status of a second-rate power, comparable to Sweden and Denmark'. In London, French motives for meddling in the revolution of 1787 in the United Provinces were construed as a disguised attempt to place British commerce and security at risk. French intrigues with Indian princes were equally distrusted, for with the Old Colonies gone, British imperial power now depended upon the sub-continent to a marked degree. And of course the antipathy was fully mirrored over the Channel. As Mirabeau predicted in 1790: 'The enmity of England will be eternal.'

Thirdly, the Ancien Regimes of continental Europe were deeply immersed in the Eastern question. The convolutions of this celebrated subject do not belong to this paper. Suffice it to say that Prussian ambitions to secure more territory by bolstering Turkey against Russia and Austria led to a definite cooling of the Anglo-Prussian association, and ultimately helped drive the vacillating Frederick William II into a *rapprochement* with Vienna in 1791 – an event that would have a bearing on the descent to war with Revolutionary France the next spring. As for France, she too regarded the survival of Turkey as vital to her interests, not least in enabling her to bring pressure to bear on Austria, and consequently made considerable efforts to woo Russia from 1787. These would prove unsuccessful – and within little more than a decade France and Russia would come into direct conflict over spheres of interest in the eastern Mediterranean and the Levant.

The foregoing paragraphs would seem to indicate that a number of ancient rivalries already bedevilled the international scene before the Revolution, and that French foreign policy would in large measure be a continuation of earlier perceived national interests. Of course there is a distinction between causes of tension and dissent on the one hand, and causes of wars *per se* on the other. Wars do not inevitably develop from the former, although they may do so for political reasons. It is to the consideration of the events and pressures that actually led to war in 1792 and 1793 that we must now turn our attention.

Although the late eighteenth century was by any standard a war-prone period, the political processes that led to the French declaration of hostilities on 24 April 1792 against Austria, and then in late-January 1793 against England, were by no means inevitable from the outset of the Revolution in 1789. Historians have been divided over this issue, as over so many more. On the one hand pragmatic analysts such as Sorel are convinced that French Revolutionary foreign policy was essentially a continuation of Bourbon concepts based upon the highly unpopular view of the treaty with Austria in 1756 – upon which all France's disasters and problems were blamed. The ideologues, on the other hand, adopt a long-term perspective based upon great waves of historical change and fatalistic purposes beyond the power of man to control. Ranke, for example, believed in a mighty clash of principles rather than one between peoples. 'It was a dual dispute which contained within it the future of the world: monarchy or republic; war or peace within Europe.' Such airy views did not commend themselves to historians such as Michon, who bluntly avowed that 'The war was desired and provoked by the Girondins.' This, as we shall see, was essentially correct. Concepts of idealism as a cause of wars need cautious handling. As the modern Australian historian Blainey sees it, war '... aims are simply varieties of power... The explanations that stress aims are theories of rivalry and animosity and not theories of war. They help to explain increasing rivalry between nations but they do not explain why the rivalry led to war.' It was to be massive misconceptions and misunderstandings of the realities of power by both parties in 1792 that underlay the descent to armed conflict – but party political reasons linked to French domestic politics triggered the final explosion.

Another contention surrounds the degree of responsibility borne by Austria and Prussia for the war of April 1792, and of England for the growth of the war in January 1793. According to Taylor, France was '... forced into war by the declared intention of the conservative powers to destroy the French Revolution'. In fact – although this is how the Brissotins chose to represent the facts for their own ends in Paris – neither Austria nor Prussia had any such desire. The former was about to emerge from a costly Turkish war, and had no wish for a further conflict. The latter – although Frederick William II was the more aggressive and acquisitive of the two rulers, and was not averse to securing choice pieces of territory to the west of the Rhine at the expense of France – was certainly not prepared to risk war alone in the hope of acquiring them. Both countries would far prefer the continued existence of a weakened and distracted France – a kind of western Poland – and even Emperor Leopold II was prepared to accept the humiliation of his royal Bourbon brother-in-law and sister if this reduction of French influence on the international scene could be continued indefinitely. Even when the French royal family's attempt to flee was aborted at Varennes in late June 1791, and the Emperor felt obliged to make a formal protest and take some form of action, he was careful to ensure that the celebrated Declaration of Pillnitz in late August was little more than sabre-rattling, the serving of a warning rather than a summons to arms. Austria and Prussia called upon the other monarchies of Europe to take concerted action with them, well aware that there was not the least prospect of England heeding the call. The very *rapprochement* between Berlin and Vienna had been partly based upon the cooling of the Anglo-Prussian alliance and partly upon a shared suspicion of Russian ambitions in Poland now that Catherine the Great's latest war with Turkey was at an end. Leopold was aware that George III would be most unlikely to intervene on the continent, and, as he wrote to his veteran minister, Prince Wenzel Anton Kaunitz, 'If England fails us, the case is non-existent.' English pacific intentions were still very pronounced as late as February 1792, as Prime

Minister William Pitt's statement to the House of Commons on the 17th of the month well illustrates. There never had been a time, he boldly declared, '... when, from the situation of Europe, we might more reasonably expect fifteen years of peace than at the present moment'. Although the statements of all politicians promising 'peace in our time' need regarding with great caution, there is no reason to question Pitt's sincerity at that moment. He was the victim, like Leopold II and Frederick William II, and indeed most French politicians, of a massive lack of perception of the realities of the situation. The continental powers totally underestimated the military capabilities of their rivals. Above all, Austria and Prussia discounted the nationalistic energy and proselytising zeal of the dominant party groupings in the French Assembly. They in their turn chose to interpret the Declaration of Pillnitz as a dire threat to French national sovereignty. As in so many cases, it is not the true nature of the threat as how it is actually perceived that is of significance in the causation of wars. In 1792 a large measure of miscalculation affected all parties in the dispute. As Heidrich described this, the French revolutionaries '... and their opponents no longer understood each other. They were breathing, as it were, in different political atmospheres.'

It is now time to examine in more detail the responsibility of France for the outbreak of war, and the ways in which revolutionary foreign policy developed to that critical point. The more immediate issues were those of the new conceptions of national sovereignty and the rights of self-determination implicit in the Declaration of the Rights of Man in the earliest days of the Revolution and the subsequent abolition of all feudal privileges. The concept of 'fraternity' could be taken to imply a threat to all old regimes, and the validity of all treaties undertaken by princes rather than peoples was thrown into question. Three matters became the focal issues. First the status of Alsace – and the Electors of Trèves and Trier – appeared in doubt. Second, the papal enclave of Avignon attracted attention to the same principle, and its eventual annexation by the French Assembly in September 1791 did not reassure the apprehensive. Third – and probably most significant – was the question of the *émigrés*. Led by the Duke of Artois and other princes who left France shortly after the storming of the Bastille in July 1789, these groups of aristocrats and officers became the voice and spirit of counter-revolution, forming themselves and their supporters into small armies in the Austrian Netherlands and other small principalities along the frontiers of France.

In fact these issues were not as serious as they were commonly made out to be. Prussia would never move over the Alsatian issue on its own. The emperor would not undertake a war over a piece of papal territory. And the *émigrés* were no more popular in most of their new homes – least of all in the Austrian Netherlands – then the PLO have proved in Jordan or Egypt in recent times. In due course the emperor expelled them from Belgium. Only a few insecure minor princes – fearful for their own futures, faced by the French undertakings addressed to all Mankind – welcomed the exiles. In sum, these matters were grounds for hostility and antipathy, but hardly *per se* for open war. It is true that the new French style of 'open diplomacy' – with foreign policy the subject for full public debate in the Assembly rather than in secret behind closed doors as heretofore – shocked many east of the Rhine. The frequent denunciations of the Austrian treaty of 1756 – which in fact both signatories had flouted when it suited their advantage – was resented in Vienna. And the florid style of the revolutionary orators was hardly reassuring. 'The French have become the foremost people in the universe,' declared Jacques Pierre Brissot de Warville to loud and prolonged applause, 'so their conduct must correspond to their new Destiny. As slaves, they were bold and great; are they to be feeble and timid now that they are free?' But most foreign observers noted the French preoccupation with domestic matters – in particular the transfer of power from the King to the Assembly – and welcomed the apparent impotence overseas that these developments incurred. Although some French leaders chose to regard Prussia as a potential ally, others considered the Austro-Prussian alliance with misgivings. It was hardly a 'Concert of Europe', and even the Declaration of Pillnitz was not widely noted in Paris at the time of its issue. When Louis XVI was induced to accept the Constitution of September 1791 it appeared to the Emperor that honour had been satisfied.

This, yet again, was a misinterpretation. The true effect of the Austrian and Prussian posturing had been to prepare the way for the surge to the left in French politics that would in the end lead to both the war and the destruction of the monarchy. When the new Legislative Assembly met, it was composed of new men of more radical persuasion than before. It set up twenty-three committees to supervise ministers, including that of Foreign Affairs. The *Feuillants* under Louis, Comte de Narbonne, and the two other politicians making up the 'Triumvirate' were the largest party, relatively moderate, happy with the new constitution, and decidedly against any talk of war. However, a right-wing split-away group, the *Fayettistes*, formed around Marie Joseph, Marquis de Lafayette, were strongly in favour of a short, sharp, successful war with Austria to restore, they hoped, the prestige of the monarchy. They found themselves in this the allies of the mid-left Brissotins, who also wanted war, but in order to finally discredit the King. The Brissotins were close to the strong Girondin faction, which also hoped to bring down Louis XVI on charges of conspiring with Austria.

Brissot set to work with a team of fine orators to create a widely based consensus in favour of a war. Using every argument, half-truth and blatant lie, the work went remorselessly forward. Above all, many appeals were made to French honour. Strong demands were made that the King should require the Emperor to disband the *émigré* armies forthwith in Trier and the Austrian

Netherlands or take the consequences. To the total disconcertion of the left, Austria at once obliged for its own reasons, expelling the exiles from Belgium. When the King reported this to the Assembly there was uproar.

Brissot was in despair; then Austria, with crass miscalculation, played into his hand. For no obvious reason, on 21 December 1791 Vienna issued a stiff note demanding French acceptance of 'the sanctity of treaties' over Alsace, and guarantees of the future of Trier, for the defence of which Austrian troops were put on stand-to ready to fight '... should French troops cross the frontier'. A concert of European powers would act ' for the maintenance of public order and for the security and honour of monarchs'. The left seized its opportunity – here was the pretext it required. From 14–24 January 1792 a great debate was held; Austria was (yet again) declared a treaty-breaker. Artois and others were indicted for high treason. A new ultimatum was dispatched with a deadline of 1 March. To bring in any remaining doubters, the advantages of war were stressed. The opposition powers were weak. French honour was at stake. 'We shall live in freedom or we shall die! The Constitution or death!' War could end civil strife in Vendée and Brittany. A cunning economic argument was added to bolster the faltering currency. 'Not to start a war is to seek to destroy the credit of our *assignats*.' Victory would be assured and easy. The might of France could not be denied. 'What is the army? It is the entire population!' Hysteria began to mount. The press was unequivocally in favour of war. Only Maximilien de Robespierre (who feared lest a successful war might re-establish the King or lead to a military dictatorship), spoke against the idea. His warnings went unheard. Once again fantasy and misrepresentation was taking its toll of level-headed reason. They would create 'one great revolution'; it would become '... a crusade for universal liberty'. When the Foreign Minister returned a timid answer he was impeached, and on 9 March the King dismissed Narbonne and appointed a Brissotin and Girondin ministry. The new Foreign Minister, General Charles François Dumouriez, issued a new ultimatum to Austria: 'Renounce the Concert – or war!' On 1 March the Emperor Leopold II had died, being succeeded by Francis II. Six weeks later he ordered his army to strengthen the frontier. The Girondins waited no longer – and on 20 April they declared war, only seven deputies voting against the proposal. The wine was drawn and would have to be drunk: twenty-three years of almost continuous warfare lay ahead.

A word must be added about the spread of the conflict to include England. As we have noted, Pitt could not foresee a struggle involving his country in February 1792. Yet within thirteen months England would be at war. Until late 1792 there had been few signs of open crisis, and although there was no love lost on either side of the Channel there was still no real reason to anticipate a war. However, as Honoré Gabriel, Marquis de Mirabeau, had asserted in 1791: 'The enmity of England will be eternal; it will grow each year with the productivity of its industry, and even more than our own.' What caused the abrupt change of attitude was first the French demand for the 'natural frontier' of the Rhine. Dumouriez claimed: 'The Rhine must be our sole frontier, from Geneva to the sea.' That implied a French assimilation of not only Belgium but also a great part of Holland. Here a cardinal principle of English foreign policy since the reign of Elizabeth I was at stake: the Netherlands must be in neutral or friendly hands or the safety of the Thames Estuary, and thus of the realm, would be gravely at risk. As Edmund Burke described it, Holland might be considered '. . . as necessary a part of this country as Kent.' As French armies – Valmy won – began to march deep into the Low Countries alarm began to mount. The gauntlet was flung down by William Wyndham, Lord Grenville. 'This government, adhering to the maxims which it has followed for more than a century, will also never see with indifference, that France shall make herself, either directly or inadvertently, sovereign of the Low Countries, or general arbitress of the rights and liberties of Europe.' The execution of King Louis XVI was the last straw. The French ambassador was dismissed. France promptly declared war. And so the most inveterate of all France's opponents – if at first the most bungling and unsuccessful (save at sea) – entered the lists.

The War of the First Coalition surprised all parties by its length (five years), its fluctuations of fortune, and ultimately its indecisiveness. Expectations of a short, cheap and glorious struggle by both France and Austria proved nugatory. Although several contestants left the ring in 1795, France and Austria – together with Great Britain – fought on remorselessly. By mid-1797 both the Directory and the Schönbrunn had come to desire a settlement. General Napoleon Bonaparte's successes in North Italy and the Frioul had to some extent been matched by French setbacks in Germany. The resultant Peace of Campo Formio (17 October 1797) conceded many points to the French – but Austria was awarded the Republic of Venice and its possessions, save the Ionian Isles.

Whether the cessation of hostilities between October 1797 and September 1798 should be called a true peace is debatable. Neither side was content with the settlement – and of course Anglo-French hostilities continued throughout. Thwarted of the possibility of a direct attack against England, the Directory settled for a feint against Ireland by General Humbert's ill-fated expedition and a major campaign into the eastern Mediterranean by General Bonaparte, his objectives being Malta and Egypt – and the posing of a possible threat towards crucial British interests in distant India.

The European powers noted the continued aggressiveness of France with misgiving. Her ambitions were not even restricted to the Orient, as became clear when French forces absorbed Mulhausen and Geneva, and then Mainz, and turned the Papal States into the Roman Republic. The so-called peace was evidently little more than a truce. As Director Louis Marie La Revellière frankly declared, France's objective was '. . . to unite Holland, France, Switzerland, the Cisalpine and Ligurian Republics by an uninterrupted continuity of territory . . . [providing] . . . a nursery of excellent soldiers and a formidable position'. As for France's ambitions in the Orient, the occupation of the Ionian Isles provided an incentive together with an exaggerated appreciation (once again) of the weakness of the Ottoman Empire. General Bonaparte had declared: 'The Republic regards the Mediterranean as its sea and wishes to dominate it.' Even allowing for Revolutionary hyperbole, these were plain warnings to those who would hear.

One power to date uninvolved in the disputes with Revolutionary France was Tsarist Russia – but stage by stage, as French interests in the eastern Mediterranean became evident, St Petersburg began to stir. Certain preliminary negotiations with Sweden and (individually) with Austria and Prussia had already been undertaken, and many French nationals expelled, when Catherine the Great was succeeded by Paul I on 17 November 1796 – but no overt hostilities had taken place, and even the precautionary moves were put in abeyance thereafter. Paul was as hostile to the Revolution as ever his mother had been, but there were good reasons for his cautious attitude. He was an enigmatic personality. 'The new Tsar Paul, a prey to whims and passions,' wrote Rose, 'was the centre of a cyclonic system all his own.' He had detested his mother – a possible reason for a policy *volte face* – Russia had a vast national debt, many of her serfs were in revolt, and Paul probably saw himself at first cast in the heroic role as mediator of a general pacification. By mid-1797, however, the French occupation of the Ionian Isles and summary treatment of Venice had led to a more realistic assessment.

From November 1797 Paul served notice of his personal interest in Mediterranean affairs by declaring himself 'Protector' of the Order of the Knights of St John of Malta, in part a reflection of his religious zeal, and in part a reaction to the Ionian situation. Russian agents were also reporting French contacts with Polish exiles and extravagant promises of aid (January 1798). French expansionism, it seemed, knew no bounds. Thoroughly alarmed, the Tsar concluded an agreement with the Turks (April 1798), next month sent two naval squadrons to aid the British blockade off the Dutch coast, and – after news of the French seizure of Malta en route for Egypt – sent another to anchor off Constantinople, its admiral authorised to offer aid to the Porte. Still Russia hesitated to engage in full hostilities – until news of Admiral Horatio Nelson's destruction of the French fleet at the Battle of the Nile (1 August) galvanised her into activity. The Second Coalition was beginning to take shape. Great Britain's isolation was ending.

The new alliance against France would not be a reality, however, until Austria could be persuaded to recommence the war. This did not prove easy to effect. On the one hand Austria was suspicious of Prussia's ambiguous attitudes. On the other Russia suspected possible double-dealing at Franco-Austrian talks being held at Selz in Alsace (May to July 1798). The first anxiety was resolved when Prussia pledged neutrality in a future general European war; the second by news of the Nile – which put new backbone into Austria's hitherto faltering resolve. But still Vienna hesitated on the brink. Even when French troops – responding to a rash Neapolitan foray into the Roman Republic – occupied Naples and set up the Parthenopean Republic (23 January 1799), the Emperor Francis II hesitated. In exasperation Tsar Paul set out to force Vienna's hand by threatening to withdraw from all undertakings. In the event the issue was decided by the French seizing the initiative: on 12 March 1799 the Directory declared war.

In summary, the immediate origins of the War of the Second Coalition can be traced to the unabated appetite of France for territorial expansion – the old demand for the natural frontiers being supplemented by additional ambitions involving further areas of Italy, Switzerland and Egypt. As in 1792–3, a whole series of French miscalculations and optimistic misrepresentations underlay the return to general war in 1799. If the Directors had been correct in estimating that the conquest of Egypt and the occupation of Naples would be relatively easy in military terms, they failed to calculate correctly in almost every other area. Their actions created new enemies in Russia and Turkey, and eventually revitalised another in Austria. Great Britain – far from cowed by threats to Ireland, her interests in the Levant and distant India – was resurgent and determined. There was instability in Switzerland, Italy and Belgium, where revolts briefly flared, and in Paris, where several *coups d'état* were undergone as the Directory changed its composition.

Nor should the role of Great Britain be overlooked. By continuing in the war after Campo Formio, she provided a basis for future European action against France. By boldly sending the Royal Navy back into the Mediterranean – despite French designs on Ireland – London demonstrated the firmness of its resolve. And above all by Nelson's victory at the Nile, Britain demonstrated that the French could still be tellingly defeated (and its best army isolated far from home) – factors that had no small effect in persuading Constantinople, St Petersburg and Vienna to re-enter the struggle against the common foe.

However, the Second Coalition was to prove ultimately as dissent-riven and ineffective as the First. Of the earlier alliance, Rose commented: 'Their aims being as diverse as their methods were disputed, the term "First Coalition" applied to this league is almost a misnomer.' Its successor proved no better. In the words of Blanning, '... flawed from the start, the Second Coalition very soon fell apart.' Austria redisplayed its '... ability to snatch defeat out of the jaws of victory', and Great Britain played its role both by treating her Russian allies as mere auxiliaries during the Helder Campaign (thereby causing the

Tsar's withdrawal from the war and, in December 1800, his formation of the anti-British Second Armed Neutrality) and by refusing her allies any share in Malta after its recapture in September 1800 despite positive undertakings to do so made in December 1798. So a combination of French victories at Marengo and Hohenlinden broke the will for the time being of Austria, and the Armistice of Treviso (15 January 1801) led to the Peace of Luneville on the 9th of the following month. These disasters left Great Britain isolated, and together with serious domestic issues – famine and Catholic relief – hastened the fall of William Pitt's ministry and the creation of a new government under Henry Addington on 14 March 1801. He at once entered into negotiations with France, and the one-sided Preliminaries and Peace of Amiens were the result. By its terms, France was to restore Naples and the Papal States, but retain Nice, Savoy, Piedmont, the west bank of the Rhine and Holland. Britain, however, was to return the Cape of Good Hope, Egypt (newly reconquered), Malta and a cluster of West Indian islands, retaining only Trinidad, and Ceylon. The Army of the Orient was to be repatriated to France with its effects.

But now a new dynamic force was on the French political scene. On 10 November 1799 Bonaparte had become one of three 'Provisional Consuls' in succession to the overthrown Directory. By early next year he was First Consul and *de facto* ruler of France. He was under no illusions whatsoever about what the future was likely to hold. 'Between old monarchies and a young republic the spirit of hostility must always exist,' he declared at the time of Amiens. 'In the present state of affairs every peace treaty means no more than a brief armistice; and I believe that my destiny will be to fight almost continuously.' And so it was to prove, even when the Republic became a Life Consulate, and thereafter an Empire. Each of the succession of devastating wars would have its own immediate causes; each of the next five great coalitions would have its specific aims; but the *origins* of the Napoleonic Wars lay in ancient frictions and rivalries, and in the events between 1789 and 1802 that have been briefly described and analysed above.

The reasons why this paper has concluded with the coming of Napoleon to power have already been indicated. How far Napoleon Bonaparte was personally responsible for the continuous series of wars that will always be associated with his name I have discussed in *The Campaigns of Napoleon* (1966). It has been a contentious subject since Napoleon's death in 1821. Unsurprisingly, on St Helena he maintained that he had acted purely in self-defence – a view much repeated by his admirers. Thus Arthur-Lévy could assert that 'during the whole of his [Napoleon's] reign, his sole aim was to arrive at a just and lasting peace which would ensure to France that status to which she is entitled. England's unchanging rivalry, the terror of ancient thrones at the spectacle of a dynasty sprung up overnight, the hopes of building a dam against the spread of libertarian ideas, and the secret appetites of all, those were the elements out of which the successive coalitions were forged and against which Napoleon's pacific attempts were ever in vain.'

Needless to say, there are other views. Some – including Louis Adolphe Thiers – have tended to the view that Napoleon's continuous recourse to war was in large measure the expression of a continuing determination to bring Great Britain – the inveterate and traditional enemy of France – to book. Peace no doubt Napoleon would have welcomed – but only on his own terms. 'One could even concede,' adjudicated Lefebvre, 'that Napoleon would have willingly kept peace, had he been left free to do everything he wished.'

The origins of wars, it has been the argument of this paper, lie deeper than immediate causes. The major, ancient contentions preoccupying and dividing the powers of Europe that resulted in war after war from 1792 to 1815 with barely a break were given new life and direction by Revolutionary France whose zeal and determination appeared to threaten so much of what the 'old order' saw itself as representing. In fact the real novelty in the 'first modern war' was the ways in which it came to be fought rather than in how it was occasioned. The ideological element in that struggle certainly helped to create hostility against France, but hardly caused recourse to war in itself. This, we have argued, was due far more to miscalculations, misrepresentations and, arising out of them, plain misunderstandings. Mutual beliefs in the other side's *weakness* had a large part to play in the original descent to war. Soon thereafter, it was fear of the newly revealed French *power* that made the continuation of war so ineluctable. But probably the most malign influence of all was mis-understanding – a factor in so many wars both ancient and modern – but rarely so graphically illustrated as in the Revolutionary and Napoleonic Wars of the late eighteenth and early nineteenth centuries.

APPENDIX

The seven coalitions against France, 1792–1815

The FIRST COALITION. Formed: 26 June 1792 – Austria and Prussia. Joined by Great Britain, Spain and Sardinia (1793). Associated: Holland and Naples. Disintegration: Tuscany, Prussia, United Provinces (Batavia) and Spain make various peaces (and in the last two cases also alliances) with France during 1795. Armistice with Austria at Leoben (18 April 1796); Peace of Campo Formio (17 October 1797). Great Britain fights on.

The SECOND COALITION. Formed: 19 May 1798 – eventually comprises Great Britain, Austria, Russia, Naples and Turkey. Associated: Bavaria, Württemberg and Mainz and other German states (but not Prussia). Disintegration: Austria makes peace at Luneville (9 February 1801); Second Armed Neutrality – Russia, Sweden, Denmark and Prussia versus Great Britain (18 December 1800); Preliminaries of Amiens (1 October 1801) become Peace of Amiens (25 March 1802) between Great Britain and France. General peace (until 16 May 1803 when Great Britain redeclares war).

The THIRD COALITION. Formed: between 11 April (Russo-British alliance) and 9 August (Austro-British alliance), 1805. Joined by Sweden (September). Associated: German princes but not Bavaria, Württemberg or (quite) Prussia. Disintegration: Peace of Pressburg (France and Austria, 26 December 1805); Franco-Russian Treaty (20 July 1806 – signed but not ratified by the Tsar). Great Britain fights on.

The FOURTH COALITION. Formed: between 1 July and 6 October 1806 – eventually comprised Great Britain, Prussia and Russia. Associated: Saxony (by compulsion) and Hesse. Disintegration: peace and treaties of Tilsit (7–9 1807). Great Britain fights on.

The FIFTH COALITION. Formed: 9 April 1809 – Great Britain and Austria. Associated: Bourbon Spain and Portugal. Disintegration: armistice of Znaim (11 July 1809) and Treaty of Vienna (14 October 1809). Great Britain fights on, with Portugal and unoccupied Spain.

The SIXTH COALITION. Formed: 20 July 1812 to 9 September 1813 by various treaties involving Great Britain, Russia, Spain and Portugal and (latterly) Prussia and Austria. The first truly effective coalition dated from the Treaty of Chaumont (9 March 1814) by which the signatories declared common aims and singleness of purpose 'for twenty years' if necessary. Associated: growing numbers of German princes during 1813, and, eventually, Naples. The Sixth Coalition ultimately triumphed: first abdication of Napoleon (6 April 1814) and the Treaties of Fontainebleau (11 and 16 April 1814). The Congress of Vienna was called.

The SEVENTH COALITION. Formed: 25 March 1815 – by all signatories of the Sixth Coalition. Crisis resolved by Waterloo. Napoleon reabdicates (22 June). End of the Napoleonic Wars.

2

THE RECONQUEST OF EGYPT:
THE BRITISH VIEW

Great Britain – for reasons examined in Chapter One – joined the War of the First Coalition in 1793, soon after the execution by the French Revolutionary authorities of King Louis XVI. In military terms, King George III's prime minister, William Pitt the Younger, attempted to carry out a maritime strategy very similar to that of his great father, the Earl of Chatham, during the Seven Years' War (1757–63). Using the Royal Navy, expeditionary forces were employed to snap up French sugar islands in the West Indies and (less successfully) to attempt to support the anti-republican risings in La Vendée, Toulon and elsewhere. Of course there was also a 'continental' strand to British policy, but Britain's attempts to participate in campaigns in Flanders in both 1794 and again in 1799 (in the new War of the Second Coalition in the second case) proved abysmal failures. Lieutenant-Colonel Arthur Wesley (as the future Duke of Wellington then spelt his family name) – commander of the 33rd Regiment of Foot under 'the Grand Old Duke of York' in 1794 – cogently remarked: 'At least I learnt what not to do – and that is always something'.

The 1799 campaign alongside Russian and other continental allies was equally disappointing – and led to a considerable success for the French General Brune, who, Napoleon commented years later on St Helena, caused the future Marshal of the Empire to be '. . . justly proclaimed the saviour of the Batavian Republic. The Romans would have awarded him the honour of a Triumph. By saving Holland he also saved France from invasion.' At this period even raids from the sea went almost consistently wrong for Great Britain – including the amphibious landings at Ferrol and Cadiz – largely due to the unwillingness of the naval and army commanders to cooperate effectively.

However, little by little the cabinet threshed out a realistic and consistent policy; and after Napoleon's return to France in late 1799, abandoning his Army of the Levant in distant Egypt, a properly coordinated inter-service campaign was arrived at with the object of eliminating the French presence in the eastern Mediterranean. The fascinating story of Napoleon's adventurous campaigns in Egypt and Syria, which I had tackled as long ago as 1966 in Part Four of The Campaigns of Napoleon, *had been described essentially from the French point of view. But how the British cabinet eventually arrived – by fits and starts largely dictated by the requirements of home defence against invasion and the need to counter French attempts to stir up major problems in restive Ireland – at an effective and ultimately successful strategy to that end, is the subject of this chapter, based upon my most recently published article for the second number of the fine new French quarterly magazine,* Samothrace.

†

From the time of the battle of the Nile (or the naval battle of Aboukir) – fought on 2 August, 1798, just one calendar month after General Bonaparte's landing in Egypt – British predictions of ultimate disaster awaiting the Army of the Orient were frequently expressed. 'This army is in a scrape,' wrote the euphoric Rear-Admiral Sir Horatio Nelson on 3 August, 'and will not get out of it.' It would nevertheless be all of thirty-nine months before General 'Abdullah' Menou's garrison of Alexandria admitted final defeat, and brought the Egyptian and Syrian episodes to an unmourned close. Even then, the terms of the capitulation required the British to provide shipping for the repatriation of the French officers and men with their personal effects, but an attempt to include the Rosetta stone (eventual key to the decipherment of the hieroglyphics of Ancient Egypt) amongst the French baggage was firmly resisted. As a result this famous artefact is to be seen today in the British Museum and not the Louvre.

The British presence on land and sea in considerable force in the eastern Mediterranean by 1801 requires examination. The loss of the naval base of Leghorn consequent upon General Bonaparte's successes in North Italy in 1796 – together with the growing threat of a serious French invasion attempt against Ireland or England itself – had induced the British government to withdraw the Royal Navy from the Mediterranean to strengthen home defence. The next year had seen the effective collapse of the First Coalition against France with the signature of the Preliminaries of Leoben in mid-April (subsequently confirmed in October in the Peace of Campo Formio signed in Paris and Vienna). There was also increased preoccupation with the invasion threat – with Bonaparte appointed to command the short-lived 'Army of England' – together with serious unrest leading to two successive mutinies affecting substantial sections of the Royal Navy (in April at Spithead and in May at the Nore, the latter being politically rather than grievance motivated and consequently the more serious). Not until Admiral Duncan's victory at Camperdown on 11 October and General Hoche's aborted attempt to land his army at Bantry Bay in December could full national confidence in the traditional shield of the 'wooden-walls' of England be restored. For all these reasons, there was scant time to consider the Royal Navy's re-entering the 'inland sea' in 1797.

The situation was even less favourable in the first seven months of 1798. Ireland exploded in a violent rising against British rule (May), and General Humbert's landing at Killala in support of the rebels in July – although ineffective and short-lived in itself – explains the British government's suspicions that the Toulon armament might be intended for a further attack upon the 'Emerald Isle'. The situation was highly unstable.

Although the desirability of creating a Second Coalition as soon as possible was being widely advocated, there were thus good reasons for David Dundas, Secretary-of-State for War and the Colonies, who placed small faith in continental allies in any case, advising caution when the sending of a naval squadron back into the Mediterranean was mooted by the cabinet in the mid-year. However, given the small size, scattered positioning and to date not very impressive record of the British Army, the Royal Navy substantially represented the 'sword' as well as the 'shield' of British policy, and this caused Lord Grenville, the Foreign Secretary, to support the bolder course of action. He was fully apprised by the Austrian ambassador to the Court of St James, that a British naval presence in Mediterranean waters was a *sine qua non* if any formation of a new alliance to contain and, if possible, frustrate French expansion were to be seriously attempted. The Court of the Two Sicilies at Naples and the 'sublime Porte' (Sultan Selim III) also required a definite indication of British good faith if they were to be cajoled into cooperative attitudes. The ambitions of 'Mad Tsar' Paul in the Balkan region at the expense of the decaying Turkish Empire in general, and towards Malta in the central Mediterranean in particular (Paul was Grand Master of the Order of St John of Jerusalem) would also bear careful watching from Britain's point of view. And lastly – but probably most significantly – the growing Toulon armament and its destination required close surveillance. So it was decided to send a strong squadron under Nelson back into the Mediterranean and on 8 May he was detached from Admiral Earl St Vincent's fleet off Cadiz and entered the 'inland sea'.

Although as late as 3 June Buckingham was advising Grenville to '... look for them in Galway Bay' (and indeed General Humbert did land at Killala in July), the true destination of General Bonaparte and Admiral Brueys had finally been identified in London by the 9th: 'I think Egypt to be their objective,' wrote Dundas to Spencer. Soon a reinforced Nelson was scouring the Mediterranean in search of the French convoy (which had used a convenient offshore gale to slip undetected out to sea on 19 May). The subsequent hue and cry, the miscalculations and narrowly missed interceptions, do not concern us here. Suffice it to say that the Army of the Orient landed safely near Alexandria (1 to 3 July) and by the end of the month was master of Lower Egypt. Nelson at last caught up with Bruey's fleet in Aboukir Bay on 2 August, effectively cutting the French off from home. The Army of the Orient was stranded. An immediate consequence was the formation of the Second Coalition between

Great Britain, Russia, Turkey, Naples and eventually Austria, completed on 22 June 1979.

But Bonaparte trapped and Bonaparte helpless were not compatible concepts. Soon the British cabinet's anxieties for India and the rich trade of the Orient were overweighing its delight at the decisive outcome of the Nile (news of which only reached England in late September – 'My heart is overflowing with joy,' wrote Grenville to Spenser on 2 October) and its subsequent diplomatic results on the broader European scene. Fears that Bonaparte might secure shipping in the Red Sea were largely allayed once Commodore Blankett arrived there with a small squadron in April 1799 and proceeded to collect local shipping at Mocha and Jeddah.

By then, however, Bonaparte was besieging Acre, having left a small garrison in Egypt while he marched the remainder into Syria intent upon pre-empting the arrival of the Pasha of Damascus and his army – an objective that was duly achieved at Mount Tabor on 16 April. But with plague raging through his ranks and news that the Royal Navy was about to escort a second Turkish force, the Army of Rhodes, to invade Egypt, the French commander abruptly abandoned both the siege of Acre (where Djezzar Pasha had been sustained by Commodore Sir William Sydney Smith's small naval squadron most effectively) and any remaining dreams of '... founding a religion, marching into Asia, riding an elephant, a turban on my head and in my hand a new Koran...,' and headed back to Egypt. By now French total losses amounted to 5344 men. He arrived there in time to crush a native revolt in Cairo and then to smash the newly landed Army of Rhodes near Aboukir on 25 July. The French position, however, remained tenuous in the extreme, and on 22 August Bonaparte slipped secretly out of Alexandria harbour with a handful of colleagues and set sail for France, promising in a letter left behind that he went to seek reinforcements and would soon return. This, of course, was never to happen: Bonaparte had no wish to be contained in Egypt whilst the main war raged elsewhere. But years later he was quite prepared to reveal his disappointment: 'If it had not been for you English I would have been Emperor of the East.'

His deserted army under General Kléber still controlled Egypt – and therefore constituted a menace to the Eastern Mediterranean and an increasingly embarrassing case of 'unfinished business' for the British government. The early Allied successes of the Second Coalition on land had given way to a series of setbacks as the Directory strove successfully to regain the initiative. The post-Nile objectives of the British naval presence in the Mediterranean had been spelt out in a dispatch sent to St Vincent on 3 October 1798. These were above all to protect Naples, Sicily and the Adriatic area, cooperating to the full with local forces; to keep the French isolated in Egypt; to blockade the French garrison of Malta; and to cooperate with the Russian and Turkish fleets. Since then, however, matters had not gone well. Stirred up by Nelson, the Kingdom of the Two Sicilies had embarked upon premature action against the Roman Republic – which by December 1798 had enforced the evacuation of the Neapolitan royal family, government, and of course Lady Emma Hamilton, to Palermo. 'Naples will be a republic within six months,' wrote the British Lothario. Austria had refused to move to its government's aid, and on 8 February 1799 Naples duly became a republic. Although Acre had been well sustained by Smith, the French were still masters of Egypt and Malta, and the mass of French transports remained untouched in Alexandria harbour whilst the paternalistic attitudes of Tsar Paul over the future of Malta (he claimed authority as the Grand Master of the Order of St John) was giving cause for concern. Thus in the main only negative, defensive goals were being achieved in the Mediterranean.

Small wonder that the British cabinet – despite the endemic problem of finding the necessary resources – demanded more action. Encouraged by the long-delayed capture of Corfu by the Russians and Turks on 5 March, a force of British troops under General Stuart made a welcome appearance in Sicily, and in March a naval blockade of Naples was started. After serious rioting in the city, the French and Neapolitan Jacobite elements (aware of French setbacks on the Rhine) abandoned Naples in April. This led, however, to the 'sicilified' Nelson using his squadron in support of land operations, which was not the intention of the Lords of the Admiralty. Captain Bull RN landed on Malta and was soon besieging Valetta, but with scant resources made only snail-like progress against the garrison. An attempt by Lord Hood to use bomb-vessels against the shipping at Alexandria failed through lack of Turkish cooperation. As a result of all these activities the British fleet was dispersed all over the region when unexpectedly Admiral Bruix's squadron from Brest threw all into complete chaos by mounting his bold attempt to resupply the French in Egypt.

The Bruix episode (15 April to 13 August) ultimately failed, but the need to meet it caused the blockades of both Malta and Alexandria to be eased, whilst fear of a possible repetition of a large French attempt to reinforce or evacuate Egypt continued to overshadow the British cabinet's deliberations. To make matters worse, the ageing Lord St Vincent resigned his post on 22 June, and his replacement, Lord Keith, was soon in furious contention with both Nelson and Smith, who resented his tighter control over their activities. Keith's orders, dated 16 July, reveal the current British view of priorities in the Mediterranean. He was to secure the safety of Lisbon, of the rich Levant convoys, and of British trade with Italy; cooperate with the Austrian army around Genoa; maintain Smith's blockade of Egypt; protect the bases of Gibraltar and Minorca; ensure the final defeat of Bruix's excursion; and for the rest to restore the former *status quo* by distributing his fleet as necessary in support of the blockades of Egypt and Malta. There was still no mention of preparing an Egyptian reconquest.

The year 1800 saw little but disaster for the Second Coalition. Insofar as

Egypt was concerned, it got off to a bad start with Sidney Smith's rash and unauthorised conclusion of the Convention of El Arish with General Kléber on 24 January – whereby 'the Swedish Knight' agreed to the repatriation to France of the Army of the Orient, its guns and baggage in its own shipping under British naval escort. Admiral Lord Keith lost no time in repudiating the agreement, although when news of these events reached London in March, Dundas tended on balance to support the proposals as being in the Turkish interest. But Grenville most certainly did not – the Foreign Secretary seeing that the terms in every way favoured the French. The idea gradually petered out through the mutual distrust of all parties: particularly British misgivings about the new First Consul. 'One is inclined to think Bonaparte more ambitious than wise,' wrote the diarist J.C. Harries. 'I think that he will overreach himself...'

In Europe, meanwhile, the situation turned from bad to worse for the Coalition. The steady French recovery in Germany, Switzerland and North Italy since the latter months of 1799 eventually was followed by First Consul Bonaparte's dramatic crossing over the Alps with Berthier's Army of the Reserve and the Marengo campaign in the River Po valley, and six months later to Moreau's great victory at Hohenlinden (3 December). These successes implied the inevitable collapse of the Second Coalition. First to go was Tsar Paul, who made peace with France in October 1800 and then threw his weight behind the formation of the Second Armed Neutrality of the North – effectively against England – which would come into existence on 16 January 1801 (only to collapse after the British naval victory at Copenhagen on 30 March the same year) and 'Mad Tsar Paul's' assassination.

Scant indeed was the success attendant upon British arms during 1800. The British expedition against Cadiz foundered in a welter of recrimination: the combined operations against Belle-Ile, Ferrol and Cadiz itself were all fiascos, foundering time after time on the rock of practically non-existent cooperation and coordination between the naval and the military leaderships. Elsewhere Genoa was captured only to be abandoned. News of Marengo in June caused renewed panic in Naples, and in July Nelson, claiming ill-health, set off overland for England escorting the Hamiltons, having shown a total incapacity to serve under Lord Keith's command. Small wonder that morale in Whitehall plumbed new depths. The only good news was the long-awaited surrender of Malta on 4 September, where the besiegers had been reinforced by General Abercromby (Stuart's successor as land forces commander in the Mediterranean) with 1500 regular troops. But what should be done next?

A growing realisation that the Second Coalition was fast dissolving around them, and that the alliance's main inspiration – Premier William Pitt the Younger – was facing George III's absolute opposition over his proposals to introduce legislation to secure Catholic Emancipation as the logical continuation of the planned Act of Union with Ireland, and that his likely successor would be the more pacifically minded Henry Addington, induced key members of the government to readdress the question of Egypt as the year of 1800 wore on. If the Turks were not to suffer total disaster (Kléber had won another large victory over them at Heliopolis on 20 March 1800), and the French not left with a permanent colony in Egypt which would inevitably pose threats to both Britain's oriental trade and above all to India (where Tippoo Sahib of Mysore had maintained a close alliance with the French until his overthrow and death at Seringapatam in May 1799), it became increasingly clear that a major expedition must be sent to dislodge the French garrison – now commanded by General Menou following Kléber's assassination by a Moslem fanatic on the same day that the battle of Marengo was fought in far-off Italy. On 15 June 1800, moreover, Bonaparte had suggested negotiations with Austria. If Great Britain was to have any meaningful asset to place on the table at a general peace conference it would have to be a reconquered Egypt. But timing was now of the very essence as Austria was in sporadic negotiation with the French Foreign Minister from mid-1800, and would indeed conclude the bilateral Peace of Luneville with France on 9 February 1801, leaving Britain alone.

Dundas had been a slow convert to this change of policy concerning Egypt. As president of the East India Company Board he had been the first cabinet member to realise the possible danger to Egypt and India posed by Bonaparte at Toulon in the spring of 1798. But for some considerable time he had been more concerned about the need to acquire trade with South American Spanish colonies than with the Egyptian question itself. Throughout 1799 he had nevertheless grown increasingly uneasy about the lack of any positive British policy designed to clear Egypt of the French, especially as Grenville was strongly mooting the possibility of handing back Britain's recent colonial conquests to France in return for the restoration of the Houses of Neapolitan-Bourbon and Orange to their lands. This possibility proved the determinant influence in converting the Secretary-of-State for War into a determined proponent of the need for the reconquest of Egypt. Aware of the immense supply and transportation difficulties such an operation would entail, he would veer back towards a cautious policy more than once during the course of 1800, but ultimately he saw that a 'second front' in the Mediterranean was indeed vital for the protection of Great Britain's long-term interests. 'If we get into negotiations [with France],' he wrote to Henry Wellesley, 'the evacuation of Egypt will be a great stumbling block. If the war continues another year, I rather think it ought to be the primary object of our share of the war.' He realised that Bonaparte secretly intended to retain Egypt.

Advising rejection of M. Otto's peace proposals, on 18 June Dundas asked the cabinet to send a strong land force to clear Egypt. The debate was convoluted and protracted over several weeks. Alternatives were fully discussed, revealing 'divided views and uncertain leadership'. Dundas strongly opposed suggestions that a new British continental commitment – to Leghorn or Portugal – should be substituted for an Egyptian expedition. He passionately advocated the case for supporting Turkey rather than Austria. Eventually he won his point when French duplicity over her true intentions towards Egypt became clear to all, even the pro-Austrian Grenville. And so on 3 October the cabinet decided by a bare majority to send General Abercromby with an army of 15,000 men to Egypt (leaving only 8000 for the expedition to Lisbon, the vital naval base). The die at last was cast. However inadequate the plan that emerged, the policy decision was correct. In the end 14,950 infantry, 1063 cavalry (many dismounted) and 586 gunners (with 38 cannon) sailed from Marmorice Bay in Turkey to land on 8 March.

The complex history of the British expedition to Egypt will be told in the following chapter. Major intelligence underestimations of French strength might well have led to disaster, but the decision to supplement Abercromby's major landing near Alexandria with a secondary expedition of 5000 men from India under General Baird to Kosseir on the Red Sea coast was clearly sound, if almost impossible to coordinate – and indeed Baird's force was hardly to fire a shot as by the time it had wearily marched through the desert to Cairo the campaign was effectively over. The death of Abercromby at the night battle of Aboukir on 22 March 1801, two weeks after the successful (although fiercely opposed) landing operation masterminded by Major-General Sir John Moore and Commodore Sydney Smith respectively, was a sad loss, but his successor in command – Lieutenant-General Hely Hutchinson – proved competent if uninspired, and with the rather questionable aid of a plague-ridden Turkish force, the 10,000 French commanded by General Belliard were induced to surrender at Cairo on 18 June; and then, after a long and complex series of combined operations against Alexandria, General Menou at last capitulated to the British with his remaining 7300 effectives on 2 September. A last-ditch attempt by a French naval force under Admiral Ganteaume to succour Alexandria had managed to reach Egyptian waters – more than Bruix had achieved – in June, only to be forced to sail back to Toulon (where he arrived on 22 July). From that moment any hope of the French retaining control of Egypt was doomed. But at least Menou and Belliard had held out long enough to secure good terms of repatriation.

With Austria having made a separate peace, and the Kingdom of the Two Sicilies again overwhelmed in March 1801, and above all with Pitt's Ministry having fallen on 3 February, it behoved the new Prime Minister, Henry Addington, to reopen negotiations with M. Otto, the French plenipotentiary. Although news of the fall of Egypt was daily expected, it is ironic to have to record that Otto, playing upon the British cabinet's fear that failure to reach terms of peace at the conference would lead to a renewed threat of invasion of the British Isles, skilfully induced Grenville to sign the Preliminaries of Peace in

London late on 29 September. On 2 October news of the surrender of Alexandria arrived – just too late to be able to influence the negotiations. Addington and Bonaparte both wanted peace, but it would not be until 29 March 1802 that Lord Cornwallis would be able to sign the definitive Peace of Amiens. Peace at last had been achieved – short-lived though it was to prove – but from Britain's point of view it was a case of 'Peace without Victory'.

3

THE EGYPTIAN CAMPAIGN OF 1801

*T*he Middle East – *comprising as it does the land-bridge joining Africa to Eurasia – has always been the scene of major campaigns from the days of the earliest Pharaohs, if not even earlier. Today, the major interest lies in the region's oil deposits. In the early nineteenth century, it was the region's strategic positioning that attracted and held international interest, commanding as the area did the western terminals of the great overland caravan trails running north-east into Muscovy and east to the so-called 'fertile crescent' of Mesopotamia (dominated by the great rivers Tigris and Euphrates, the supposed site of the Biblical 'Garden of Eden') and thence the landward and seaward approaches to the Indian sub-continent – the location of supposedly inexhaustible riches.*

British interest in the area had long been focused upon the Levant Company, trading out of London to Syrian ports such as Aleppo and Smyrna, and at one remove with the powerful 'John Company' – the East India Company – which dated back to 1601. British interests would most certainly not have been advanced by a permanent French presence in Egypt, nor in the collapse of the increasingly decrepit 'Porte' – the Ottoman Empire (or rather its remains) governed by successive Sultans from Constantinople. As was mentioned in the last chapter, Bonaparte's personal return to France in late 1799 in due course signalled the sending of a major British expedition to undertake the liberation of Alexandria, Cairo and Upper Egypt and the area's return to Turkish or Mameluke hegemony, thus removing the potential threat to India.

This article was the first I had published, appearing in two parts in 1962 – and thus by sheer coincidence 'closing a circle' with my most recent publication – namely the pre-ceding chapter. I wrote it on the basis of the research I had undertaken into the War of the Second Coalition during my third year at Oxford, under the benign but strict supervision of the late C.T. Atkinson, Fellow-Emeritus of Exeter College. The circumstances that led to the subject's eventual acceptance for publication (a case of 'second time lucky') have already been touched upon in my General Introduction to this volume and need no further reiteration here. But as it led to the invitation to write my first major book – and, as it has turned out, probably my most influential one – it occupies rather a special place amongst my publications. To this day, there has not been a definitive monograph devoted to this successful British combined operation of 1801, most of the attention still being paid to the Napoleonic conquest and the period to August 1799. So there is room for further scholarly research and writing from the British, Mameluke and Turkish points of view.

✝

'You may depend upon it, there is a certain devil in this army that will carry it through thick and thin. It is the first fair trial between Englishmen and Frenchmen during the whole of this war, and at no former period of our history did John Bull ever hold his enemy cheaper.' Thus wrote Colonel Paget of the 28th (the Gloucesters) as the storm-bound British Fleet prepared to disembark the British Army on the beaches of Aboukir Bay – 7 March 1801. At long last Nemesis was about to overtake the French Army that had landed near the very same place four years earlier.

The French Directory had come regretfully to the decision, in 1797, that a direct invasion of the British Isles was beyond their resources. In place of this military undertaking, they had substituted a second plan to undermine British resistance by means of a threat to India and the vital East India trade through Asia Minor. This plan greatly commanded itself to all parties concerned: the zealous and brilliant young general – Napoleon Bonaparte – fresh from his triumphs in Italy, was already fascinated by the Eastern scene; while the members of the Directory were not too displeased to remove this embarrassing young firebrand to a theatre remote from the political intrigues of Paris; furthermore, they were able to saddle him with some of the most violently Republican and Jacobin units of the army – who were also a political liability nearer home. Militarily speaking, this conception of a flank attack on a vulnerable and vital part of the British war-effort and resources left little to be desired, at least strategically. But politically it was bad statesmanship. The political weakness lay in the fact that the Directory mistook effect for cause; British prosperity, and Britain's determination to combat the menace of Revolutionary and regicide France, were due far more to the overall energy and commercial genius of the British people than to her possessions and trade in any one corner of the world, however lucrative. Nevertheless, the destruction of the East India trade would have been a heavy blow.

The Indian enterprise was rendered almost impossible by Nelson's great victory at the Nile in August 1798, barely few weeks after the French Army had landed. Indeed, it was only sheer bad luck that had prevented Nelson from intercepting the French Fleet and transports at sea: then Bonaparte's destiny might have taken a very different form. But with all communications by sea with France severed, and the French Fleet all but destroyed, the necessary build-up of reserves and supplies in the Delta that would have to precede any waterborne attack on India down the Red Sea through the dug-out ancient Suez Canal, or overland through the 'Fertile Crescent', was clearly out of the question. But this did not deter Bonaparte: he turned to a slightly less grandiose scheme of conquest: India might be beyond his grasp for the

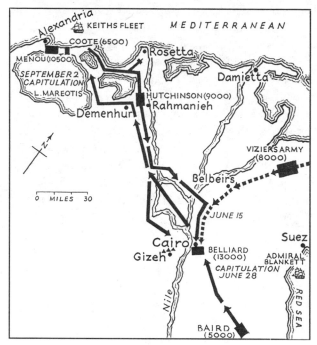

THE EGYPTIAN CAMPAIGN OF 1801

moment, but the far-flung and corrupt rule of the Turk throughout Asia Minor lay open to his aggressive genius. He dreamed of recreating the empire of Alexander the Great on an even vaster scale. But once again the Royal Navy, in the person of the eccentric Sidney Smith with his small squadron, was at the right place at the right time, and thus for a second time altered Bonaparte's destiny. This Smith achieved by reinforcing the Turkish garrison of Acre until plague and frustration forced the French forces to retire on Egypt. 'If it had not been for you English, I should have been Emperor of the East,' Bonaparte admitted many years later. This second victory of the Royal Navy was wholly the outcome of the first at the Nile – which secured the vital naval control of the Eastern Mediterranean. Thus the ultimate result of Nelson's great victory was to restrict the French Army to the Nile valley – there either to await reinforcement in strategic isolation, or to accept the reality of complete defeat.

The morale of the Army of Egypt was shaken by these defeats; captured correspondence showed marked despondency and home-sickness. 'This army is in a scrape,' wrote Nelson to Hamilton, 'and will not get out of it.' It is probable that Bonaparte felt the same about his position: and he resolved to leave the dismal Egyptian scene at the most favourable moment to restore his fortunes. News of the generally worsening situation in Europe, and the slow crumbling away of French armies on almost every front, was cunningly supplied to Bonaparte by Smith from his blockading squadron off Alexandria by means of month-old copies of English newspapers. This decided Bonaparte: if he could escape away to France and retrieve the situation in Europe, his failure in Egypt would be overlooked – and, indeed, he would again be hailed as the saviour of France. He felt no compunction about abandoning his men: his armies were no more than animate instruments for his genius to employ: if one was blunted, or broke in his hand, he would throw it away and take up another. So he left his army – as he was again to do in Russia thirteen years later – and sailed secretly, with his favourite generals, for France on 21 October 1799, ordering General Kléber to hold the country at all costs until the following May, by which time, Bonaparte promised, reinforcements would be dispatched from Toulon.

The Army of Egypt soon became convinced that it was forgotten and deserted. Nelson confidently informed Wyndham: 'I have little doubt but that the Army will be destroyed by plague, pestilence, famine and murder.' And at that moment the French government was not in a position to waste a single man: the Army of Egypt's negative role of tying down a handful of British naval vessels could not be compared to the potential value of forty-thousand veterans as a reinforcement on any of the shaky European fronts. Continual plans for the relief and evacuation of Egypt were under consideration by the Directory.

Any such scheme, however, the British cabinet was equally determined to prevent. The unauthorised conduct of Commodore Smith in negotiating the Convention of El Arish with Kléber in January 1800, led to a crushing repudiation and reprimand – administered on the government's behalf by Lord Keith, newly appointed to the Naval Command in the Mediterranean. The official British attitude at this stage is typified by Lord Grenville's letter to Lord Minto, dated 3 June 1800: 'Kléber and his army can annoy us much less where they are than in almost any other possible situation.'

But both the French and British attitudes to the fate of the Army of Egypt underwent a complete change by the end of the year. Bonaparte's campaigns in Italy laid the Second Coalition in ruins – and indeed spasmodic negotiations for a general peace were re-opened. Large areas of southern Europe fell under French control. In these new conditions, French plans for evacuation gave way to schemes for reinforcement; Egypt under the Tricolour would be a valuable pawn in any full-scale peace negotiations, especially as the garrison there was no longer vitally required elsewhere.

In similar fashion, British views altered. The complacency of June gave way to the anxiety of September. Deteriorating relations with Russia gave much cause for alarm, and there was real danger that the French might renew their project against India. The desire to clear the land of the French was freely expressed – even at the price of the evacuation terms so haughtily denounced in January. But this was not the first time that military action in Egypt had been suggested. As early as December the previous year, Lord Keith had urged Dundas, the Secretary-of-State for War, to send a 'respectable European force' to bolster Turkish resistance; but it was not until September 1800 that this course of action was officially adopted, when Dundas wrote to Lord Spencer, the First Lord of the Admiralty, stressing the value of Egypt as a bargaining counter.

The British Army was in dire need of real action after two years of almost unalleviated frustration and failure. The record for 1799 and most of 1800 was abysmal. First, there had been the failure of the Helder campaign in Holland. The army had then been switched, too late, to aid the Allies in the Mediterranean theatre. This met with little better success. Lieutenant-General Sir Ralph Abercromby – General Stuart's successor as Commander-in-Chief – was able to give but little help to the Italian mainland. The combined operation of the fleet and the army, which attempted to destroy the military installations of Cadiz, had to be abandoned owing to unsuitable weather – and friction between the respective commanders – after three days of inactivity within sight of the objective. Farther north, operations against Belle-Ile and Ferrol had been equally unsuccessful. Against this record of failure there could only be placed the long-awaited surrender of Malta. It was thus imperative for British military prestige and Allied morale that some successful land operation should take place. Egypt was the most obvious and practicable choice: the only alternative was Naples – but a speedy decision in Egypt was made all the more desirable by the collapse of the Second Coalition after the battle of Marengo. The Peace of Luneville left the First Consul free to attend to the relief of his old comrades-in-arms in the East, with the greater part of the Italian coastline and its ports available to him for a mounting area.

Once the decision to attack Egypt had been taken, the British Government lost no time in dispatching fresh orders to the Commanders-in-Chief. On 6 October, the Admiralty instructed Lord Keith to hold his fleet in readiness to transport Abercromby and a force of 15,000 men to Egypt. A second force was to land on the Red Sea coast from the squadron of Sir Home Popham. Keith was further notified that the French forces were to be allowed repatriation. For information on local conditions, he was told to rely on the only two Englishmen who possessed an on-the-spot knowledge of the Egyptian coast: Commodore Smith and Captain Hallowell. On the same date, Dundas wrote to Abercromby appointing him to the command of the Expeditionary Force, stressing the need to deny France a permanent garrison in the Eastern Mediterranean – and the general inconvenience such an attack would occasion the 'stubborn' French government. At all costs, Bonaparte was to be deprived of the advantages of the Orient. Abercromby was consequently to attack before the French had time to reinforce their occupation forces.

What appears to have been in Dundas's mind was a trial of strength by concentric sea-power against a purely military force operating on interior lines but separated from its base. The first, and major, effort was to be the landing of

Abercromby's 15,000 men from the Mediterranean. In conjunction, Popham was to land General Baird and a force of 5000 men (drawn from the garrisons of India and the Cape) on the Red Sea coast, with the role of clearing Upper Egypt. Dundas, the politician, sanguinely hoped that the Expeditionary Forces would reach Egypt by December and complete the campaign by April or May of 1801.

This plan, though majestic in conception, was both visionary and unrealistic. In the first place, Dundas's conviction that 20,000 men – split into two unequal forces – would suffice for the campaign was based on hopelessly faulty intelligence, which estimated the foe's strength at a mere 16,000 men, whereas in fact Kléber had fully 32,000 at his disposal. Secondly, Dundas's hope that the two parts of the expedition would be able to cooperate across hundreds of miles of desert was further complicated by the fact that the secret codes of the two forces were different. Thirdly, he failed to take into account the difficulties that would face Lord Keith's fleet, and the leaky transports, with only Minorca, Sicily, Algiers and Tunis open to them as potential sources of supply and refit. Finally, Dundas's estimate that three or four months would suffice to bring the French to capitulation – a conclusion based on the French home-sickness and Kléber's eagerness to make terms in January – was by September equally unrealistic. The siege of Malta had lasted long enough. As Mahan wrote: 'An army powerful enough to hold in submission and reap the use of the fertile Nile Valley, albeit very discontented, could never be reduced like the port of a rocky island.' Dundas was hoping for miracles.

Nevertheless, the die was cast, and preparations were at once begun, and the new orders reached the theatre. On 28 October, Sir John Moore noted in his diary that he had heard the army was to leave Gibraltar – where it was recuperating after its latest fiasco off Cadiz. Six battalions, under General Pulteney, were to be detached for service in Portugal; the remainder was to sail, initially, for Malta. The ultimate destination was also known to Major-General Moore: 'Sir Ralph goes to Egypt.'

The Army sailed in three divisions and, after a rendezvous off Minorca, the whole force joined Abercromby at Malta on 22 November. A Council of War was at once held, to decide the best methods of executing Dundas's orders. Abercromby wavered between the advantages of a direct attack on Alexandria, with consequent mopping-up operations, and an alternative campaign based on a landing at Damietta, leading to the capture of Cairo with the aid of a Turkish army. Major-General Sir John Moore favoured the first plan: 'If we are able to force a landing at Alexandria and make ourselves master of that port, the business will be soon done. But if we are forced to land first at Damietta and move on Cairo, the operation will be more tedious. The season of the year is much against us.' This last point was very much in the minds of the sailors: the prevalent north-easterly winds of the Eastern Mediterranean winter would make naval operations off that treacherous coastline difficult indeed. The actual landing, however, was not considered to be impossible: it would be relatively easy if the Turks could be induced to move from Jaffa to cover the operation. In any case, Moore thought that the French would not be able to oppose the landing in force without abandoning either Cairo or Alexandria – if they possessed only 16,000 men. Moore was, however, a soldier experienced enough not to ignore the friction of chance in war: 'All this, however, is subject to a degree of uncertainty.'

On 20 December, the expedition sailed for its final pre-invasion concentration area – Marmorice Bay, close to the island of Rhodes. By 20 January, the forces were all disembarked there. They were made up as follows: – 14,144 infantry; 1063 dismounted cavalry; 630 guns (to include the fleet's armament) – in a total of 138 ships. The expedition lacked horses, wagons, interpreters and maps: the staff depended on the Turks for the supply of all these vital items. But, as Abercromby and his officers had more or less expected, little aid was forthcoming. The Turks were suspicious of this new 'infidel' force on their territory; moreover, the Sultan's loyalty was wavering. The expedition was consequently delayed.

Two developments had changed the overall situation since the expedition had sailed from Gibraltar. The first – favourable from the British point of view – had been the assassination of General Kléber in December by a Moslem fanatic. His successor in command – General 'Abdullah' Menou – had little of Kléber's ability and was, moreover, the laughing-stock of both his men and the local population for having adopted the Moslem faith in order to marry the 'elderly, ugly daughter' of the Shereef – a descendant of the Prophet. The other disquieting development was the increasingly hostile attitude of the Russian Tsar Paul: Russian cooperation in the Mediterranean had been an enigma since 1797, and only a formality since 1800, but her designs on Malta were of long standing. After the battle of Marengo, the insane Tsar came increasingly under the spell of his hero, Bonaparte. The situation rapidly deteriorated as the 'Armed Neutrality' came into being. On 16 December, an Admiralty Order sanctioned the detention of Russian shipping, in reply to the Russian embargo on all British ships in Russian ports. The likelihood of hostile Russian intervention in the Mediterranean was now more than a mere possibility. Far more alarming, from Abercromby's point of view, was the pressure being exerted on the Sultan by the Court of St Petersburg: the Turks were wavering before the threats of their powerful northern neighbour. Consequently, the British received sparse supplies and assistance from the Vizier's army, originally designed to support their operations.

Sir John Moore was dispatched to act as liaison officer with the Vizier's army, stationed at Jaffa, to try to win its commander's support for the projected Damietta landing; and also to urge the prompt supply of provisions and water-transport. Of this latter item the expedition was desperately short: on 11 January, Keith reported to the Admiralty that the supply of gunboats and landing-craft was far behind schedule. Moore's mission met with little success: nor was he impressed with what he saw of the Vizier's army. Its supply system, he reported, was non-existent; its soldiery a 'wild ungovernable mob'; its commander 'a weak-minded old man without military talent or any knowledge'. To cap it all, plague was rampant in the ranks, and had claimed 6000 lives in the last six months. Abercromby, never markedly optimistic, was not very much reassured by this gloomy tale when Moore returned to Marmorice on 20 January.

These new factors determined Abercromby to follow his first plan – a landing near Alexandria, an operation less dependent on Turkish cooperation. Throughout January and February, the army made preparations and trained to the best of its ability. Small craft were coaxed from local pashas: supplies rounded up by the fleet; siege materials prepared. The troops, meanwhile, were continually exercised in disembarkation practices that were to result in the most efficient landing operation of the Napoleonic Wars. Meanwhile, the nerves of the High Command became a little frayed. Remembering the dissensions that had existed between the naval and military staffs off Cadiz the previous October, Abercromby formally requested a guarantee of full naval support for the landing and the consequent operations. Keith at once replied that the Navy would do its duty, but that his first care, in an emergency, would be for his ships. The rumours of quarrelling that reached Whitehall, however, were emphatically denied by both commanders, and, indeed Keith's cooperation with Abercromby was admirable. For instance, he placed all the marines from the fleet under Abercromby's orders for assault-training. 'It will be my duty,' Keith wrote, 'and it is strongly my inclination, to comply to the greatest possible extent.' His relations with Abercromby's successor were not, however, to be marked by such cordiality.

The fleet off Marmorice totalled 164 vessels: five ships-of-the-Line, two frigates, 100 transports and fifty-seven Turkish vessels. Captain Cochrane – the naval officer in charge of the actual landing operation – had boats for 16,000 men. Everything was nearly ready.

Nevertheless, Abercromby was not too happy about his situation or prospects. News that two French frigates had eluded the blockade off Alexandria, bringing vital ammunition and 800 reinforcements – probably the precursors of a larger relief force – was not calculated to cheer. In a letter to the Military Secretary he wrote: 'I never went on any service entertaining greater doubts of success . . . there are risks in the British service unknown to any other.' The task before him was to all appearances arduous indeed. He was about to sail on a risky operation, with a force of untested quality and Allies of very doubtful value – against a largely unknown foe on a shore that had been but sketchily reconnoitred. In spite of all his misgivings, the order to sail was issued on 21 February. The next day, escorted by the fleet of Lord Keith, the mass of transports raised their anchors and put out to sea.

On 1 March 1801, the combined Anglo-Turkish fleet sighted the Egyptian coast, slightly to the west of Alexandria. In full view of the town, the vessels sailed eastward to their planned beach-head in a small bay almost under the guns of Aboukir Castle. All hope of surprise was thus lost. The only advantage of the site chosen was the possibility of finding fresh water close to the beach. That evening the fleet anchored off Aboukir Bay, and the landing was ordered for the morning of the 4th, at dawn. During the night, however, a gale blew up, and the landing had to be postponed, much to the chagrin of all concerned in the crazily pitching transports at anchor. Sir John Moore had even more reason for rage – since he had accompanied Abercromby on a reconnaissance of the beach at considerable peril – for the landing was once again postponed on the 6th. No wonder the mood of the seasick soldiers was 'grim', as Moore described it: it appeared to be the Cadiz story all over again. The staff were equally perturbed by the delay, as it would give Menou ample time to reinforce the defences of the bay. A second reconnaissance on the evening of the 7th, however, revealed no new positions, and, as the wind and sea were both dropping, the landing-order was again issued for the next morning.

Very early on the 8th, the boats of the fleet began to assemble. The honour of leading the first landing had fallen to the Reserve commanded by Moore, strengthened by detachments drawn from the Guards. These troops entered the boats at 2 am. The attack was scheduled for dawn, but because of some delays in organizing the flotilla, the boats were not all at their rendezvous until 9 am. The troops, therefore, had to land in broad daylight and under fire from round-shot, which sank several boats. The weeks of drill at Marmorice now showed their value: the troops remained calm, and the landing proceeded according to plan. The troops went ashore in three waves: in the first were 3000 men, conveyed in fifty-eight flat-bottomed boats, supported on each flank by cutters with 6-pounders mounted in their bows. This was followed by a second flotilla of eighty-four boats, each carrying thirty men. Both flotillas were under Captain Cochrane's personal command. Close inshore was a force of two bomb-ketches and three sloops, engaging the shore-batteries as they revealed their presence. Waiting beyond these craft was the third flotilla, consisting of fourteen ships' launches towed by thirty-seven cutters, carrying the guns, commanded by Commodore Smith. Five miles offshore lay the transports – the shallows made it impossible for them to come in closer – and two miles beyond the troopships lay Lord Keith's battle fleet, ready to deal with any enemy intervention from the sea.

The outline of the operation resembles in many features landings of modern times. It was a masterpiece of organisation on the part of Captain Cochrane – even allowing for the initial delay: within an hour of the first boat touching the beach, 6000 well-supported soldiers were ashore.

As the boats came within range, a sharp musketry fire caused casualties. On the left, French cavalry rode down to the water's edge to sabre the troops staggering ashore from the tightly packed boats. In spite of these initial losses, the troops formed up as taught at Marmorice under Moore's personal command. Sword in hand, he led the men of the 40th, 23rd and 28th Foot against the central sand-dune that comprised the key of the enemy's position. An attack with cold steel overwhelmed the 61st Demi-Brigade and flung it back in retreat. Meanwhile, the French cavalry were driven off the beach by the Coldstream, the Third Guards and the 42nd Highlanders. At the cost of 600 casualties, the landing had been safely effected by 6000 men facing several thousand enemies entrenched among the dunes. Moore was justifiably pleased: 'Our attempt was daring and executed by the troops with the greatest intrepidity and coolness.' General Menou had made his fatal mistake: had he mustered but half of his available forces to oppose the landing, he might well have flung the expedition back into the sea. But internal dissensions and lack of determination in the French command enabled the British troops to survive the most dangerous moment of the campaign.

During the rest of the day, the landing of the guns and stores continued, under the spasmodic fire of Aboukir Castle. The entire army was ashore by 4 pm, and the outposts pushed inland for two miles. Moore in person led patrols forward to gather intelligence. All night there were patrol clashes. On the beaches, supply difficulties were encountered – in particular a shortage of fresh water. Hallowell soon dug a well which eased this anxiety. By nightfall the bridgehead was secured, and the most dangerous phase of the expedition had passed.

On 12 March, a general advance was ordered along the narrow peninsula towards Alexandria. This gradually made progress in the face of stiff opposition from the slowly retiring foe, at a cost of a further 1300 casualties in a sharp action on the 13th: 'But the undaunted spirit of the troops made them constantly advance in spite of every loss, so that we gained ground, which is the great object of every action.' By the 18th the army was securely camped half way across the heights that divided Alexandria from the beaches. The same day, the Castle of Aboukir capitulated. There was still no sign of Menou, though, in fact, he was not far away: most fortunately for the army, on the 20th one of Sidney Smith's Arab spies brought news of French preparations for a large-scale surprise attack on the British camp, planned for early next morning.

In the hour before dawn on the 21st, a force of 12,000 Frenchmen attacked the encampment of the British reserve – sited amongst the ruins of a Roman palace and a half-built redoubt. Menou had at last reinforced the Alexandria garrison with 10,000 men, and had determined to attack the British army before it could be reinforced by the Turkish army, now advancing from Jaffa. A preliminary feint attack on the left flank of the reserve's position did not long deceive Sir John Moore: the right of his position in the Roman ruin was the real objective. But by the time this attack fully developed, the British troops were in position. For a while chaos reigned – so common a feature of night actions – but the steadiness of the infantry of the line saved the battle. A body of French cavalry and grenadiers penetrated into the rear of the British right wing – that is to say, behind the 28th Foot and the 42nd Highlanders, who found them- selves assailed on both sides at once. Colonel Chambers's cool order: 'Rear rank 28th; Right about Face,' saved the situation, however, and, incidentally, earned the Gloucesters one of their most prized battle honours – the badge on the back of their headgear. Eventually, the enemy was decisively repulsed with heavy loss. The crack French grenadier unit – 'the Invincibles' – lost 650 casualties; total enemy losses reached the figure of 3000 men, including three generals. The British army lost seventy officers and 1306 other ranks.

But the army suffered its gravest loss in the wounding, and subsequent death, of its gifted and beloved commander, Sir Ralph Abercromby. He had undergone an active night: at one moment, in the confusion, he had almost been captured by French dragoons. This he managed narrowly to avoid, only to be struck in the thigh by a musket-ball. He allowed himself to be carried from the field only after the final repulse of the foe. A story tells how a young officer improvised a pillow for Sir Ralph as he was being carried away: 'What is that you are placing under my head?' 'Only a soldier's blanket, sir.' ' "Only a sol- dier's blanket, sir?" A soldier's blanket is of great consequence. You must send me the name of the man to whom it belongs that it may be returned to him.' He died nine days later, and Sir John, himself fated to fall in the moment of victory, recorded that 'Sir Ralph had fallen in a moment most unfortunate for his country'. He was universally lamented; the victory had been a triumphant justification of the quality of his men and their training. 'We have beaten them without cavalry, and with inferior artillery,' exulted Moore, himself slightly wounded in the action. With the aid of a flotilla of naval gunboats on the army's left wing in Lake Aboukir, the expedition had proved its valour. One certain fact that had emerged from the fortnight's fighting was the inadequacy of Dundas's intelligence about the enemy's strength. As Moore wrote to his father on the 25th: 'The French forces and their situation are far better than the government originally believed,' but, he continues cheerfully, 'we have beaten them three times.' Only eleven days earlier he had gloomily written: 'It is impossible to foresee the outcome of this expedition.'

Everybody was now optimistic, and a few hoped for a rapid conclusion to the campaign. Major-General Sir Hely Hutchinson had succeeded to the command, and although he was a competent officer who had enjoyed the full confidence of his former general, several of his colleagues had lower opinions of his ability. Moore, however, was constantly loyal, and endorsed most of Hutchinson's orders: the one that caused the most dispute was his decision not to attack Alexandria immediately, although it appeared ready for occupation. Had he at once followed up the night battle of Lake Mareotis, he might have taken the town in the general confusion. But the sudden and unexpected assumption of the supreme command found him unready for the responsibilities and instant decisions required, and in consequence he missed the opportunity. He lacked the heavy artillery for a regular siege, and while he made up his mind what to do with his main body, he detached a force to besiege Rosetta to the East. Eventually he decided to advance on Cairo, marching with a force of 5000 British troops and 4000 Turks under the Captain Pasha, who had put in a belated appearance with a Turkish fleet on the 25th. Lord Keith and Captain Cochrane opposed this decision, favouring instead a scheme to flood the dry-bed of Lake Mareotis by cutting the dyke containing Lake Aboukir, thus isolating the town of Alexandria from the south. Hutchinson allowed this to be done on 13 April, but, nevertheless, refused to permit any attempt at an assault: his troops were not numerous enough. A few days later, the Allied force marched for Damietta (which fell on the 19th), leaving Sir Eyre Coote and 6500 men to contain Menou in Alexandria. Early on the march, Hutchinson was forced to request Lord Keith to recall Sidney Smith, who had mortally offended the Captain Pasha over the terms he had afforded some prisoners at Rosetta. The command of the boats on the Nile was handed over to a Captain Morrison, but Hutchinson was never satisfied with the number of boats the Navy provided. Attacking Keith, he wrote on 27 April: 'If no attention is to be paid to our most pressing needs, it will be useless to attempt any further military operations. There are not twelve British boats on the Nile...'

The sad fact was that the new commander lacked Abercromby's ability for handling sailors. Lord Keith privately regarded Hutchinson as a clever, but indolent and slovenly, man and was continuously urging him to hasten his operations. Not unnaturally, Hutchinson bitterly resented this intervention. Lord Keith, however, had other problems on his mind besides that of amicable relations with his opposite number. The danger of the fleet's situation owing to the prevailing winter winds troubled him considerably. Moreover, and even more disturbing, he had received information that a French squadron had slipped the Toulon blockade and put out to sea: its probable objective was the relief of Alexandria. 'It is surely no desirable situation,' he wrote, 'to be performing duties of an agent of transports when the enemy have a squadron at sea.'

This naval force was that of Rear Admiral Ganteaume, which had originally escaped from Brest on 29 January, and had subsequently made two attempts to reach Egypt from Toulon. On the first occasion, it was forced to return to port following an epidemic of plague in the ships crowded with soldiers. On the second attempt, Ganteaume conveyed 4000 troops to Derna, 400 miles west of Alexandria, but did not dare to approach closer owing to Keith's vigilance. On 8 June, Keith had informed the Army Headquarters that 'an enemy force is in the offing and I may have to leave this area.' But Ganteaume was unable to land his troops owing to the fierce surf, thus saving them from virtual suicide on the inhospitable coast. Two days later Keith was off Derna, writing to Warren, commanding the naval units pursuing the French, 'Ganteaume's squadron was here two days ago but has retreated.' After detaching Bickerton with a squadron to follow the enemy, Keith returned to his station off Alexandria to face a bitter dispute with some of his captains over the allocation of fresh vegetables and firewood to the fleet. Nevertheless, the return of Ganteaume to Toulon, and the eventual victory of Captain Saumarez over a combined Franco-Spanish Squadron, marked the failure of the last serious attempt to relieve the beleaguered French Army in Egypt.

Meanwhile, on 11 May, Hutchinson reached the important junction of the Rosetta and Cairo–Alexandria roads. Here he was faced with the final decision of which objective to tackle first. A combination of circumstances led him to continue the advance on Cairo. In the first place, the French covering force had abandoned Rhaminie and fallen back towards Cairo, and not Alexandria as had been expected. Secondly, on 12 May, news arrived of Admiral Blankett's arrival off Suez. This officer was commanding the squadron conveying Baird's troops from India, and Hutchinson assumed – wrongly as events later proved – that the reinforcement of 5000 men was still aboard ship, and thus also close to Cairo. In fact, Blankett was merely reconnoitring Suez with two ships. Baird had already been landed at Kosseir, farther down the Red Sea coast, and was not to leave his camp there until 21 June. A final factor influencing Hutchinson's decision was the rumour that the Vizier's army – marching from Belbeirs towards Cairo – was in danger of a French attack.

The decision was taken. On 1 June, the army made a junction with the Vizier's forces near Belbeirs. The Allies held a Council of War, and again it was decided to march on Cairo – Moore noting the rumour that the Vizier had forced Hutchinson's hand in the matter. The combined army, now totalling some 12,000 men, finally reached the outskirts of Cairo on 15 June. Had the French garrison made a determined defence, the outcome could have still been in doubt; the Turks were of little effective value, as the Vizier and the Captain Pasha were on the very worst of terms and refused to cooperate with one another. At the same time, a serious dissension broke out amongst the senior British officers – at one time almost amounting to a mutiny against Hutchinson's authority. A serious situation was only averted by the good sense and loyalty of Sir John Moore, who, from his sick-bed, persuaded his brother-officers to be reasonable and return to their duty. It is typical of the man that no word of the affair is recorded in his diary.

It was fortunate, under these circumstances, that the French garrison of 13,000, commanded by General Belliard, had no stomach for a fight. The Cairo garrison was, indeed, depleted by 8000 sick, so that the effective strength numbered a mere 5000. This force was wholly inadequate for the defence of the walled perimeter of Cairo, as the defences, though extensive, were in a very poor state of repair. Moore inspected the fortifications after the capitulation and gave it as his expert opinion that only one small sector was in a condition to withstand a determined assault. French morale was very low: isolated for the last twelve months, with no news from France, thanks to the effectiveness of the British naval blockade, continuously assailed by the clandestine attacks of the local population, and terrified of the bloodthirsty reputation of the Turkish army for atrocities, the French had little fight left in them. For these reasons, General Belliard was anxious to capitulate to Hutchinson rather than risk the Vizier's tender mercies, and he at once applied for an armistice so that terms could be discussed. After long negotiations, the final terms were signed on 28 June; the conditions were close to those offered by Commodore Smith the year before. The French agreed to abandon Cairo, and leave Upper Egypt within twelve days. The Royal Navy was to be responsible for their repatriation to France, together with their arms and personal baggage. Thus half the French Army of Egypt passed into British hands with hardly a shot fired in the defence of Cairo. They secured honourable terms, but in Moore's eyes the capitulation was the work of a coward. On 30 July, he wrote in his diary: 'Belliard's conduct in surrendering seems to me one of the basest acts I have heard of.'

Two days after the surrender of Caito, General Baird's army limped into camp after an extremely arduous march from Kosseir. Far away on the coast, Lord Keith was furious when news of the surrender reached him second-hand. In an angry tone he wrote to Hutchinson on 5 July, demanding a full explanation why he had not been consulted over the terms in his capacity as joint commander-in-chief. He was justified in his complaint insofar as his vessels had been committed for the evacuation of the French army and its effects. Hutchinson replied that he felt fully justified in seizing the offered opportunity to secure half the military objective of the campaign.

But in spite of occasional friction of this kind, cooperation between the army and navy remained efficient. At the same time, the British government was doing its best to keep the expedition up to strength and fully supplied. Reinforcements from the Brigade of Guards sailed from England on 29 May, followed a week later by the 25th and 26th Regiments of Foot. These reinforcements represented a considerable sacrifice to the home forces, reducing them to the barest minimum.

By 10 July, the French army had moved to Gizeh. Already the Turks had murdered several men, and everybody felt that the sooner the prisoners of war were on their way for the coast, the better. The march began on the 15th, under close escort by the British army. Hutchinson was taken ill, and the march to the embarkation point was under Sir John Moore's command. After fifteen days, the coast was reached, and by 3 August the embarkation was proceeding at Rosetta. Moore hoped that the whole operation would be completed in six to eight days, and, thanks to the magnificent work of the sailors of the fleet, the British army was free to march to the siege of Alexandria by 8 August. Ever since Ganteaume's failure, Bonaparte, the First Consul, had been convinced of the final outcome in Egypt, and ordered his envoys to hasten the negotiations for a general peace with Great Britain. The fall of Alexandria was merely a matter of time.

By 16 August, the full siege was in operation. Plans to capture the town were settled between Keith and Hutchinson – now once more in command. Five thousand of General Coote's force, who had been observing Alexandria since July, were transferred by boats across the flooded Lake Mareotis to seal off the western approaches to Alexandria along the remaining narrow isthmus of land. This movement was covered by diversionary attacks against the cliff defences to the east of the town. Coote reported that there were no fortifications apart from the Marabout Redoubt that were capable of long withstanding an assault on the western side. But the question was different facing the Heights of Necropolis; Moore reported: 'The eastern fortifications are formidable.'

Preparations for a preliminary 'testing' assault were hurried forward. The army was re-brigaded, and 2000 further reinforcements dispatched to Coote under cover of darkness. On the 21st, his force made a determined attack on Fort Marabout, which was soon captured. The command of the harbour fell with it into British hands. Two nights later, a flotilla of boats from the fleet attacked the harbour installations – commanded by Sydney Smith and Cochrane. A French counter-attack against Coote was thwarted by further diversions against the Eastern Heights.

26 August saw Moore in person on the western approaches, judging the position immediately prior to the final assault. He reported to headquarters that the Fort de Bains was the last remaining obstacle – in fact, the key to Alexandria. Troops were rapidly deployed for the morrow's assault: batteries began a heavy fire. The attack never took place. On the very eve, General Menou's personal aide-de-camp entered the Allied lines under flag of truce, requesting a three-day armistice. During this period, Menou promised to draw up what he considered to be reasonable terms for capitulation.

The time limit expired without the appearance of the French proposals, but on Menou's urgent entreaty, it was extended for a further period. On 1 September the French terms were submitted. But Hutchinson held all the cards and was in a position to dictate. In spite of Menou's protests, the terms were gradually whittled down to exactly the ones that Belliard had accepted. The French were to be repatriated with their arms and baggage by the Royal Navy, but all public property and vessels sheltering in the harbour were to be handed over. An attempt to smuggle the famous Rosetta stone to France as a 'personal possession' gave rise to a bitter argument, but once again the French had to give way. On 2 September, the capitulation was signed, and the garrison of Alexandria – 10,528 strong – marched out of the town with the full honours of war. They were accompanied by 685 scientists and civilians who had originally accompanied Bonaparte. Thus the French adventure in Egypt came to an end. The last French soldier left Egypt on 15 September.

The campaign had not been an easy one for the British expedition – least of all the conditions faced by the men in the ranks. The Memoirs of Sergeant-Major Coates of the 28th Foot, published in 1836, reveal that his regiment was on front line duty for every day of twelve weeks without respite, and that the night of 3 June was the first occasion since the landing that the troops were allowed to sleep without wearing full equipment. The European-pattern uniforms, with stiff, buckled collars and tight-fitting coats, made of serge, were not the ideal dress for campaigning in the heat of the Nile Valley. But the troops bore these agonising discomforts cheerfully, though there were many cases of heat-exhaustion and sunstroke.

It only remained to announce the victory to London. On 2 September, Keith wrote to the Secretary at the Admiralty: '... the important object of this campaign is fully accomplished', and he went on to give a full measure of praise to the officers and men of his ships that had been engaged in the operation in all its phases since March. A few weeks later, orders arrived from the War Office disbanding the British army in Egypt. Four thousand men, under Craddock, were to be sent to Corfu; a garrison of 6000, together with Baird's force, were to remain in Egypt; 7000 were to be transferred to Malta; and 4000 to Gibraltar. These figures reveal that the army totalled 26,000 men at the close of the campaign – after the reinforcements dispatched in May had joined the army. Moore was originally designated for the unpopular duty of commanding the Egyptian army of occupation, but he succeeded in evading this irksome task by pleading sickness and anxiety for his father. Since the beginning of the campaign, some 3000 British casualties had been suffered, and many more had died from sickness and exhaustion.

The achievement of the military aim had been unquestionably accomplished: the French no longer held Egypt, and their influence in the region had been eliminated. But it is ironic to have to record that the political aim of the campaign was not achieved, for on 1 October, M. Otto, representative of the French Republic and the First Consul, had signed the Preliminaries of the Peace of Amiens with Lord Hawkesbury. News of the fall of Alexandria only reached London the next day – too late to be of use as a bargaining counter in the negotiations. But it was common knowledge that the fall of French Egypt was only a matter of time – and this, no doubt, hastened the French eagerness to conclude the negotiations. Indeed, Bonaparte had learnt on 17 September that Alexandria was doomed, and had at once ordered that the negotiations were to be concluded before the news of Menou's capitulation came to improve the British position at the conference table. But although Bonaparte's wiles had averted the political consequences of the Army of Egypt's final defeat, the military significance of the campaign was enormous. As Sir Arthur Bryant has described it, the campaign 'resulted in the most humiliating reverse the French arms had received on land since 1793.' Thirty-thousand veterans, with 600 guns, had been routed at every point by an expeditionary force of smaller numbers, bereft of cavalry and with inferior artillery. From the British point of view, it was a significant example of a combined operation efficiently carried out – in spite of shocking intelligence – based largely on the vital factor of command of the sea. The defeat of her fleet cost France the island of Malta and, ultimately, Egypt itself. British tactics of fighting in line had repulsed the assaults of the French attacking in column during the night battle of 21 March.

The nation was properly grateful to its armed forces. On 12 November, the thanks of both Houses of Parliament were moved 'for the services of the army and navy in Egypt.' Keith and Hutchinson were made barons.

The morale effect of the campaign was indeed vast, if its political significance was minimised by events outside the theatre. To quote the words of Sir Henry Bunbury: 'It revived confidence and pride in our military service.... The miserable warfare in America, the capitulation of Saratoga and Yorktown, and the more recent disasters to our troops in Flanders and Holland, had fixed a deep distrust in the public mind of the military men. It was believed that our commanders, nay, even our officers and soldiers, were degenerate and unequal to cope in battle with the conquerors of Italy and Germany. The trial that had now been made under great disadvantages first dispelled the prejudice. Our service regained its ancient standing in the estimation of the British people.' The last word on the success won by the British army in Egypt was spoken several years later on the field of Maida by General Sir John Stuart. On that occasion he could find no higher praise for the army's efforts than: 'Begad, I never saw anything so glorious as this. There was nothing even in Egypt to equal it! The finest thing I ever witnessed.'

4

ADJUSTING THE RECORD: NAPOLEON AND MARENGO

*T*he battlefield of Marengo, alas, remains one Napoleonic battlefield I have not yet managed to visit. Twice I have come very close to doing so. As recently as April 1993 I visited Ivrea to preside over the third annual general meeting of the Union of European Re-enactment Societies – an organisation which now has a dozen member-countries (but not, I am sad to say, Great Britain), and an estimated 40,000 European re-enactors who represent every period from the legions of the latter-day Roman Empire to the Austrian Deutschmeister-Schützenkorps of fin-de-siècle Vienna, but deliberately avoids the strife-torn twentieth century; but our programme was so full of official events (above all a memorable visit to Turin as the guest of the regional and city authorities where we inspected the superb '1706' local regiments and artillery commemorating the great city's siege and battle of that year) that there was no chance to visit Alessandria and the nearby battlefield of Marengo. In 1992 I came even closer while attending a fine conference at Turin organised by the Italian commission of la commission internationale d'histoire militaire comparée. A visit to Marengo was actually on the programme, but a pressing engagement to lecture at Fort Meade in Maryland compelled me to fly on across the Atlantic the day before the scheduled trip.

Nevertheless, I have read so many pages, pored over so many maps, and studied a myriad of photographs kindly provided by more fortunate friends and colleagues, that I feel I know practically every yard of this great battle of 14 June 1800's 'haunted acres'. Marengo holds a special place in Napoleonic history on several counts. It ended, of course, in a major French victory over the Austrian forces – but (and here lies much of its fascination) only just. The French Army of the Reserve had lost the day by mid-afternoon despite (and in part because of) the inspiring presence of First Consul Napoleon Bonaparte, and it was only the largely fortuitous return of General Desaix with Boudet's detached division that swung the fortunes of the day. What might have happened – in Europe and above all at Paris – if the outcome had been a major defeat, as was so nearly the case? To surmise is fascinating but useless.

Marengo's main fascination for me lies elsewhere, however. Napoleon – as First Consul, then Consul-for-Life and ultimately as Emperor – went to special pains to 'adjust the record' in order to represent the outcome as a personal triumph, which it was far from *being. No less than four successive 'official accounts' (to include the last – that dictated on St Helena) succeeded one another. The earlier versions – particularly the version of 1803 – were ordered to be destroyed and left without trace. But there sometimes the worm turns. An unknown clerk of the archives at Vincennes took care to tuck away in an inaccessible place – one version says it was under a blotter – a single copy, which duly survived to resurface many years later; in so doing he threw the history of Marengo once more into the melting pot, and in the process showed up one of the less scrupulous aspects of the dynamic little Corsican, namely his* penchant *for 'tuning the pulpit' (or tidying-up official records), thus justifying the cynical French contemporary* bon-mot '. . . mentir comme un bulletin'.

Napoleon found the time to revisit the battlefield in 1805 on his way to his second coronation – this time as King of Italy – at the Duomo in Milan. I must surely follow on the earliest possible occasion – and I look forward to doing so. The battle is mentioned in several of the facsimile reprints of contemporary memoirs and accounts made available in recent years in Greenhill Books' 'Napoleonic Library', not least The Note-books of Captain Coignet.

The dramatic events that took place near the River Bormida on 14 June 1800 occupy a special place in Napoleonic history – and myth. That this is the case can largely be attributed to Napoleon's determination to adjust – a less charitable word would be 'fake' – the official record in order to present his contemporaries and posterity with the impression of a personal triumph in which everything was foreseen and nothing went seriously wrong from the French point of view. The intention of these pages is to examine what really took place at the battle of Marengo, and to trace the various steps taken by Napoleon as First Consul, then Emperor, and ultimately as an exile, to pull the wool over men's eyes by misrepresentation of the facts.

Napoleon's personal obsession with Marengo can be illustrated in many ways. Numerous orders of the day and victory bulletins of the Grand Army contain comparative and emulative references to the events of 14 June 1800. According to Baron de Marbot, the Emperor spurred on his hurrying columns towards the battlefield of Friedland in 1807 by repeatedly calling out to them, 'Today is a happy day – it is the anniversary of Marengo.' Eight years later on the eve of launching his ill-fated campaign into Belgium in 1815, he recalled to his soldiers that 'Today is the anniversary of Marengo and Friedland which twice decided the destiny of Europe.' He also named his horse after the battle, and christened a favourite dish with the same name, and countless diners to this day pay homage – albeit mostly unconsciously – to the triumph of the French

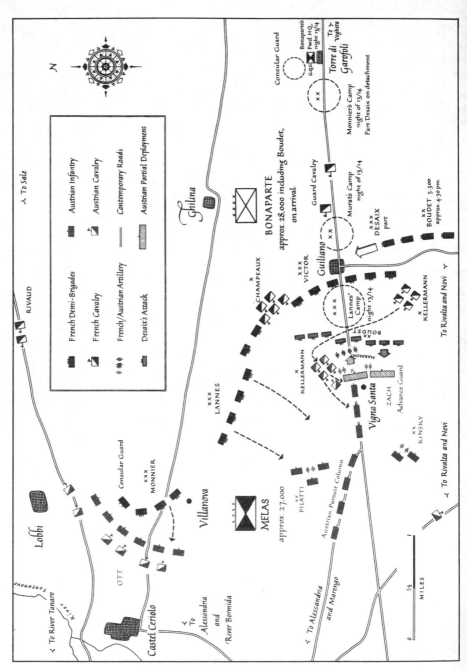

MARENGO, 1800: THE AFTERNOON BATTLE

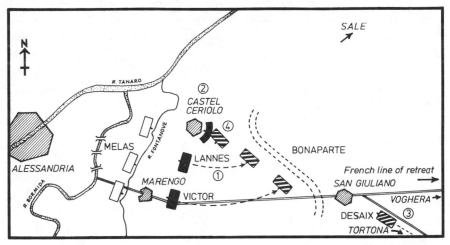

THE 1803 RELATION: ADDITIONS AND CHANGES

① Deliberate, phased French retreat.
② Practically continuous occupation of Castel Ceriolo, the pivot
③ Deliberate placing of Desaix.
④ Deletion of all mention of Monnier in favour of Carra St.Cyr.
‐‐‐‐ Actual line held by the French c.3p.m.

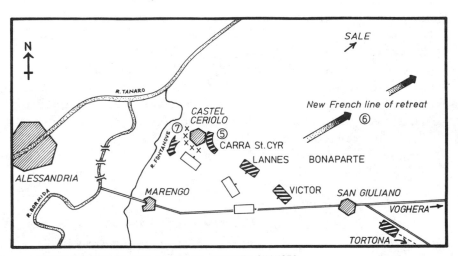

THE 1805 AND St.HELENA RELATIONS: FURTHER CHANGES

⑤ Carra St.Cyr
⑥ ➤ New French line of retreat
⑦ Envelopment of Austrian left by French right.

85

First Consul long ago when they order *Poulet à la Marengo* from the menu. Twenty French regiments boast 'Marengo' among their battle honours; Paris inevitably contains a thoroughfare named after the victory (albeit a small one) and several towns in the North American continent also bear its name, while the rather dejected skeleton of Napoleon's one-time charger of that name occupies a prominent place in the British National Army Museum at Chelsea. All this would seem to show that Napoleon succeeded to a large extent in securing Marengo a hallowed place in the history of his military triumphs.

There are, however, indications that the immediate impact of the news of his victory on the French populace was very slight. The Marquise de la Tour du Pin, for instance, recorded in her *Journal* how she attended the official celebrations of 14 July 1800 on the Champ de Mars in Paris. 'After the review of the National Guard and the Garrison,' she recalled, 'a small force of a hundred men dressed in torn and dirty clothing, some with arms in slings, others with bandages round their heads, bearing the standards and banners captured from the Austrians at Marengo, entered the arena. I waited for a wild and well-merited applause, but contrary to my expectations there was not a cry and hardly a sign of joy. We were as surprised as we were indignant.' This popular apathy is significant. One possible reason for it was that the populace as a whole was disappointed that the victory had failed to bring the ardently desired peace that the First Consul had so frequently promised he would secure since his elevation to the position of head of state in the months after the *coup d'état de Brumaire*. Indeed, it required a further eight months of protracted negotiation and costly military effort, including a renewed offensive over the River Adige by General Brune and a full scale drive on Vienna by General Morceau, culminating in his victory at Hohenlinden (3 December) before the Habsburgs were prepared to sign the Peace of Luneville (8 February 1801). Napoleon's success at Marengo, therefore, was only one step towards securing a favourable pacification and hardly the knock-out blow he had so confidently predicted. In this slightly unpalatable fact lies, no doubt, one clue to the Emperor's subsequent determination to convince everybody – even himself – that Marengo was a typical Napoleonic engagement of standard pattern and brilliance, and that almost from the outset its successful conclusion was assured. For if Marengo was to take its intended place in history as the true moment of departure for the locust years of Napoleonic splendour, both military and civil, no less an image would suffice the exacting requirements of Napoleonic propaganda.

From the outset, the future Emperor's servants certainly did their best to project the 'right' image of the campaign of 1800, and in the process produced an interesting number of distorted facts and misleading images. Napoleon's secretary, for instance, is responsible for propagating the celebrated, but almost certainly apocryphal, story of his master lying stretched full length across a large map of North Italy driving a coloured pin into the village of San Giuliano, three miles to the east of Marengo and exclaiming: 'I shall fight him [Melas] here, on the plain of Scrivia.' Such prescience, coming as it is supposed to have done several weeks before the battle, is barely credible. Similarly, the court artist, J. L. David, painted a famous, but highly idealised picture of Napoleon crossing the Alps astride a prancing charger, whereas, in fact – as Delaroche depicted in a far more accurate, though less well-known portrayal of the same scene – the First Consul traversed the Great St Bernard in rather less dramatic fashion huddled rather insecurely on the back of a mule! It is necessary, therefore, to distinguish fact from fiction, however difficult this may be.

In trying to determine what actually happened on 14 June, the military historian is deprived of Napoleon's exact orders to his subordinates, for there is a significant gap in the official *Correspondance* from the early hours of the 13th to the victory bulletin issued on the 15th. As a result, any analysis has to rely largely on what Napoleon subsequently cared to record about the battle, and on the impressions of other soldiers present. A comparison of these two main sources of information shows several marked discrepancies; many accounts seem to challenge the legend of Napoleonic infallibility so seduously fostered, as we shall see, by the cunning and unscrupulous Corsican. Of course, all first-hand evidence has to be treated with caution. The passage of time can play tricks with men's memories; and, even when participants wrote down their impressions soon after the battle, it must be recognized that the vast majority of them could have possessed only the haziest of ideas about what took place a small distance away from their own narrow and smoke-obscured sectors. Similarly, it is a well-known fact that two neighbouring eye-witnesses of the same historical phenomenon will rarely agree on all the details of what both observed at close quarters. From the mass of depositions assembled by the *Dépôt de la Guerre* in the years immediately after the battle, however, and the many detailed analyses that have been made by generations of distinguished military historians over the last century and a half, it is possible to paint a credible picture of the events of the battle of Marengo. As we shall see, this impression, drawn from such a kaleidoscope of sources, differs in several important respects from Napoleon's own 'final version' of events set down in 1805 and later repeated with minor alterations in the Memorials of St Helena.

It is not possible here to enter into a full consideration either of the campaign of 1800 or of Napoleon's fully developed system of strategical envelopment and grand tactics, but it is necessary to outline the background in order to place Marengo in its proper context.

Faced, after his elevation to the dignity of First Consul, with the need to procure peace with Austria (and later England) in order both to secure his political position and afford a respite to a weary France, Bonaparte – as he should still properly be called at this period – had formed a new Army of the Reserve around Dijon during the early months of 1800 (giving its nominal command to Berthier, as by the Constitution of the Year VIII a French Consul was debarred from taking the field in person). His original intention was to employ this force in conjunction with Moreau's Army of the Rhine in a concerted drive over the Rhine and through Switzerland towards the Danube and Vienna, destroying the main Austrian Army of General Kray in the process, and thereafter compel the stubborn Hapsburgs to sue for terms. In early April, however, General Moreau's obstructive attitude led to a complete change of plan; the First Consul now decided to use the new army in a sweep over the Alps into the Po valley, hoping to sever the Austrian General Melas's communications with Mantua and the Tyrol while General Massena's Army of Liguria pinned Austrian attention near Genoa. It was hoped that the destruction of the Austrian Army in Italy would compel the Aulic Council to come to terms. In the event, Melas struck first (5 April) and the subsequent defeat of Massena (which led to one part of his army being besieged in Genoa from 22 April and another being driven back behind the River Var) compelled the First Consul to hasten his plans for intervention in the theatre.

The crossing of the Alps commenced on 15 May, and by the 22nd the bulk of the Army of the Reserve, accompanied (in fact commanded) by Napoleon in the guise of Berthier's adviser, had reached Ivrea. But the mass of the French artillery remained bottled up in the Great St Bernard Pass owing to the stubborn resistance of Fort Bard, and rather than press on immediately towards Genoa, the First Consul decided to swing away to the east to take Milan, where he could hope 'to find guns in the enemy's arsenals'. At Milan he was joined by a corps tardily released by General Moreau from the St Gotthard Pass, which raised his strength to over 60,000 men. The eventual surrender of Fort Bard (5 June) enabled his artillery to move forward to join him. Meantime, French contingents were securing crossings over the Po, for the First Consul was determined to capture the town of Stradella, a move that would effectively sever Melas's line of retreat and compel the Austrians to fight in order to restore their communications. The main transfer of the army to the south bank of the Po started on 7 June and was completed over the next three days.

Away in Genoa, however, General Massena's stalwart defence had already come to an end (4 June) and his troops were in the process of being repatriated to join their colleagues behind the Var. Although he placed the destruction of Melas before the relief of Genoa, this setback (which Napoleon first learnt about on the 8th) compelled a further change of plan. Instead of waiting for Melas to try to blast his way through the Stradella position, Napoleon determined to advance towards Alessandria, where the Austrians were concentrating. He was very anxious lest Melas might now fall back upon Genoa where he could be sustained, and if need be evacuated by the Royal Navy. Napoleon now desired to forestall any such complication and compel Melas to accept battle at the earliest possible moment.

Advancing through Montebello, where Lannes won a stiff action with an Austrian force on the 9th, the Army of the Reserve pressed on over the River Scrivia, and entered the plain of Marengo during the afternoon of 13 June. At this juncture – after providing for the security of Valenzia, Milan, the St Gotthard Pass and the bridgeheads over the Po – the army numbered no more than some 31,500 men, but at least the greater part of its artillery had caught up with it. Melas was in immediate command of a similar number of troops which he proceeded to withdraw over the Bormida into the fortress of Alessandria. This move somewhat surprised Napoleon, for the Austrians had apparently sacrificed a good battle position where the open plain would have favoured their superior cavalry. The only logical reason he could conjecture for this move was that Melas had no intention of fighting a serious engagement, but instead was determined to commence a retreat before the arrival of Massena and Suchet, marching from the River Var, could place him between two fires. Determined to prevent the foe from moving either north over the Po, or south towards Genoa, Napoleon decided to detach Lapoype's division (3462) northwards and Boudet's division (5316), accompanied by General Desaix, towards Rivalta and Novi southwards to serve as blocking forces. These decisions, which were put into effect on the afternoon of the 13th in the case of Desaix and early on the 14th in that of Lapoype, almost cost the French the campaign. Napoleon was left with barely 23,000 men and twenty guns under direct command, facing a superior adversary supported by 100 cannon. Of course, he had no real belief that Melas would attack, and the erroneous report of a staff officer that the Austrians had destroyed their bridges over the Bormida (when in fact there were still three in position) confirmed his general impression that it was both tactically safe and strategically desirable to make these detachments, and to encamp his army in an extended line along the road running from Alessandria towards Voghera as a preliminary to attacking the retiring Melas.

As a result of these very considerable miscalculations and errors, which include the under-estimation of his opponent and an over-confidence in his own ability and reputation, Napoleon was taken completely by surprise when the Austrian army in three columns sallied forth across the Bormida early on the 14th and proceeded to attack General Victor's exposed formations in the vicinity of Marengo village and the Fontanove stream. The main Austrian onslaught went in about 9.00 am; but the First Consul still chose to believe for a period of several hours that this unexpected activity was merely a ruse designed to conceal Melas' withdrawal: accordingly he sent off Lapoype towards the River Po as planned, and dispatched a message to Desaix instructing him to press on for Novi. It was only at about 11.00 am that the full gravity of the situation seems to have dawned on Napoleon's comprehension. By that time Lannes and Murat, as well as Victor, were fully engaged with

15,000 men in trying to contain the heavy Austrian attacks. Soon everybody was appealing for reinforcements; but in reserve stood only the 900 strong Consular Guard, Monnier's division (3614) and part of the cavalry. Napoleon decided that these slender resources must be employed to extend the French battleline northwards towards Castel Ceriolo in order to avert the growing danger of General Ott's column of 7500 Austrians enveloping the right of the French line. By early afternoon practically every man of the 23,000 strong Army of the Reserve was committed. There were thus no reserves to help bolster the tiring French left and centre where Victor's and Lannes' hard-pressed men were fast running out of ammunition, particularly the former who had already sustained three hours of combat against heavy odds.

By this time aides-de-camp were spurring north and south with desperate and peremptory orders of recall for Lapoype and Desaix. 'I had thought to attack Melas,' allegedly ran the First Consul's message to the latter; 'He has attacked me first. For God's sake come up if you still can'. The desperate tone of this summons disposes of Napoleon's later assertion that this move was pre-conceived. Lapoype only received his order when his men were half-way over the Po at about 4.30 pm. Why it took the messenger so long to cover the intervening twenty-two kilometres has never been explained, but he came too late to enable the northern detachments to reach the field before nightfall, and Lapoype's division eventually camped near Voghera after covering forty kilometres over atrocious roads during the day. Thus, no assistance materialised from the direction of the Po. Fortunately for Napoleon, his second messenger reached Desaix about 1.00 pm, by which time Boudet's division had managed to put only fifteen kilometres between the main army and itself owing to the swollen River Scrivia which had delayed its march the previous evening. Some accounts assert that Desaix was already retracing his steps towards the sound of the cannon before the message reached him, and if that were true, it is just conceivable that he was acting on contingency orders, but be that as it may, he soon had Boudet's men stepping out for the village of San Giuliano (which they eventually reached between 4.00 and 5.00 pm in time to reverse the fortunes of the day), while he himself rode off ahead to seek his commander-in-chief.

Back on the main battlefield, a lull had descended over the fighting between the hours of noon and 1.00 pm, as the Austrians regrouped their forces for another all-out onslaught, and thereafter a little more desperately needed time was gained while Ott turned to deal with Monnier's division in the vicinity of Castel Ceriolo. But once the full fury of the engagement was resumed it soon became clear that any French hopes of holding their forward position were ill founded, and by 3 pm the French left and centre were reeling back in con-siderable exhaustion and disarray towards the hamlet of San Giuliano. The battle seemed on the point of being disastrously lost – the French line of retreat towards Torre de Garofoli and distant Voghera appeared in imminent danger.

So thought the weary General Melas, who chose this moment to hand over command to General Zach before retiring to his headquarters in Alessandria; so thought General Desaix, who covered in mud, reached Napoleon shortly after 3 pm. 'This battle is completely lost,' the newcomer asserted, 'However ... there is time to win another.' While they awaited the arrival of Boudet's troops, the First Consul rode up and down the main line encouraging his men. 'Soldiers, you have retreated far enough; you know that it is my custom to bivouac on the field of battle.' But it would clearly be a race against time.

Fortunately for the French, General Zach was no hustler, and the time he took to reform the Austrian right and centre into a massive column for the final attack enabled Boudet's men to make their appearance behind Victor's practically shattered corps. Napoleon ordered Desaix to counter-attack the Austrians without delay. Marmont extemporised a battery of guns to give supporting fire, and Kellermann and his heavy cavalry jingled up to assist the infantry. Then Boudet's division, formed into an oblique line of three demi-brigades, the two outer adopting '*l'ordre mixte*' formation and the central one forming in line, swept forward from the left. A bitter struggle developed. Boudet's relatively fresh troops hesitated when Desaix was shot down near Vigna Santa, but Marmont rushed to the front with a few guns and began to discharge canister into the dense Austrian column. Then an ammunition wagon exploded; the Austrians were momentarily stunned by the concussion. Sensing a fleeting opportunity, Kellermann plunged forward at the head of his cavalry into the paralysed left flank of the Austrian column. 'A minute earlier or three minutes later and the thing could not have succeeded, but the timing was perfect, and North Italy was recovered in that moment for the French Republic'. The Austrian column – 6000 strong – was soon a mass of fleeing fugitives. The panic spread, and soon the entire Austrian army was streaming back for the bridges over the Bormida. Their left, however, conducted a cool retreat under General Ott while the exhausted, but now jubilant French line advanced in a final attack all along the front.

Napoleon had won his victory. Probably 6000 Austrians lay dead and wounded, and something between 6000 and 8000 more were taken prisoner in the cramped bridgehead area. The rest, abandoning fifteen colours and forty cannon, made good their escape into Alessandria and beyond. The French losses were also very high; perhaps as many as 7000 were *hors de combat*; the survivors were on the verge of utter exhaustion. There was no question of forcing a crossing over the Bormida either that night or the following day, and the First Consul was pleased to grant Melas' request for an armistice which eventually was transformed into the Convention of Alessandria. By its terms, the Austrians were permitted to retire behind the River Mincio after handing over all fortresses to the west and south; the armistice was to continue pending an appeal to Vienna for a general pacification. So ended the First Consul's celebrated

Italian campaign of 1800; much of North Italy had been freed from Austrian control, but it had hardly been the anticipated victory of annihilation.

Napoleon had, in fact, been fortunate to win the battle of Marengo at all. The morning and early afternoon engagements were indisputably lost by the outnumbered French, and it was only the arrival of Boudet's division in the very nick of time – the gallantry of Desaix – and the initiative displayed by Marmont and Kellermann, that enabled a considerable victory to be snatched from the very jaws of disaster. They, rather than Napoleon himself, were the true heroes of the day. Until the arrival of Desaix, it had been a sheer battle of attrition allowing of scant subtlety. The First Consul had, it was true, made wise use of his slender reserves during the late morning phase, and doubtless his inspiring presence helped sustain his men in the firing line, but he was completely responsible for the near-fatal decisions to detach Desaix and Lapoype, for being duped by Melas, and in the final analysis, for risking the destruction of his numerically inferior troops at the very climax of the campaign. The best that can be said for him is that he hung on grimly until help came.

How then was he ever able to represent the events of 14 June 1800 in any other light? The fact that he took so much trouble to do so shows that he was secretly very disturbed by the events of Marengo. To his credit, he never denied his debt to Desaix, although he soon tried to make out that his timely intervention was all according to plan. Desaix's role was too well known to be ignored – and besides he was killed, and 'stone-dead hath no fellow'. Nor could Napoleon deny that his troops received the worst of the initial encounters near Marengo. But for the rest, Napoleon began deliberately to change the emphasis of events, making his personal role ever larger and more significant. This process of pseudo-rationalisation went through four clear stages, and the progressive changes in the 'official history' are worth noting in the order in which they occurred. Not the least interesting aspect is the light it throws on one of the less scrupulous sides of Napoleon's personality.

The first description of the battle was contained in the Bulletin issued on 15 June 1800. This was brief and fairly factual, admitting that the enemy did surprise the French advance guard, confessing that 'four times during the battle we were in retreat', and giving credit to the Consular Guard for its staunch stand in the plain on the French right 'until the arrival of General Monnier who captured Castel-Ceriolo at bayonet-point', placing this event at about 3 pm. The bulletin goes on to state that 'the battle appeared lost' until the troops of the shaken French left were able to rally behind Desaix's newly-arrived division near the village of San Giuliano. General Dupont then described Desaix's and Kellermann's attacks, and the collapse of the Austrian resistance. 'The whole army followed this movement. The enemy *right* [this author's italics] found itself cut off; consternation and fear spread through their ranks.' The Bulletin ends with estimates of casualties (the French being considerably understated at 3000 in all), and a tribute to Desaix, struck by a ball at the start of the charge of his division; he dropped dead on the spot. Reputedly he only had breath enough to whisper to the young Lebrun: 'Go and tell the First Consul that I die regretting that I have not done sufficient to live in posterity.' Hardly a convincing swan-song if his wound was truly so quickly fatal! According to Napoleon's account, his only reaction when these tidings were brought to him in the midst of the battle was to say 'Why am I not allowed to weep?' It would be possible to suggest several reasons, but it is evident from this account that Napoleon was already at pains to represent himself fully as 'riding the whirlwind and directing the storm' at all stages of the day. Perhaps this was natural enough. We know of no instance of a victorious general stressing his errors in his victory bulletins.

As time passed, however, Napoleon became increasingly dissatisfied with this record of the battle, which gave insufficient attention to his own part in the victory, and left a definite impression that it was on the Austrian right that the outcome was decided after Desaix's timely arrival. At last, in 1803, he ordered the officers of the *Dépôt de la Guerre* to investigate the action, instructing them to base their enquiries on the account by the Reserve's chief of staff, General Dupont, published in *Le Moniteur*, but embellishing and adjusting it in accordance with the results of new interviews with selected participants. In due course, Colonel Vallongue sent in a draft accompanied by seven maps for Napoleon's comments. He was far from content with what he read, and the criticisms he levelled at this document mark the beginning of the myth. The First Consul was displeased to note that Lannes' Corps was represented as making a headlong retreat to the rear, instead of a carefully phased tactical withdrawal towards San Giuliano (although almost all the deposed evidence strongly supported Vallongue's view). Secondly, Napoleon insisted that the role of the extreme French right should be redrafted. As it stood, the 1803 account – based on the evidence of participants – mentioned that Carra St Cyr's brigade of Monnier's division occupied the village of Castel Ceriolo briefly and beat off some Austrian light infantry before falling back eastwards in conformity with the general retreat of the French line. Only after they had fallen back through vineyards for between one and one-and-a-half hours, so the witnesses' stories went, did they meet an aide-de-camp who turned them around and sent them back to regain the village, which they succeeded in doing at dusk. This account – however factual – did not fit in with the picture the First Consul was now determined to depict. 'This point cannot have been abandoned until shortly before the arrival of General Desaix,' he minuted, 'and the French troops *must* have reoccupied it in strength at the moment when the army began to move forward again.' The reason that underlay this apparently petty concern with a point of detail was that Napoleon was determined to have it officially recorded that the French line *deliberately* pivoted on Castel Ceriolo; in other words, that the French left and centre swung back according to plan to lure the Austrian right into putting more distance between themselves and their bridges, thus drawing them straight into the arms of the approaching Desaix, and at the same time leaving their own lines of communication dangerously exposed to the French right wing. Now we can see the retrospective mastermind at work! The Austrians were to be represented as being lured to their doom by a carefully designed plan of the First Consul's making.

An even greater exaggeration was the emphasis Napoleon wished to be laid on the role of Desaix's detachment as the carefully positioned *masse débordante* or enveloping force. The impression was to be fostered that Desaix was deliberately placed in a situation from which he could either proceed towards Novi (his strategic function) or return towards the main army to play a decisive part on the enemy's flank *if* a major engagement developed near Alessandria after all. Although Napoleonic warfare was consistently fluid and adaptable, it is highly probable that this particular claim is a case of special pleading, or making the facts fit into a supposedly preconceived scheme of action in order to represent Desaix's critical intervention at Marengo as a typical French tactical outflanking manoeuvre such as was employed in many Napoleonic battles. Such a theory, however, does not fit in with the swollen River Scrivia (which alone accounts for Desaix being within reach of the battlefield), nor with the fact that Desaix appeared *in rear* (or *en potence*) of the collapsing French left, and not on the Austrian flank, as Bonaparte pretended.

A final change was the dropping of all mention of General Monnier from the official account. Since 1800 this officer had incurred Napoleon's displeasure, and was consequently to be written out of the record. Monnier's senior General of Brigade – the favoured Carra St Cyr – was to be henceforth described as the right wing commander. But it is important to note that no objection was raised at this juncture to the statement that the French army's line of retreat lay along the Alessandria, San Giuliano and Voghera highway.

The loyal historians of the *Dépôt* accordingly revised their account, and duly incorporated their master's amendments in the text; 'their's not to reason why.' There the matter rested until the early summer of 1805, when Napoleon travelled to Italy on a state visit, culminating in his coronation in the Duomo at Milan. Part of the splendid celebrations surrounding this august occasion included a sumptuous military review on the battlefield of Marengo timed to commemorate the fifth anniversary of the victory. Napoleon ordered a large memorial to be erected, and conscientious and hard-working Berthier, then Minister of War, deemed that this nostalgic occasion would be the ideal moment and place to present the Emperor with the *Dépôt*'s revised draft of the 1803 Relation. (The passage referring to the French preparations to meet Zach's attack, for instance, runs as follows: 'The movement that the French had made on their left and centre, bringing them closer to their reserve, was now complete, and the genius of their commanding general triumphed as a result of making this move. Bonaparte sized up the foe's position and faults; in a flash a new plan of attack was fashioned.') This proved an error. Although the new version contained flattering – not to say unctuous – references to Napoleon's personal contribution to victory, and obligingly stressed the deliberate nature of the French withdrawal on the left, and the skilled placing of Desaix to support the flank, the Emperor once again changed his mind. His on-the-spot battle-field tour had shown him what he should have done in 1800, and he was henceforward set upon foisting the *ideal solution* as the true account of what had taken place. He accordingly ordered the destruction of the revised 1803 Relation and demanded that a *third* account should be prepared.

It would be interesting to know in detail the reactions of the sorely tried Vallongue and his researchers to this news! Unfortunately history has drawn a tactful veil. Doubtless the *Chef de Séction* could console himself with his recent promotion to the rank of general, but his patience must have been sorely tried. What Napoleon now wished to have incorporated in the record were the following changes and additions. First, he was determined to establish that San Giuliano remained firmly in French hands *throughout* the second (early after-noon) phase of the battle. At the most he was prepared to concede a temporary withdrawal of a few hundred paces, but even this concession eventually dis-appeared. As he minuted in the margin of a draft of one of the maps being prepared for the new 1805 version, 'The division of Carra St Cyr was *inside* Castel Ceriolo; it had barricaded itself in there.' This was the first time any such claim had been put forward. A second major insertion was an intentional attempt to complete the tale of the deliberate French withdrawal on the left, with their line pivoting on Castel Ceriolo. The Emperor now recognised that such a move would have placed his line of retreat down the Alessandria – San Giuliano – Voghera highway in jeopardy, as, of course, had indeed been the case. Although no attempt to deny this had been incorporated in either of the previous Relations, such a weakness could no longer be allowed to survive. Accordingly, the Emperor fabricated the myth that after the beginning of the battle he had changed his line of operations, or retreat, from the actual road running east–west to a safer series of tracks running away to the north-east between Tortona [or Voghera] and Sale on the Po. If this concept received widespread credence, then Napoleon's skill at Marengo would be proved beyond question, and the whole sequence of the battle would fit into a neat pattern! The French, recovered from their initial setback, would be seen to have swung back their left and centre as part of a deliberate movement on their 'fortified' pivot of Castel Ceriolo, luring the Austrian right further and further from their bridges, and closer to Desaix's approaching troops. The French 'manoeuvre towards the rear' would be seen to have brought their battle-line back into the ideal position of being at right-angles to their new line of retreat, whilst the Austrians fooled themselves into thinking that they were about to cut the main French communications, whereas in fact the Alessandria – Voghera road was now completely irrelevant. The story now needed only one finishing touch to present Marengo as a Napoleonic masterpiece, and the Emperor did not hesitate to add it in direct contravention to the known facts. If the French right – Carra St Cyr at Castel Ceriolo – could be represented as sweeping round the Austrian left towards the crucial bridges, the First Consul's genius would be unquestionable, and so this entirely bogus concept was also added to the 1805 Relation. Never before had there been any suggestion of a French envelopment from the right. . . .

> The first echelon of the second line of reserve, commanded by General Carra St Cyr, occupied Castel-Ceriolo. He barricaded himself in the village, and kept the enemy cavalry at a respectful distance; they were also under threat from along the Sale road.
> The foe, who had bypassed the farm of La Ventolina on our left, and who believed the moment had come to sever our line of retreat, found himself turned on his left; our divisions that stretched from Castel Ceriolo to San Giuliano took up positions on his flank; his battalions received a fusillade from all sides at once – from the front, from the left flank, and from the rear. . . .

There is barely any corroborative evidence for these claims. It is true that two pontoon bridges had been established over the Po near Sale to facilitate the operations of Lapoype and Chabran, but these hardly provide incontrovertible proof that the switch of communications actually took place. Nor is there any evidence that Carra St Cyr on the Castel Ceriolo sector was in any position to do anything more than reoccupy that village at dusk. So much for the 'barricaded' assertion and the even more far-fetched idea of the enveloping attack developing from the village as the *coup de grâce*.

The final version of Marengo, as seen by Napoleon, was written in exile at St Helena and published in France in 1830. This added little that was new, but merely reiterated and strengthened the old claims, as a few quotations will reveal. 'The First Consul ... directed Carra St Cyr's division towards the extreme right at Castel Ceriolo, in order to outflank the enemy's entire left wing ... (later, at the time of Desaix's attack on the opposite flank) ... Carra St Cyr marched forward on the extreme right and by means of an inward swinging movement, turned the enemy's left.' Meanwhile, believing that the army's line of retreat lay along the road to Tortona, 'he [General Zach] sought to penetrate on to the highway beyond San Giuliano; but, at the opening of the battle, the First Consul had changed his line of retreat and had redirected it between Sale and Tortona in such a way that the Tortona [or Voghera] highroad no longer had any importance for the French army.'

As it made its retreat, Lannes's Corps constantly refused its left, thus aligning itself with the new line of retreat; 'and Carra St Cyr on the extreme right wing found himself almost upon this line of retreat at the very time that Zach believed these two corps to be completely cut off.' Then, after describing (reasonably accurately) Desaix's attack against the Austrian right, the Emperor put the final touch to his tale of exaggeration and carefully engineered false-hood. 'General Lannes swept forward at the *pas de charge*. Carra St Cyr, finding himself *en potence* behind the enemy's left wing, was far closer to the Bormida bridges than the enemy himself. In an instant the Austrian army was in the most frightful confusion. Eight to ten thousand cavalry, holding the plain, retreated at the gallop riding down everyone who stood in their way, in the belief that St Cyr's infantry would reach the bridge before them.'

Thus Napoleon left his final version of this confused day's fighting. It was an interesting engagement that he described, but it certainly was not the real battle of Marengo.

It is evident that by the time he arrived at St Helena, Napoleon had come to believe every detail of his Marengo story. His loyal aide, General Gourgaud, recounts how Napoleon suddenly remarked one day when he was working on his final account of Marengo:

> The great art of battles is to change your line of operations during the fighting; this is an idea that is suddenly quite new to me. It is what made me conquer at Marengo. The enemy advanced towards my line of operations to cut them; but I had changed them and it was he who found himself cut off.

The 'history' of Marengo was now complete. But there was one last sequel to be played out in 1821. As the deceased Emperor's body passed to its first resting place in St Helena, it was recorded that 'the pall spread over his coffin ... [was] ... the military cloak which he wore at Marengo'. Whether this was by his express direction or the result of an inspired gesture by a subordinate, we shall never know; but even if the latter be true, it is ironically consistent and fitting that the 'myth' of Marengo should have literally accompanied Napoleon to the grave – and beyond.

Why did Napoleon take so much trouble over the years to hoodwink pos-terity? We have already mentioned one reason, the need, real or imagined, to upgrade Marengo as a success in order to make it a suitably grand moment for the start of his years of greatness. Secondly, there was the Emperor's desire to conceal his mistakes and make the battle conform with the pattern of great battles that emerged from 1805 onwards. At Austerlitz, for example, Napoleon undoubtedly changed his line of retreat to run towards Brünn instead of Vienna, deliberately luring the Austro-Russian army to attack his right in the belief that this would cut the French off from their communications, and then produced Davout's III Corps (like Desaix) to bolster his retiring right while a sweep from the French centre surrounded two-thirds of the enemy army and drove part of them into the frozen meres. Similarly, at Friedland, the Emperor employed Lannes's isolated corps as a bait to lure Bennigsen into crossing the River Alle with his Russians in the hope of a quick success. Then after compelling his adversary to fight with a river to his back (like the Bormida), Napoleon proceeded to rush up his main forces to escalate the battle, and finally unleashed Ney to turn the Russian right and drive for their bridges over the river. It is clear, therefore, that Napoleon wished to date the full development of this successful system of 'grand tactics' from Marengo. As General Camon has written: 'The corrected version of 1805 has not redrawn the battle of Marengo; but it did inspire the underlying plans of Friedland and of Waterloo, and the admirable set-battles of Austerlitz and Wagram.' In most ways, therefore, the Emperor's account of the battle was based on dreams of what might, what *should* have been done to achieve a complete victory of annihilation that would have ended the war. The real attritional nature of the struggle, the fact that few plans survive the first minutes of battle, the parts played by sheer good luck and inspired subordinates in achieving victory, and, above all, the grave errors of Napoleon's judgement – these features were carefully hidden beneath successive layers of myth. Yet from these same dreams there eventually emerged the refined Napoleonic battle method that led to his greatest successes in the field.

5

THE NAPOLEONIC MARSHALATE

N ot even a military colossus such as Napoleon could achieve much without appointing key subordinates. The twenty-six Marshals of the Empire who received the coveted baton from the Emperor between 1804 and 1815 were essentially the recipients of a civic honour rather than a military rank, and, as I discuss below, formed the Emperor's inner circle of soldiers. Yet political considerations within the French army figured as importantly as displayed military skill in determining the actual choices.

Rarely has a more colourful band of warriors – drawn from every type of social background, displaying conflicting character traits and abilities as senior commanders – been assembled in a single generation, army or country (although Poniatowski, of course, was a Polish prince by birth).

Napoleon above all required obedience rather than brilliant military flair in his carefully considered appointees. He firmly believed that '... in war, it is not men that matter but the man. It was not the Roman army that crossed the Rubicon – it was Caesar' – in other words, himself. As a Corsican he trusted few men or women outside the immediate famiglia (and most of them ended by letting him down too), so he regarded the marshalate as mere instruments of his all-embracing will. He took some pains to encourage clashes of personality between his paladins, believing in Caesar Caligula's precept: 'Divide and Rule'. This was possibly all very well while the marshals were close at hand and under his direct control, but disaster was all too often the result when their duties carried them far away from their master, when they could neither cooperate effectively with one another nor show much original thought.

There were exceptions: Massena, Davout and Suchet would have risen to high rank in any army, and were great commanders in their own right. The remainder showed various and contrasting talents – but surprisingly few revealed outstanding attributes as generals above army corps level.

In 1987 my edited Napoleon's Marshals was published, and much of what follows forms part of my General Introduction to that volume. The memoirs of individual marshals make compulsive reading – not least those of Berthier. Paul Britten Austin's chef d'oeuvre 1812: The March on Moscow which draws brilliantly from the recollections of survivors of all ranks, not least those of the marshalate involved, contrasts *interestingly with George F. Nafziger's earlier* Napoleon's Invasion of Russia *which stresses the statistical approach.*

Here, however, are my views upon the men who rowed, snapped, snarled and feuded with one another in campaign and out during the dramatic years of the Napoleonic Empire from 1804 to Waterloo.

†

Few military careers – whether considered individually or collectively – can have rivalled the drama, the opportunities proffered or the penalties incurred – than those of the twenty-six officers who in due course formed the Napoleonic Marshalate. The men concerned came from all strata of French society, including a number from the officers and non-commissioned officers of the pre-revolutionary French Bourbon army, who may truly be said to have had their batons '. . . in their knapsacks'.

The reasons that led to individuals being selected by the Emperor Napoleon I for this distinction were complex. A reputation for courage in action and perseverance on campaign figured high amongst the qualities desired, but internal army politics played as great a part as proven ability in high command.

The favoured eighteen of the original promotion of August 1804 and the eight appointed later were very much of a mixed bag. Glory-seekers, feuders, barely disguised (if at all) looters on the grand scale – they left their mark on the early nineteenth century which saw their exploits. Some were cultivated men; others the very reverse. Two would become kings, a number more received princedoms. Almost all received vast grants of land and sums of money from the Emperor. On the other hand, three would die of wounds received in action; five more would meet violent deaths, and all, without exception, suffered the strains of seemingly perpetual warfare, involving (for many) periods of disgrace and, after Waterloo, persecution.

On 18 May 1804, Napoleon Bonaparte was proclaimed Emperor of the French people by formal decree of the Senate. The change from the Consulate to the Empire was embodied in the 'Constitution of the Year XII', which in Article 48 announced the creation in principle of sixteen active 'Marshals of the Empire' and a further unspecified number of honorific appointments to the same dignity whose main purpose was to represent the army's interests in the Senate. On 19 May, the day after the issue of the *Senatus Consultum* of *28 floréal an XII*, the names of the first promotions (fourteen active and four honorary marshals) were made public. The list was headed by Alexandre Berthier, Napoleon's indispensable chief-of-staff, followed by Joachim Murat, imperial brother-in-law and *beau sabreur* of the French army. In eighteenth place came the name of Jean Sérurier, sixty-two-year old veteran, one of the honorific appointees. The oldest on the list was François Kellermann the Elder, nine days short of entering his seventieth year. The youngest – not half the age of the hero of Valmy – was Louis Davout, who had celebrated his thirty-fourth birthday just nine days earlier.

Over the next eleven years a further eight distinguished soldiers – seven Frenchmen and one Pole – would also receive their batons from Napoleon: Victor in 1807; Macdonald, Marmont and Oudinot (all three at or soon after Wagram in 1809); Suchet in 1811; and Gouvion St Cyr, Poniatowski and Grouchy (the twenty-sixth and last) in 1812, 1813 and 1815 respectively. The average age of the eighteen marshals of 1804 was forty-four years (the inclusion of the four veterans of the Revolutionary Wars having an effect), and that of the later eight was also forty-four on appointment. At the time of his coronation, Napoleon was thirty-five. Only two of the Marshalate were younger – namely Davout and Marmont; eight were ten or more years older; a further seven were his senior by between four and nine years; the remaining nine were under two years older – three of these (Ney, Soult and Lannes) sharing Napoleon's birth year of 1769.

Inevitably, the uncertainties and balancing opportunities of the Revolutionary Wars launched the careers of the future Marshalate just as they did that of their chief. Many enjoyed spectacular promotion. Bernadotte, for instance, was first commissioned a lieutenant in the 36th Regiment on 6 November 1791 and just under three years later was promoted general of division in the Army of the Sambre-et-Meuse on 22 October 1794. Gouvion St Cyr's early rise was even more meteoric. Enlisted as a volunteer on 1 September 1792, two years and one day later he received confirmation of his promotion to general of division in the Army of the Rhine from the Committee of Public Safety. But at a troubled time when ideological probity was as important as military valour or skill, there were many pitfalls awaiting the unwary or just plain unlucky. Between August 1792 and November 1799, no less than 994 general officers out of 1378 holding commands during that seven-year period were disciplined in some degree for one reason or another – no less than 75 per cent. A total of eighty-one were condemned to death (forty-one for alleged political crimes) and fifty-five were actually executed by firing-squad or 'sneezed' into the basket of Mme Guillotine. However, if a thrusting general officer was fortunate enough to keep his head upon his shoulders through the revolutionary period *and* to earn the ultimate accolade of selection for the award of the baton from Napoleon for reasons to be discussed later, there were indeed many glittering prizes awaiting the faithful, the relations, the favourites (very few) and the deserving. Every marshal – and indeed at least 5000 soldiers of every rank – could anticipate membership of that celebrated honours system, the *légion d'honneur*. Naturally, the Marshalate came in for the lion's share of other orders and distinctions, many of them foreign. The most decorated of the marshals was *not* Murat but probably Berthier who accumulated no less than thirteen orders (to include his Grand Eagle) in just over three years.

If decorations and orders were one form of recompense, titles of nobility were another as Napoleon set out to recreate a social hierarchy around his throne. In 1805, Murat – his brother-in-law – was made a prince. Next year Berthier was created Prince of Neuchâtel, and Bernadotte Prince Ponte-Corvo, both endowed with principalities. Sixteen of the Marshalate became dukes, and six became Princes (Berthier for good measure twice, in 1806 and 1809); Murat was Grand Duke of Berg and a prince of the blood by marriage; the others were Bernadotte, Davout, Massena and Ney (we exclude Poniatowski who was a Polish prince in his own right). Only Brune and Jourdan held out against this flood of honours because of republican principles, but both ultimately succumbed to become peers of France in 1815 during the Hundred Days, and the latter was made a count by Louis XVIII in 1816.

To support their new dignities, Napoleon distributed very substantial sums of money amongst the 'military' princes, the twenty-three dukes, 193 counts, 648 barons and 117 knights who eventually made up his military aristocracy. In all, he disbursed over sixteen million gold francs in 1261 awards in favour of 824 generals. The actual sums varied enormously, but once again a majority of the marshals did very well for themselves. Berthier – besides his principality – received eight *dotations* (endowments) to a total value of over 1,254,000 francs. Ney – close on his heels – benefited from five awards to a total value of 1,028,973 francs (receiving 800,000 in a single gift in late 1812). Davout received six awards totalling 910,840 francs and Massena some 638,375 francs in five (besides his notorious 'little savings' which were another matter entirely). Lannes received almost 328,000 francs – and doubtless would have had more but for his premature death in 1809. Others of the Marshalate did not do so well. Gouvion St Cyr reputedly received only 30,000 francs – and Brune and Jourdan received nothing at all. As we shall see, many another marshal besides Massena looked after his own interests in foreign parts – causing many a problem thereby – not least Brune, who earned the nickname of 'the intrepid looter' from the Emperor himself, although Soult was apparently the worst depredator.

But if wealth, honours and rewards were one part of the story of being a Marshal of the Empire, there was (as already mentioned) another, darker side to the coin. Apart from the honorary senatorial appointees, few marshals were allowed much time to enjoy their privileges – unless like Brune, Gouvion St Cyr, Macdonald and (ultimately) Massena, they fell out of favour with the Emperor and were consequently not employed in the Grand Army for long periods. He was a relentless master, and when not engaged on active service most marshals were required to undertake time-consuming administrative tasks or tedious court functions. And of course, the marshals were by no means immune from shot and shell. Over half would receive wounds as marshals, and three would succumb – Bessières killed outright at Rippach on 1 May 1813, Lannes as a result of wounds sustained at Essling on 22 May 1809, and Prince Poniatowski, drowned whilst trying to swim the Elster with severe wounds at Leipzig on 19 October 1813. Lannes had also been hit at Pultusk in 1807. The invincible Oudinot received at least eight wounds as a marshal, three of them in Russia, 1812, to add to his incredible total of battle injuries which did not prevent his living to the age of eighty. Davout, Bernadotte, Marmont and Ney were all wounded on two occasions (the first-named in fact sustained two injuries at Borodino and so really counts as three-times stricken), whilst Murat, Augereau, Suchet, Gouvion St Cyr and Victor were individually laid temporarily *hors de combat* on one occasion in a whole range of battles from Eylau on 8 February 1807 to Craonne on 7 March seven years later.

It would be quite wrong to assert that the 'untouched' marshals tended to hang back or avoid the firing line. Many had been wounded in their service before 1804. Only Massena, Kellermann, Moncey and Brune survived their entire active careers without sustaining a wound in battle – but the first-named had performed legendary feats in full view of his men and the enemy on numerous occasions, as at Rivoli and Essling. As for Brune, his luck on the battlefield did not extend to the events of 2 August 1815, when he was attacked and murdered by royalist 'white' terrorists in a particularly brutal manner – hacked to death, flung into a river, his body then used for target practice for several hours. Such exceptions, however, only serve to prove the rule. Officers of all ranks were closely involved in physical terms in the battles of the early nineteenth century.

Clearly high command brought high physical risks as well as considerable recompenses and privileges. The tough old Duke of Danzig, Lefebvre, twice wounded himself (the first time while protecting the Royal Family from the attentions of the Paris mob outside the Tuileries in 1791), assuredly said it all when an old friend was enviously admiring his fine Paris mansion. 'So you're jealous of me,' exclaimed the veteran. 'Very well; come out into the courtyard and I'll have twenty shots at you at thirty paces. If I don't hit you, the whole house and everything in it is yours.' The friend hastily declined to take the chance, whereupon Lefebvre remarked drily, 'I had a thousand bullets fired at me from much closer range before I got all this.'

The future Marshals of the Empire came from widely differing social and family backgrounds. It is interesting to note that all of seven of the Marshalate came from aristocratic families, although most of these belonged to the *petite noblesse*.

Poniatowski was of course a Polish prince, and Grouchy a French marquis, in their own rights, but Berthier, Davout, Macdonald, Marmont and Pérignon were also men of good family, the descendants of officers in the Royal Army or of important officials. Some would also place Sérurier in this category. Not only was he a major and a chevalier of St Louis before the Revolution, but his father certainly regarded himself as a landowner and office-holder under the Bourbon monarchy as the royal mole-catcher at Laon. Augereau, Lefebvre, Murat, Mortier and Ney – sons of a fruit-dealer, a miller, an inn-keeper, a peasant-farmer and a barrel-cooper respectively – were men of relatively humble origins. The remaining thirteen came from professional, commercial or lower middle-class backgrounds.

Equally significant and revelatory is the study of the marshals' educations and of their previous military experience. Napoleon laid some stress on the former. 'There are scant resources to be found in men who have not received a primary education,' he once reflected. 'They can feel keenly, they can sense, but they cannot analyse anything; and when they come up against novel circumstances they only perpetrate stupid mistakes.' According to Guy Godlewski, eight of the marshals – like Napoleon himself – had received some formal military education. Six more were students (in the case of Murat a seminarist) in early life, but all abandoned the pen (or, in Murat's case, the *soutane*) for the sword, and the book for the barrack-room, at an early stage; Ney was training to be a notary, Mortier to be a merchant's clerk, Gouvion St Cyr to be an artist. All the remainder were literate in varying degrees, although Augereau, Lannes and Lefebvre owed more to their native wits than to any formal education. But in terms of innate intelligence all rated quite highly - especially Berthier, Davout and Soult, Massena and Suchet. Napoleon did not surround himself with fools – far from it.

There was also a great reservoir of variegated experience – both military and civil – amongst this band of twenty-six men. When Louis XVI was arrested at Varennes in June 1791, nine future marshals were serving as officers in the Royal Army. At that moment in time a further ten future marshals were either serving as NCOs or other ranks, or had recently done so. At the same date in 1791 the remaining six (discounting Poniatowski who was serving with the Polish army) were all still civilians following various employments, although once again several were already part-time members of the National Guard. All six were members of the bourgeoisie, and clearly every man was patriotically inclined and probably politically aware, as their association with National Guard of Volunteer formations might indicate. In troubled times it was prudent to be seen as actively committed to the defence of the Revolution.

Politically the future Marshalate represented a wide spectrum, from crypto-royalist to rabid republican – but most of them representing various shades of tactful 'centerism'. All, however, save possibly Jourdan, were opportunists to a marked degree, as indeed was Napoleon Bonaparte himself – and only a few would stay loyal to the end. A high degree of ideological flexibility was a desirable characteristic in a revolutionary period with its abrupt swings and *volte-faces*; and the relative ease with which many of the marshals were re-assimilated after the First and Second Bourbon Restorations of 1814 and 1815 would also seem to reinforce this impression.

Rarely has any group of men called to high military rank at a single period been more varied in terms of temperament and character. The flamboyance and quarrelsomeness of the touchy Murat contrasts with the icy-coolness of Davout or the reserved, stalwart fidelity of Bessières, or again the sensitivity of Moncey. The red-headed Ney had a flaring temper to match, not least in battle, the coarseness of Augereau or the drive of Lannes. Soult was both able and vain. None seems to have been highly religious, although Bernadotte made much of being a Protestant in later years, and Lefebvre made no secret of his Catholicism. Gouvion St Cyr was a confirmed agnostic. A few had a feeling for music and the arts. In their private lives, the great majority were unremarkable – they were good, if unspectacular, husbands and fathers in the main. The exceptions only proved the general rule. Marmont had a miserable marriage, Bessières was notorious for his casual affairs, and Massena's taste for women was apparently insatiable. Massena's mistress Silvia Cepolini accompanied him for most of the First Italian Campaign; and in 1810 the Prince of Essling took another, Henriette Renique, fetchingly if wholly unconvincingly disguised as an officer of cavalry, to Portugal – although this caused much trouble with his corps commanders, who refused to talk to her at mealtimes.

If the Marshalate shared one vice other than quarrelsomeness, it was venality. Their appetite for riches seemed bottomless, and represents the more sordid side of the ambition that drove them forward without exception. The names of Augereau, Brune and Massena are often associated with tales of peculation and looting on an impressive scale, with Victor only a shade behind them. Their bare-faced depredations became legendary. Soult looted in the grand manner – holding towns and provinces to ransom, and gathering the finest collection of paintings in Europe in the process (compelling us to recall Reichsminister Goering in a later century). Napoleon, of course, knew every detail of what was going on from his spies, and occasionally used his knowledge ruthlessly to control – even blackmail – his subordinates. Sometimes he insisted on ill-gotten gains being returned: both Brune and Massena were on occasion made to disgorge. More often he turned a blind eye on such irregularities. 'Don't talk to me about generals who love money,' he enjoined Gourgaud on St Helena. 'It was only that which enabled me to win the battle of Eylau. Ney wanted to reach Elbing to procure more funds.' It seems the Emperor had hoped to check the cupidity of his senior generals by awarding them proud titles, with appanages and monetary grants to match – but if anything it proved the opposite. The newly ennobled needed fine houses, hunting-lodges and all that went with them, and above all to outshine their rivals. But not all were tarred with the same brush, or to the same degree. Some, including Davout (save when the French interest was involved), Bessières, Mortier or Suchet and certainly Bernadotte were all men of some financial probity who set an example to their men and enforced similar standards. It must be admitted, however, that these fine examples were exceptional. They were for the most part rough men set in rough times, and acted accordingly. Napoleon had few illusions on this score. Once on St Helena he reproved General Gourgaud who was reminiscing in glowing terms about Lannes and Ney. 'You are fooling yourself if you regard Lannes thus. He, and Ney, were both men who would slit your belly if they thought it to their advantage. But on the field of battle they were beyond price.'

That was indeed the point: military valour and performance rated higher than the moral virtues, at least in the Emperor's book. The basic requirements Napoleon sought in a senior commander were as follows. 'A general's principal talent consists in knowing the mentality of the soldier and in gaining his confidence,' he once asserted. Or again: '... a military leader must possess as much character as intellect – the base must equal the height.' Before appointing a general he would enquire *'Est-il heureux?'* ('Is he lucky?' – and by 'luck' the Emperor really meant a flair for taking properly calculated risks). In 1804 he advised Lauriston that a successful general must achieve concentration of force, display activity of body and mind, and firmly resolve 'to perish gloriously. These are the three principles of the military art that have disposed luck in my favour in all my operations. Death is nothing, but to live defeated is to die every day.' And brave men the marshals certainly were – and for the most part very able, a number definitely gifted. One only has to think of Lannes wrestling with his aides to take up a scaling-ladder outside Ratisbon when the spirit of the storming-party faltered. Or Ney, commanding the rearguard, sword over arm, during the retreat from Russia, arriving at last in safety totally unrecognisable even to close associates. Or again, Massena, fighting intrepidly amongst his men in a desperate situation two years later at Essling, are further well-known examples of the personal valour of these famous figures, and many another example might be cited. Inspirational leadership of this type was much appreciated by both Napoleon and the ordinary soldiers – but there was sometimes a price to be paid. The instincts of the warrior sometimes overwhelmed the cool calculation of the strategist. Murat's cool demonstration of *sang-froid* at Vienna does not conceal the fact that he was not supposed to be anywhere near the Austrian capital – and his presence there was in fact allowing the Russian army to escape.

All the marshals were brave men without doubt, but only a few were 'great captains' in their own right. Davout and Massena, and probably Suchet, merit such a description, being men capable of independent command, strategic insights and intuitive flashes of inspiration. As for the rest, most were, if the truth be known, pretty mediocre commanders. Marmont was something of a paradox but Berthier – the chief of staff *sans pareil* – was hopelessly at sea in command of the army in Austria at the outset of the campaign of 1809. Some generals of division – including Lasalle, Lecourbe and Vandamme – were probably capable of more initiative than Marmont, Macdonald or Oudinot. But then, Napoleon, as we shall see, did not always encourage independence of mind in the men he chose for the highest honours, and took scant pains to inculcate in them an appreciation of the finer points of the art and science of war (*pace* certain historians).

That many of the chosen twenty-six were awkward subordinates to control, with their fits of feuding, quarrelling and plain insubordination, there can be no denying. Napoleon was not above playing the game of Caesar Caligula, *divide et impera* ('Divide and Rule'), to keep the hounds at bay by encouraging them to savage one another, but at times his patience must have been sorely tried. Murat became ever more difficult to handle, partly because of his sense of being a ruling monarch and needing to act out the role accordingly. Soult's aspirations to an Iberian crown reached near-treasonable proportions. Gouvion St Cyr – after clashing with Murat and Massena – had to be ordered back to Naples on pain of death after abandoning his duty station in 1806 for a visit to Paris in order to protest his treatment. So the marshals rowed, snarled and snapped at each other in campaign and out, and were repeatedly complaining to the Emperor about one another's behaviour. Thus Davout – whom Berthier thoroughly disliked – loathed Bernadotte and despised Murat, who in turn was barely on speaking terms with Ney from 1805 onwards. Brune gave as much blatant criticism as he attracted. Ney rowed with his superior Massena in 1810, and was as a result removed from his command, but so a little later was the Prince of Essling himself. Murat and Lannes prosecuted a lively feud from 1799, and Oudinot had scant time for Ney, and achieved possibly the perfect revenge at Dennewitz in 1813 when, smarting from being superseded in command by his rival, he *obeyed* an order knowing it to be wrong. The list could go on almost indefinitely. But, as disasters began to mount, so the morale of his key subordinates began to sink in the later years. 'It would be difficult for me to describe the gloomy inquietude which I saw on the face of the gold-spangled courtiers and generals assembled in the Emperor's apartments,' recalled the Austrian statesman Metternich of peace negotiations in early 1814. 'The Prince of Neuchâtel said to me in a whisper – "Do not forget that Europe needs peace – France above all wants nothing but peace."' And in the end the system let him down when a group of marshals, led by Ney, totally demoralised and wearied beyond bearing by the incessant demands of warfare, mutinied at Fontainebleau on 4 April 1814, and refused to obey orders to march on Paris.

When it came to selecting the men to carry the baton, Napoleon was again the subject of conflicting pressures and priorities, in which politics within the army had an important part to play. Prominence in the army and personal valour were certainly basic criteria, but military distinction *per se* was not the sole, or even the most important consideration. Relationship by marriage with the Bonaparte clan was a factor in the appointment of both Murat and Davout to the dignity, and the inclusion of a number of staunch heroes of the early Republican period such as Kellermann, the other honorific marshals, and Lefebvre, was clearly a sound decision. This at once helped quell any charges of anti-Republican bias in the selection process and stressed the continuity of the institution. But it was even more important to strike a balance between significant power groupings within the army itself, and to keep them under control, allowing no single cabal to exert a decisive influence and to avoid the danger of possible *coup* attempts.

There were two main groups, and one minor, to be placated, controlled and integrated. These were in the first place the generals who had served under General Bonaparte in the famous Army of Italy, many of whom had followed him on to Egypt and Syria. Then there were those soldiers who had made their reputations serving on the northern and eastern frontiers of France under such notable commanders as Dumouriez, Kellermann, Moreau, Pichegru and Kléber without any recourse to Napoleon, or experience of serving under him; and in third place there were commanders who had mainly served on the southern frontiers in the Armies of the Pyrenees, of whom the same might be said. There was considerable mutual suspicion, even a degree of antagonism, between the groups, particularly the first two. The 'Italians' considered themselves as the élite owing to their former proximity to Napoleon's person – and some were inclined to take liberties on this basis – another tendency the Emperor was determined to check. The 'men of the Rhine', on the other hand, believed that they had carried the brunt of the Revolutionary Wars and achieved just as much, if not considerably more, than the Corsican's *mafioso* who had fought on what could be deemed the secondary front against, in the main, second-class opponents in Italy. By 1804 Dumouriez had defected, Moreau had been disgraced and Pichegru and Kléber were dead, but Napoleon realised the need to rally the remaining veterans of the Rhine Armies in order to avoid any danger of schism and conspiracy, and to achieve his determination to create a single, united French army without strong regional loyalties and attitudes that might cause problems. Accordingly, the list of eighteen names was a carefully conceived balancing act designed to unite the factions, giving each a fair share of representation. Seven of the 'active' marshals were drawn from the generals of the Army of Italy – namely Berthier, Murat, Massena, Augereau, Brune, Lannes and Bessières. Seven were selected from the Armies of the Rhine – namely Jourdan, Bernadotte, Soult, Mortier, Ney, Davout and Lefebvre. The

Armies of the Pyrenees (which had been largely quiescent since 1795) were represented by two of the honorific appointments, namely those of Moncey and Pérignon; the remaining two batons were awarded to an old soldier from each of the two main factions – Sérurier representing the veterans of 'Italy', Kellermann those of 'the Rhine'. All four incarnated the achievements of the first armies of the Republic, and also represented a salute to the old Bourbon Royal Army that preceded these, and in whose ranks at least three had earned considerable distinction. So much for the 'Promotion of 1804'. It is interesting to note that roughly the same balance was preserved in the later appointments, although the distinction between 'soldiers of Italy' and 'men of the Rhine' had become less critical with the passage of time. Thus Victor, Marmont and Suchet had originally served under Bonaparte in 1796–7, whilst four more – Macdonald, Oudinot, Gouvion St Cyr and Grouchy – had first earned their spurs on the eastern frontiers. Poniatowski, of course, as a foreigner belonged to no French faction.

Napoleon would live to regret some of the appointments he made, and even to question the wisdom of restricting the award of key commands to marshals alone, above all in the later years. 'He found fault with himself for having made so much use of the marshals in these latter days,' recorded Caulaincourt in 1814, 'since they had become too rich, too much the *grands seigneurs* and had grown war-weary. Things, according to him, would have been in a much better state if he had placed good generals of division, with their batons yet to win, in command.' But in the great years, before disillusion set in, he owed much to the men he had selected to wear *les gros bonnets*.

In conclusion, it remains to reach some sort of an estimate of Napoleon's opinion of his twenty-six marshals, and also some of their feelings towards him. He was always aware of his debt to them individually. Anyone criticising, for example, Augereau would be reminded, 'Ah, but remember what he did for us at Castiglione!' Ney's conduct during the retreat from Moscow was frequently recalled in the last years of the Empire as at least partial absolution for his errors of judgement. The Emperor could equally be devastatingly scathing to those he regarded as having let him down. He rarely minced words, either face to face or on paper. 'I cannot approve your manner of march,' he wrote to Murat in 1805. 'You go on like a stunned fool taking not the least notice of my orders.' On another occasion, he compared his latest splendid uniforms to 'Franconi the circus rider'. Again, after Bernadotte's major *faux pas* in mid-October 1806, Napoleon declared: 'This matter is so hateful that if I send him before a court martial it will be the equivalent of ordering him to be shot . . . (However) I shall take care he shall know what I think of his behaviour.' When Marmont was responsible for a near-disaster in the Festieux Defile (March, 1814), the Emperor fulminated at '. . . the crass stupidity of the Duke of Ragusa, who behaved himself like a second-lieutenant', which at least gave him some seniority over Ney at Jena, compared scathingly to 'the last-joined drummer boy'. 'Write him a truly dry letter,' directed the master, sacking Victor for idleness in 1814; and no man was better at phrasing a telling expression of imperial displeasure than Berthier, of whom Napoleon once admitted '. . . no one else could replace him.'

There is no question but that the Emperor drove his key subordinates hard. As we have also seen, he could be generous – but few were given much chance to enjoy their privileges. The system worked well enough in the great days of the Empire – but several grave penalties had to be paid in later years. First, because Napoleon demanded absolute obedience, few of the marshals were happy when situations arose which demanded genuine initiative in their master's absence. This became particularly evident in Spain from 1809, when successive teams of marshals – deprived of the Emperor's dominating presence – proved incapable of fully effective action, and furthermore wasted much time and energy prosecuting their personal feuds against one another. Even the great Massena fell prey to this tendency in 1810–11 with dire results. Moreover, if even Napoleon was incapable of controlling events on the Tagus or Ebro from Paris, what hope had he of doing so from Moscow in 1812 or central Germany in 1813? Thus the strictly centralised direction of campaigns upon which he insisted – and was operable enough in the campaigns he personally commanded with armies of up to 250,000 men – eventually broke down when the size of armies burgeoned to half a million and more, as war zones extended ever more widely, and as a second front – and a Russian one at that – was finally added to compound the problem.

On his return from Elba in 1815 for the final gamble of the 'Hundred Days', he took his revenge. After Waterloo, the Bourbons exacted their vengeance by shooting Ney and by depriving several more marshals of their batons at least temporarily.

How then did Napoleon see his marshals? The long years of exile on St Helena gave him plenty of leisure to consider their strengths and abilities, their failings and foibles, and the services of Count Las Cases and General Gourgaud to record his verdicts. Here it will only be possible to cite a single recorded opinion (or at the most two) on each of the marshals. Of course some allowance has to be made for the circumstances of disillusion and bitterness that surrounded the exile of St Helena which inevitably coloured his verdicts at least to some degree, but they do provide a guide to Napoleon's innermost feelings at that time. The justice or otherwise of the Emperor's sometimes inconsistent views will have to be judged by individuals. The marshals are placed in alphabetical order:

Augereau: 'It is a long time since the marshal was truly a soldier; his courage, his outstanding virtues certainly elevated him far above the crowd; but honours, titles, and money plunged him back into it. The conqueror of Castiglione could have left a cherished name to France; but she will recall the memory of the deserter of Lyons.'

Bernadotte: 'I can only say that Bernadotte betrayed me. He had become a sort of Swede, but never promised or declared an intention to stay true. I can therefore accuse him of ingratitude, but not of treason.'

Berthier: 'I have been betrayed by Berthier, a true gosling whom I had made into a kind of eagle' (1814). 'There was not in the world a better Chief of Staff; that is where his true talent lay, for he was not capable of commanding 500 men . . .' (St Helena).

Bessières: 'If I had had Bessières at Waterloo, my Guard would have brought me Victory.'

Brune: '. . . was justly proclaimed the saviour of the Batavian Republic. The Romans would have awarded him the honour of a Triumph. By saving Holland he also saved France from invasion.'

Davout: '. . . will have his place in History because of Auerstädt. He also performed well at Eylau, but, urged on at Wagram, he was the cause of the loss of a possible battle the previous day . . . He also made mistakes at the Moskowa [Borodino].'

Gouvion St Cyr: 'My mistake was to have employed St Cyr; he never exposed himself to fire, made no visits, left his comrades to be beaten, and should have been able to save Vandamme' [at Kulm, 1813).

Grouchy: 'Marshal Grouchy, with 34,000 men and 108 cannon, solved the apparently undiscoverable secret of being, on the morning of the 18th [June 1815], neither on the battlefield of Mont St Jean nor on that at Wavre . . . His conduct was as unforeseeable as if his army, on the march, had undergone an earthquake and been swallowed up.'

Jourdan: 'I certainly used that man very ill; nothing would be more natural than that he should think that he owed me little. Ah well! I have learned with great pleasure that since my fall he invariably acted very well. He has thus afforded an example of that praiseworthy elevation of mind which distinguishes men one from another. Jourdan is a true patriot, and that is the answer to many things that have been said of him.'

Kellermann: 'I think that I was probably the boldest general who ever lived, but I wouldn't have dared to take post there [the ridge topped by a windmill at Valmy].'

Lannes: 'In the case of Lannes, his courage in the first place carried him further than his spirit; but each day his spirit rose to the occasion, and restored the balance. He had truly become a superior being by the time he perished; I found him a pygmy, but I lost a giant.'

Lefebvre: 'A truly brave man . . . whose only thought was to fight better . . . He had no fear of death . . . He possessed the sacred fire.'

Macdonald: 'He was a reliable man, good to command between 15,000 and 20,000 men. Brave, but slow and lazy.' 'Macdonald and others like him were good when they knew where they were and under my orders; further away, it was a different matter.'

Massena: '. . . was once a very superior man who, by a very special dispensation, possessed that greatly desired coolness in the heat of an action; he came alive when surrounded by danger. Massena, who was endowed with rare courage and such remarkable tenacity, also had a talent that increased the greater the danger; when defeated, he was always ready to begin again as if he was in fact the victor.'

Marmont: 'The ungrateful fellow – he will be much unhappier than I' (1814). 'Many others were worse than he, who did not have the sense of shame that he felt . . . Vanity was his undoing – an excess of folly.'

Moncey: '. . . was an honest man.'

Mortier: 'The three best of my generals were Davout, Soult and Bessières. Mortier was the most feeble.'

Murat: 'I cannot conceive how so brave a man could be so lax. He was only brave when confronted by the enemy, and then he was perhaps the bravest man in the world . . . but if he was placed in council he was a poltroon with no judgement and was quite incapable of making a decision. Murat's character, however, was nobler than Ney's, for he was generous and frank.'

Ney: 'Ney only got what he deserved. I regret him as a man very precious on the battlefield, but he was too immoral, too stupid to be able to succeed.' 'He was good for a command of 10,000 men, but beyond that he was out of his depth.'

Oudinot: 'He was a brave man, but none too bright. He let himself be dominated by his young wife of good family.' 'I should not have made either Marmont or Oudinot marshals. We needed to win a war.'

Pérignon: Napoleon is not known to have ever commented upon this deserving officer.

Poniatowski: 'He was a man of noble character, brimming-over with honour and bravery. I intended to make him King of Poland had I succeeded in Russia.'

Sérurier: '... retained all the characteristics and the severity of an infantry major – an honest man, with integrity and reliability, but unfortunate as a general.'

Soult: 'I should have made a great example and had Soult shot; he was the greatest pillager of them all.' 'Both [Soult and Talleyrand] put money before everything else; they wanted a royal suite and money, always money.'

Suchet: Asked by Dr O'Meara to say who was the ablest of his generals, Napoleon replied: 'That is difficult to say, but it seems to me it may have been Suchet; once it was Massena, but eventually one had to consider him as virtually dead; Suchet, Clausel and Gérard were the best French generals in my opinion.'

Victor: '... was better than you might think. At the passage of the Beresina he commanded his corps very well indeed.'

So much for the master's views on his key military subordinates (save the shadowy Pérignon). They, of course, also had some very decided views about him. In 1796 Massena recalled how the newly arrived General Bonaparte 'suddenly put on his hat, and seemed to have grown two feet.' Augereau commented: 'This little bastard of a general actually scared me.' Even the hardened and totally intractable republican general Vandamme later admitted: 'So it is that I, who fear neither God nor Devil, trembled like a child when I approached him.' All respected, most admired, but by no means all liked Napoleon. Massena was for many years not wholly his man, and during the Consulate pointedly asked an officer of the Consular Guard when he had joined 'the janissaries', and how was 'Sultan Bonaparte' getting on? On another occasion he pointed out to a friend that the stream that watered Malmaison had its source on Massena's property, and that accordingly, 'I piss on him when I want to.' Augereau could be even blunter. In 1814, as the Empire collapsed, the Duke of Castiglione issued a proclamation at Valence releasing his soldiers from their oaths to Napoleon, '... a man who, having sacrificed millions of victims to his cruel ambition, has not known how to die like a soldier.' Little wonder he found himself struck off the list of marshals on the Emperor's return to France next year. Ney's 1815 comment about bringing Napoleon back to Paris 'in an iron cage' is well known, but Bernadotte, when changing sides to the Allies in 1812, referred to Napoleon as 'that rogue, that scourge of the world who must be killed'. Again, given his pusillanimous behaviour the previous year, we are not surprised that Napoleon rejected Murat's proffered services in 1815.

Even Lannes, loyal though he basically was to Napoleon and something of a favourite, never accepted all his pretensions; nor did Gouvion St Cyr – perhaps the least-favoured of the Marshalate. But Napoleon had their measure. As he once confided in a realistic if disillusioned moment to Minister Molé in 1813, 'I have nobody I can put in my place, neither here (in Paris) nor in the Army. Without a doubt I would be very happy if I could make war through my generals. But I have accustomed them too much to knowing only how to obey; amongst them all there is not one who can command the others, for all they know is to obey me alone.'

The marshals, like so many others, succumbed to the tremendous personal appeal that Napoleon could exert. I conclude with the celebrated passage from Hendrik van Loon (written in 1921) which goes some little way to explaining this phenomenal appeal and personal magnetism:

> Here I am sitting at a comfortable table loaded heavily with books, with one eye on the typewriter and the other on Licorice the cat, who has a great fondness for carbon paper, and I am telling you that the Emperor Napoleon was a most contemptible person. But should I happen to look out of the window, down upon Seventh Avenue, and should the endless procession of trucks and carts come to a sudden halt, and should I hear the sound of the heavy drums and see the little man on his white horse in his old and much-worn green uniform, then I don't know, but I am afraid that I would leave my books and my kitten and my home and everything else to follow him wherever he cared to lead. My own grandfather did this and Heaven knows he was not born to be a hero... If you ask me for an explanation, I must answer that I have none. I can only guess at one of the reasons. Napoleon was the greatest of actors and the whole European continent was his stage. At all times and under all circumstances he knew the precise attitude that would impress the spectators most and he understood what words would make the deepest impression – at all times he was master of the situation... Even today he is as much of a force in the life of France as a hundred years ago...'

6

NAPOLEON'S MASTERPIECE:
AUSTERLITZ, 2 DECEMBER 1805

*T*he dramatic events that took place over the frost-covered fields of Moravia (part of
the modern Czech Republic) near Brünn on 2 December 1805 hold a central place
in Napoleonic military history – both fact and legend.

Austerlitz is one of the most satisfactory battlefields to visit. I have done so twice in
recent years – first, while I was writing Austerlitz, 1805 (1991) in the company of the
Napoleonic Association of Great Britain. I learnt for the first time of the size and number
of similar Napoleonic societies of students and re-enactors existing in (the then) Eastern
Europe – and this discovery provided much of the impetus for the foundation of the Union
of European Re-enactment Societies which I have already mentioned. The ground was
barely altered since 1805: the villages, streams, and heights are clearly identifiable from
the Santon to the Pratzen and Zurlan Heights, from Aujedst Markt to Sokolnitz and
Telnitz. The meres and lakes of 1805 that witnessed the dramatic and terrible last act of
the battle on its southern extremity have long been drained to form rich farming land and
thus have disappeared – but their former location can be traced without much difficulty.
A fine map-table and orientation point is to be found on the summit of the Zurlan
Height, although I have been informed that the former has recently been disastrously
vandalised. Eheu mores! Eheu tempora! But at least eastern Europe is now open for
visits.

My second visit was in 1992, when I accompanied a videofilm company, Seventh Art,
over the area for the purpose of making a film on Napoleon and the battle of Austerlitz as
part of Channel 4's 'Great Commanders' series. On each occasion I learnt a great deal
about the battle area; and I can only encourage fellow-enthusiasts in the Napoleonic
period to make a point of making such visits to the battle-sites and supporting museums.
Each anniversary Czech and other Napoleonic Associations put on a commemoration –
often in snow and icy conditions. A second commemorative re-enactment is performed each
2 December by the officer-cadets at the French military school of St Cyr-Coëtiquidian,
where the training-area has been named 'the Pratzen'.

Much scholarly work remains to be done in order to make Russian and Austrian
studies and memoirs available to English students, and I feel sure that this effort will be

forthcoming. Grenadier Coignet's account of the battle forms an important section in his Notebooks – *already mentioned in the introduction to Chapter 4.*
Austerlitz was without a doubt Napoleon's greatest battle.

†

Even after, the soldiers called it 'the sun of Austerlitz'. The blood-red globe, magnified several times by the dense fog it was dissipating, was a spectacle that few who saw it – and survived the battle – would ever forget. Near the summit of the frost-capped Zurlan Height stood two men, a cluster of cloak-wrapped staff officers and aides-de-camp drawn up at a respectful distance behind them. As a muffled church clock somewhere below began to chime nine o'clock, the shorter figure, clad in the grey overcoat and black cocked-hat that became synonymous with his name, snapped shut his telescope (with which he had been closely observing the mist-free top of the Pratzen Heights, a mile away to the east over the fog-filled valley of the Goldbach stream) and turned to Marshal Nicolas Soult at his side; 'the first manoeuvrer in Europe', he would soon dub him. 'One sharp blow and the war is over,' declared Napoleon. 'I have no need to remind you to comport yourself as you have always done.' But the emperor's companion had already swung himself into his saddle and disappeared down the steep hillside. It was the morning of 2 December 1805 – and the 'battle of the Three Emperors' was about to reach its first climax.

The battle of Austerlitz takes its name from a medium-sized town (now known as Slavkov) in Moravia (today part of the Czech Republic). Four miles west of the township are the Pratzen Heights, in 1805 the centre of a mighty battle fought by 158,000 men equipped with 417 cannon – 36,000 of whom would become casualties before dark on that freezing December day. Exactly one year earlier Napoleon had crowned himself Emperor at Notre Dame – as his soldiers now reminded him, shouting *'c'est l'anniversaire'* and forming an impromptu torchlight procession as he strolled through their bivouacs in the dark early hours of that fateful Monday morning. Deeply touched by this evidence of his soldiers' loyalty and affection, he could find no words to thank them but slowly moved his hand to and fro in recognition of their spontaneous demonstration. 'This has been the finest evening of my life,' he was heard to murmur as he lay back to snatch a few hours rest in his straw-floored tent. But an even finer one lay close ahead. Before sunset that same day he would have established his place in history as one of the truly 'great captains' of all time. For Napoleon personally, Austerlitz would forever afterwards rank as his favourite battle. It was destined to be his masterpiece of operational art – of battlefield command.

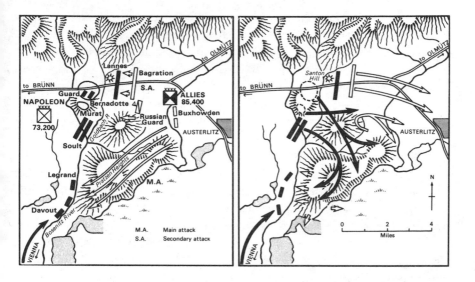

AUSTERLITZ 1805
ALLIED ATTACK

AUSTERLITZ 1805
NAPOLEON'S COUNTERATTACK

The origins of the War of the Third Coalition go back to the seizure on neutral soil and subsequent hasty execution of the Bourbon prince, the Duke of Enghien in March 1804. This ruthless deed – intended to serve as a warning to would-be assassins – caused a storm of European outrage, creating a Franco-phobic atmosphere that British premier William Pitt the Younger hastened to exploit. As Napoleon's ruthless Minister of Police, Joseph Fouché, trenchantly remarked, 'It was more than a crime – it was a mistake.' Napoleon further eased the task of his inveterate British foe by next crowning himself Emperor in late 1804 and then King of Italy (May 1805). These political acts, added to the 'judicial murder' of the Bourbon royal princeling, inalienably affronted the ancient royal houses of Europe. The Habsburg Emperor Francis II in Vienna and the Romanov Tsar Alexander I in St Petersburg – the two crowned heads who would share with Napoleon the events of 2 December 1805 – proceeded to negotiate alliances with Great Britain, and were joined by Sweden, Naples and other Germanic states to put a joint 400,000 men into the field against France. A decidedly complex seven-part strategic plan evolved, but so shoddy was the staff work of the Allies of the Third Coalition that Vienna even failed to realise the twelve-day difference between the west European and Russian calendars.

Through his well-placed spies Napoleon was kept abreast of the main developments, and on 25 August he ordered the breaking up of the Camp of Boulogne (formed in 1803 for the mounting of an invasion of England across the Channel) and the stealthy transfer of the newly designated Grand Army to the Rhine. His intention was to launch a rapid pre-emptive strike on a broad, initially 100-mile front through Germany to crush Austria (whose army was already attacking France's ally, Bavaria) before the Russians could arrive. Warlike preparations under Marshal Massena in Italy (where Napoleon knew his foes expected him to take his main effort) were effectively used to conceal his true intentions. Of all the European powers, only Frederick III of Prussia continued to conceal his intentions behind a supposedly neutral stance.

On the night of 24 September the first French soldiers crossed over the Rhine. Organised into six front-line army corps commanded by Bernadotte, Marmont, Davout, Soult, Ney and Lannes, supported by Marshal Augereau's VII, the 210,000-strong Grand Army moved in a vast concentric sweep through Germany. Just eleven days later their leading elements were crossing the Danube well to the east of Ulm in Bavaria, where a near-mesmerised Austrian Quartermaster-General Mack and the Archduke Ferdinand were attempting to concentrate their 72,000 men. The events that followed this *blitzkrieg* leading to the surrender of Mack at Ulm cannot even be summarised here. Suffice it to say that by the end of the month Napoleon had, without recourse to a major battle, accounted for 64,000 Austrians for a loss of under 2000 casualties. His bold opportunistic sweep to encircle Ulm – adapting his original plan to suit actual circumstances – caused a stunned Mack to capitulate with 21,000 men on 21 October (the same day that far away to the west Rear-Admiral Horatio Nelson won the decisive naval victory off Spanish Cape Trafalgar). The French had then proceeded to mop-up Austrian detachments with remorseless efficiency.

The main secrets of Napoleon's success to date were surprise, the seizure and keeping of the initiative, and the superb mobility and flexibility that the army corps system conferred. Each corps was in effect a miniature army, 17,000 to 30,000 men strong. It was a balanced, all-arms, self-sufficient formation, capable of operating alone (thus easing road problems and facilitating 'living off the countryside') and, if necessary, of fighting a far superior force for up to twenty-four hours. Napoleon placed his corps in a flexible strategic net, capable of rapidly reinforcing any threatened sector by 'marching on the sound of the guns'. 'March dispersed, fight concentrated' was another key Napoleonic maxim. This system had been tried out before, but only now in 1805 was its full potential being demonstrated. Small wonder that Napoleon's foot-sore soldiers remarked: 'The Emperor has discovered a new way of making war: he makes use of our legs instead of our arms.'

Mack and Ferdinand crushed, Napoleon next turned his full attention to the approaching 58,000-strong Russo-Austrian army of General Kutusov. This one-eyed sixty-year-old veteran of many campaigns against the Turks was a redoubtable commander despite his addictions to the bottle and young women.

He immediately ordered a retreat from the River Inn, intent upon transferring his army north of the Danube so as to unite it with General Buxhowden's 30,000 Russians who, accompanied by the Tsar, were approaching Olmütz from Poland. Despite frequent skirmishes at successive river lines, Napoleon failed to bring the wily Russian to battle, and on 3 November Kutusov safely recrossed the Danube at Krems. This setback was largely due to Prince Joachim Murat, Napoleon's brother-in-law, the exceptionally brave *beau sabreur* but unthinkingly headstrong commander of the French cavalry, who ignored orders and rode ahead to seize Vienna. This earned him a blistering reprimand, followed by a second when, after brilliantly bluffing his way over a bridge prepared for demolition at Vienna, Murat was fooled in his turn by guileful talk of an armistice by the Russian Prince Bagration's rearguard at Hollabrünn on the 15th. 'I am lost for words with which to express my displeasure,' fulminated the Emperor, ordering Murat to resume hostilities immediately. But it was now too late to catch Kutusov, who duly joined the Tsar and Buxhowden near Wischau on 20 November. The joint-army, now totalling 86,000 men, pulled back to Olmütz.

Napoleon reached Znaim on the 17th. But growing exhaustion and worsening weather forced him to halt his pursuit at Brünn. Forty miles now divided the two main armies. News from Italy and the Tyrol was still mainly favourable, but the equivocal attitude of Prussia now necessitated the sending of Bernadotte's I Corps to Iglau as a precaution against a sudden Prussian attack. This and many other garrison detachment reduced Napoleon's strength around Brünn to barely 53,000 men under immediate command.

With the far stronger Allied army only forty miles away, Napoleon was in an increasingly precarious position. So at least thought the bright sparks around the Tsar, who were strongly supported by the Austrian General Weyrother, 'a veteran of the Viennese offices' (or military bureaucrat). These pressure groups demanded an immediate counter-offensive. Francis II and Kutusov advised caution, only to be contemptuously scorned and ignored by the firebrands, who included the twenty-eight-year-old Alexander.

Napoleon was well aware of the peril – but determined to turn it to his own advantage. To redress part of his manpower shortfall, he summoned by forced marches I Corps from Iglau (mercifully there were still no firm signs of Prussia entering the war), and also Davout's III Corps from Vienna all of eighty miles distant, creating a dense cavalry screen to mask these vital transfers. Meanwhile, the French deliberately gave every appearance of irresolution further to fool the allies. Cavalry outposts were ordered to fall back from near Wischau, Austerlitz was evacuated, and even the dominating high ground of the Pratzen Heights abandoned – all in order to create an impression of French weakness and low morale. Napoleon next switched his lines of communication from the dangerously exposed highroad to Vienna to that running west towards Iglau.

He began to feign weakness, requesting an armistice and peace negotiations (both were brusquely refused), and step by step he set about inducing the Russo-Austrian high command to attack his exposed right (which the foe was induced to consider but weakly held, although Davout's secret arrival in the area would swing the balance) and the road to Vienna beyond it. As early as 21 November he had required his staff to study the area west of the Goldbach stream: 'Gentlemen, examine this ground carefully. It is going to be a battlefield: you will have a part to play upon it.'

On 1 December it was clear that the Allies were duly falling for the bait dangled so temptingly before their eyes, blinded as they were by the prospect of an easy and decisive victory. After a two-day advance along the Olmütz to Brünn road, most Allied divisions swung off to the south to occupy the undefended Pratzen area ready to envelop Napoleon's right wing and thus cut him off from Vienna. Their commanders and staffs met at Krzenowitz late on 1 December. Little did they realise that before nightfall the French strength had been raised to over 66,000 men following Bernadotte's unostentatious arrival from the west, or that 6600 more reinforcements under Davout's command were near Raigern Abbey after a heroic march of eighty miles from Vienna in just fifty hours. As news reached Napoleon that masses of the enemy were collecting on and to the south of the Pratzen Heights, his confidence grew. 'Before tomorrow evening this army will be mine!' he prophesied. '*On les aura!*' ('We shall have them!').

The field of Austerlitz stretches for six miles, north to south. The mile-wide valley between the Zurlan and Pratzen Heights is watered by the Goldbach stream, joined by the Bosenitz stream near Puntowitz village. To the east, just north of the highway, stands a cone-shaped hill called the Santon, topped by a small chapel beyond which the Goldbach Heights develop. The hillsides were bare, encouraging manoeuvre. Only the valley floor was scattered with villages and enclosures. This sector Napoleon entrusted to the fiery thirty-six-year-old Marshal Lannes' V Corps (12,700 men and twenty guns strong). Around the Zurlan (his first battle headquarters) facing the Pratzen over the valley were Murat's Reserve Cavalry (7500 men with thirty-six pieces of horse artillery), Bernadotte's I Corps (13,000 and twenty-four guns), the Imperial Guard (5500 veterans and twenty-four guns), and General Oudinot's special force of grenadiers (5700 strong) drawn from all the line regiments. Soult's IV Corps (23,600 men with thirty-five guns) comprised three divisions, two of which (commanded by Generals Vandamme and St Hilaire) were hidden away on the valley floor west of the villages of Puntowitz and Kobelnitz, whilst the third (under General Legrand) – the bait – was thinly spread over a two-mile sector running from Kobelnitz Pond past Sokolnitz castle and its village to Telnitz, facing the iced-over Satschan Mere. To the south-west rested the short-sighted but valiant thirty-five-year-old Marshal Davout's exhausted men of Friant's

Division, still out of close contact. Four miles away to the east was Austerlitz, a medium-sized town that contained the fine palace of Prince Kaunitz, destined to give its name to the impending battle.

Napoleon's plan was to lure the foe into making a heavy attack against his apparently weak right flank, which would, however, be reinforced at the critical moment by Davout's nearby formations. If necessary, Davout and Legrand could give ground towards the north, giving the enemy the illusion of success – and be reinforced by Oudinot's special force. Meanwhile, on the French left flank, Lannes (aided as necessary by Murat's cavalry) was to hold the cone-shaped Santon hill at all costs against the enemy right wing. Once the mass of the enemy was committed to these attacks, Napoleon intended to launch Soult's two concealed divisions from the valley floor against Pratzen village and its surrounding heights, and thus occupy the denuded enemy centre. Reinforced by Bernadotte and the Guard, Soult would then roll up either the enemy left or right according to the prevailing circumstances. The various corps were to be linked by visual telegraph – a line of intervisible flag stations – once the fog lifted. To put his men on their mettle, a flamboyant order of the day was issued.

That he had divined his opponents' intentions was indicated by the campfires burning to the southward and the fierce skirmishing around Telnitz about midnight. Napoleon and his escort rode over to observe, and almost ran into a patrol of Cossacks, but safely returned to the French lines. Napoleon then walked through his cheering army as described. By 2.30 am, all was quiet once more.

In fact the Allied plan of battle reflected most of Napoleon's hopes. The final 1 am staff conference at Krzenowitz was chaired by dozing Kutusov, who fell asleep before its conclusion. Weyrother described his plan – which was unanimously adopted by everyone else present. A diversionary attack was to be mounted in the north by Prince Bagration and 13,000 Russians, while the main effort was to be launched by the Allied centre and left, in all some 59,300 men under overall command of General Buxhowden. This massive force was to sweep south off the Pratzen to capture Telnitz and then, after crossing the shallow but marshy-banked Goldbach, Sokolnitz and its castle. These objectives were entrusted to Kienmayer's (Austrian) advance guard (5100 men), General Doctorov's (Russian) First Column (13,600) and General Langeron's (Russian) Second Column (11,700 strong). These powerful forces would be supported by Generals Miloradovitch's and Kollowrath's Russo-Austrian Fourth Column (23,900 men with seventy-six cannon), and would in due course be joined by General Przbyswski's Russo-Austrian Third Column (7700), whose particular role was to move west down the Pratzen at the correct moment to attack Puntowitz. All these forces were then to surge north and west to bend back the French right to Turas, cutting the supposedly vital Vienna highway in the process. The taking of Puntowitz – the hinge of the hairpin-bent French battle-line – would then reduce Napoleon's army to shambles. Meanwhile Lichtenstein's 3600 cavalry (after being repositioned from their overnight camping-ground) was to be ready to support Bagration on the right as necessary. Finally, in ultimate reserve, Prince Constantine's Russian Imperial Guard Corps (6730 élite infantry, 3700 superb cavalry and forty guns strong) was placed near Krenowitz. This was a complex plan, which the dense late- night fog did nothing to assist in the forming-up stages at 4 am. Some measure of chaos was immediately experienced when Lichenstein's horsemen, en route for their correct station, demanded right-of-way as they crossed the heads of several infantry columns.

Napoleon was roused once from his sleep to approve a minor change to strengthen the French right. And so the scene was at last set for Napoleon's greatest battle. A final briefing of senior officers was held atop the Zurlan at 5.30 am. Concern that Lannes would come to blows with Soult over a mis-understanding of several days' standing proved unnecessary. 'We have more serious things to engage our attention,' Soult loftily informed the fire-spitting Gascon – who growlingly concurred and stood aside. The last orders given, all save Soult and Berthier departed to their prescribed battle stations.

After a hearty breakfast, the fur-wrapped Russian Tsar and Austrian Emperor met Kutusov near the peak of Staré Vinohrady to the north of the Pratzen. 'Mikhail Hilarionovich!' the Tsar exclaimed testily. 'Why haven't you begun your advance?' 'Your Highness, I am waiting for all our columns to get into position.' 'But we are not on the Empress's Meadows [at St Petersburg], where we do not begin a parade until all the regiments are formed up.' 'Your Highness, if I have not begun it is precisely because we are *not* on parade and *not* on the Empress's Meadows. However, if such be Your Highness's order...'

After a stumbling and confused descent to the valley, at 7 am the Austrian Kienmayer attacked the village of Telnitz. An hour later, a massively out-numbered Legrand pulled his men back west of the Goldbach, and a jubilant Buxhowden directed Doctorov's and Langeron's columns (which had been badly delayed by the transfer of Lichtenstein's cavalry across their front towards the right) to prepare to attack Sokolnitz. But abruptly out of the fog came Friant's leading brigade of Davout's III Corps to give timely assistance – just as Napoleon intended: Telnitz was eventually cleared, and as the Allies tried to deploy over the Goldbach they were taken in the flank by yet more men of III Corps, and found themselves repulsed from Sokolnitz as well by 10 am. The fierce and confused fighting amidst the fog was not without some local setbacks for the French. Near Telnitz, as Corporal Blaise of the 108th Line Regiment of Friant's Division recalled, '... we were halted by a stream too broad for us to cross. General Heudelet thereupon ordered our colonel to move us over a bridge away to our left. This necessary movement was the cause of our undoing, for the soldiers were so eager to come to grips with the vaunted enemy infantry that they disordered the ranks despite the wise orders of our officers; and when we tried to reform our battle order under heavy fire, some Austrian hussars . . . in the thick smoke and fog . . . wounded a great many of us and captured 160 men including four officers.' But this untoward event did not prevent some 10,300 French troops from tying down 50,000 Allies – as they were to continue to do for six more hours. But in the meantime critical events were taking place further north.

By 8.45 am the sun's rays were fast piercing and dissolving the fog. Napoleon could now see that the Pratzen was almost clear of Kutusov's troops as more and more Allied formations were sucked into the fighting against Davout and Legrand. 'How long will it take you to move your divisions to the top of the Pratzen Heights?' Napoleon enquired of Soult. 'Less than twenty minutes, Sire.' 'When we will wait for another quarter of an hour.' A sense of timing is everything in war. Just after nine o'clock, drums beating, Vandamme and St Hilaire's divisions emerged from the mists of the valley floor, bayonets glittering in the sunlight, dispersing the fog clinging to their flanks like two terriers shaking themselves on emerging from water. They soon cleared Pratzen village as an aghast Kutosov tried desperately to recall Kollowrath and Miloradovich, who were now two-thirds of the way down the slopes. But as these foes were some way distant the French retained the advantage of the initiative. By 11 am the summit of the Pratzen Heights, and several abandoned Russian batteries, were firmly in French hands. These events also eased some of the pressure on the hard-beset French right.

The battle had also been joined for two hours on the northern flank, where by dint of hard fighting Lannes was containing Bagration. As Prince Lichtenstein's squadrons attempted to fall on V Corps' flank, they were countercharged by seven regiments of Murat's cuirassiers. The two forces of cavalry met with a crash that was heard throughout the field. Soon the French had gained the upper hand, and Lannes sent part of Caffarelli's division to take Bläsowitz. By 11 am both of V Corps divisions were gaining ground, and at midday Lannes called a halt lest his men should press too far ahead of the main battle that was now raging with renewed ferocity on the Pratzen. Bagration eventually rallied behind the Raussnitz stream, having lost 2500 killed and 4000 taken prisoner. The French had lost 2000 casualties, but they were now undeniably masters of the left-wing sector.

On the Pratzen, Soult's tired but victorious troops began to re-order their ranks. They received only a short respite, however, for counter-attacks by the troops of the Allied centre recalled by Kutusov soon began to mount. Kaminsky's part of the Second Column almost overwhelmed St Hilaire's right-hand brigade under Paul Charles Thiébault. Heeding one of his colonel's warnings that his men could not withstand another attack at the halt, he boldly decided to charge rather than retire – probably the single most critical decision of the battle for the French – but soon reinforcements arrived. A renewed Allied onslaught was met with the fire of IV Corps' twelve-pounders (brought up by Soult in person) at point-blank range. Loaded with canister as well as round-shot, the guns tore great gaps in the enemy formations. 'Ten more minutes of this – and that will suffice!' remarked a French onlooker. But yet more Allies appeared, led up by Weyrother and Langeron – only again to be repulsed all the way back to the wall enclosing the woodland of the Sokolnitz pheasantry in the valley floor. Langeron reported these untoward events to General Buxhowden whom he found complacently sitting with his staff taking a little refreshment. 'My dear general,' the left-wing commander airily informed Langeron, 'you seem to see the foe everywhere!' 'And you, Count, are in no state to see the enemy anywhere!' snapped back his subordinate. Allied tempers were clearly becoming a trifle frayed.

Meanwhile Vandamme was not having exactly an easy time on St Hilaire's left. His men had secured the peak of Staré Vinohrady, and soon had a battery established. But suddenly Kollowrath's men counter-attacked – watched by both the Tsar and Kutusov. They found themselves too close to the action for comfort. Alexander was covered with earth by a near miss, while Kutusov received a slight head wound amidst the combat. Again the French triumphed, and Kaminsky's shattered regiments reeled back in their turn. At this juncture Napoleon decided to move his command post over the valley to the Pratzen, followed by the Guard, Oudinot's grenadiers and Bernadotte's I Corps. The Music of the Guard struck up the famous march *On va leur percer le flanc* as Guardsman Coignet later recorded, and the élite '. . . climbed the far heights to cries of *"Vive l'Empereur"*', as Guardsman Barrès recalled. Napoleon had meanwhile reached Staré Vinohrady and studied the battlefield anew. The weather had clouded over, but visibility was good, and he arrived just in time to witness the last throw of the Allies – the counter-stroke by the Russian Imperial Guard, under Grand Duke Constantine.

Parts of this élite force had fought in several local engagements during the morning, but by 11.30 am the Prince had regathered his complete command behind the Raussnitz stream, where it covered the withdrawal of Bagration already described. Now, as cannon-balls from Vandamme's battery began to find its ranks, the Guard – infantry and cavalry – began to move impressively forward. Constantine at first only intended to mount a demonstration in strength, but this grew into an all-out attack by 1 pm. Three thousand mitre-capped guardsmen of the Semenovsky and Preobrazhensky Guard Grenadiers surged panting towards the summit of the Pratzen, there to smash through the first line of French units before withdrawing to reform in excellent order. On Napoleon's order, Vandamme swung to his right to bring more fire to bear, but in doing so uncovered his left flank. Fifteen squadrons of Russian Guard cavalry, accompanied by horse artillery, immediately attacked. Two French regiments – the 4th Line and 24th Light – broke and fled past the Emperor and his staff. As staff officer Philippe de Ségur recorded: 'The unfortunate fellows were quite distracted with fear and would listen to no one; in reply to our reproaches ... they shouted mechanically *"Vive l'Empereur!"* while fleeing faster than ever.'

This gap in Vandamme's line presented a serious danger: Napoleon signalled to Marshal Bessières, and six squadrons of Guard cavalry spurred into action. However, Russian reserves arrived at the same moment, and French casualties mounted. The situation was saved by the timely arrival of the leading brigade of Bernadotte's I Corps – which won a brief respite, gaining time for ADC General Jean Rapp to charge at the head of the Mamelukes (the gorgeously apparelled cavalry Napoleon had first raised in Egypt in 1798) and two squadrons of *chasseurs-à-cheval* of the Emperor's escort. The Russian Guard staggered, halted – and began to recoil. The crisis was over. Rapp – wounded himself – led up to the Emperor 200 disarmed Chevalier Guards. 'Many fine ladies of St Petersburg will lament this day,' commented Napoleon drily. It was a little after 2 pm. The Pratzen was securely in French hands at last. Napoleon had effectively won the battle.

It remained to convert victory into triumph. Napoleon now decided to engulf the Allied left wing – still fighting against the stalwart Davout and Legrand in the valley below. Bernadotte was ordered to secure the Pratzen and Staré Vinohrady, while the Imperial Guard and the two battered but triumphant divisions of Vandamme and St Hilaire swung south. As Napoleon's men began to line the edge of the cliffs overlooking the frozen lakes, Legrand launched a new attack against Sokolnitz – village, castle and walled pheasantry. Assailed on two sides at once, Buxhowden's only thought was retreat. Various formations of his force began to try to break out: some were successful – many were not.

Napoleon's third command post had now been established at the Chapel of St Anthony, near the cliffs overlooking the scene of developing confusion below. To his chagrin it took longer than anticipated to capture Aujest Market, commanding the road towards Austerlitz – the best line of retreat for the Allies. A battery of fifty Russian guns took some time to silence, and in the growing dusk there was some confusion during which substantial numbers of the Allied left wing made good their escape. Eventually the gap was plugged by the French. Many Austrians and Russians remained in the trap, pinned against the frozen ponds. Taking a desperate gamble, Buxhowden ordered his men to head for the single bridge over the Littawa south of Aujest Market. The general and his staff passed over safely, but just behind them a gun-team smashed through the planking and blocked the bridge; whereupon hordes of infantry began to scramble over the ice. Another column of artillery tried to use a narrow causeway linking two parts of the mere. But they were observed by French artillery officers on the Pratzen, and a lucky French shot detonated an ammunition wagon: a thunderous explosion ensued – and another escape route was blocked. In desperation a number of gun-teams gingerly swung round on to the ice. Napoleon ordered his artillery to line the southern edge of the Pratzen to fire at the ice. Seconds later a desperate scene developed as men, horses and guns crashed through into the icy water. The Thirtieth Bulletin of the Grand Army subsequently claimed that 20,000 Allies perished in this way – but this was a wild exaggeration. The meres were shallow, and although a fair number of exhausted soldiers doubtlessly drowned, estimates of their numbers vary between 200 and 2000. The only certain statistic is that thirty-eight cannon and the corpses of 130 horses were subsequently recovered from the ponds after the battle. But everywhere now Allied soldiers were surrendering. Up to this point very few captives had been taken. Davout had indeed ordered: 'No prisoners! Let not one escape!' But now, as the dusk deepened, it was possible to exercise leniency. 'Up to the last hour of the battle we took no prisoners,' recalled General Thiébault. 'It would just not do to take any risks; we could stick at nothing, and thus not a single living enemy remained to our rear.' Perhaps 12,000 Allied prisoners was the final total of the 'battle of the Three Emperors'.

By 4.30 pm the last shots had been fired. Napoleon, accompanied by Berthier and Soult, rode slowly down to the valley, and then northwards, to the plaudits of his troops. The cost of victory had not been slight: more than 9000 Frenchmen had become casualties (12 per cent of the whole). Inevitably, the Allies had fared far worse. Besides their captives, another 15,000 were dead or seriously wounded (or some 32 per cent).

There was no immediate pursuit – both sides were equally exhausted. As he rode towards the post-house of Posoritz, where he would spend the night, Napoleon repeatedly paused to organise succour for the wounded. On his orders, his escort stripped greatcoats from the Russian dead to lay them over the wounded. Sometimes it was noted that the Emperor dispensed brandy with his own hand. Arrived at his lodging, he took a simple supper before starting to write a short note to Josephine: 'I have beaten the Austro-Russian army commanded by the two Emperors. I am a little weary. I have camped in the open for eight days and as many freezing nights. Tomorrow I shall be able to rest in the castle of Prince Kaunitz, and I should be able to snatch two or three hours sleep there. The Russian army is not only beaten but destroyed. I embrace you. Napoleon.' Taking a second sheet of paper he began to write the Order of the Day: 'Soldiers! I am content with you ...', he began. But then weariness overwhelmed him. Next morning the pursuit of the shattered Allies commenced: Murat and Lannes up the Olmütz road, Bernadotte and Soult towards Göding down the road through Czeitsch. Davout marched further south, collecting Gudin's division and Beaumont's dragoons en route before turning east to sever more possible Allied lines of retreat. Meanwhile, Napoleon's completed communiqué lavished praise on his men, and distributed favours and monetary rewards wholesale.

The results of Austerlitz were impressive in both military and political terms. There was no further thought of the Allies continuing the struggle. Two days later an open-air interview took place between Napoleon and the Emperor Francis at the latter's request. It was agreed that an armistice would come into immediate effect, and that peace talks would begin at Vienna. These resulted in the Peace of Pressburg, signed on 26 December. By its terms, Venice was added to the Kingdom of Italy, and Istria, Croatia and Dalmatia ceded to France, Swabia was awarded to Württemberg, and the Tyrol, Vorarlberg and other Alpine enclaves given to Bavaria. Thus the two loyal French Germanic confederates received their rewards. Meanwhile the Russians continued eastwards. Davout's hard-marching columns caught up with the Russians at Göding, and renewed hostilities appeared imminent. But the Tsar and Kutusov claimed that they had already concluded an armistice – in fact this was not the case, but Davout chose to accept their declarations at face value. Observed by Savary, chief of intelligence, the Russians comprised '... no more than 26,000 ... all arms included. Most of them had lost their knapsacks, and a great number were wounded but they marched bravely in the ranks.' The Tsar sent Davout and Savary a message for transmission to Napoleon. 'Tell your master that I am going away. Tell him that he has performed miracles ... that the battle has increased my admiration for him; that he is a man predestined by Heaven; that it will require a hundred years for my army to equal his.'

When news of Austerlitz reached England, it proved the last blow for the ailing William Pitt, who would die in January 1806. Shortly before the end, he told his niece, Hester Stanhope: 'Roll up that map of Europe. It will not be wanted these ten years.' As for Napoleon, he was now well on the way to becoming master of Europe.

For the rest of his life Napoleon drew pleasure from recollecting the battle of Austerlitz and its surrounding events. When, in 1808, consideration was being given to suitable ducal titles for award to the Marshalate, Soult suggested that his might be 'Duke of Austerlitz'. The idea was abruptly rejected; Davout might be created Duke of Auerstädt, Ney Duke of Elchingen and Massena Duke of Rivoli, but 'the first manoeuvrer of Europe' as Napoleon had dubbed him in 1805, had to be content with the dukedom of Dalmatia. Austerlitz was one title that Napoleon was determined not to award – but keep for himself.

Why did the Emperor accord the battle such priority' Why did he deem Austerlitz more important than, say, Rivoli, Friedland or Wagram? In the first place it was the first full trial-of-strength since the creation of the Empire, and the refinement of France's soldiery into the unified Grand Army. It is sometimes overlooked that this was Napoleon's first major campaign, and great battle, for five-and-a-half years. Not since Marengo (14 June 1800) had he been in a major engagement (if we exclude Ulm, which was a special case). It represented, therefore, the full testing of his martial skills and genius – and the result had been triumph. After Austerlitz, Napoleon's reputation as a great commander – first gained in 1796 – had received confirmation.

The plan of campaign – rapidly extemporised in August 1805 to meet the new challenge posed by the Third Coalition – had illustrated Napoleon's mastery of strategy. Appreciating the chance to catch Mack's and Ferdinand's Austrians on their own, as we have seen he had moved 210,000 men in a bold sweep through central Europe. Not every detail had been foreseen – the anticipated battle on the River Iller had never materialised, for instance – but Napoleon's strategic system had proved flexible enough to adjust to circumstances. Nor had the subsequent pursuit of the retreating Kutusov been as successful as hoped. It was not Napoleon's wish to see the Russians able to rendezvous with their second army at Wischau, nor to be drawn in his turn ever deeper into Moravia in search of a decisive battle in the very depth of a bitter winter. His remaining men – when the effects of strategic consumption had been taken into account – were exhausted, tattered and nigh-starving. But the carefully planned web of army corps still permitted Napoleon substantially to redress the numerical imbalance on the eve – and even the very day – of battle. Here indeed was the hand of a great master of war at work. He took huge risks, but they were calculated ones.

Using his actual weakness to delude his superior opponents, Napoleon had then excelled in imposing his wishes upon them at the operational level. To produce substantial reserves was one thing; to induce the enemy into adopting the battle-plan that best suited the French, quite another. True, not every detail of the bitter day's fighting was foreseen in advance: 'one engages, and then one sees' – a maxim that was very much illustrated by the touch-and-go and critical battle for retention of the Pratzen Heights between 10 am and midday. 'There is a moment in engagements when the least manoeuvre is decisive and gives a victory,' runs another Napoleonic maxim; 'It is the one drop of water which causes the vessel to run over' – in this case probably the decision of General Thiébault to order his wavering brigade to charge Langeron's masses rather than retire. Battle control of a very high order had then been needed to overcome the crisis in the centre as the Russian Imperial Guard attacked. And it was only at about 2.30 pm that Napoleon made up his mind which wing of the staggering but still powerful Allied army to envelop: once again, essentially an extemporised decision.

But successful extemporisation is one necessary aspect of a demonstrable genius for waging war, just as 'an infinite capacity for taking pains' is another, and an ability to inspire soldiers at times of great peril, a third. Above all, perhaps, the determination to fight a fluid battle, one of continual movement, lay behind the great success. The key, as the percipient General Savary wrote later, '... was that we moved about a great deal, and that individual divisions fought successive actions on different parts of the field. This is what multiplied our forces throughout the day, and this is what the art of warfare is all about ...' These gifts – and many more – Napoleon had demonstrated at many levels during 1805. Small wonder that an important boulevard in Paris is named after the battle, or that the main training area at St Cyr-Coëtiquidian is named 'the Pratzen', where each 2 December a large re-enactment of Austerlitz is performed by all the French officer-cadets under training before a select audience of staff and quests. For Austerlitz had once and for all set the seal on the creation of the French Empire and upon Napoleon's reputation as a soldier of pre-eminent ability. Such has been posterity's verdict. Austerlitz had proved one of the greatest battles in modern military history.

7

COLUMN VERSUS LINE –
THE CASE OF MAIDA, 1806

*A*s already stated, '. . . in strategy there is no victory'. Unless the actual fighting at the tactical or Forward-Edge-of-the-Battle-Area (FEBA) is successfully controlled and coordinated, everything else may prove to nil effect no matter how brilliant the higher concepts and planning. The instance of the battle of Maida, fought in early July, 1806, near the Calabrian coast of southern Italy between a small British force under Sir John Stuart, conveyed and landed from its Sicilian base by courtesy of the Royal Navy (demonstrating some of the advantages of 'command of the sea' gained at Nelson's battle of the Nile almost eight years before), against the troops of General Reynier, forming the major part of the French army of occupation in Naples, is a good example to make the point. It also highlights another military historical peril – that of the regrettable tendency for errors of interpretation to be repeated by historians one generation after another.*

The celebrated Sir Charles Oman set events in motion by writing an essay – much acclaimed at the time – declaring Maida to have been the perfect example of the British line formations meeting, and defeating, a series of French attacks in column, thus creating a pattern that would be repeated many times under Wellington in the Peninsular War (1808–14) and indeed at Waterloo in 1815, where, the great Duke laconically remarked some time after the climacteric battle: 'They {the French} came on in the same old way and we saw them off in the same old way'. In fact, later research proved that the French at Maida had indeed approached the British position in column but had then formed into line as directed in the Drill-Book of 1791 before actually coming to grips. In other words, the battle was fought – and won by Stuart – in line against line formation and not pace *the legend, in line against column.*

Oman acknowledged his error in a later edition of his celebrated studies, but unfortunately publishers have always preferred to republish in facsimile the original version, while historians tend to prefer the first edition of a celebrated work, assuming (often erroneously) that it is the most important. Thus, although '. . . history never repeats itself, historians seldom differ'; and also in their serried ranks must stand the weighty figure of the present commentator. Quis custodiet ipsos custodes? Mea culpa; mea maxima culpa.

Indeed, it is a sad case of 'e'en Homer nods' where the coverage of Maida is concerned in both editions of my Dictionary of the Napoleonic Wars, *but at least I can claim to be amongst a memorable list of fellow-sinners in this respect. Perhaps I will be able to put matters right in the third edition, if any. The whole matter came to light in an exchange of views in learned journals during the 1980s, inspired in large measure by the fine article on the subject in the pages of the* SAHR Journal, *written by the up-and-coming young American military historian, James Arnold.*

What follows comprises a paper I presented at the International Military History Conference on the Peninsular War organised by my friends, Professor Donald Howard of the University of Florida at Tallahassee and Dr John Esdaile of Liverpool University, at Lisbon in the spring of 1989. The conference was memorable for many things, not least the farewell dinner, which was given by our Portuguese hosts on a perfect evening in a fortress forming part of the third (re-embarkation) fortifications of the Lines of Torres Vedras, complete with conscript guard of honour dressed in caçadores *(light infantry) uniforms of 1810. Military history certainly provides much enjoyment to its* aficionados!

†

'In strategy there is no victory' runs an ancient military adage. If this is demonstrably true, then it behoves military historians looking into the history of specific campaigns and battles to pay special attention to the factors that bring (or brought) success or failure in particular instances to contesting armed forces – and amongst these factors the development and application of force at the tactical level is clearly an important consideration. For overall victory and defeat is often the outcome of a myriad small engagements. The further one goes back into history, the harder it becomes to draw significant conclusions on the details of tactical operations. And although the period of the French Revolutionary and Napoleonic Wars is comparatively well documented (no pre-twentieth-century struggles have left more by way of first-hand sources, memoirs and the like) and has probably been more thoroughly analysed time and again by soldiers and scholars than *any* other military period – and I must confess to having contributed a book or two myself to the mountain of published works – yet it has to be recognised that the tactical methods of the contending powers, most particularly those of Great Britain and France, remain the subject of considerable scholarly contention and (occasionally) heated debate.

There remains to this day an ongoing fascination with the subject of 'column versus line', for it is the area of infantry tactics that attracts most discussion and disagreement. The long list of British infantry successes over their French counterparts, whether in Egypt (1801), Calabria (1806) – the subject that forms the basis of this paper – in the long-drawn-out Peninsular War (1808–14), and ultimately, of course, at Waterloo – cannot today be explained in terms of a cool, typically modest, inborn, insular, even racially-blue-blooded British superiority in such matters (although in the past some Victorian historians in the great 'Storm in Channel, Continent isolated' tradition have tended towards such tactless simplifications).

The reason must therefore lie in certain details of comparative tactical technique, linked to consideration of available weaponry and, last but not least, certain morale factors, for was it not the great Emperor Napoleon himself who reminds us that '... in war, the moral is to the physical as three is to one' – and who am I to query the master's dictum? The challenge has been taken up time and again by military historians – from the days of Jomini and Clausewitz, to those of Commandant Colin, the great Sir Charles Oman and Sir John Fortescue, to the modern groups of analysts including the Americans Quimby and Weller, the Englishmen Glover and Griffith, not to overlook the contributions to the debate of a new rising generation of historians including James R. Arnold.

The Duke of Wellington's laconic comment on the French attacks at Waterloo – 'they came on in the same old way and we saw them off in the same old way' – reveals little over the tactical controversy save the continuity of basic methods, and the Duke's notable degree of *sang-froid* for which he was famous. Nevertheless, the belief has steadily developed that the higher fire-power obtainable from the two-rank deep British battalion line was remarkably superior to both the fire-production and shock-value of a French attack in column. Napoleon himself allegedly went on record at St Helena as declaring that '... the formation of infantry in line should be always in two ranks, because the length of the musket only admits of an effective fire in this formation. The discharge of the third rank is not only uncertain, but frequently dangerous to other ranks in front.' (Maxim XLVIII). It is nevertheless notable that throughout the First Empire the *régiments de la ligne* – when deployed in line – were invariably drawn up three ranks deep.

Accordingly, the purpose of this chapter is to examine the tactical contention, particularly as regards the claims and deductions of Sir Charles Oman, some of whose conclusions have been challenged by modern research, at least in part.

Sir Charles Oman was a remarkable historian by any measure of calculation. Although his great seven-volume *History of the Peninsular War* will always stand as his scholastic monument, his area of study also extended to embrace the history of warfare in the Middle Ages, the art of war in the sixteenth century, and large numbers of studies and collected essays including *Wellington's Army* and his *Studies in the Napoleonic Wars*. Besides his knighthood, he was an Honorary Doctor of Common Law in the University of Oxford, held equivalent degrees from Cambridge and Edinburgh universities, was for sixteen years the parliamentary representative for the University of Oxford, and held the Chi-

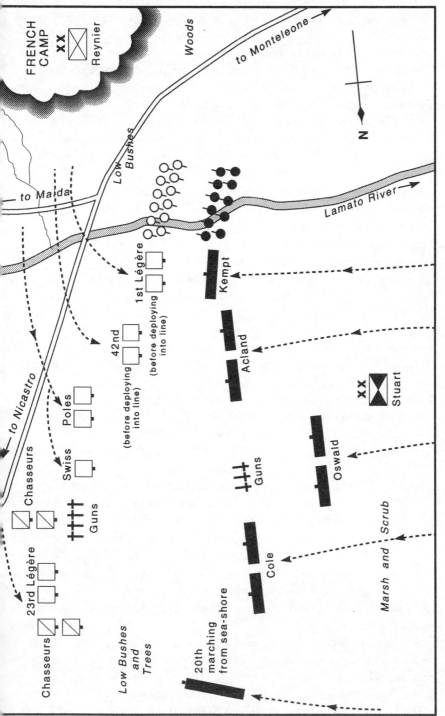

FRENCH CAMP

XX Reynier

Woods

to Monteleone

N

Low Bushes

to Maida

Lamato River

1st Légère

(before deploying into line)

42nd

(before deploying into line)

Kempt

Acland

Poles

XX Stuart

Swiss

Oswald

Chasseurs

Guns

to Nicastro

Guns

Cole

23rd Légère

Chasseurs

Marsh and Scrub

Low Bushes and Trees

20th marching from sea-shore

THE BATTLE OF MAIDA, 1806

chele Professorship in the Art of War and Modern History as well as a Fellowship of All Souls' College, and was also an Honorary Fellow of New College, Oxford.

Before proceeding to examine Oman's somewhat contentious views on the battle of Maida, it is necessary to pay some passing attention to the grand tactical (or 'operational') and tactical realities of the period, especially as they affected the French army of the early nineteenth century.

Marshals or senior officers were responsible for orchestrating the activities of their horse, foot and gun detachments to the maximum effect, including the proper handling of reserves. They delegated the detail of minor tactics at brigade, squadron or battalion level to subordinate commanders. The following passage gives some idea of the sequence of a corps 'grand tactical' battle – the level at which most marshals operated (although some, like Massena and Soult, were given command of armies of Napoleon's absence, particularly in Spain and Portugal, and of course Reynier was on detached duty in Calabria in 1806).

Let us summarise the tactical sequence of an imaginary Napoleonic battle. As will be seen, the true secret of success in the field lay in the careful coordination of cavalry, infantry and guns into one continuous process of attack, each arm supplementing the activities of the other two. Through interarm cooperation lay the road to victory.

At the outset, a heavy bombardment would be loosed against the enemy formations, causing fearful losses if they failed to seek shelter, and generally lowering their power of resistance. Under cover of this fire, swarms of *voltigeurs* would advance to within musketry range and add a disconcerting 'nuisance' element by sniping at officers and the like. The preliminary phase would be followed by a series of heavy cavalry and infantry attacks. The secret of these was careful timing and coordination. The first cavalry charges were designed to defeat the hostile cavalry and compel the enemy infantry to form squares rather than to achieve an immediate breakthrough. This task was left to the hurrying infantry columns, which under ideal circumstances would have moved up to close range before the horsemen fell back, and before, therefore, the enemy could resume his linear formation. Clearly, a unit drawn up in square or rectangular formation could produce only a greatly reduced output of fire in any one direction, and this diminution of fire-power enabled the French columns to get to close grips without suffering phenomenal casualties – providing all went well. If the attack succeeded, the newly deployed French infantry would blaze a gap through the enemy lines; their accompanying batteries of horse artillery would unlimber and go straight into action at point-blank range, and finally the French cavalry, after reforming, would sweep forward again to exploit the breakthrough.

The description is very generalised as every action or battle was of course unique, and details varied according to circumstances. However, the broad principles outlined above supply a broad indication of a sequence that was often attempted, in whole or in part.

The weapons of the French infantry were not of particularly high quality. The firearms were invariably muzzle-loading, smooth-bore flintlocks, capable of mass production thanks to the new industrial technique developed by the expert Blanc. The French used coarse black powder as propellant, which resulted in excessive fouling of the barrels and a general obscuring of the battle-scene with clouds of dense smoke. Exposure to undue damp soon placed these weapons out of action. Each man carried into action fifty cartridges (the balls weighing four-fifths of an ounce apiece, the powder-charge being 12.5 grammes) and three spare flints.

The standard small arm was the Charleville '1777' musket, a weapon of .70 calibre, measuring one metre 57 centimetres – or approximately 50 inches – (without bayonet), which remained in the French service until the 1830s. For all its longevity, it had severe practical limitations. Its maximum range was officially over 1000 metres, but it was almost useless against even large bodies of formed troops at more than 250, while for use against individual enemies a range of less than 100 metres was advisable. Excessive fouling occasioned by the coarse powder meant that the barrel required washing after every fifty rounds, while the flint needed changing after ten or twelve discharges. Misfires were experienced on an average of once in every six shots, and in the din and heat of battle this could often lead to double-loading, with unfortunate results to both weapon and firer. Reloading required five separate evolutions: first the soldier took a paper cartridge from his pouch and bit off the end containing the ball, which he retained in his mouth; next he opened the 'pan' of his musket, poured in a priming charge, closed it and ordered arms; thirdly, he tipped the remainder of the powder down the barrel, spat the musket ball after it, folded the paper into a wad, and then forced both ball and wad down the barrel on to the powder charge with his ramrod; finally, he brought the musket up to the present, took aim and fired. This loading system was open to many oversights and abuses. An inexperienced recruit might easily double-load after an unnoticed misfire, or forget to withdraw his ramrod before pulling the trigger; similarly, a clumsy or malingering *fantassin* could easily contrive to spill most of the powder charge on to the ground and thus avoid the shoulder-dislocating kick of the weapon.

It has been claimed that an expert marksman could loose off as many as five shots in sixty seconds under favourable circumstances, but once the barrel became fouled this rate dropped to four rounds in three minutes. Probably one or two rounds a minute was the average rate of fire. The French very often neglected musketry practice; this was partly due to a desire to conserve ammunition, partly to avoid the probability of casualties caused by burst barrels or idle practice, and not a little to the conviction of many senior commanders that it was the task of the gunners to inflict casualties through fire upon the enemy rather than that of the infantry, whose true *métier* was to follow up with the bayonet to exploit the gaps in the hostile formations so caused. The proven unreliability of the '1777' firearm greatly reinforced the arguments of this school, and it became the exception for the ordinary soldier to attain a high degree of proficiency with the weapon.

At the very best the musket was an inaccurate weapon. Towards the close of the eighteenth century, the Prussian army conducted some field-firing experiments with their own musket which differed little from its French counterpart in terms of accuracy. After setting up a canvas target 100 feet long by 6 feet high to simulate an enemy unit, they drew up a battalion of line infantry at varying ranges and ordered the men to fire a volley. At 225 yards distance, only 25 per cent of the shots fired hit the target; at 150 yards the proportion was 40 per cent; at 75 yards, 60 per cent of the shots told. It would appear, therefore, that the number of casualties caused by deliberately aimed rounds fired at normal range were comparatively slight; most troops were killed or wounded by artillery fire or 'casual' bullets. However, when fire was held until the troops could literally see 'the whites of the enemy's eyes' – say 50 yards – horrific casualties could result, often as many as 50 per cent of a unit's personnel – or even more. Thus at Austerlitz the 36th Regiment lost 220 out of 230 of its grenadiers, while at Auerstädt (1806) Gudin's division lost no less than 124 officers and 3500 men killed and wounded out of a total of 5000 men committed to action.

Little wonder, then, that many French experts advocated shock-action with the bayonet rather than fire-action with powder and ball in the hope of avoiding such crippling casualties in a straightforward stand-up fire fight. Every French infantryman was armed with a 15-inch triangular-shaped socket bayonet. The real effectiveness of this sidearm, however, is also open to doubt. It would seem from the result of researches conducted by Surgeon General Larrey that the havoc wrought by 'cold steel' was more moral than material; after studying the casualties – French and Austrian – in two separate units that had been engaged in a hand-to-hand mêlée, he could discover only five wounds directly attributable to the bayonet, whereas wounds inflicted by bullets during the same actions numbered 119. As a general rule, therefore, it was fear of the bayonet rather than its actual application that caused units to turn and flee. Perhaps this was all for the best, for the quality of the French bayonet was far from good; we know, for instance, that after the battle of the Pyramids in 1798 the French infantry found little difficulty in bending their bayonets into hooks for the purpose of fishing the corpses of richly clad Mamelukes out of the Nile. So this was hardly a dependable weapon, and many classes of infantry carried swords for additional personal protection.

In the place of the Charleville musket, a few rifled carbines were carried by certain soldiers, mostly officers and NCOs of the *voltigeur* companies. It was a lighter weapon of smaller calibre, but the rifling made the bore extremely tight, and to drive the ball home an iron mallet had to be employed on the ramrod. The French were less impressed with this type of weapon than their British and Prussian contemporaries, who armed a considerable proportion of their light infantry with rifled muskets. Another type of firearm occasionally issued to the French infantry for counter-insurgency or anti-guerrilla operations was a bell-mouthed blunderbuss, loaded with a handful of loose powder and whatever hard objects were readily available. However, the vast majority of soldiers used the '1777' musket.

At first the infantry tactics varied little from those of the revolutionary forces in whose ranks most of the officers, including Napoleon Bonaparte himself, had learned so much of their trade. *L'ordre mixte* and attacks in battalion column were commonly employed. Dense clouds of skirmishers – sometimes whole regiments were employed in this role – would engage and harass the enemy formations while the columns of attack drew near, bayonets at the ready. If the morale of the attacking troops left something to be desired, the élite grenadier company would often be placed in rear of the battalion columns to force their comrades forward; if, on the other hand, the *esprit de corps* was high, they would lead the right of the attack. Normally, the battalion formed up for the attack in 'column of division' (in other words, a two-company frontage), every company being drawn up in three ranks with about a yard between them. Thus at the beginning of an attack, a battalion column (consisting of four 'divisions' or eight companies) would cover a front of 50 yards and a depth of approximately 21 yards (twelve ranks). In later years, when the battalions were reduced to six larger companies, a battalion column would contain only three 'divisions', thus reducing its depth to 15 yards (nine ranks) and at the same time broadening its frontage to 75 yards. As the *voltigeur* company would usually be serving as a sharp-shooter screen ahead of the rest, a straight-forward 'column of companies' was often resorted to, especially when negotiating a narrow defile.

A large-scale attack would be mounted by a whole series of battalion columns in line or echelon. The interval between each individual column was at least 150 yards – this space being needed to enable the column to deploy into line for fire-action if required and at the same time permitting the skirmishing screen to fall back through the intervals without having to cease fire; for it was very important that the harassment of the enemy's formations by the skirmishers should continue until the actual moment of contact so as to distract a proportion of their fire and prevent the deliberate concentration of every musket against the advancing columns, which were very exposed during the last stages of their advance.

Although he rarely intervened in tactical matters, Napoleon clearly favoured *l'ordre mixte* formation. It was ideally adapted for the exploitation of success, the assumption of the defensive or an abrupt change of front; in other words, it could perform almost any role with a minimum of delay. Various adaptations of *l'ordre mixte* were evolved to counter the solidarity of the Russian infantry, the most notable being the formation of a division with linked brigades, which produced a maximum degree of fire-power for defence and yet still retained sufficient depth for an immediate attacking role. The great advantages of column formation were that it permitted great mobility and boundless flexibility; a unit could advance to the attack, form square to repel cavalry, or adopt the tactical defensive in *l'ordre mixte* with a minimum of delay and confusion. Above all there were no time-wasting delays to check the alignment of the ranks, which always bedevilled troops advancing in the old type of formal linear formations. Perhaps a perfect example of the adaptability of the system was the handling of Morand's division at the height of the battle of Auerstädt (1806); within a short space of time it was put through five separate evolutions to meet changing situations, but not for one minute was the pressure against the Prussians even slackened.

In later years, as the quality of the French infantry deteriorated, their generals had occasional recourse to huge, divisional squares and columns (as used by Macdonald on the second day at Wagram and by d'Erlon in the first attack at Waterloo – on both occasions with scant success), but these vast formations presented an unforgettable target to artillerymen and infantry alike and were far too bulky to move with ease.

However, even the perfected system of battalion column could go wrong, and even at its prime the French attack had serious drawbacks which a determined and cunning adversary could exploit. At the outset of the advance, the ranks would tend to open out, as the individual soldiers sought sufficient elbow-room, but as the column approached its target, the reverse became the case. The men would tend to crowd in upon one another until ranks became disordered and cohesion began to disappear – as Guibert had prophesied long before. General Bugeaud has left a vivid description of the limitations of over-hasty attacks in column against troops drawn up in line as experienced during the Peninsular War:

> The English generally occupied well-chosen defensive positions having a certain command, and they showed only a portion of their forces. The usual artillery action first took place. Soon, in great haste, without studying the position, without taking time to examine whether there were means to make a flank attack, we marched straight on, taking the bull by the horns. About 1000 yards from the English line the men became excited, called out to one another, and hastened their march; the column began to become a little confused. The English remained quite silent with ordered arms, and from their steadiness appeared to be a long red wall. This steadiness invariably produced an effect on our young soldiers. Very soon we got nearer, crying '*Vive l'Empereur! En Avant! À la baionnette!*' Shakos were raised on the muzzles of muskets; the column began

to double, the ranks got into confusion, the agitation produced a tumult; shots were fired as we advanced. The English line remained silent, still and immovable, with ordered arms, even when we were only 300 yards distant, and it appeared to ignore the storm about to break. The contrast was striking; in our innermost thoughts we all felt the enemy was a long time in firing, and that this fire, reserved so long, would be very unpleasant when it came. Our ardour cooled. The moral power of steadiness, which nothing can shake (even if it be only appearance), over disorder which stupefies itself with noise, overcame our minds. At this moment of intense excitement, the English wall shouldered arms; an indescribable feeling would root many of our men to the spot; they began to fire. The enemy's steady, concentrated volleys swept our ranks; decimated, we turned round seeking to recover our equilibrium; then three deafening cheers broke the silence of our opponents; at the third they were on us, pushing our disorganised flight.

It was axiomatic that the columns were intended to deploy into line before delivering their final attack – and yet this was neglected on a number of critical occasions with unfortunate results. Some commentators, led by the great historians Oman and Fortescue, have argued that this failure to deploy was intentional; that the French commanders, brought up in the revolutionary tradition when the rawness of the troops made any complex evolution out of the question, purposely attacked right home in column, hoping to crash a way through the opposition by a combination of sheer weight and psychological advantage (the appearance of a column advancing at the charge being sufficient to instil fear in the bravest heart). However, this school of thought has been convincingly challenged by Commandant Colin and Hilaire Belloc. They claim that the French attempted to launch their final attacks in column by error and not design. Many existing battle orders mention the need for deployment before making physical contact with the foe, and the fact is that the French columns habitually attempted to carry out these instructions, but often delayed the final evolution until it was too late.

Most of the system's failures were experienced when fighting Wellington; he had discovered the perfect counter-tactic to the French method. By keeping the bulk of his men concealed behind reverse slopes, he not only protected them from the worst attentions of the French artillery and skirmishers (he also habitually pushed swarms of light infantry onto the forward slopes to keep the latter at bay), but also upset the calculations of the officers commanding the French attacking columns. Unable to locate the exact position of their adversaries, they tended to retain their troops in column until they reached the crest, and then it was too late; for, just below the top of the ridge, 'silent and impressive, with ported arms, loomed a long red wall', and before the French could deploy or charge, raking volleys – often directed from three sides at once – would obliterate the head of the column and send the survivors reeling back along their tracks or at least halt them in stupefied confusion. This is what happened to some units of the Imperial Guard in the final phase at Waterloo: the famous grenadiers, after advancing along an incorrect line of approach, came upon Wellington's waiting battalions before they expected to do so, and although they immediately attempted to deploy they received such a riddling fire from three sides that they proved incapable of completing the evolution, and were soon decimated and sent back in headlong retreat.

Nevertheless, the fact that the system could be countered should not be allowed to disguise the fact that it brought the French ten years of almost unbroken victory on the field of battle. The fluidity, aggressiveness, *élan* and mobility of the French infantry proved too much for a succession of Austrian, Prussian, Spanish, Russian and Neapolitan armies. Properly applied, it held the secret of tactical success against opponents committed to rigid concepts of linear tactics; only when improperly executed – or when faced by the tactical genius of Wellington and the proverbial coolness of his British troops – did the system fail and lead to disaster.

It is time to turn our attention to the battle of Maida, and its interpretation. The major factors are not in dispute. Following Napoleon's deposition of Ferdinand IV, King of Naples, in favour of his brother, Joseph Bonaparte, the British government ordered Lieutenant-General Sir John Stuart to land with an expeditionary force in Calabria, southern Italy. This body of troops, conveyed by Sir William Sidney Smith's naval squadron on Admiral Collingwood's orders, left Messina in Sicily on 27 June, and three days later the force anchored off the Gulf of St Euphemia. At dawn on 1 July 1806, the first of 5200 officers and men made a virtually unopposed landing (a small force of 300 Poles had to be brushed aside with a loss of two officers and fifty men) followed by four field guns, two mortars and ten light mountain cannon. There was no cavalry to support the advance guard and three small brigades commanded by Acland, Cole and Oswald. Unfortunately General Stuart decided that the occupation of the village of St Euphemia was sufficient for the day – and indeed he made no attempt to leave the coast over the following seventy-two hours. It appears he was waiting for an anticipated popular rising in his support.

This pause enabled General of Division Jean Louis Ebénézer Reynier – the senior French commander in Calabria (Marshal Massena being engrossed in the siege of Gaeta and General Gouvion St Cyr fully engaged in distant Apulia and Capitanata) – to gather some 6440 men, including 328 cavalry and one battery of horse artillery, organised into two brigades under Generals Compère and Digonet – the cavalry being commanded by Peyri – and with it to cover eighty miles in three days marching from Reggio to the approaches to San Pietro de Maida, camping on the high ground above the town on the evening of 3 July.

Next morning both forces advanced to seek contact, Stuart pressing over a low-lying area of bushes, marshes and scrub to the north of the River Lamato,

Reynier sweeping down from his encampment on the ridge in four columns to cross the same rivulet further to the east before pivoting on his left, to face the advancing British brigades – having his cavalry and horse artillery on his open right flank. Stuart halted his men in two-deep line along a low ridge at 9 am. The British held their fire and then advanced in a menacing red line to discharge three crippling volleys – at 150, 80 and 20 yards range – into the French, following this up with a determined bayonet charge led by the light infantry. The French gave ground at once, and soon their left wing – comprising Compère's élite 1st Légère and the 42nd of the Line – was totally defeated. Retreat became rout, and the French left the field. Behind them they left 700 killed and 1000 wounded, and as many prisoners. Perhaps 2000 is a fair total. Stuart's casualties amounted to 327 men.

The victorious general marched his men back to the beaches to rest after their exertions. His subsequent actions have been justly criticised. Instead of making use of his advantage to attempt to raise Massena's siege of distant Gaeta, he proceeded to march them south intent on returning to Sicily, and thus achieved very little in lasting terms. Indeed, Gaeta fell on the 18th. But we are concerned with the reasons for the defeat of Reynier's force on the morning of 4 July, for Oman's interpretation of these events has led to major tactical misconceptions, repeated time after time but now once and for all convincingly challenged on the basis of modern analysis of all available documentation.

Two passages from Sir Charles Oman's pen form the basis of the trouble: 'The first clash of Compère's heavy battalion columns ... gives the key to the whole tactical superiority of the British infantry which lay at the base of Wellington's victorious schemes during the years 1808–15' (see *Studies in the Napoleonic Wars*, Oxford 1929, p. 37). 'The Maida campaign then had, as its sole good result, the confirming in the minds of the more intelligent British officers who had taken part in it, of the great truth of the superiority of line tactics over column attacks.' (*ibid* p. 68). At another place – in his essay on 'Column and Line in the Peninsula' – Oman goes still further: 'It cannot be said that the efficiency of the two-deep line against the column was publicly demonstrated by a crucial experiment of the most conclusive sort till three years after the commencement of the second half of the Great French War. But for all those who were present, or who received the report of an intelligent eye-witness, the little-remarked Calabrian battle of Maida was an epoch-making day in British Military History. On the sandy plain by the Lamato, 5000 infantry in line received the shock of 6000 in column, and inflicted on them one of the most crushing defeats on a small scale that took place during the whole war. The troops and the order of battle won the victory, for the commander, Stuart was an incapable officer whose personality had no influence on the fight, and who sacrificed all the fruits of his success by his torpidity. But the march was unmistakable – on the critical part of the field four battalions of the best Troops of the old French Army of Italy (2800 men of 1st Légère and 42nd Line opposed to 2100 of Kempt's Light Battalion and Acland's 78th and 81st), in column of divisions, has been met in frontal shock and blown to pieces by British battalions in two-deep line. The four French battalions lost 1080 men. The three Dutch only 320.' (*ibid* p. 97–8)

Oman had first drawn this deduction as early as 1907 in a lecture given to the Royal Artillery Institution at Woolwich. Speaking of the critical clash on the French left he called it '... the fairest fight between column and line that had been seen since the Napoleonic Wars began – on the one side two heavy columns of 800 men each, drawn up in column of companies... The front of each was not more than 60 yards. Kempt, on the other hand, had his battalion in line ... every {soldier] could use his musket against either the front or flank of the two columns'. His view had immediate impact. Sir John Fortescue, in Vol. 5 of the first edition of his famous *History of the British Army*, published in 1910, adopted the same conclusion. Both, however, were wrong.

Five pieces of clear contemporary evidence show this to have been the case. Two French sources are the following: Lieutenant Grisois, of the 1st Légère, wrote in 1828 that 'General Reynier gave the order to advance and engage the enemy, and in order to accomplish this to form on the left in line'. And secondly there is the evidence of the French commanding general himself, who wrote on 5 July 1806 to Joseph Bonaparte as follows: 'The 1st {Légère] and 42nd regiments, 2400 strong, under the order of General Compère, passed the Lamato and formed into line.' The other three are British: Sir Henry Bunbury, present in the field, wrote in his *Narratives of the Great War with France* (London, 1854): 'The French infantry formed for attack and marched rapidly upon us... Their 1st Légère advanced in line upon the brigade of British Light Infantry... A crashing fire of musketry soon opened the battle on both sides, but it was too hot to last at so short a distance... Kempt gave the word, and his 800 Light Infantry pressed eagerly forward to close with their antagonists. But the two lines were not parallel; the light companies of the 20th and 35th encountered the extreme left of the French, but the rest of the enemy's brigade broke before their bayonets crossed. They had, however, come too close to escape, it was headlong rout.'

The second British contemporary source for this point was Charles Boothby, in his book *Under England's Flag from 1804 to 1809* (London, 1900). Boothby wrote the account from 'subsequent observation and inquiry'. He mentioned the charge and the equal shock of opposing forces in 'lines of troops'.

And lastly, Ensign Joseph Anderson of the 78th Regiment, in *Recollections of a Peninsular Veteran* (London, 1913) described the incident as follows:

'As soon as these formidable French columns came sufficiently near, and not till then, our lines were called to "attention" and ordered to "shoulder arms". Then commenced in earnest the glorious battle of Maida, first with a volley from our brigade into the enemy's columns and from our artillery at each flank without ceasing, followed by independent firing as fast as our men could load; and well they did their work! Nor were the enemy idle; they returned our fire without ceasing, then in part commenced to deploy into line.'

This evidence is reasonably conclusive on the issue. The French approached in column, then deployed into line. To his credit, Oman did see the need to amend his account in 1912. In his famous work, *Wellington's Army*, he wrote: 'Till lately I had supposed that Reynier had at least his left wing ... in columns of battalions, but evidence put before me seems to prove that despite of the fact the French narratives do not show it' – in fact, of course, they do – 'the majority at least of Reynier's men were deployed.' Clearly he issued this recantation on British evidence brought to his notice. Fortescue, in the second (1921) edition of his work, also adjusted his account.

Unfortunately the damage was already done, and the erroneous account has persisted to the present day. In the 1929 *Studies in the Napoleonic Wars*, we find Oman repeating his 1907 version, and the latest reprint of the volume is a facsimile of the 1929 publication, so the misinformation will continue to spread. Indeed, I stand before you a self-condemned historian. In my *Dictionary of the Napoleonic Wars* I end the entry on Maida with the sentence: 'Maida is important tactically as demonstrating the inherent superiority of British tactics over the French column of attack'. To make it even worse, an unnoted literal has the date as '6' July, not the 4th. *Eheu mores: eheu tempora!* All I can say in my defence is that I remain in good company on the first point.

This is, of course, a small matter involving a relatively insignificant battle in an almost forgotten campaign. The trouble is that Oman's original misinterpretation influenced his later tactical conclusions – and hence those of generations of English language historians. The fact is it was British shock action – the bayonet charge after the volley – that won the battle of Maida. It is quite clear that French 'columns of divisions or *d'assaut*' were methods of manoeuvre before the final attack rather than an actual assault formation, as has been so often asserted. Of course there were occasions when French infantry columns did not deploy but attempted to crash their way through the revealed opposition – as when columns, deprived of their skirmish screen or 'eyes', approached an apparently undefended hill-crest only to find the 'solid red wall' advancing to meet them up the other side and already at close proximity – but these were the exceptions. The French Drill-books of 1788 and 1791 are clear that troops in columns were required to deploy into line before the clash of arms – as I described it earlier – and in almost every battle in central Europe and Spain in fact proceeded to do so. The exceptions – such as the calculated attack of the Middle Guard in the last act at Waterloo on 18 June 1815, when the Guard was caught trying to deploy by the British Guardsmen rising out of the sheltering corn to pour in devastating volleys at short range – are the particular instances that only go to prove the rule. It was the combination of British volley fire with, above all, the feared blood-curdling 'English Cheer' and the dire psychological threat of the bayonet attack, that decided the vast majority of Anglo/French infantry confrontations at battalion and brigade level. Thus the shock element of the British formation was the essential ingredient of victory, rather than the supposed effect of their fire-action alone.

Two final observations. The first is a plea. We welcome the profusion of re-printed sources now becoming available, but would publishers please be sure to go to the trouble and extra expense of having them properly edited and introduced so as to bring them up to date in the light of recent scholarship. The second is a sad reiteration of the old saying: 'History never repeats itself, but historians seldom differ.'

8

THE BATTLE OF SAHAGUN
1808

B *ritish seaborne expeditionary forces sent to Egypt in 1801 and to Naples in 1806 proved but precursors to the comparatively immense and sustained Peninsular War, fought against the French armies of occupation in Portugal and Spain, which ran from the autumn of 1808 until the spring of 1814 with never a pause. Once again, as in both earlier instances, it was the Royal Navy that made such a huge undertaking feasible by conveying, supplying and reinforcing the British army ashore – and in large measure their allies too. It was a RN squadron that whisked General La Romana's hostage corps from the Danish coast in 1808 after the rising of the people of Madrid in the* Dos Mayo *forever immortalised in Goya's well-known painting of that name in the Prado Museum.*

This rising enabled Great Britain to intervene actively on the continent of Europe in the military sense, and brought to an end the period of virtual insular isolation that – apart from raids-in-strength such as the Maida (1806) and Copenhagen (1807) incidents, not to forget the failed expeditions against Buenos Aires (1806 and 1807) in South America – had persisted since late 1805. Sir Arthur Wellesley's successes at Roliça and Vimeiro in Portugal (August 1808) were overshadowed by the Convention of Cintra subsequently imposed by his two newly arrived superiors, and all three were summoned back to London to face a court of enquiry.

During their absence, command of all British troops in the Peninsula devolved upon Sir John Moore. With orders to assist the Spanish regular forces locked in battle against Napoleon in person, Moore marched his army into Spain by way of Salamanca (leaving 10,000 men to garrison Lisbon, the vital base) and had reached the approaches to the Spanish capital when news reached him that Marshal Soult's IV Corps was strung out north of Madrid, inviting defeat in detail, which would effectively sever the French main line of communication running from Madrid to Burgos and thence towards Bayonne – the French main base – over the Pyrenees in France. Moore determined to strike at these inviting targets, and sent a force of two cavalry regiments to reconnoitre Soult's dispositions. The result was the celebrated cavalry battle of Sahagun in December 1808, the subject of this chapter. The small but significant victory there gained by Lord Henry Paget (the future Lord Uxbridge and Anglesey) on 21 December 1808 was significant for three reasons. First it proved that, man for man, the British cavalry was in every way more than a match for the French mounted arm. Secondly, it raised morale throughout the army at a very critical moment. And thirdly, it led in 1842 to the rarest issue of a battle clasp to the first General Service (or Peninsular) Medal, which was awardable only to the British cavalry regiment present, the 15th Hussars.

I have visited Sahagun with various battlefield tours that I have led over the years for the British Military History Society and Captain Gordon Battlefield Tours, and in the spring of 1994 I had hoped to take a party for Holt's Battlefield Tours. It is most rewarding to follow Paget's approach route to Sahagun from Mayorga at dead of night amidst difficult wintry conditions to attempt a dawn surprise-attack – that most perilous of military operations – against General Debelle's dragoons and chasseurs-à-cheval occupying Sahagun, before following the course of the action beyond the town and the subsequent controlled pursuit of the defeated foe. Moore and the main body of the army reached Sahagun later that same day – but so did alarming intelligence that Napoleon was hot on the British tail after swooping from Madrid over the Guadarramas Pass, Spanish regular resistance having ceased over a week earlier. Moore was left with no choice but a rapid retreat to Corunna but Vigo, but that, as they say, '. . . is another story'.

✝

'We saddled our horses, and away we did go
O'er rivers of ice and o'er mountains of snow,
To the town of Sahagun then our course we did steer
'Twas the Fifteenth Hussars, who had never known fear.'
    Anon. Regimental Ballad, c. 1809

British cavalry exploits during the course of the Napoleonic Wars tended to be notable for their combination of great gallantry, considerable initial success – and ultimately near-fatal consequences. The fates of the 20th Light Dragoons at Vimeiro, or of the North British Dragoons (later the Royal Scots Greys) at Waterloo, show the sad tendency for the instincts of the hunting field to override the dictates of prudence and discipline – particularly during the exploitation and rallying phases of a successful charge. As a general rule, there is no denying the superiority, man for man, of the British cavalry trooper over his French equivalent. Although the standard British cavalry sabre tended to be inferior to the longer and better-tempered French weapon, British mounts were of better quality in most cases and the physique of the cavalryman somewhat superior to that of his enemy. But when it came to the vital matter of rallying after a successful charge, the British cavalry had much to learn, and proved notably stubborn in its unwillingness to reform its ways.

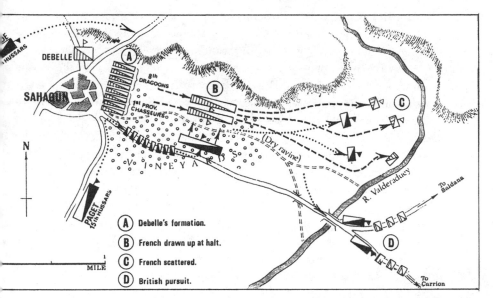

A Debelle's formation.
B French drawn up at halt.
C French scattered.
D British pursuit.

TOP: SAHAGUN, 1808: Cavalry Action

LEFT: SAHAGUN, 1808: Troop Movements

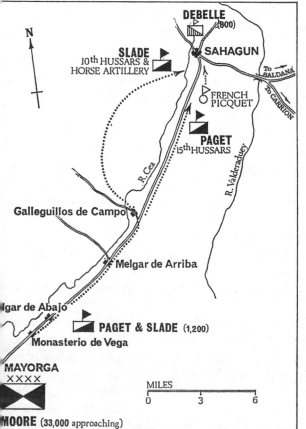

Fortunately for the record, there are a number of occasions when British cavalry was handled superbly well. Its notable feats at the difficult battle of Fuentes de Oñoro, or General Le Marchant's celebrated charge at Salamanca, are both cases in point – but no incident in the long history of these wars redounds more to the credit of British cavalry than the celebrated action fought at Sahagun on 21 December 1808, when a small detachment of horsemen under command of Henry, Lord Paget (destined, as Marquess of Anglesey, to lose a limb at Waterloo and earn the nickname of 'One-Leg' throughout the service), decisively defeated a larger French force under General of Brigade Debelle in the early hours of a bitterly cold, snow-bound winter's morning.

To the celebrated historian of the British army, Sir John Fortescue, this success was '. . . a brilliant little affair – and very creditable to Paget'. To the great historian of the Peninsular Wars, Sir Charles Oman, Sahagun was '. . . perhaps the most brilliant exploit of the British Cavalry during the whole six years of the war'. As will be seen, contemporary opinion was no less effusive. Consequently this incident – it hardly deserves the appellation of action, let alone battle – merits some description and investigation.

As the climax of the campaign of 1808 approached, the army of General Sir John Moore, 33,000 men strong, was advancing from Salamanca in the general direction of Burgos, intent upon surprising and, all being well, defeating in detail the dispersed forces of Marshal Soult, and thereafter creating a threat to the vital French lines of communication running from Bayonne through Burgos to Madrid, which Napoleon had recently occupied at the head of his army corps. Ahead of Moore's main body moved his screening light cavalry under command of the forty-year-old Henry Paget, Lt General of cavalry, who was described at about this time by his younger brother Edward as '. . . always at the head, and in the thick of everything that has been going on. He is, in this respect, quite a boy, and a cornet instead of a Lt General of cavalry, but in every other he is the right hand of the army.' His present command comprised two cavalry brigades under John Slade, 'that damned stupid fellow' as his superior regarded him with some justice, and Charles Stewart respectively. The first brigade, with which we are concerned, comprised the 10th and 15th Hussars and a detachment of horse artillery; the second was made up of the 3rd and 18th Hussars, some King's German Legion cavalry, and the 7th Hussars, Henry Paget's own regiment.

As Moore marched for Mayorga, his questing cavalry moved towards Melgar de Abajo. Unknown to the British command, Soult was in fact already aware of the proximity of an enemy force, but he had no accurate notion of Moore's strength (Baird would join him with 10,000 men on only 20 December); nor had he any idea that he was so close at hand. As a sensible general precaution, however, the Duke of Dalmatia had concentrated infantry divisions at Carrion and Saldana, and sent cavalry forces to Sahagun and Mayorga under Generals of

Brigade Debelle and Franceschi. It would be the former force, comprising the French 8th Dragoons and the 1st Provisional Chasseurs (a formation of Hanoverians absorbed into the French Army of Spain) that was destined to have its rest rudely shattered before dawn on the 21st.

Four days earlier the presence of this French formation in the vicinity was established by British patrols – and an estimated strength of between 700 and 800 troopers calculated. Sir John Fortescue doubts that there were more than 400 in fact; but Oman accepts the higher figure. Be that as it may, late on the 19th, amidst a storm of driving snow, the 10th and 15th Hussars entered Mayorga, after a thirty-mile march, to receive further tidings that Debelle's cavalry had moved to Sahagun that same afternoon. That night Paget moved forward to Melgar de Abajo as the main army closed up on Mayorga. The 20th was devoted to a well-earned rest.

That evening, however, Paget issued his orders for a night attack on Sahagun in the early hours of the 21st. Dated from 'Morgel de Alaxo (*sic*), 20 December 1808, $\frac{1}{2}$ 9 pm (*sic*)' these ran as follows:

> The 10th Hussars with four guns will march from Monastero so as to arrive at the Bridge of Sahagun precisely at half-past six tomorrow morning. The whole will march as light as possible, leaving the forage to be brought forward by the country carts with the baggage, which will march at daybreak under escort of such men and horses as are not fit for a forced march. The guns will move without ammunition waggons, the two remaining ones, with everything belonging to the artillery, will come on with the baggage. The object of the movement is to surprise Sahagun. The picquet at the Bridge will be driven in briskly. If serious opposition is made, a squadron or more may be dismounted, who, followed by a mounted squadron, will enter the town, make for the (French) General's and principal officers' quarters to make them prisoners. It is only in case of absolute necessity that the guns must be used. The grand object is to drive the enemy through the town, on the other side of which Lt Gen. Lord Paget will be posted with the 15th Hussars. The moment this object is in way of being accomplished, two squadrons of the 10th must be detached to the left of El Burgo Ranco, where the enemy has a picquet of from sixty to 100 men. These must be briskly attacked and made prisoner. This done they will return to Sahagun.

Such was the plan – one cavalry regiment to act as beaters, the other as stops on the further side of the town. But as happens so often in military operations, events were destined to take rather a different form. As von Moltke would remark sixty years later, '... no plan survives the first five minutes of battle.'

Paget's scheme involved a twelve-mile approach march, starting at 1 am through snow and ice on a bitterly cold night. Much clearly depended on proper coordination of the moves of the two regiments – but a combination of bad weather and Brigadier-General Slade would prove daunting odds against a full and successful implementation. The die was cast, however, and shortly after midnight Lieutenant-Colonel C. Grant of the 15th began to muster his men. Their number was probably about 400 troops of the 15th Hussars – we know that of the 700 men and 682 horses that embarked for the Peninsula there remained 527 still present with the regiment on 19 December – as many more of the 10th Hussars, and a dozen of the 7th Hussars, forming the personal escort of Lord Paget, not to forget the brigade, four guns strong, of horse artillery. Perhaps 1200 men in all mustered to the bugle's command that chill early morning of Christmastide 1808. Their gathering was not a little complicated by the inopportune outbreak of a fire in the village of Melgar, and there was some confusion as the church bell rang the alarm. Despite this unlooked for diversion, the march began on time.

'Our march was disagreeable, and even dangerous,' reminisced Captain Alexander Gordon of the 15th, whose *Journal of a Cavalry Officer in the Corunna Campaign, 1808–9* forms one of the major sources for the action of Sahagun, 'owing to the slippery state of the roads; there was seldom an interval of many minutes without two or three horses falling, but fortunately few were hurt by these falls. The snow was drifted in many places to a considerable depth, and the frost was extremely keen. We left Melgar in the midst of a heavy fall of snow...' At first the entire force travelled together, following the road running parallel to the River Cea, but at either Melgar de Amba or Galleguillo de Campo, Slade led off his column (comprising the 10th and the Horse Artillery) over the stream by a bridge, and continued independently towards the rendezvous of Sahagun.

Any remaining hope – after the fire – that the enemy would be taken by surprise was dashed when the advance guard of the 15th ran into an alert enemy picquet some way short of the town soon after 5 am. A sharp, confused encounter resulted, in which '... the Frenchmen ran away, and in the pursuit both parties fell into a deep ditch filled with snow. Two of the enemy were killed, and seven or eight made prisoners (other accounts say five); the remainder escaped and gave the alarm to the troops at Sahagun,' continues Alexander Gordon. The need to cross a number of narrow and slippery causeways in single or double file at this juncture impeded any attempt at 'hot pursuit'.

Although aware that the chance of catching the foe unawares was now gone, Paget pressed on for Sahagun with all possible despatch. Within the town the cavalry trumpets were now shrilling as Debelle's 700-or-so chasseurs and dragoons came tumbling out of their billets; but it is significant to note that their horses had been left ready saddled and bridled overnight – clearly the French were aware that something was in the wind. Of course there was no sign of Brigadier Slade and the 10th Hussars – and the French were able to form up unhindered at the east gate of the town. Exact timings are difficult to determine; but it is more than possible that the time was in advance of the 'half-past-six' enjoined in Paget's orders already quoted; to that extent, together with the problems of the way, Slade can be absolved at this juncture, although it also appears that he had seen fit to treat his shivering men to a lengthy speech which he eventually concluded with '... the energetic peroration of "Blood and Slaughter! March!"'

Lord Paget nevertheless decided to implement his own part of the plan – and led his hussars on a detour round the south of Sahagun, keeping them in double column of divisions – or half-troops of about twelve files, each squadron comprising some 280 men at full establishment, subdivided into four 'divisions'. His aim was to intercept any attempt by the French to evacuate the town. Dawn was now breaking, but visibility was far from clear that wintry morning.

In fact, Debelle and his men were further ahead with their preparations than Paget had anticipated, and the French were already about to ride off to the eastwards towards Carrion. This Paget was determined to forestall, and his column was soon moving along the road in hot pursuit, moving parallel to his quarry who chose to move cross-country over an area of vineyards, having a fair-sized ravine between themselves and their pursuers. As a result, the French, despite their head start, found themselves slowed by the icy conditions amid the stumps of the vines, and the British began to make ground. Thereupon, after failing to cross the head of Paget's column, and recognising that he had a fight on his hands, Debelle halted his squadrons and, wheeling right, formed them for action into close column of regiments, some six ranks deep, using the dyke to cover at least part of his front. At this juncture, misled by the mist, the French apparently believed that they were facing a force of Spanish cavalry, and were not unduly anxious about the outcome. Their flankers, riding close to the British, continually cried out the challenge '*Qui vive?*' in an attempt to identify their foes, but received no reply. In the half-light Paget noticed that the French had halted, and after riding on a short distance he, too, ordered a halt, wheeled his half-troops into line to the left, and, without the least delay, he ordered the bugles to sound the charge, '... just as you have seen us do at Ipswich', as he prosaically recalled in a letter written after the battle. His hussars gave three fierce cheers, the bugles blared, and with a great shout of 'Emsdorf and Victory!' the squadrons charged.

The lateral ravine behind which the French were standing at the halt delayed Paget not one instant; however, his charging line did not exactly coincide with that of the enemy – the British left extending beyond the French right flank. Still labouring under the belief that they were facing a Spanish force, the French were surprised by this impetuous attack – and sat gaping on their horses at the mist-shrouded sight of cheering hussars charging in upon them. 'The interval between us was perhaps 400 yards,' recalled Gordon (although some accounts put it at as little as eighty yards), 'but it was so quickly passed that they (the French) only had time to fire a few shots before we came upon them ... 'The shock was terrible; horses and men were overthrown and a shriek of terror, intermixed with oaths, groans and prayers for mercy, issued from the whole extent of their front.'

The area of the engagement is easily recognisable today – an open area of cultivated ground some five square miles in extent, bounded to the north and east by a bend of the River Valderaduey, a tributary of the Cea, which the Sahagun road crosses by a bridge before dividing towards Saldana and Carrion respectively. A fair rise also lies to the north of the battle area before descending steeply into the valley. The vineyards of 1808 are not in evidence today, nor is the lateral ravine, but several drainage ditches intersect the ground.

The 1st Provisional Chasseurs – Hanoverian allies of France – formed the front three ranks of Debelle's static formation. As Gordon noticed, the men tried to fire their carbines, but in an instant the 15th had swept up and broken them entirely. The chasseurs were flung back upon the three ranks of the French 8th Dragoons standing in rear, plunging them, too, into sad disorder. The chasseurs were commanded by Colonel Tascher, a nephew of the Empress Josephine, although there is some doubt as to whether he was himself present. The dragoons looked imposing enough in their '... brass helmets of the ancient form, and the long horsehair streaming from their crests', but within a very few minutes the entire French force was in full flight from the field – their commander Debelle being first dismounted and then trampled in the crush of the 'sauve qui peut'.

Within ten minutes the mêlée was over, and the action became a disjointed series of isolated fights as spurring hussars hotly pursued fragments of their shattered foe over the mile and a half to the banks of the river. 'We found them broken and flying in all directions, and so intermixed with our hussars that, in the uncertain twilight of a misty morning, it was difficult to distinguish friend from foe,' wrote Gordon. At this juncture who should appear on the scene from the north-west but Slade and the 10th Hussars; they narrowly avoided being charged by their victorious compatriots who at first took them for a further force of Frenchmen. 'Nevertheless,' continues Gordon, 'there was a scant firing of pistols, and our lads were making good use of their sabres.' The confusion prevalent at this period is well evidenced by the captain's brush with an officer he suddenly thought was Lieutenant Hancox of the regiment from his fur cap and half-glimpsed features, whereupon the hotly pursuing Gordon sloped his sword and rode off – only to find later that Hancox 'was not the person I had followed, who, I conclude, was an officer of the grenadiers à cheval or compagnie d'élite ... and doubtless was much astonished at my sudden appearance and abrupt departure.' Another hussar, to the amusement of his unfeeling fellows, managed to shoot his own horse. A few acts of wanton cruelty were committed by the success-drunk horsemen: one cut down a wounded and dismounted French dragoon, later seeking to explain his action on the grounds that he did not '... like to let the day pass without cutting down a Frenchman and could not let such a favourable opportunity to slip'.

As the hussars approached the banks of the river, the strident bugles sounded the 'rally' – a wise precaution as the squadrons were fast becoming sadly disordered. This allowed some 200 Frenchmen to make good their escape in different directions. A force was detached to pursue what was left of the *Chasseurs-à-Cheval* towards Carrion while the rest followed the Provisional Dragoons towards Saldana, where a battered and distracted Debelle, who had somehow survived the action, strove to rally them.

The French were fortunate to get so many men away, and would not have done so had not Lord Paget – who fought with the left centre squadron – sent an officer with a handkerchief as flag of truce to offer the enemy the chance to surrender. In fact, they only fled all the faster, using the pause to gain both time and distance – and so got away. Nevertheless, the bag was impressive, although once again the details are disputed. The French seem to have had 120 killed and all of seventeen officers and 150 men taken prisoner – including both Colonel Dud'Huit of the 8th Dragoons and Colonel Dugens of the Chasseurs – many captives being severely wounded by sabre strokes. The French also lost all their regimental baggage, including their records and, 'it appeared by the returns found in his (Debelle's) portfolio that the French had about 800 men mounted and in the field, whilst we only mustered betwixt three and 400, independent of various small detachments, above a hundred men and horses were left at Melgar de Abaxo.' Thus wrote Captain Gordon. The historian Sir John Fortescue, however, claims that Paget had at least 500 sabres in the field to Debelle's 450; but, he concedes, 'apart from all questions of inferiority in strength, Debelle seems to have been overawed by Paget's quickness in manoeuvre and by the beautiful accuracy of the movements of the Fifteenth'. To achieve this much cost the Regiment only two men killed besides three officers and twenty men wounded.

The outcome of this brief but spirited action well demonstrates the advantages conferred by superior military intelligence, the achievement of tactical surprise associated with determined shock action pressed against a foe unwise enough to receive a charge at the halt. Although British sabres tended to be shorter, broader and blunter (through having metal scabbards) than French weapons, their mounts – despite the ravages of Peninsular campaigning and the adverse weather – were indubitably superior. The French chasseur cap, however, reinforced by an iron hoop that helped protect the wearer from a downward cut, was an improvement on the current British hussar headgear, which tended to fall off at the least exertion.

There is no faulting the tactical conduct of Paget's attack. As Captain

Carnock, Adjutant of the 15th Hussars wrote, 'the French officers who were taken declared they had never seen such determined charging, which they should not have stood in the manner they did, but that they thought us Spanish cavalry, and their error owing to the mist of the morning was not discovered until we were upon them.'

Paget himself, although naturally delighted by the outcome, was nettled by the failure of his attempt at a parley, and berated his reassembling officers and men for the disorder of their pursuit. 'I gave them a good scolding for it after the affair was over, and the answer they gave me was three cheers, and a request that I would accept as a token of their regard the two best officers' horses that were taken. You would be pleased if you were to hear all they say about me. I cannot write it . . .' This incident forms an interesting parallel to the Duke of Marlborough's experience at Elixhem just over a century earlier, when he, too, was cheered by his cavalry in the moment of victory. 'This gave occasion to the troops with me to make me very kind expressions, even in the heat of the action, which I own to you gives me great pleasure, and makes me resolve to endure anything for their sakes.' From such incidents a rare bond is forged between leader and led.

The effects of Paget's success proved transitory. Moore's army entered Sahagun on the 21st to be awarded a day's rest, but on the 23rd news arrived that Napoleon was in hot pursuit from Madrid, intent on cutting off 'the hideous leopard' from Lisbon. Moore at once abandoned all further thought of his offensive, and on Christmas Eve the long and arduous retreat to Corunna was commenced. But this in no way detracts from the achievement of the future Marquess of Anglesey and the 15th Hussars three days earlier. 'Although the success of the action was rendered incomplete, owing to the very extraordinary conduct of General Slade and some mistakes of Lord Paget,' wrote Gordon, 'it nevertheless impressed such an idea of the superiority of our cavalry on the mind of the enemy as induced them to avoid as much as possible coming in contact with us . . .' Sir John Moore justly described the affair as '. . . a handsome thing, and well done.' And the 15th Hussars, who later became the 15th/19th The King's Royal Hussars (and today 'The Light Dragoons'), are quite correct to celebrate the events of 21 December and the gallantry of their forebears by the dawn band parade followed by a regimental holiday which marks each anniversary of the occasion that also earned them the unique distinction, for a cavalry regiment, of bearing on their standard the proud honour, 'SAHAGUN' – an honour they share with no other regiment. This was a significant moment in the history of the British cavalry.

9

WELLINGTON IN THE PENINSULA: A REASSESSMENT

*O*ne of the duties of a military historian is to reassess famous historical figures – however well known – in the light of the most recent generation of discoveries and evaluations, taking into account the shifts in popular interest and scholarly fashions.

Arthur Wellesley, First Duke of Wellington, Field Marshal of five nations and sometime Prime Minister of Great Britain, is – second only (and this is arguable) to Vice-Admiral Lord Horatio, Viscount Nelson and Duke of Brontë – the greatest British national hero of the Napoleonic Wars and, indeed, of the first half of the nineteenth century. There have been several hundred biographies – good, bad and indifferent – devoted to this commanding figure, the latest published as recently as 1992. Yet legends and inaccuracies die hard. Lawrence James, author of The Iron Duke – a Military Biography *(1992), should have sought for a less anachronistic title. As every schoolboy ought to know (but, alas, I fear that is not always the case in these educationally turbulent days), the sobriquet relates neither to the Duke's toughness as a soldier nor to his determined character, but to his period as a rather controversial prime minister, when his attitudes to such matters as Catholic Emancipation and Parliamentary Reform inspired the London mob to turn up (when it had nobody better, such as King George IV, to harass) outside the railings of No. 1 London (Apsley House) and proceed to heave stones and bricks through the ducal windows. These democratic demonstrations became something of a habit, so the Duke – not wishing to be a spoil-sport but in order to save on his glazier's bills – had iron shutters fitted.*

What follows in this chapter is a brief introduction I was invited to give as an overall 'keynote address' at an International Conference organised by the tireless Professor Howard at Ciudad Rodrigo in 1986 – devoted to the study of the Great Duke and his opponents in Iberia. This was attended by their Graces the Duke and Duchess of Wellington, the present Prince Massena, Duke of Rivoli, and Comte Clausel, and also the descendants of Don Herrasti (Spanish hero of the French siege of the town in 1810) as guests of honour. In deference to our Spanish hosts it was necessary to modify certain views held by Wellington and many another British officer (after all, 'War', as Napoleon once somewhat untypically remarked, 'is, like government, a matter of tact') who served through those tumultuous years in the 'Spanish Ulcer' which have inspired so much scholarly attention. A great deal of value came out of the conference.

But there is still, perhaps surprisingly, much work to be done – particularly in the political area and (the subject of the next chapter) in respect of the guerrilla aspects of the struggle, not to forget the often neglected roles of the remaining Spanish regular soldiers which have been taken under the able wing of Dr Charles Esdaile of Liverpool University, who was at the time the first Wellington Papers' Fellow at Southampton University. A mass of unedited documents from Stratfield Saye House are still in course of evaluation. Dr David Gates's fine book, The Spanish Ulcer, *has recently provided an excellent one-volume summary of the Peninsular War in emulation of Napier and Oman. Every year new biographies and studies continue, amazingly, to appear – including* Thomas Browne's Papers, *published in 1989. This is indeed the most popular period of British military history, with the sole exceptions of the two titanic struggles of the first half of the twentieth century – and the more one reads into it the more one comes to understand why.*

The significant role of the Peninsular War in defeating the ambitions – some would doubtless say thwarting the genius – of Napoleon Bonaparte, probably the most important military commander in modern history, is today widely acknowledged by historians, although there is considerable variation in national bias and interpretation. The physical cost to the Empire is usually put at 240,000 men over an eight-year-period, almost 100 casualties a day when averaged out. The maintenance of an intractable and (from 1812) a worsening political and military situation required the presence of between 320,000 and some 200,000 French and Allied troops (to give the highest and lowest annual estimates, those for 1810 and 1813 respectively). Even more important than this manpower problem was the logistical strain the effort imposed in a country where, it has been said, 'small armies are defeated and large armies starve'. This became marked from 1812, when the Emperor's ministers had to find the wherewithal for supporting, equipping and supplying another army of half a million men in Russia – Moscow being all of 1500 miles from Paris and at least 2200 from Madrid. But perhaps the most devastating effect of all caused by the 'Spanish Ulcer' (as British historians often describe the Iberian struggle) was the psychological strain it placed on the individual soldiers called to follow the tricolours of France – whether Italians, Westphalians, Poles or Frenchmen. Marching orders for Spain from 1810 came to be regarded with the same lack of enthusiasm by the hapless conscripts as was a posting to another daunting corporal's Eastern Front in the Soviet Union from 1943. It was widely regarded as a one-way ticket to an early death – and not without reason. As Napoleon remarked in a famous aphorism, 'In war, the moral is to the physical as three is to one.' General Mathieu Dumas, father of the future famous French romantic and historical novelist, described his sensation as follows: 'I used to travel over that assassin's countryside as warily as if it were a volcano: every day saw the deaths of several Frenchmen. I cannot describe the sense of oppression and anxiety that afflicted me at this time.' The tension induced reprisals. 'Our men did not want to take any prisoners,' recalled Castelanne. 'They said, "These men are brigands – they kill us when we march alone!"'

Napoleon was correct when he ascribed a great deal of the trouble he found in Spain and Portugal to Great Britain. 'The hideous leopard contaminates by its very presence the peninsula of Spain and Portugal,' he grandiloquently proclaimed to his troops. 'Let us carry our victorious eagles to the Pillars of Hercules.' Indeed, once the earlier Spanish rejection of the French takeover had been signalled by the famous rising of 10 May 1808 in Madrid, and the provinces began to arm for an all-out struggle, it was the *junta* of Seville's appeal to the British government for armed and financial support – passed through the British governor of Gibraltar (one occasion, at least, when Britain's presence on the Rock was both welcome and of use to the Spanish people) – that set in train events of momentous implication. Great Britain's prompt response may have been motivated in part by its own strategic concerns: the Andalusian invitation – subsequently endorsed by the Supreme Junta in Cadiz – was accepted in London during June, and before that month was out the British cabinet had decided to send Sir Arthur Wellesley and an army to the Peninsula. It was not long before the Royal Navy gave practical evidence of its power to influence Spanish events. A squadron spirited away General La Romana's corps from the miseries of Gothenburg under the very noses of Bernadotte's forces, and thus repatriated 15,000 Spanish regular troops to the land of their birth.

Wellington's role in the Peninsular War has been variously interpreted according to national attitudes. Some French historians rely heavily on Napoleon's remark that he would prefer to have the British army safely committed to Spain and Portugal, rather than waiting, 40,000 strong, in transport vessels off the Isle of Wight, ready to mount a hit-and-run attack against some point of the French controlled seaboard of continental Europe. In sum, the failure in Spain is seen as merely one aspect of a huge design that failed. British historians tend to rate the significance of Wellington's contribution very highly indeed, claiming that it was probably the major factor in causing the decline and fall of the French Empire. This is similarly an extreme view – tending to discount the contribution of the British allies – who besides the Spaniards and Portuguese, included Russians, Prussians, Swedes and Austrians at various times and in various combinations, generally backed by British subsidies to a greater or lesser extent but – save in the first two instances – not supported by British troops as such. However, the importance of the Peninsula in providing Great Britain with an access point to the continent cannot be stressed too highly, and there is little doubt that Wellington's army made critical contributions to the Iberian wars in ways to be detailed below. The Portuguese – 'England's oldest ally' with links going back to John of Gaunt in the fourteenth century – tend in their historical evaluations to concur to a marked degree with the British interpretation, freely acknowledging our vital role in training, officering and equipping their army, and in playing a determinant part in securing first the liberation, and then the effective defence, of their country during three successive French invasions. Spanish historians, however, take another view, and I feel it would be fair to say that the British role in the titanic eight-year struggle tends to be written down. To Spaniards, as I read it, the Peninsular War is seen as 'the struggle of a whole nation against a tyrannical foreign government, a movement in which the British army plays but a marginal part'. As the Dutchman Professor Geyl remarked, 'History is indeed an argument without end', and without a doubt the real truth lies somewhere in the middle ground shared by all interpretations.

In attempting to evaluate Wellington's contribution to the Peninsular War we must start from his own conception of the struggle. He first described it on 1 August 1808, and elaborated it on 7 March 1809 and many times thereafter. At the heart was his awareness that he was in command of Great Britain's only field army – which therefore he deemed it to be his supreme duty to preserve. Second, he saw that to achieve this overriding requirement he must ensure that Portugal – and above all Lisbon – was maintained as his inviolable base of operations, as a sanctuary or even as a re-embarkation point if all went wholly wrong. His various major advances into Spain in 1809, 1812 and then 1813 were all dependent upon the security of Portugal, the base. If Lisbon was threatened, Wellington would abandon all other operations and fall back to undertake its defence. This happened in 1809 after Talavera della Reina, in 1812 after the failure to take Burgos, and it would have happened again in 1813 had not the issue of the whole Peninsular War been settled once and for all by the crowning victory of Vitoria.

Aware that he had rarely more than 35,000 British troops and that the foe had seldom less than 250,000, his view of operations was both steadfast and audacious, and above all realistic. The impregnable triple Lines of Torres Vedras were to be the key to his strategy, 1810–12.

His base once established, Wellington was also clear on how best to proceed. Although Napier, Fortescue and Oman have tended to concentrate on the conventional operations Wellington undertook at the head of his Anglo-Portuguese army, it is today quite clear that he also set the greatest store on exploiting the opportunities offered by the guerrilla war. This began to be really important following the defeat of the Spanish regular forces by late 1808 – which had the effect of scattering numbers of the most determined soldiery into the hills of Spain, where they formed or joined already-existing bands of *guerrillos* under new leaders and then proceeded to evolve a novel style of warfare – one that proved that, in suitably difficult terrain and with civilian cooperation, men who are fighting for survival on their own soil can be more than a match for a vastly superior opponent.

Wellington set himself to exploit the advantages the widespread popular resistance spearheaded by such fine leaders as Don Julian Sanchez could confer. First there was the matter of military intelligence. Thanks to the skilled placing of his secret 'correspondents' (or collecting agents) in numbers of Spanish towns and cities, the future Duke was rarely short of the latest news of French movements and strengths. The distribution of rewards for information was well worth the financial outlay involved. The simple fact is that Wellington stumbled upon the secret that made a permanent French occupation of Spain as impossible as that of a permanent United States and ARVN (Army of the Republic of Vietnam) presence in South Vietnam in the mid-1970s. That is to say, that the combination of a small but well-trained regular army operating in association with, and in support of, widespread guerrilla forces, is bound to make a permanent occupation by a far larger army not enjoying the full support of the local population, impossible to achieve. Sir Basil Liddell Hart was amongst the first in Britain to realise the error of the conventional accounts of the Peninsular War, which concentrated on Wellingtonian set battles, and the linked French movements, at the expense of the Spanish and Portuguese contributions, which tended to be relegated to a peripheral, rather than a central role.

Perhaps we would question the effectiveness and scale of the associated 'scorched earth' aspect of this analysis – as recent research by Professor Howard and others has tended to reveal that even in 1810 the French were able to find at least a modicum of supply in the supposedly totally swept-bare countryside north of the Lines of Torres Vedras – but the main observation by Liddell Hart is wholly supportable, and there is an analogy with US experience in Vietnam. The French could not both 'occupy' the country and hold down the popular, guerrilla war, and at the same time collect conventional field armies to counter, meet and fight Wellington's regular Anglo-Portuguese army on one of its deep incursions into French-held Spanish territory.

Thus the French in 1810 or 1811 were strong enough to contain the guerrilla menace and occupy the majority of towns and key communication centres – but only just so long as Wellington did not intervene and force them to con-centrate. When that happened, the French control of the countryside slipped, and the pressure was removed from the guerrillas, who made the most of their opportunities to reoccupy vacated areas and harass French convoys (which, by 1812, needed an infantry escort of at least 1200 men, some as many as 3000 according to the French hussar officer M. de Rocca). It has been estimated that the guerrillas at any one time never numbered more in total than between 36,500 and 50,000 under arms; yet they have been credited with causing an average of thirty French deaths a day. Thus, of the 240,000 Frenchmen who died in Spain, some 45,000 can be attributed to direct battle action, 76,650 to guerrillas and the balance to disease and accidental causes. King Joseph's aide, General Bigarré, put the figure of French deaths from guerrilla action as high as 180,000 men over five years, and total guerrilla losses over the same period as under 25,000 – but his estimates are probably exaggerated on both counts.

Whatever the correct figures, Wellington was well aware of the central significance of the War of Independence, and until 1813 adapted his strategy accordingly. That, probably, was his greatest contribution to ultimate victory. By 1813 The French were both physically weakened by losses and detachments for eastern Europe, and generally demoralised – and then the campaign of full liberation of Spain could be implemented. At the same time, from mid-1812 Wellington began to use selected guerilla units for conventional operations – again in a remarkably prescient way reflecting Mao Tse Tung's 'Stage 3' of Revolutionary Guerrilla Warfare. Spanish irregulars were used to seal off the French-held forts in Salamanca, and in due course Don Sanchez's colourful horsemen became the most effective Spanish cavalry. They were used, for example, to cover the movements of the main army following the capture of Burgos in mid-1813.

It was in the cooperation between the two very different types of struggle that were being waged simultaneously and the high degree of coordination of effort achieved – sometimes consciously and sometimes almost unconsciously – that the secret of success ultimately lay. There is a lesson there, I feel, for NATO planners and strategists of the late twentieth century as well as for historians delving into the events of the early-nineteenth. A balanced view is essential.

This is no way to deny Wellington's immense personal contribution to victory, and I propose to devote my remaining space to considering some of his specific attributes as a great commander, for me second only to John Churchill First Duke of Marlborough (and possibly Oliver Cromwell) amongst soldiers produced by Great Britain and Ireland. It was not without good reason that the Spanish government made Wellington *Duque de Ciudad Rodrigo* and a Grandee 1st Class of Spain in 1812, and then *Duque de Vitoria* in 1813; nor that the Portuguese bestowed the title of *Marquez de Torres Vedras* to supplement that of *Conde de Vimeiro* awarded in 1811. Nor, ultimately, was his own country slow to recognise his achievement. On 28 June 1814, he was admitted to his seat in the House of Lords shortly after his first return to England after five years abroad, and heard his patents as Baron, Viscount, Earl, Marquess and Duke, all read out in succession – a unique honour.

To his officers, he was known as 'The Beau' or 'the Peer'; to his rank and file

'Douro', 'Our Arthur', 'Old Hookey' (a reference to his prominent nose) or, more prosaically, 'that long-nosed bugger that beats the French'. To his Portuguese 'fighting-cocks' (trained up under Marshal Beresford), he was 'El Duero' – as they chanted in unison on his appearance on the battlefield of Sorauren in July 1813. To the British public his name was to become synonymous with a form of short riding boot that he favoured, and, years later, he would become known for very different reasons as 'the Iron Duke'. It must be said, however, that famous soldiers do not necessarily make the most successful prime ministers or presidents, at least in Anglo-Saxon countries.

Of his many skills as a commanding general, I would first wish to emphasise his thorough knowledge of his opponents, whom he respected and understood, but did not fear. Nothing is more revealing in this respect than the famous conversation with his friend Croker, shortly before he embarked for the Peninsula in 1808 to face the French in battle for the first time since 1794, when, as a Lieutenant-Colonel under 'the Grand Old Duke of York' in Flanders, he 'had learned what not to do, and that is always something'. Asked what he was thinking about, he replied:

> Why, about the French I am going to fight against to be sure. They were capital troops in Flanders, and a dozen years of victory under Bonaparte must have made them better still. They have, besides, it seems, a new system of strategy which has outmanoeuvred and overwhelmed all the armies of Europe. 'Tis enough to make one thoughtful, but no matter. My die is cast. They may overwhelm me but I don't think they will outmanoeuvre me. First, because I am not afraid of them, as everybody else seems to be; and secondly because if what I hear of their system of manoeuvre is true, I think it is a false one as against steady troops. I suspect all the continental armies were more than half-beaten before the battle was begun – I, at least, will not be frightened beforehand.

This highly revealing passage indicates Wellington's understanding of the French method of making war – a case of 'fore-warned is fore-armed'. He had read the omens and was psychologically prepared.

Secondly, mention must be made of his great skill in the tactical field at making use of ground, and at devising suitable tactical methods to achieve the defeat of his foes. His battlefields – from Vimeiro to Talavera, from Salamanca to Orthez, yes and Waterloo, were skilfully selected. It is often said that he fought defensively. This is only a half-truth. In many battles he preferred to lure the enemy into making ill-judged onslaughts – which he would repulse with heavy loss before unleashing his own devastating counter-attack. In this he was only reflecting the concepts of Napoleon himself who advised '... a well-reasoned and circumspect defensive followed by a rapid and audacious attack'. Just as he knew the likely forms and stratagems of a French strategic attack, so he knew the well-tried sequence of their tactical onslaughts, and set about exploiting the weaknesses they incorporated. By keeping the bulk of his men concealed behind reverse slopes, by dominating 'no-man's land' to the front with his riflemen and Portuguese *caçadores*, he disrupted the progression of French attacks – meeting them at the summit with the massed volleys of 'the long red wall', followed by the feared British cheer and bayonet charge. Time and again this became the time-honoured format for British tactical conduct – and the French never really discovered the answer to it.

Of course there were battles where Wellington fought aggressively from the outset – one thinks of the launching of Packenham's 3rd Division at Salamanca to head off the advanced elements of Marmont's army, or the massive series of coordinated attacks over an eight-mile front that 'opened the ball' at Vitoria. But enough has been said to indicate Wellington's mastery in the use of ground to confound his enemies' plans of attack and thus increase the chances of his own success. But it is necessary to point out again that too much significance is often placed on the formal battles of the Peninsular War.

The third special attribute of Wellington's relates to his mastery of logistical concepts. Once again, his geographical skills were very much to the fore. To secure his Portuguese base, he had to deploy his limited resources so as to cover the five invasion routes leading into the country from Spain – the approaches through Valnca and Chaves in the north, the important 'northern corridor' between Almeida and Ciudad Rodrigo (which became the scene of so much activity in 1810–12), the Castelo-Branco route just north of the Tagus, and lastly the significant 'southern corridor' between Badajoz and Elvas threatening Lisbon from the east – or, worst of all, a combination of two or more at once. To be able to do this called for a sound supply system, and this he developed in accordance with principles learnt during his campaigns in India. The subject has been well analysed by S.P.G. Ward, and can only be touched upon here. The system operated out of the rear depots of Lisbon (replaced, from late 1813, by Santander) and had three distinct components: the rear-line of barge-traffic linking Lisbon to intermediate depots; then the ox-wagon convoys to forward supply depots; and last the divisional and regimental mule-trains supplying the individual units at the front.

Wellington once stressed the importance of '. . . following the history of a biscuit from its leaving Lisbon until it reaches a soldier's mouth on the frontier.' By attention to detail – the loading of mules, the weight of equipment carried by the individual soldier, the daily distance an ox-cart could be realistically expected to cover – Wellington brought victory to his armies and great assistance to the peoples of Portugal and Spain in their great struggle for liberation from the foreign yoke. The climax came at Vitoria – which took 400 miles in forty days to reach in 1813. As Fortescue well remarked, 'Wellington's supplies were always hunting for his army. Joseph's army was always hunting for its supplies.'

To conclude this examination of Wellington in the Peninsula, I wish to examine his relationship with his officers, troops and allies. It would be true to state that he was respected and feared rather than loved. Where his officers were concerned, he adopted a tough and critical attitude. 'There is but one way – to have a hand of iron. The moment there was the slightest neglect in any department I was down on them.' 'Nobody in the British Army ever reads a regulation or an order as if it were a guide to his conduct, or in any other manner than an amusing novel . . .; when it is found that the arrangement fails, they come upon me to set matters to rights, and thus my labour is increased tenfold.' Some officers – a very few – he trusted implicitly, Picton, Uxbridge and above all Graham; some he praised wholeheartedly – including his intelligence expert, Major Somers Cocks, killed at Burgos, 1811. 'Had Cocks outlived the campaign . . . he would have become one of the first generals of England'. On the other hand, the Horse Guards sent him some unsatisfactory material – Sir William Erskine, General Lumley and General Lightburne amongst them, occasioning his famous outburst to Henry Torrens, Assistant Military Secretary. 'Really, when I reflect upon the characters and attainments of some of the General Officers of this army, and consider that these are the persons on whom I am to rely to lead columns against the French Generals, and who are to carry my instructions into execution, I tremble; and as Lord Chesterfield said of the generals of his day, "I only hope that when the enemy reads the list of their names he trembles as I do." Sir William Erskine and General Hay will be a very nice addition to this list! However, I pray God and the Horse Guards to deliver me from General Lightburne and Colonel Sanders.'

His views on his rank and file were equally direct. 'The army was, and indeed still is, the worst army that was ever sent from England' (1810). 'There is no crime recorded in the Newgate Calendar that is not committed by these soldiers, who quit their ranks in search of plunder.' The most often-quoted comment of all was, of course, the following: 'It is quite impossible for me or any other man to command a British Army under the existing system. We have in the service the scum of the earth as common soldiers, enlisted for drink . . . It is really a disgrace to have anything to say to such men as some of our soldiers are.' There were times – as in the appalling aftermath to the storming of the great breach at Badajoz in April 1812 – that his army deserved such harsh strictures. But of course there was the reverse of the medal, as he freely admitted: '*Their* soldiers (the French) got them into scrapes; *mine* always got me out.' Or again, to his confidante Lady Salisbury, 'I could have done *anything* with that army, it was in such splendid order.'

Clearly, his attitude towards the British soldier was ambivalent – and with some reason – but he and his officers ultimately forged the British Peninsular Army into a redoubtable weapon. Wellington's views of his allies were also, as is well known, mixed. In his letters he does not always express the greatest confidence in, or (let us admit it) respect for, the governments in Lisbon and Cadiz. Writing from near Badajoz on 12 June 1811, he complained that '. . . no crime that I know of has been punished in either (country), excepting that of being a French partisan'. And again, 'The cause of this evil is the mistaken principle on which the Governments have proceeded. They have imagined that the best foundation for their power was a low, vulgar popularity . . . and to obtain this bubble, the Government of Portugal as well as the successive governments in Spain, have neglected to perform those essential duties of all Governments, viz, to force those they are placed over to do their duty . . .'. The Portuguese soldiers – once trained up by the gigantic Irishman, Marshal Beresford and given adequate arms – he came to regard very highly: 'the fighting cocks of the army', he called them. His views of the Spanish army were typically direct. 'The Spaniards make excellent soldiers,' he assured Viscount Mahon years later. 'What spoils them is that they have no confidence in their officers . . . The men are all very fine fellows; but the officers have no knowledge or discipline. "*No lo se*" is their answer on every occasion.' (Browne has several stories indicating British scorn.) In 1809 he found that it was wiser to rely on his own supply and transport arrangements than upon the promises of his allies: 'The Spanish army has plenty of everything, and we alone, upon whom everything depends are actually starving.' The Spaniard, he observed, '. . . obeys no law, despises all authority, feels no gratitude for benefits conferred or favours received and is always ready with his knife or his firelock to commit murder'. They were also intrepid looters. Well, no doubt Spanish contemporaries had their views, as well, of their British allies.

Happily, there was a reverse to his coin of disillusion and hard critical appraisal. He proved capable of cooperating with the most diverse guerrilla leaders. The plaque inscribed near the present tomb of Sir John Moore at La Coruña records his words addressed to his troops in 1813 after the action of San Marcial: 'Warriors of the civilised world, follow the example of the men of the 4th Division which I have the honour to command. Every single soldier of that Division deserves better than I do to wear the insignia of a Commander. We have all been the witnesses of a heroic courage. Spaniards! All of you model yourselves on the inimitable Galicians . . .' He could, therefore handle allies pretty effectively – we get a glimpse of him with Don Julian Sanchez, the colourful guerrilla leader, the two men clearly regarding themselves as comrades-in-arms. Many British soldiers had first seen the famous guerrilla chieftain at a Te Deum sung in Salamanca cathedral to celebrate the surrender of the French forts in the city on 27 June 1812 – admiring his 'furred pelisse and immense Hussar cap with the eagle of Napoleon symbolically reversed'. But it was at Frenedas, during the winter of 1812–13, that Edward Costello, rifleman of the 52nd Regiment of Foot, recorded in his Journal that, 'Here, for the first time, I saw Don Julian Sanchez, the noted guerrilla leader, linked arm in arm with the Duke – an instance peculiar to the time of obscure merit rising of its own impulse, to an equality with the greatest man of the age.' This moment was symbolic of the critical association, through thick and thin, of Wellington and the Spanish people.

As for Wellington's role in the Peninsular War, it is evident that he would not have been able to win the struggle on his own. However, I feel it is equally clear that the War of Independence would have been far more protracted and even more costly but for the presence of the Duke at the head of his 'great little army'. His generalship was a blend of calculated example, of 'heroic general-ship' at many a critical moment and place on the battlefield, and of cool realistic appraisal of strategic realities and military capabilities. That remains as clear today as it has ever done before. But from first to last he was well served by the regimental officers and men of his army, of whom Captain Thomas Henry Browne stands as a typical example.

10

WELLINGTON AND
THE GUERRILLAS

*T*he methods of guerrilla warfare – although not the name – are probably as old as history. Prehistoric tribes strove to fight their rivals on a hit-and-run basis, attempting to avoid conflicts when not the stronger, and fleeing without shame after a successful raid so as to avoid retribution. Similar methods were adopted in more recorded times. Fabius Maximus of Rome earned the title of* cunctator *('the delayer') when he avoided large-scale action against the conquering Carthaginians until Roman recovery from Cannae and Lake Trasimene were well on the way to completion. Instead of seeking major confrontations, therefore, he harried his enemies with what today would be called 'low intensity operations', allowing them scant rest or time to enjoy their booty.*

The word 'guerrilla' was born in Spain at an unknown moment in late 1808 or early 1809. 'Little war' connoted a popular struggle of the last resort in defiance of a foreign conqueror – and it was in this sense that Clausewitz addressed what he termed 'war of the people'. That it tended to be a peasant-based resistance was due to circumstances rather than design, and internal political connotations only truly emerged after the expulsion of the French from Spain in late 1813 – when some guerrilla leaders proved averse from surrendering the power of terror, and hostility to King Ferdinand's reactionary rule created a backlash. Great Britain first learned to cooperate with irregular forces during the Peninsular War under Wellington, but promptly forgot all it had discovered in the usual manner, and it was not until Caldwell's Small Wars *appeared later in the nineteenth century that it took on much importance. Guerrilla wars of a type were encountered in India, Africa and the Middle East as the British Empire spread '. . . in a fit of absence of mind', but were usually confined to conflicts against badly equipped native peoples – 'the lesser breeds beyond the Pale' in the revealing words of the supposedly Christian hymnal – as Victorians manfully '. . . took up the White Man's Burden'. The military realities of such struggles as the Ashanti or Afghan wars (not that the latter were in any way a walk-over – far from it, as the famous memoirs of Lady Sale reveal) were soon being reflected in music hall doggerel, and by the 1880s rumbustious lower-middle class Victorian audiences were being regaled with such jingoistic ditties as:*

'Pity the hapless Hottentot;
We have the gatling – he does not.'

Then the Boer Wars shook the British army out of its post-Crimean complacency as its soldiers met for the first time European-type irregular opponents armed with accurate Mauser rifles and equipped with artillery. The army abruptly awoke to the urgent need for reform and modernisation – processes it completed just in time for Armageddon in 1914. Two further refinements followed. The use of irregular forces acting in concert with conventional British armies was relearnt by General 'Bull' Allenby fighting the Turks in Palestine with the aid of Captain T.E. Lawrence and his Hashemite Arab friends. Chapter 33 of The Seven Pillars of Wisdom *is devoted to Lawrence's sophisticated view of guerrilla warfare – which earned Mao Tse Tung's approbation a little later, and became partially assimilated into the Chinese doctrine of Revolutionary Guerrilla War – which, with its basic intention of creating political, social and economic revolutions from within, and with its 'rural', 'urban' and 'terrorist' forms, has been taking up much of the British army's attention and energy ever since 1945 – from Palestine to Ulster.*

The following chapter formed the basis for another keynote address, first given at an international conference held at Southampton University in 1987 – again to study the Wellington period in its military and political aspects – and also drawing on an earlier talk given to the Special Staff Course at the US Army Staff College, Fort Leavenworth, in April 1985.

†

'Nothing new under the sun', runs the dog-eared adage. The significance of the interrelated *conventional* war and the popular or *guerrilla* struggle in the Peninsula, has long been appreciated – but it has only recently become clear – in the light of painfully acquired experience in the 1960s and 1970s in several areas of the world – how closely Wellington's experience of fighting a serious, six-year war, 1808–14, alongside irregular forces in Portugal and Spain, may be said to coincide with supposedly 'modern' principles of guerrilla warfare. As Wellington always forebore to commit his military convictions formally to paper, we have to *deduct* from his actions and occasional mentions in dispatches how his ideas evolved, but the tentative conclusions we can draw are of some interest. As an introduction to our subject, however, a very brief background résumé of the Peninsula War may be appropriate.

In late 1807, Napoleon dispatched his first troops over the Pyrenees – ostensibly with the Bourbon Spanish government's approval and cooperation – to attack Portugal, 'England's oldest ally', and at the time – after Tilsit – almost only friend in continental Europe. Lisbon was duly occupied, but overplaying his hand, Napoleon – always the supreme opportunist – used his military deployment to take over not only the Portuguese but also the Spanish government, exiling the decrepit royal house of Bourbon and replacing it by his unwilling brother Joseph.

These high-handed actions gave rise to waves of spontaneous popular insurrection in both countries – events which provided Great Britain with the opportunity to emerge from its post-Tilsit insular isolation and, thanks to the Royal Navy, send Sir Arthur Wellesley and a small British army – 15,000 strong eventually – to the region in early August of 1808. Within three weeks he had broken the French hold on Portugal and induced the French to evacuate, lock, stock and barrel. Meanwhile the as yet unaided Spanish armies (amalgams of regular units and local militias) – following up a remarkable success over General Dupont at Bailen – had driven King Joseph and his armies back beyond the Ebro. These unpropitious events – in both Spain and Portugal – caused Napoleon to intervene in person in October at the head of the Grand Army, and in a whirlwind campaign of conquest the Emperor defeated a clutch of half-trained and ill-led Spanish armies, restored his *fratello* to his throne in Madrid, and forced Sir John Moore (Wellesley's temporary successor) pre-cipitately to evacuate the British army through Corunna (at the cost of his life) before leaving the Peninsular for ever to turn his attention to new central European crises (not least that Talleyrand and Fouché had been seen talking – and worse, laughing – together in Paris), handing over the final stages of pacification to a group of his marshals.

The British retention of Lisbon enabled Wellesley – restored to command – to return to Portugal. Within months he had flung Soult, Duke of Dalmatia – or 'Duke of Damnation' as the British troops called him – out of northern Portugal – and set out into Spain for his first attempt at direct cooperation with the remaining Spanish forces in-being and the popular resistance. It proved a daunting experience. As Winston Churchill was to express it: 'The Good Lord knows it is difficult to fight wars *with* Allies' (a point with which Sir Arthur would have heartily concurred): 'but it is still *more* difficult to fight wars *without* them.' In the case of the next five years, this was also to be borne out by events – indeed *without* the aid of the guerrillas, the struggle would have been wholly insupportable.

Wellington – as we may call him after Talavera – found Spanish promises valueless, and a forced retreat back to Portugal proved the prelude to the defensive campaign of 1810 – during which Soult advanced to Cadiz in the south, whilst the great Massena mounted a major invasion of Portugal through the Northern Corridor and marched on Lisbon. The attempt to expel the British once and for all foundered on the 'surprise' of the revealed Lines of Torres Vedras, and the French were then forced to retreat in part because of the pressure against their lines of communication exerted by the Portuguese *orde-*

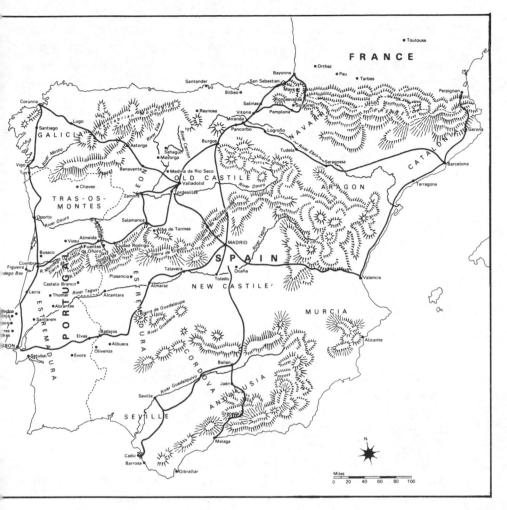

THE PENINSULAR WAR

nenza and partisan forces. Four years of heavy fighting ensued – with Wellington using his small Anglo-Portuguese army in association with the by now better conducted Spanish guerrillas to overcome far stronger French forces overall. From 1812 Wellington was able to assume the offensive – only to lose the initiative after the Burgos débâcle – but in 1813 the campaign of conquest was resumed, and by early 1814 the new Duke had thrown the French back over the Pyrenees, contributing substantially (with a little help to be sure from Marshal Ney and a few other disillusioned marshals at Fontainebleau) to Napoleon's first abdication. Throughout these four years Wellington was managing his irregular allies with rare skill and great profit. Enough by way of overall outline.

We must now describe and differentiate between the successive stages of the *popular* struggle, the 'War of Independence', which went through three distinct phases.

First, the spontaneous risings in Portugal and Spain in early 1808 were *not* of a truly guerrilla type. Rather they were violent manifestations of hatred for the French by a large section of the indigenous populations, leading to ill-coordinated results. That of 2 May in Madrid, immortalised by Francisco Goya – which took the French by surprise and cost them one hundred casualties – was brutally repressed in forty-eight hours – some thirty Spanish being shot on the night of the 3rd (Spanish sources claim 1500!) although its symbolic significance was to far outweigh its practical effects. Similarly, the Portuguese rising – only partially orchestrated by the militant Bishop Castro of Oporto – was also of a somewhat ineffective nature. In both countries, the revolts led to the formation of armies organised on essentially regular lines – although composed largely of militia. These half-trained forces then tried to fight regular battles against the occupiers – but were usually slaughtered by the far-superior French forces. On 28 December 1808, the Supreme Junta – now fled to Cadiz – gave legal existence to what they called 'a new kind of militia' – the *partides* or *guerrillas*, and the 'little war' was born.

From April 1809, Wellesley effectively took over all Portuguese males capable of bearing arms aged between sixteen and sixty. Part – including what was left of the original regular army – he formed into regular units which contained about 20 per cent British officers, and trained them with British NCOs. This task he largely confided to Beresford, who did so good a job that within a year the new Portuguese formations – his 'fighting-cocks' – were deemed capable of standing beside the British divisions at Busaco in the regular line of battle. Another part of Wellington's work led to the reform, reorganisation and retraining of the Portuguese militia. A third force – far larger than the other two several times over – was the distinctive Portuguese *ordenenza*, which was essentially guerrilla in nature. These irregulars – such as the force commanded by the English Colonel Trant – proved their value in carrying out the 'scorched earth' policy (however incompletely executed) during the retreat to Torres Vedras, and then harassed the French mercilessly through the late autumn and winter in such operations as the notorious massacre of the French wounded from Busaco in the hospitals of Coimbra in October which eventually induced Massena to retreat.

In Spain, the situation was far more confused. The instability of the Supreme Junta and the extensive and ruthless nature of the French occupation, and above all the dislike of any form of centralised direction by the guerrilla chieftains, deprived the popular resistance at the outset of any true centralised control or reliable logistical support. Following the dismal story of defeats of their regular armies culminating in the loss of Saragossa (sturdily defeated by Palafox at the close of the siege), guerrilla attacks proliferated rapidly in many areas of the country, but with a wide variety of leaders and in a wide variety of forms. Owing to the strongly particularist proclivities of the proud Spaniards, regional and local loyalties predominated over any sense of a 'national' cause, making coordination of effort all but impossible to achieve. This was 'the war of the flea' with a vengeance. However, Wellington and his staff were able to supply clear, simple advice when approached – which proved effective when taken. Still more to the point he was able to provide money, arms, ammunition and vital supplies. He rapidly came to receive better cooperation from reward-seeking guerrilla chieftains, robbers and terrorists though most of them were, than he did from such Spanish regular commanders as Gregorio de Cuesta.

Gradually, from mid-1809, an operational pattern began to evolve which posed the French with an insoluble problem, and the second phase of the popular war began gradually to manifest itself. With a maximum of 340,000 troops (as in mid-1810) at their disposal, the French might have been able to combat the guerrilla war on its own and overwhelm it. But to do so forced them to disperse into town-garrisons, convoy-escorts, bridge guards, and 'seek-and-destroy' punitive units. However, when Wellington undertook a strong probe, raid or serious invasion from his secure sanctuary of Lisbon into Spain – as, on various scales, in 1809, 1811, 1812 and 1813 – the French were compelled to concentrate – and accordingly the heat was taken off the popular bands, which immediately swarmed out of their hillside sanctuaries to occupy all areas evacuated by the French and to terrorise the collaborationist sections of the Spanish population which were *not* negligible in size, especially in the towns. Indeed, most of the liberal, educated and aristocratic sections of the Spanish people were more pro-French than anti, a fact sometimes overlooked. The guerrilla movement was essentially peasant-based and fanatic-led – really a lower-class revolutionary movement strengthened by an admixture of former regular soldiers who had taken to the hills after the defeat and scattering of their original armies. However, as Dr Charles Esdaile has recently revealed, the

Spanish regular forces continued to make a considerable (if often unsung) contribution to the war in Spain.

The terrain of the Peninsula favoured the 'tip and run' of guerrilla harassing operations to a marked degree and deserves a brief mention. Much of the area is an immense plateau of between 2000–3000 ft, bordered by the Cantabrian Mountains in the north, the Ebro Valley to the east, the Sierra Morena and River Guadalquivir to the south, and the mountainous spurs running westwards into Portugal. The main ranges run east to west – Pyrenees, Cantabrian Mountains, the Guadarramas, the Sierras de Guadalupe and de Toledo, the Sierra Morena. Some 8000-ft peaks are incorporated. So movement from east to west is easier than from north to south. The rivers, partly navigable, conform – Ebro, Douro, Tagus, Guadiana, Guadalquivir. The barren nature of much of Spain – 'a country where small armies are defeated and large armies starve' (Henry IV of France) makes only a few areas suitable for cavalry action – the plains of Salamanca and Vitoria, the area around Madrid, the Ebro valley and the plain of the Guadalquivir.

In sum a rugged, barren country of few roads – ideal for waging a popular war by a proud, fierce, implacably xenophobic people, as the Spanish certainly were.

As for Portugal, the barren frontier regions restricted practicable routes for invasions to five – three minor (Tuy, Chaves or Salvaterra) and two major – the northern and southern corridors. Two-thirds of the area is mountainous – only south of the Tagus is there any really fertile country. Everything north of Lisbon, therefore, was well designed for partisan activities.

To summarise – the Peninsula was well-suited in geographical terms for a desperate last-stand, war-to-the-death against a foreign conqueror, as the French were to come to realise to their terrible cost.

To be effective, *any* guerrilla war must achieve the following: create casualties by continuing harassment amongst its foes; deny the enemy the use of economically important and population-dense areas for long periods of time; physically hold – and be seen to hold – all territory not actually occupied by the enemy; and whilst achieving these intermediate objects, lastly, avoid being defeated by using hit-and-run tactics.

The guerrillas achieved all four requirements in varying degrees: first in terms of casualties. It is estimated that the eight-year main struggle cost the French 240,000 casualties – or something like 100 a day. A close examination of the French battle losses throughout the period reveal that only some 45,000 can be deemed action casualties against formed forces. We must not discount the ravages of illness, starvation or accident – perhaps another 50,000. That still leaves 145,000 French deaths unaccounted for – and these may fairly be attributed to the guerrillas. Some French sources place the losses higher. King Joseph's ADC, General Bigarré wrote as follows:

'The guerrillas... caused more casualties to the French Armies than all the regular troops during the whole course of the war in Spain; it has been proved that they murdered a hundred of our men daily. Thus, over the period of five years they killed 180,000 French Soldiers without on their side losing more than 25,000'.

This was certainly an economic cost-effective effort considering that it is calculated that never were more than 50,000 guerrillas under arms in global terms: some sources assert that there were only 36,500 at most. Wellington's English army never surpassed 40,000 men, perhaps plus a further 25,000 attached and trained Portuguese and Spanish 'regular' forces. The French forces in Spain fluctuated between a peak of 340,000 (1810) and a low of 200,000 (1812 and after). These figures speak for themselves. The 'Spanish Ulcer' tied down a wholly disproportionate amount of the French and their allied forces – and bled them white: with dire psychological repercussions. May we not at least suggest a parallel to the scale of US involvement in Vietnam?

In the second place, the *denial* of free use of population or economic resources to the enemy by the guerrillas can also be illustrated without difficulty. The French were never allowed to disperse in search of food in their time-honoured central European fashion – or if they did so, or tried to snatch a quick siesta – they would all too often soon come to rue it. Similarly, the guerrillas waged a pitiless war of terror against Spanish collaborators (the only 'crime' ever truly punished in Wellington's opinion). Perhaps 30,000 Spanish 'liberals' – ranging from aristocrats to townsfolk – were eliminated in a bitter side of the struggle that receives scant notion in formal terms. Terrible examples were made in public of known, or suspected, pro-French collaborators – such as torture, garotting and burning at the stake – *pour encourager les autres*. Sometimes whole villages were wiped out. The fact that the death of an estimated 4000 Spaniards at the hands of the British army at Badajoz in April 1812 following the famous 'storm' caused so little stir in Spain itself was that the townsfolk of that critically placed fortress were widely considered to have a poor record of resistance against the French in the period of French occupation from March 1811. The desperate treatment handed out to San Sebastian in September 1813, where only a dozen houses are reported to have been left standing, is another instance.

Wellington soon realised the value of denying the enemy easy inter-communication between geographically separated columns and persuaded guerrillas to observe French movements and report back, or to capture dispatches for which he would pay good prices. Sir John Moore's windfall in 1808 – the message revealing that Marshal Soult had no idea of his presence near Madrid and was still strung out – was an early case in point of invaluable intelligence information. As guerrilla activity intensified – all-out struggle was decreed by the Seville Junta on 17 April 1809 – so the French had to revert to sending two or three copies to ensure that one got through, and that also increased the likelihood of a duplicate or even a complete set reaching Wellington. French recourse to codes availed them little, as in Captain George Scovell Wellington discovered a gifted cryptographer who could break French messages in very short order. As a result Wellington's military intelligence windfalls were often little short of miraculous: French orders of battle, operational instructions, routine returns to Berthier – all fell into his hands in profusion.

He took great pains to develop the network. A substantial number of 'correspondents', or agents, were placed in towns throughout Spain; they collected, collated and sent on the fruits of guerrilla forays and their own observation missions. Well-mounted courier-officers – whose thoroughbred English and Irish horses could outdistance a French pursuit any day – clung on the flanks of French forces on the move, reporting every visible detail.

Equally important was to keep the guerrillas supplied with the necessities of war – not only money, but perhaps even more important, weapons, ammunition and supplies. Of course the guerrillas captured substantial amounts from French sources, but these needed to be supplemented. Here the Royal Navy proved of inestimable value.

The activities by which the Spanish guerrillas harassed the occupation forces will be well known those who have boyhood memories of reading the fictional accounts of Conan Doyle based on the Memories of Baron Marbot or those fine tales by C.S. Forester – *The Gun* and *Death to the French*. Couriers were so regularly ambushed that as early as the late summer of 1808 an escort of 200 cavalry was required to guarantee a dispatch getting through, and five years later on the 'Royal Road' it needed 1000. Convoys needed similarly large escorts – and by late 1812 it is calculated that the French had to deploy 90,000 men – 30 per cent of their total strength – to keep open the Burgos to Bayonne arterial road. General officers were occasionally captured and horrifically tortured – General Franceschi, for example. Atrocity bred counter-atrocity as the French reacted harshly – often on Napoleon's direct order – the volumes of the *Correspondance Inédits* of the Emperor holds many instances. Goya's terrible 'Horrors of War' scenes were not at all the product of an unbalanced mind and feverish imagination. The bitterness steadily grew, and the struggle became wholly intractable.

The psychological strain of operating under such conditions is to be found in many contemporary French memoirs. There are clear indications that French soldiers came to regard orders for Spain from 1810 onwards with as much enthusiasm as a member of the Wehrmacht received a posting order to the Eastern Front in 1943– 4. In other words it became regarded as very much of a 'one way ticket'. As early as December 1807 Bourienne was writing of Junot's invasion of Portugal that: 'Many men met their deaths through sheer misery – or at the hands of the peasantry.' General Mathieu Dumas wrote: 'These men are brigands; they kill us when we march alone. I shall always remember how I was afflicted with great anxieties; every day saw the murder of several Frenchmen, and I travelled over this assassin's countryside as warily as if it were a volcano'.

The French high command tried to come to terms with the terrible experience. Marshal Suchet recorded: 'This new system of resistance defended the countryside more effectively than a war regulated by disciplined armies, because it conformed to the localities and the character of the inhabitants.' Gouvion St Cyr left possibly the best description: 'Ready for all sacrifices, free from 'soft' needs or prejudices ... they formed irregular corps, chose their leaders, operated by whim, attacked anywhere that numbers or conditions favoured them, fled without shame whenever they were not the strongest, and disappeared by a combined dispersion... In the long term, such a system of implacable hostility must suffice to destroy the most numerous and valiant of armies, obliged as they were to fritter their strength away in mobile columns and convoy escorts.'

One is reminded of Mao Tse Tung's formula:

'The foe advances – we retreat
The foe halts – we advance;
The foe attacks – we withdraw
The foe retires – we pursue.'

Thus Colonel de Grandmaison: 'Yes, really a war to the death, for to kill the enemy became the general aspiration, the brutal goal pursued unceasingly wherever there was hope of its achievement: in the silence of the night, in the shelter of a house, in the repose of one's bed, in a corner of the woods, at the turning of a pathway – unexpectedly – through a hedge, behind a rock, on the highway – just as on the field of battle.'

The variety of Spanish guerrilla organisations throughout the country further baffled the French – and, it must be admitted, Wellington himself on occasion. Well-known leaders such as Longa, or Don Julian Sanchez, controlled large numbers of men, but in widely different ways. Local leaders were often, *pace* Napoleon's deprecatory remark about 'bandits led by monks', men of some education and local standing. They were able, if utterly unscrupulous men, and a distressing characteristic – as Wellington soon discovered – was a tendency to regard neighbouring bands with almost as much hostility as the common French enemy. Feuds were common – as between Mina and Echeverria in 1810 (resolved at Estelle), genuine cooperation was rare, and all leaders frequently disregarded any orders from the Cortes or the Junta if they clashed with their own selfish designs.

Don Juan Pilarea – 'El Medico' – was the leader of a mounted band who expended his activities from upper La Mancha to Toledo and the approaches to Madrid. On 6 April 1811 he captured the famous painter Colonel Lejeune (who was fortunate to live to tell the tale), on a mission for King Joseph, after wiping out his escort.

Juan Diaz Porlier – 'El Marquesito' (a former marine who had fought at Trafalgar) – led the struggle in the Asturias and in Galicia. In 1809 he led 1500 men, and two years later he was at the head of more than 4000.

Francisco Espoz y Mina – Commandant-General from 1810 – was possibly the most cunning leader, who had no less than 3000 followers. He succeeded his nephew Xavier Mina after his capture by the French in March 1810. A former peasant, he proved a strict disciplinarian and forbore to hold villages to ransom and so gained popular support. He was highly active in Navarre, controlling the 'Royal Road' and, waging 'war to the death' in the most atrocious manner. He avoided many man-hunts, and destroyed two large convoys in May 1811 and April 1812. His lair was at Ronda.

Don Juan Diaz – 'El Empecinado' – 'the stubborn' – was a former soldier turned farmer, who set up his first band after Medina del Rio Seco in July 1808. Uniquely, he insisted upon a form of uniform, and operated in Castile around Aranda, Segovia and Guadalajara. He had his defeats as well as his victories, but continued to offer a legendary resistance.

These are but a few of the better known: we might equally feature Delica, 'the Monk' Jiminez, Camilo Gomez, Clavos, Longa, Barrid, Jouregau 'El Pastor', Longa 'Papel', Albiur 'El Manco' or Alvarez, or several dozen more. They were a dangerous if somewhat disreputable gang.

The hostility of such leaders and the guerrillas they led indubitably demoralised the French army, who were not used to fighting whole populations. Proud, easily offended, and spurred on by the minor clergy, the Spanish were obsessed with the idea that the French were instruments of the devil. Although the French were nominally masters of half the country, in reality they controlled only 'the ground upon which the soles of their feet rested'.

Step by step, Wellington began to induce the guerrillas to carry out a coordinated strategic plan and the third phase of the popular struggle began. As the French enjoyed at least a four to one superiority in terms of regular troops, it was vital to keep them dispersed so as to prevent a daunting concentration of force. When the French *did* concentrate, the guerrillas at once occupied the vacated territory. Perhaps most important of all, their pervasive if unseen presence in an area fatally hampered thorough logistical 'living off the country' – never easy in Spain – which severely restricted French operational freedom.

In early 1812 – as Wellington at last prepared to go onto the offensive as Napoleon ordered large transfers from the Peninsula to swell his armies in eastern Europe – extensive plans were made for utilising the guerrillas for diversionary attacks. The aim in 1812 was to isolate the target – Marmont's Army of the North in north-central Spain – from reinforcement once Wellington launched his offensive. An orchestrated furore of guerrilla attacks was inspired not only by British supplies but also by British soldiers and sailors in direct cooperation with them. Guerrilla attacks – and threats of naval activity from the sea – kept Soult in Andalusia and Suchet in Valencia off-balance and apprehensive. Along the Biscay coast, Commander Sir Home Popham with two ships of the line, five frigates and two sloops, carrying two battalions of Royal Marines and one company of Marine Artillery, cooperated with Porlier, Longa and Mina and others – and had done so since 1810. Sudden landings were followed by quick sieges of coastal towns and equally quick evacuations.The capture of Santander in August 1812 – the new lines of communication route – was Popham's crowning achievement. General Caffarelli – French sector commander – was kept in a feverish state of insecurity, and he was unable to detach a single battalion, despite the orders of King Joseph, to reinforce Marmont. In July the previous year, an Anglo-Spanish squadron landed 1500 guerrillas at Santona, and took them off again four days later – just ahead of the French arrival in force. Even Joseph's Army of the Centre was effectively pinned down by Julian Sanchez's bands of *mounted* guerrillas who for twelve days captured every dispatch sent out by either Jourdan or Marmont. At the time of the battle of Salamanca, the two forces were *only fifty miles apart* but neither had the least idea where the other was situated. This guerrilla-induced isolation permitted Wellington to fight and win on equal terms in numbers at Salamanca: but whereas he had 70 per cent of the total Allied regulars in the Peninsula on that battlefield, Marmont had barely 20 per cent of his overall French forces present.

As guerrilla successes mounted, Wellington had to guard against one risk: that over-emboldened popular leaders would be tempted to resort to open warfare on their own initiative – and thus risk elimination by a sudden French concentration. In Andalusia, the chieftain Ballesteros suffered just this fate, but was able to regroup his shattered forces under the guns of Gibraltar.

In 1813 the guerrilla war was again coordinated to play a big role in the campaign. Despite the losses of 1812, the French in Spain would have been able to concentrate a daunting force against Wellington's army – but for the guerrilla effort. Suchet was kept tied down on the east coast – with all of 30,000 men – whilst Popham and his allies continued to keep the French dispersed along the north coast. Once again, two French armies in central Spain were kept apart until Jourdan's force (in fact the remnants of *three* former 'armies') had been eliminated as an effective force at Vitoria. Thereafter both Jourdan and Soult were driven back over the Pyrenees.

By this stage Wellington was cautiously allowing the guerrilla forces to carry out semi-regular operations in association with his Anglo-Portuguese Army. Thus at Vitoria it was Longa who cut the road over the River Zadorra that severed the French line of retreat. In every successful guerrilla war, the time comes when the loose organisation has to be tightened. Wellington achieved this by easy stages. As early as mid-1810 selected units of the Portuguese *ordenenza* were formally trained, armed, and provided with British officers under Marshal Beresford – and allowed to take a place in the line of battle at Busaco. As the French recoiled, so the opportunities for purely guerrilla action against them also decreased.

Wellington in due course converted Sanchez's mounted men into the best available Spanish cavalry – and used them to conceal the advance of the allied army after the French abandonment of Burgos in early 1813. They also helped capture Bilbao. Once the northern littoral was clear of the occupiers, Longa's mountaineers were used for regular operations from before the battle of Vitoria. Mina and Copons were similarly transferred to regular roles in Navarre and Catalonia respectively. But once over the Pyrenees, the Duke soon had to decide to send the Spanish formations back to Spain, for their actions on French soil were hardly commendable. So ended the long relationship of Wellington and the Spanish guerrillas.

Unlike Napoleon, Wellington left no maxims. He was never over-communicative – but perhaps we may, following a convincing analysis made by Jac Weller in 1963 – suggest four basic ideas on the proper use and treatment of guerrillas drawn from his actions.

First – guerrilla forces come in many different guises; their leaders and men will have many strengths and weaknesses: often unusual ones. The regular commander operating with them will be better advised in cajoling and persuading rather than ordering them in arbitrary fashion. The provision of munitions and money will often win their full cooperation.

Second – guerrilla forces must be aided to survive. They must be encouraged to do the things they are adept at, and to avoid risking total defeat. Their organisation should be simple, and their supply system should not outstrip their resources.

Third – guerrilla forces' main importance is their ability to deny an enemy permanent or real control of any area not physically dominated by military presence, and to demoralise the foe by inflicting a steady drain of casualties. They can further be extremely useful in the intelligence role – and in preventing the enemy from gaining information or even achieving inter-communication. Whatever their possible contribution to regular operations, their greatest use is to keep the foe off-balance and dispersed. A blow threatened is often more valuable than one delivered.

Fourth – guerrilla forces must be kept supplied with essentials and encouraged to cooperate and coordinate with one another – and with the regular forces. Operating alone, they can only achieve success against weak, inefficient, unpopular opponents.

Sir Charles Oman has said:

'By treating the Peninsular War as a chronicle of battles and sieges, it becomes meaningless – the predominant influence on the issue was that of the Spanish guerrillas.'

This is, I feel, a just – if often disregarded – summation. The guerrillas probably accounted for *twice* the casualties (or more) the Anglo-Portuguese regular forces ever caused. They also gave the 'flavour' to the struggle in terms of its stress-pattern, and as 'force-multipliers' effectively made it impossible for the French to complete or consolidate their conquests. To a degree, they also prepared the way for the 1812-and-after Wellingtonian reconquest. In the longer term in the post-War of Independence view, they also prepared the way for a long period of internal turbulence for Spain and the restored autocratic Bourbon Monarchy of Ferdinand VII – culminating in the liberal revolt of 1820, the loss of colonies in South America and elsewhere, and to the French intervention of 1823 and the Carlist War. Thus there was a price to be paid for the dedicated and implacable ferocity of the guerrilla resistance to the French.

If the Spanish resistance was central to the struggle, the contribution of Wellington's army and the remaining Spanish regular forces should not of course for one instant be belittled. The two aspects of the war were wholly intertwined and interdependent. Without British intervention in 1808 and 1809, both Spain and Portugal would very probably have gone under. By drawing away the French forces, compelling them to concentrate for important periods of time, the British fostered the spread of guerrilla warfare throughout the Peninsula by providing practical relief to the hard-pressed popular movement. The British army also gave moral support to the guerrillas: by its very presence, 'the hideous leopard' (as Napoleon dubbed it) indicated the possibility of ultimate victory over the hated invader. They did more: with the invaluable and irreplaceable aid of the Royal Navy, the British were able to supply, equip and reward the guerrilla forces, and both keep them in existence and encourage their growth. In return, Wellington was provided with first-class military intelligence and much logistical and interdictive assistance of the first importance.

It was then the inter-action of regular and irregular warfare that posed the French an insoluble politico-military problem. The French could not both contain the guerrillas *and* win the conventional war against Wellington: as a result, they lost both struggles, and the result was cataclysm. Their attempts to terrorise the Spanish and Portuguese populations failed lamentably; only in Catalonia did Suchet's attempt – aided by his able Duchess of Albufera – to gain the 'hearts and minds' of the local population, bear any fruit. Elsewhere, French depredations and severity bred hatred, mounting resistance and ever more brutal atrocities – which in turn led to counter-atrocities and an ever-escalating level of violence. Of course the French found similar problems elsewhere – Hofer's revolt in the Tyrol, the rebellion against their rule in Calabria in southern Italy, the partisans of Davydov in Holy Russia, to mention but three. But nowhere did they come to realise the problems of 'a war without a front' (to cite Napoleon's own words), or to pay more serious penalties, than in Spain and Portugal between 1807 and 1814.

As for Great Britain, it was practically a unique experience to find her army acting in *cooperation* with such fervently nationalistic allies – and Wellington's acquired skills in coordinating the vengeful fury of the 'tip and run' guerrillas with the steadier fighting qualities of his Anglo-Portuguese line regiments, and in directing the overall strategic thrust and purpose of the campaign, were perhaps the most important aspect of all in ensuring that 'the Spanish War' continued to fester and suppurate until French will-power and determination at last gave way.

11

THE RUSSIAN ARMY AT WAR 1807 AND 1812

*S*o *far the essays and articles included in this collection have dealt mainly with western European or Mediterranean subjects. Any consideration of the vast canvas of the Napoleonic Wars would be hopelessly incomplete without consideration of the troops and achievements of 'Holy Russia' – foes of Napoleon as members of the Third and Fourth Coalitions, his allies from Tilsit in July 1807 until at least mid-1811, and then his enemies once more as members of the Sixth and Seventh Coalitions. This takes us through the great drama of the French invasion of Russia in 1812, Napoleon's retreat from Moscow and utter defeat, followed by the liberation of central Europe from French hegemony in 1813, the invasion of France the following year – and reappearance as part of the Allied army of occupation in 1815 after the 'Hundred Days' episode (in which the denizens of distant Muscovy arrived too late to play any form of active military part). Many, many books have been devoted to the immense saga of 1812 since Clausewitz wrote his pages, but its fascination and grim, epic appeal remains ageless.*

The origins of my article on The Russian Army at War *were somewhat unusual, and the events surrounding its first delivery as a lecture in Moscow form something of a cautionary tale which perhaps throws a little light upon the prevalent conditions during one of the bleakest periods of the Cold War (after the Soviet intervention in Czechoslovakia, the crushing of the Prague Spring and the attempted reforms of Mr Dubcek). In 1970 I was sent to Moscow with Dr Christopher Duffy to attend the XIIIth International Historical Congress or, more precisely, the part of it devoted to consider 'Soldiers at War', hosted by the Soviet Commission for Military History under the benign presidency of my good friend (as he became before 1970 was out) Major-General Pavel Jiline, Senior Historian of the Soviet Institute of Military History.*

I had been invited – as president of the recently reformed British Commission for Military History – to present a paper. For its subject, I hit upon an analysis of the views of a British liaison officer, General Wilson, who spent 1806–7 and late 1812–13 attached to the Russian army of Tsar Alexander I. The views of an erstwhile ally, I innocently supposed, would be welcome to our hosts. So I duly prepared my twenty-minute paper (a fuller version would be published in the Acta *appearing after the conference), and sent it off to the Organising Committee three months in advance for translation. The ominous silence that then fell should have warned me that something was amiss – but as an optimistic 'ambassador of Sandhurst' I thought nothing of it, and duly arrived in Moscow on the appointed date to find a decidedly frosty reception.*

When the day came for my paper to be delivered in Moscow University, I was flattered by the larger than usual and indubitably expectant attendance on the 'home team' benches. As most conferences do, the morning ran late, and I was the last speaker before lunch. As I advanced to the podium I was told by General Jiline, presiding at the session, that I could have only fifteen minutes – which was to prove my salvation as it turned out, although at the time it seemed a drastic curtailment.

Somehow I managed to excise passages – most of them direct quotations from Wilson's Journals – as I went along, and squeezed home in the stipulated time; I then returned to my seat high in the semi-circular auditorium to distinctly lukewarm applause from the packed eastern benches. I was soon to discover why. Usually, after a paper had been given, a designated Soviet professor would make a brief speech thanking the speaker for his scholarly effusion. This was not to be the case in my instance. As the perfunctory clapping died, a Soviet professor strode to the vacated podium, and (to my surprise, and the amusement of the 'western' benches) proceeded to denounce, in order, my General Wilson (a '... typical bourgeois imperialist of the early nineteenth century'), myself (an '... obviously decadent Soviet-hater of a modern historian') and Great Britain ('... hotbed of unrestructured imperialist-capitalism'), larding the whole effort with quotations from my (full) paper which had obviously been made available to him for some time in order for him to prepare his diatribe on behalf of the peace-loving Soviet Motherland. As he stopped, perspiration gleaming on his brow, a thunderous burst of applause broke out from the eastern tiers.

When the general excitement settled down, I was on my feet waving a paper. For a while nobody wished to notice such an non-koltorny *foreigner, but suddenly General Jiline (who had been watching me sardonically throughout the incident) dug a nearby colonel in the ribs and sent him up to take my note. In it, I had scrawled three sentences: 'Despite Professor B....'s allegation, I did* not *say so-and-so' (and indeed I hadn't, owing to the curtailment of my communication on his direct order). Receiving my missive, the general read it, looked up at me, smiled – and winked. He then proceeded portentously to the microphone. 'I have, from Professor Chandler, a most important communication to make,' he began. An expectant hush fell over the hall. Was the newly uncovered capitalist perverter of historical science, this Chandler, about to confess his ideological errors?*

I must admit General Jiline did me proud. He expanded on each of my brief denials at some length – and then handsomely conceded that Professor Chandler had not *in fact uttered the passages at issue. Sensing a turning in the wind, poor Professor B.... sat slumped in his seat, a picture of total despair, while all his serried rows of colleagues as one man rose to their feet, turned towards me, and gave me an extended ovation. Phew! It had been '... a near run thing' indeed, but there was no denying who had won on points. Putting on my most modest yet nobly determined and vindicated expression, I swept from the hall – the cheers of Muscovy ringing in my ears – and proceeded by car to the British*

Embassy to take lunch (as had been prearranged) with the cultural attaché. A day or two later I made my peace with Professor B. . . . ., whose own chief had after all effectively thrown him to the wolves, by purchasing a copy of his Life of Kutusov *and asking him to autograph it for me. Anglo-Russian relations promptly improved by one degree centigrade – and I could feel that I had done my small part in the search (in those days) for meaningful* détente.

†

When the poet Fitzgerald wrote: 'How sweet the music of a distant drum', he was clearly not considering the problems of twentieth-century military historians, striving to gain some insight into the lives, experiences and attitudes of military men belonging to earlier generations and distant countries. The more remote the period, the greater grows the difficulty. For, until the present century, the serving soldier has, all too often, proved reluctant – or simply incapable – of recording his impressions of the military life, and this is particularly true of the rank and file. This problem of martial taciturnity takes a further daunting dimension when the British historian turns to consider the soldiers of East European countries, for here, all too often, one meets the language barrier.

If difficulties of identification with the fighting men of distant countries still hamper the modern historian, with all the apparatus of modern research techniques at his disposal, how much harder it must have been for our ancestors to gain even the remotest conception of conditions of service within distant, contemporary armies. During the Napoleonic Wars this was particularly true of the Russian army which must have seemed, in terms of distance and time, to many British subjects of circumscribed outlook virtually to have belonged to another planet. Hence the importance of General Sir Robert Wilson, whose unparalleled acquaintance with Russian forces in 1806–7 and 1812–13 was fortunately matched by an insatiable desire to record and disseminate his firsthand impressions to the more enlightened sections of the British public, and thus performed a valuable service both to his contemporaries and to posterity. His writings also demonstrate the major problems faced by a soldier of one nation when trying to evaluate the performance of soldiers and leaders of another at first-hand. The distracting and often distorting elements of preconceived opinions, of national and political prejudices, or even of the heat of the moment, are often evidenced in Wilson's writings, but they nevertheless form a valuable source of eye-witness opinion by an outsider, despite the modern opinion of Soviet military historians who go to some pains to discredit Wilson, since his views of Field-Marshal Kutusov, in particular, are at variance with the current official line.

In this paper it will be possible only to examine two aspects of Wilson's reporting, namely, his impressions of the Russian fighting man, and his view of certain Russian commanders. His equally interesting accounts of military action, and above all of the terrible French retreat from Moscow, have regretfully had to be omitted.

First, let us consider Wilson's career, character and publications, with a view to establishing his credentials and degree of reliability. Born in 1777, he was first commissioned in 1794. That same year, as a young cavalry cornet, he greatly distinguished himself in Flanders by helping to save the Emperor Francis II of Austria from imminent capture by the French at Villiers-en-Couche (14 April). This exploit in due course brought him several Austrian awards, and earned him the *entrée* into European high society. Five years later he served alongside Russian troops for the first time in the abortive Helder campaign, but of this episode he left no record. The autumn of 1800 found him in Vienna in a minor diplomatic capacity, and next year he served in Egypt. By 1805 he had purchased a cavalry lieutenant-colonelcy before being sent to the Cape of Good Hope. The triumph of the Whig party – with which he had strong affiliations – on the death of William Pitt, brought Wilson back to London, and in late 1806 he was attached to Lord Hutchinson's mission to Prussia. He was soon serving with fair distinction with the Russian army, receiving the Cross of St George for his part at Eylau, and subsequently fighting at both Heilsberg and Friedland. The Tilsit agreements grieved him greatly – 'How false is royalty! How disloyal to itself!' he wrote of Tsar Alexander, but this did not substantially alter his strong Russophile leanings. In *The Dynasts*, Thomas Hardy claims that Wilson hid aboard the raft on the Niemen, disguised as a Cossack; although, in fact, he was at Memel at the time, he did gain a brief glimpse of Napoleon on 9 July at no little personal risk. Several diplomatic journeys followed between St Petersburg and London. His personal popularity with the Tsar enabled him to inflict several snubs on the French ambassador, General Savary, but could do nothing to avert the breakdown of Anglo-Russian relations. He was required to leave Russia in October; but, by furious journey, he forestalled the Russian declaration of war and enabled the British authorities to detain the Russian frigate *Sperknoi* before the official news broke.

Promoted brigadier-general in the Portuguese army in 1808, he formed the Lusitanian Legion, and next year took part in the Talavera campaign. Disagreements with Marshal Beresford ended this episode, and after a lengthy sojourn in London, he eventually secured the appointment of military adviser, with the local rank of brigadier-general, on the staff of Mr Robert Liston, newly appointed ambassador to Constantinople. The circumstances of his transfer to Russia will be noted a little later.

He spent 1813 with the Allied armies in the liberation of Germany, being promoted major-general and taking part in all the major battles, but the enmity of Lord Cathcart, British ambassador to St Petersburg, resulted in his being sent, protesting vigorously, to serve in Italy. His later career can only be hinted at here. In 1816 he was jailed for three months for aiding the escape of Comte Lavallette from a death-cell in Paris. In 1821 he was dismissed from the British army by George IV for championing the unfortunate Queen Caroline, but was later restored by William IV and promoted lieutenant-general. For several years he sat in Parliament as a Whig, but later was promoted full general and governor of Gibraltar. He died in May 1849, ripe in years and experience, survived by thirteen children. As he commented, '... I have seen more of it (the world), been more acquainted with its rulers and ... with every class of society ... than has perhaps fallen to the lot of any other individual'.

As the fluctuations in his fortunes indicate, in character Sir Robert was something of a 'stormy petrel'. In many ways he invites comparison with his naval counterpart, Sir William Sydney Smith, the 'Swedish Knight'. Like Smith, he was vain and outspoken, given to boundless enthusiasms and unauthorised initiatives – characteristics that did not endear him to his British superiors. It is noteworthy that not one of his eight orders of chivalry was bestowed by the country of his birth. Again like Smith, he waged what amounted to a personal vendetta against Napoleon Bonaparte, who once referred to him, revealingly, as 'General Smith'. Yet his *rapport* with both Tsar Alexander I, the Austrian emperor and many other influential European soldiers and statesmen, probably based upon his superb personal courage and dash, gave Wilson a considerable influence over matters pertaining to both the field and cabinet. In sum, to quote Sir George Jackson's opinion, Wilson was 'popular with the army ... though decidedly a little maddish'.

By the standards of his time, Sir Robert was also a prolific author. Ignoring his purely political works of later years, we should mention his substantial *History of the British Expedition to Egypt* (1802), and *The Tender Mercies of Bonaparte in Egypt! Britons Beware!* (1803) which earned him the nickname of 'Jaffa Wilson'. Next year he published *An Enquiry into the present state of the Military Forces of the British Empire* which demanded the abolition of flogging. Then, in 1810, appeared his important *Brief Remarks on the Character and Composition of the Russian Army; and a Sketch of the Campaigns in Poland* ... which proved both popular and influential in forming British opinion. Wilson's equally celebrated *Narrative of Events during the Invasion of Russia ... 1812*, and his *Private Journal ... in the Campaigns of 1812, 1813 and 1814* only appeared posthumously in 1860 and 1862 respectively, being edited by his nephew and son-in-law, the Rev. Herbert Randolph. The last-mentioned work was republished (1969) in an edited form by my friend and colleague the late Antony Brett-James.

On reaching Constantinople in early July, 1812, Wilson soon found a way to be sent on a mission to Russia. News of the French invasion of 21 June reached his ears on 16 July – an indication of how slowly news travelled in those days – and he persuaded Liston to detach him on a mission to Bucharest and St Petersburg designed to bring about an improvement in Russo-Turkish relations. His departure was delayed by the death of the Sultan's only son, although, as Wilson acidly commented, 'as he has four wives already pregnant the loss of Prince Murad is not irreparable'. He eventually received his passports on 26 July.

An execrable journey covering 511 miles in five days brought Sir Robert to Bucharest, where his formal mission to Admiral Tchichagov was a success, if we may judge from Liston's 'high satisfaction' communicated in a letter of 13 August. Wilson then pressed on for a meeting with the Tsar, and after a hard and eventful journey he reached Smolensk in time to share in the celebrated battle of 17–19 August. As the Russian army resumed its retreat, Wilson headed for St Petersburg, and thus was not present at Borodino or the evacuation of Moscow. At court he soon gained an audience, but made no further progress in his Russo-Turkish mediation. Indeed, he was soon in trouble. Lord Castlereagh in London was infuriated to learn of Wilson's largely unauthorised initiatives, and instructed the British ambassador, Lord Cathcart, to have Wilson's competence restricted to military matters only. This message was passed, with relish, on 12 September; but, nothing daunted, Sir Robert set off five days later to serve as British Military Commissioner at Kutusov's headquarters. In this capacity, he would take part in many staff intrigues as well as the battles of Vinkovo, Malo-Jaroslavetz, Viasma and Krasnoe alongside his Russian comrades-in-arms, despite the frequent protests and remonstrations of the super-critical Cathcart who distrusted and disliked Wilson from first to last.

Whatever his defects as a diplomat, and however over-optimistic were his views of certain events, Sir Robert Wilson was an acute observer of military affairs in general, both in 1807 and 1812. 'I never saw a more martial army,' he had written shortly before the battle of Eylau. 'Their discipline is good. Their marching is regular, and, considering what they have gone through, their appearance is admirable... How lamentable, then, that such formidable means should be committed to the direction of those who are altogether unequal to the trust....' This observation gives the key to Wilson's view of the Russian army throughout the period: he fervently admired the men, but seriously criticised the senior leadership, whether it was by Bennigsen (1807) or Barclay de Tolly and Kutusov in 1812 – as we shall note a little later.

He enlarged on the characteristics of Russian officers and soldiery in his *Brief Remarks* ... of 1810. 'The infantry is generally composed of athletic men between the ages of 18 and 40, endowed with great bodily strength but generally of short stature ... (They are) inured to the extremes of weather and hardship; to the worst and scantiest food; to marches for days and nights of four hours repose and six hours progress ... ferocious but disciplined, obstinately brave, possessing all the energetic characteristics of a barbarian people, with the advantages engrafted by civilisation.'

Wilson's view of the Russian officer is also revealing:

The Russian soldier in general is extremely subordinate, and attached to his officer who treats him with peculiar kindness, and not as a machine, but as a reasonable being whose attachment he ought to win, although he has authority to command his service. Punishment is not so frequent as in other armies, nor is it very severe. . . .

   The Russian officer, although frequently making the greatest physical exertions, is, however, inclined to indolent habits when not on actual duty; loves his sleep after food, and dislikes to walk or ride far. This is one of the defects of education. At Petersburg or Moscow no person of rank moves on foot, and a journey of fifty miles on horseback would be an expedition for the city's talk. The Emperor met one morning at Petersburg an English officer (Wilson himself), and stopped his *padroskin*. 'Where is your carriage?' 'Sire, I am walking about to look at your capital.' 'Ah!' said his Majesty. 'I would give a great deal if my officers would imitate such an example, and appreciate justly the great value and utility of that custom which I hear so much prevails in your country!'

Wilson also approved of the Russian artillery and cavalry – and above all of the Cossacks. 'No troops can and do defend ground in retreat better than the Russians,' he wrote in reminiscence of 1812. 'Their artillery is so well horsed, so nimbly and so handily worked, that it bowls over almost all irregularities of surface with ease, lightness and velocity that give it great superiority. The vivacity of the cavalry, and the unquailing steadiness of their infantry, make it a pleasure to command them even in extremist difficulties; for, like the British soldier, the most unbounded confidence may be reposed, to use a sailor's expression, "in their answer to the helm" . . .'

Wilson had already described the Cossack in his *Brief Remarks* of 1810. 'Mounted on a very little, ill-conditioned, but well-bred horse, which can walk at the rate of five miles an hour with ease, or, in his speed, dispute the race with the swiftest – with a short whip on his wrist (as he wears no spur) – armed with a lance, a pistol in his girdle, and a sword, he never fears a competitor in single combat; [Cossacks] ... attack in dispersion, and when they do reunite to charge, it is not with a systematic formation but *en masse* . . . the swarm attack.'

Their reputation was formidable in 1812. Captain Roeder of the Hessian Lifeguards, for instance, recalled in his diary for 17 August how 'everything was thrown into ridiculous uproar (at Vitebsk) because a few Cossacks had been sighted'. The entire French garrison ran to arms and rode out, to discover only a few dozen opponents, 'dodging about hither and thither'. 'In this way,' he glumly prophesied, 'they will be able to bring the whole garrison to hospital in about 14 days. . . .'

Cossack courage and stoic endurance of pain were legendary. 'The day before yesterday,' Wilson noted in his *Journal* for 8 October 1812, 'I saw a Cossack have his arm extracted from the shoulder-joint, who had ridden 20 miles after being struck by a cannon shot. He never spoke during the operation . . . but he talked afterwards quite composedly. The next morning he drank tea, walked about his room, and then got in a cart, which carried him 14 miles. He is now proceeding several hundred miles to the Don, and is, according to the last report, doing very well.' If General Wilson is to be credited, it would seem that the Russian soldier of the early nineteenth century was a pretty hardy representative of the military profession.

It is Wilson's view of the Russian generals that lends a particular interest to much of his writing. Some he admired, others he criticised loudly. In August 1812, he soon noted the general distrust felt for Count Barclay de Tolly, a Livonian by birth, Minister of War and senior commander in the field during the long retreat from Vilna to Smolensk. 'General Barclay as Commander-in-Chief has totally lost all confidence,' Wilson reported to Lord Cathcart. 'It is therefore a duty . . . to state that I consider General Barclay as terrorised . . . by the reputation of his enemy. That I am certain he is not making a War of Manoeuvres upon any fixed or prearranged system, but a war of marches without sufficient arrangement and method to avoid serious misfortune if the enemy should press with more energy. . . . In the moment of battle I have seen him brave, active and capable, but these qualities alone are not sufficient, especially for the command of a Russian Army. His troops want (lack) general direction . . . I should hope that a sense of this necessity and of his inability to acquire the confidence of his army will induce the General to resign. . . .'

Yet Wilson admired Barclay's courage in action, as when he led a charge by the Russian staff crying 'Victory or Death! We must preserve this post or perish!' to extricate the rearguard at Lubino. He also had nothing but praise for his administrative ability, recording in May 1813 that 'the Russian Army is much strengthened and greatly improved by Barclay's regulations'. But in August the previous year Wilson welcomed Barclay's replacement by Kutusov – although he was very shortly to discover that the Russians, in the metaphor of Aesop's fable, had only replaced 'King Log' by 'King Stork', at least in Wilson's highly biased opinion.

Robert Wilson's view of Prince Mikhail Hilarionovich Golenischev-Kutusov deteriorated from admiration to detestation as the war progressed. The great Russian commander tried to enlist Wilson's support. At their first meeting he perciptiently informed him '*Vous êtes un galant homme – et Anglais*', and pressed him to: 'Lose no time to return; I have great need of such a comrade as yourself in the cabinet and in the field'. Although susceptible to flattery, Wilson was soon disillusioned, but he fairly recorded Kutusov's earlier services, describing him as 'shrewd as a Greek, naturally intelligent as an Asiatic and well instructed as a European ... more disposed to trust to diplomacy for his success than to martial prowess, for which by his age and ... constitution he was no longer qualified'. It is instructive to compare this (shortened) description with the opinions of Carl von Clausewitz and Comte Philippe de Ségur. 'Kutusov,' opined the Prussian, 'no longer possessed either the activity of mind or body which one sometimes finds in soldiers of his age. However, he knew the Russians and how to handle them... he could flatter the self-esteem of both populace and army, and sought by proclamation and religious observances to work on the public mind.' The Frenchman went further: Kutusov's 'valour was incontestable, but he was charged with regulating its vehemence according to his private interests; for he calculated everything. His genius was slowly vindictive and above all crafty – the true Tartar character – knowing the art of preparing an implacable war with a fawning, supple and patient policy.' Such, then, were three contemporary impressions of the septuagenarian, corpulent, one-eyed mastermind of the Russian forces. It is highly probable that Wilson, blinded by his personal lust for determinant military action, never fully understood Kutusov's devious character, and therefore tended to underestimate his intentions and grasp of other strategic realities during the French retreat.

His mission to St Petersburg completed, Wilson rejoined the Russian army near Kaluga on 27 September. He at once became the mouthpiece of those members of the Russian staff who bitterly resisted all attempts by the French to open private discussions with Kutusov. Some talks were held with General Lauriston, but nothing came of them, and Wilson played no small part in thwarting several further initiatives by would-be emissaries. He was delighted when action flared again at Vinkovo (17 October), and at the subsequent battle of Malo-Jaroslavetz (23/24 October) claimed in person 'the honour to open the ball and plant the first guns that saved the town'. From that same occasion dated his full disillusion with Kutusov. 'The Russians,' he wrote, 'accuse *one person* of being deficient in example ... Marshal Kutusov affords a memorable instance of incapacity in a chief, of an absence of any quality that ought to distinguish a commander. Although within five *versts* of the action from daybreak, he never had the curiosity to appear until five in the evening...'

As the French, repulsed from the Kaluga route towards Smolensk, reverted to their original invasion route via Borodino, Wilson's criticisms of Kutusov became increasingly bitter. In Wilson's view, the commander-in-chief was deliberately avoiding closing with the French. By 30 October he was declaring that Kutusov's 'feebleness outrages me to such a degree that I have declared, if he remains Commander-in-Chief, that I must retire from the army'. A week later he asserted that 'the misconduct of the Marshal makes me quite wild.... Our marches were studiously made to avoid the enemy.' Sir Robert never appreciated the finer points of the Russian strategy designed to trap Napoleon at the Beresina river line, but attributed the most devious of intentions to his allies. 'I am by no means sure', he makes Kutusov assert in his *Narrative*, 'that the total destruction of the Emperor Napoleon and his army would be such a benefit to the world: his succession would not fall to Russia or any other continental power, but to that which already commands the seas, whose domination would then be intolerable'. This was going too far, even for Wilson. Kutusov's age may have reduced his dynamism, but his Fabian strategy ultimately paid a large dividend. Although the Beresina trap failed, the French forces would soon be driven to the point of ultimate moral and physical collapse by the combined effects of 'General Winter' and the Russian and Polish partisans and peasantry.

Wilson, however, continued to castigate the Russian chief. He championed Bennigsen against Kutusov – but this row only resulted in the second-in-command being dismissed from the staff. As Lord Cathcart wrote to Castlereagh on 16 January 1813, 'Sir R. Wilson was very imprudent on the subject of the commander-in-chief, and too openly took part with the second-in-command. Unfortunately opening letters is not confined to one office, and Prince Kutusov's family and friends and many others deeply resent Sir R. Wilson's interference...' In his frustration, Wilson rode with the Advance Guard and hurled himself into action whenever possible, returning to his written offensive each night. 'Wilson is in the hottest part of every action...' reported F.P. Werry to the Foreign Office. 'He gets into *mêlées*, scours the country; and at night, I verily believe, never sleeps, for he writes folios of dispatches.... He is an astonishing fellow. The parties, jealousies and intrigues in the army are too numerous for him to escape their vortices; he reconciles the Russian generals but gets himself into hot water.'

On the other hand, Wilson had great and lasting admiration for other Russian generals. General Prince Peter Ivanovich Bagration, commander of the Second Army of the West until his mortal wound at Borodino, 'was beloved by everyone and admired by all who witnessed his exploits. No officer ever excelled him in the direction of an advance or rear guard; nor had any officer's capacity in these commands ever been more severely tested'. For Matvei Ivanovich Platov, Hetman of the Don Cossacks, Wilson's regard verged on the idolatrous; he ever dreamed of forming an Anglo-Cossack cavalry division under his command, but nothing came of it. Regarding Admiral Pavel Vasilievich Tchichagov, the commander Napoleon outwitted at the Beresina, Wilson's early impressions were somewhat guarded – 'a commander not selected for his military experience or talents', he commented on 9 July 1812 – but before the year was out he was describing Tchichagov's harrying of the French survivors towards Vilna as 'a lesson to us of energy'.

At this point we must leave the peppery, energetic Sir Robert Wilson. The strident tone of his criticisms of Russian inaction must in large part be attributed to his flaming desire to destroy the French by the most immediate and direct means possible; he was a veritable firebrand, as both his own pages and the recorded impressions of others reveal. There is no time here, however, to describe his many adventures, nor even his accounts of the harrowing scenes that took place behind the retreating French army. On a different level, he also has much to say on the subjects of Russian country roads, the price of food, and peasant customs. For all his faults and inaccuracies, Wilson was without a doubt in a unique position to record his impressions of the Russian campaign of 1812, for the friendship of the Tsar and the greater number of his generals and officers opened all doors and not a few hearts to the fiery and impatient British Commissioner. If he often proved incapable of overcoming his strong personal inclinations and prejudices in his attempts to assess the leading soldiers of another major power, we should in no way impute base motives to his strident and outspoken criticisms. His basic honesty and integrity are above question. His writings, therefore, remain a major source, and probably the most important British source, for the events of these dramatic months. Every page reveals Sir Robert's genuine attachment to Russia and its peoples. 'Every hour endears Russia more and more to me', he wrote. His lasting achievement was to present his British contemporaries and posterity with a striking picture of life in the headquarters and camps of the Russian army during those great days of early nineteenth-century history which saw the turning of the tide against a common enemy.

12

BORODINO
1812

*T*he battle of Borodino, one way and another, has figured several times in my professional life. When I helped found the Sandhurst War Games Society in the late
1960s, it was Borodino that I chose for my first set-piece battle game. In August 1970,
after the contest-of-wills at Moscow University over General Wilson, the Soviet authorities fell over themselves to arrange a car to take Dr Duffy and myself – properly escorted
by Lilia, our special Intourist guide and escort – to visit the battlefield and its museum
seventy miles west of Moscow. An interesting battlefield tour was the result. In 1912 the
Tsarist regime had made every effort to commemorate the centennial of the battle – raising
many individual monuments – and as a result it resembles Gettysburg more than any
other battlefield I know. One is surprised – even shocked – at the relative compactness of
the site, the scene of the worst effusion of blood in the nineteenth century. Between dawn
and dusk that day in 1812, an area of some eight square miles saw some 70,000
fatalities, both sides included. It was the equivalent – as Dr Gwynn Dyer was the first to
mention in a Canadian documentary in 1984 – to a jumbo-jet load of passengers
crashing every five minutes for eight hours with no survivors: a thought that gives one
reason to pause awhile.

Many of the key features have been preserved or restored: the rebuilt Borodino church,
the three flêches in the centre, the site of the Russian Great Battery, the knoll of Utitsa
and the rest. A 360-degree panoramic painting was moved to the western outskirts of
Moscow in the 1960s after a mad moujik had attacked it with an axe, and next to its
new location stands a replica of the hut at Gorki where Kutusov held his fateful council-
of-war after the battle – the subject of one of Versachigin's best-known paintings. The
area certainly repays a visit.

Hardly had we returned to England than Dr Duffy and I found ourselves invited –
together with the late Antony Brett-James – to serve as a troika of military historical
advisers to the BBC for the making of the twenty-episode television series devoted to the
great Tolstoy's War and Peace. There followed one of the most interesting years of my
life. We split the tasks between us, and covered for one another at Sandhurst when a spell
of work on location came up for us in turn. My special tasks included travelling to Rome
with Charles Knode, the costume designer to the series, to select possible uniforms from the

1970 epic Sergei Bondarchuk film, Waterloo, *and then two weeks of winter-filming of the retreat from Moscow sequences at Novi Sad in Yugoslavia – aided by a couple of thousand Serbian soldiers of the local equivalent to the Territorial Army. The producer, David Conroy, and director, John Davies, had many a cross to bear – not least the refusal of snow to fall (for the first time in two decades) because it was so bitterly cold. In the end two acres of artificial snow had to be laid at great expense, and the 'large scenes' moved up into the mountains where deep fogs helped conceal the inaccurate terrain and the relative paucity of our military resources. Back in London many visits to help advise on studio shots followed – and then the excitement of watching the series in late 1971. It was not quite so splendid as Bondarchuk's earlier film version, but it was the BBC's first major epic shot in colour – and the result was first rate. Indeed, the video-film rates amongst the top dozen BBC productions for sales to foreign countries – and it is high time it was shown again, there having been only one reshowing (in 1975). There are interesting side-lines to being a military historian.*

✝

Borodino stands on the banks of the River Kalatsha near its confluence with the Moskva, some seventy-five miles west of Moscow. On 7 September 1812 it was the scene of one of the goriest major engagements of the Napoleonic Wars. The combatants were the Emperor Napoleon at the head of the 135,000-strong Grand Army of Russia, and General Prince Golenischev-Kutusov commanding the combined armies of the West which totalled some 120,000 men.

Franco-Russian relations had been steadily deteriorating for five years before war broke out in June 1812. Many contemporary observers had regarded the famous Tilsit meetings of 1807 – when Emperor and Tsar had met on a raft moored in the River Niemen to settle their differences – as the inauguration of a lengthy period of amicable cooperation between the two autocrats. The *entente*, however, had proved more apparent than real; from the first, fundamental clashes of interest remained unresolved, and these were soon the subject of bitter diplomatic exchanges.

From Tsar Alexander I's point of view, there were three particular bones of contention. In the first place, his agreement to join the Continental System (Napoleon's attempt to close all European ports to British trade) offended many powerful court interests at St Petersburg; although eventually the Tsar was persuaded to turn a blind eye to evasions of the regulations prohibiting trade with Britain. Secondly, the Russians disliked the presence of French forces east of the Oder; Napoleon seemed to be interfering in Russia's front-yard. And thirdly, they resented the Emperor's determination to restrict Russian expansion in the Balkan region at the expense of Turkey.

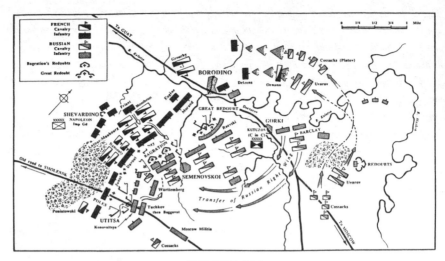

BORODINO, 1812

Of course, Napoleon had his grievances against Russia as well. He could not tolerate the barefaced flouting of his Continental System; if the dyke were once breached, the flood would sweep in, and every French ally and coerced satellite would hasten to evade the hated sanctions. Furthermore, the French resented Russian intrigues in Poland. Napoleon could never tolerate either a backslider or a rival, and by 1811 Tsar Alexander appeared to be both. Soon, charges of warlike intentions were being exchanged, and by 1811 France was openly preparing for a final struggle in eastern Europe. Alexander had also begun his defensive preparations as early as 1810. The outbreak of war did not, therefore, come as a great surprise to those in the know, and few predicted anything but a quick French triumph. The more discerning, however, foresaw a herculean struggle; if the massing of over 500,000 French and allied troops in East Prussia and Poland did not bring Alexander to accept Napoleon's demands, it was possible to forecast a long war.

The war between France and Russia was ten weeks old before the climax of Borodino, when Napoleon's repeated efforts to force a decisive battle on his adversaries at last bore fruit. Kutusov's predecessor in command, Baron Barclay de Tolly, had conducted a strategy of evasion, trading space for time, drawing the French almost 500 miles into the depths of western Russia, the Russians deliberately ravaging the territory they abandoned. How far this policy was dictated by circumstances as opposed to deliberate choice is still in some doubt.

True, Tsar Alexander I had informed the French ambassador shortly before the outbreak of hostilities that Napoleon would have to go 'to the ends of the earth' if he desired victory, and equally certainly the Russian strategists had planned to fall back as far as the fortified river lines of the Dvina and Dnieper before making their main stand in 'the River Gap' to the west of Smolensk, but it is unlikely that they envisaged a further withdrawal of some 160 miles to a position so close to Moscow.

When the French forces crossed the Niemen on 22 June 1812, there was no idea in Napoleon's mind of going so far in search of his victory. Napoleon's concept of war was based upon forcing his opponent into major action at the earliest possible moment. As it had turned out, the two Russian generals, Barclay and Bagration, had proved adept at side-stepping the clumsy French lunges, and had eventually reunited their armies near Smolensk, thus thwarting Napoleon's plan of annihilating them in turn. This was not wholly due to Russian military skill. The Grand Army of 1812 was a huge, unwieldy, multinational force, hindered by unaccustomed reliance on slow-moving convoys for its supplies. So large an army could not live off the land in the bleak plains of western Russia. The 460,000 men of the three armies and two semi-independent corps that constituted its first-line strength (a further 200,000 reserves were echeloned all the way back to the River Oder) comprised over a dozen nationalities, and only slightly over half the total were Frenchmen. Even of these a high proportion were raw conscripts, experiencing their first taste of war, for large numbers of veterans were tied down 2000 miles away fighting the British army under Wellington and the guerrillas in Spain.

On top of the problems posed by unwilling allies, different languages and equipment, inadequate supply arrangements, and raw troops, was superimposed that of control. It was one thing for Napoleon personally to command armies of some 250,000 men in the campaigns of Austerlitz and Jena; it was quite another to try to do the same with an army of more than twice the size in Russia. It was not only a question of poor roads delaying the transmission of orders and reports by mounted messengers over ever-growing distances, but also of the unwillingness of outlying commanders to take the smallest decision without prior reference to the *Grand-Quartier-Général*.

Furthermore, subscribing to his innate Corsican tendency to rely only on the clan, Napoleon had chosen to appoint his senior commanders from his immediate family, regardless of their military calibre. His brother-in-law Joachim Murat, King of Naples, was certainly the best man to command the cavalry, but to hand the 2nd Support Army to Napoleon's brother, Jérôme, King of Westphalia, was to court disaster (although fortunately Jérôme left the army in a huff on 17 July after amply demonstrating his inadequacies in the first major manoeuvre of the campaign). The 1st Support Army was entrusted to the Emperor's stepson, Eugène Beauharnais, Viceroy of Italy, who, despite gloomy predictions, proved a commander of fair ability. But even Napoleon's genius could not manage to weld the different components of his army into an effective whole.

As a result of these difficulties, three successive major offensives had failed to trap the Russians into battle. It is true that there had been a tough three-day engagement at Smolensk (17–19 August) against the recently reunited Russian armies, but even the fact that the two Russian commanders, Barclay and Bagration, were on the worst of personal terms had not enabled the French to achieve a decisive result. After Smolensk, Napoleon had taken the momentous decision to press on towards Moscow rather than halt until the following spring, and one result of this had been to diminish alarmingly his fighting strength. The ever-lengthening flanks of his arrow-head advance into Russia and ever-extending lines of communication needed many troops to guard them, while the toll of death and sickness caused by the heat of the Russian summer had reduced the numbers of both horses and men still more. 'Between Kovno and Vidzeme,' noted Captain Roeder of the Hessian Life Guards, following in the wake of the invasion, 'we found a good 2000 horses lying by the roadside . . . and even more rotting human corpses.' Napoleon, therefore, was able to field rather less than a third of his original front-line strength at Borodino, and many of his men were sick, exhausted and half-starved by the endless succession of marches which had far out-distanced the cumbersome supply convoys.

Almost at the same time as Napoleon was reaching his critical decision to advance beyond Smolensk, Tsar Alexander and his advisers at St Petersburg were reconsidering the war situation. To date, the Tsar had shown the greatest confidence in his Minister of War and senior field commander, Barclay de Tolly, who, since 1807, had performed miracles in reconstructing the Russian army along French lines. The continuous tale of retreat and surrendered territory, however, was having an adverse effect on both civilian and military morale, and the 'Little Father' was aware that he could not afford many further setbacks. Consequently he heeded the mounting clamour against Barclay de Tolly, and decided to replace him in the senior command with Mikhail Golenischev-Kutusov. This corpulent, one-eyed, native-born veteran, sixty-seven years old, was beloved and trusted by the rank and file in a way the Livonian-born Barclay could never be. Half a century of campaigning in Europe and the Balkans had made Kutusov a cunning and tenacious commander, who, in the words of the military scientist Clausewitz, 'knew the Russians, and how to handle them'. Charged by his master with the specific task of fighting in defence of Moscow, he assumed command on 29 August, and at once set about selecting a favourable battle position.

Very soon, the new commander-in-chief's single eye lighted upon the countryside in the vicinity of Borodino. Here his army would turn and fight the foreign invader. With great psychological skill the general began to play upon the simple superstitious souls of the peasant-soldiers under his command. Religious and patriotic fervour were brought to a climax the day before the battle, when the sacred icon known as 'the Black Virgin of Smolensk' was paraded through the kneeling ranks. Thereafter, the Russian soldiers redoubled their preparations for the morrow, chanting, Philippe de Ségur tells us, ''Tis the Will of God!'

The chosen battle area lay between and around the two post-roads, the old and the new, that linked Moscow and Smolensk. The countryside was undulating, broken by numbers of ravines and small streams with steep banks, and contained several villages and woods. The Russian right lay along the east bank of the Kalatsha (a narrow river fordable at most places, but difficult to approach) from its confluence with the River Moskva, to Borodino, which stands on the west bank near the bridge bearing the new post-road. The whole of this sector Kutusov entrusted to Barclay's I Army, three infantry corps (II, IV, and VI) with as many formations of cavalry in rear. Borodino itself constituted at once the hinge and the advanced position of the Russian forces, and was given a garrison of Chasseurs of the Russian Imperial Guard. The Russian left started from the Great Redoubt, a massive earthwork containing twenty heavy guns overlooking Borodino from the east across the river, ran on over the broken plain to the ruined village of Semionovskaya (where several more earthworks, known as *flèches*, had been constructed), and from there through forested country to the village of Utitsa, through which ran the old post-road.

A knoll to the east of the hamlet formed the limit of the Russian line. This two-mile sector was held by Bagration's II Army, three infantry corps (the III, VII, and VIII) and one of the cavalry. Kutusov placed the Grand Duke Constantine's V (Guards) Corps in central reserve on a second ridge near Psarevo, and set up his headquarters near Gorki. To give early warning of the French approach, Prince Gorchakov was sent with an infantry division to hold a redoubt near the outlying village of Schivardino, about a mile west of Semionovskaya. From these dispositions it would appear that the Russian commander anticipated a French attempt to turn his right flank rather than his left, hence his decision to hold the lower reaches of the Kalatsha. Altogether, Kutusov disposed of 17,000 regular cavalry, 7000 Cossacks, 72,000 infantry, and 10,000 Moscow Militia, together with 640 cannon (14,500 gunners), along an initial front of five miles.

The French approached the area in three columns during the morning of 5 September. The evening of the 5th saw a stiff action before Gorchakov relinquished control of the outlying Schivardino position, and fell back to the main Russian line. By midday on the 6th the bulk of the French Imperial Guard, I and III Corps (Davout and Ney), Junot's VIII Corps and Murat's cavalry were camping near the village, with Eugène's IV Corps and Poniatowski's V Corps protecting the left and right flanks respectively. All in all Napoleon enjoyed an advantage of perhaps 15,000 men, but he was lighter in artillery (587 guns), and many of his men and horses were out of condition.

Barely a mile separated the two armies during the 6th, but the day passed in a state of unreal calm as Napoleon reconnoitred Kutusov's positions and the Russians put the finishing touches to their earthworks. The Emperor rejected the suggestion of Marshal Davout that he should be sent overnight with 40,000 men to turn the extreme left of the Russian line beyond Utitsa. 'Ah, you are always for turning the enemy,' the Emperor remarked. 'It is too dangerous a manoeuvre.' He did not consider his numerical superiority sufficiently great to justify so large a detachment, he was aware that his cavalry was exhausted, and he was continually haunted by the fear that the Russians might slip away yet again under cover of darkness, along the new post-road, if they gained even a hint of a French movement to the south. Similarly, he ruled out any attack against the Russian right; the Kalatsha was too difficult. Instead he decided that the battle should turn round a frontal attack against the Great Redoubt and Semionovskaya by Davout and Ney, with a preliminary attack against Borodino by Eugène's command early in the morning. Poniatowski, on the right, would capture Utitsa and attempt to tactically outflank the Russian left. The Guard and much of the cavalry, together with Junot's VIII Corps and one division of the I, would constitute the reserve. The battle would open with a heavy bombardment by 120 massed guns.

His orders given, Napoleon returned to his quarters to rest. He was suffering from a heavy cold and an old bladder complaint. Nor was the Emperor unduly cheered by the recent news of Wellington's victory at Salamanca in Spain. On the other hand, the simultaneous arrival of a new portrait of his son, the infant King of Rome, helped rally his spirits before he retired to rest. All through the night, however, he was constantly rising from his camp-bed to reassure himself that the Russians were still in position. Only at 2 am did he feel sufficiently confident of this to issue the prepared bulletin to his troops, who were spending a miserable night huddled around inadequate campfires in a vain attempt to combat the pervading drizzle. 'Soldiers!' the bulletin ran, 'Here is the battle you have so long desired. Henceforward victory depends on you ... Conduct yourselves as you did at Austerlitz, Friedland, Vitebsk, and Smolensk, so that posterity will for ever acclaim with pride your conduct on this day; let them say of each one of you: "He took part in the great battle beneath the walls of Moscow."'

The 7th dawned finer, the sun being visible through the mist. Several hours earlier the troops had taken up their appointed battle-stations, and, after a delay occasioned by the need to resite the main battery, which had been drawn up too far back, the initial bombardment opened at 6 am.

As usual, the French were determined to seize the initiative and attack. In most respects the standard tactical sequence of a dozen major Napoleonic battles was repeated at Borodino. The heavy bombardment was designed to shake enemy morale and inflict as much damage as possible on his most exposed formations. Under cover of the firing, swarms of *tirailleurs* (light infantry) would advance in open order to within musketry range, and add a disconcerting 'nuisance' value by sniping at officers and gunners. Once this preparatory phase was thought to be accomplished, a series of heavy cavalry and infantry attacks would be launched. The secret of these was careful timing and coordination. As the light infantry drew aside, the massed squadrons of cuirassiers, lancers and dragoons would thunder past to defeat the enemy cavalry and then, if all was going well, proceed to attack the infantry lines beyond. These charges were designed to force the regiments to 'form square' rather than to achieve an immediate breakthrough. Although infantry squares were rarely broken by cavalry attack, provided the troops remained cool and steady, they presented good targets for the batteries of French horse artillery which accompanied the cavalry and proceeded to unlimber and go into devastating action at point-blank range. All this activity was designed to facilitate the main attack, entrusted to the hurrying columns of French infantry. These formations were originally based on a two-company frontage, say fifty men, with three double-companies in support, making a depth of twelve ranks, but by 1812 more massive formations had been substituted as the quality and reliability of the French and allied infantry decreased, the commanders relying on sheer weight and the bayonet to see them through to success.

If the infantry attack was properly timed, the columns and their supporting battalions drawn up in line to provide close fire support would be near to the enemy lines before the French cavalry drew off to re-form. Ideally, the French columns would, therefore, catch the rival infantry still in square – a formation that obviously greatly reduced the amount of fire-power that could be deployed against the new menace. By this time, the excitement and enthusiasm of the columns would have become intense, and after a few scattered volleys they would hurl themselves upon their weary opponents and as often as not rout them. This was the moment for the reserves to move up to exploit the break-in – fresh columns and horse-artillery batteries forming and widening the walls of the corridor being driven into the enemy line of battle. Into and through this would come the French light cavalry – hussars, chasseurs and more dragoons – their sabres ceaselessly rising and falling as they fell upon the last knots of enemy troops still offering resistance, their effect being to convert the enemy's setback into a full-scale rout. Such was the typical tactical battle of a French army corps – those highly adaptable all-arm formations that constituted one major reason for Napoleon's greatest battle successes. A whole series of such major formations would be operating along these lines on different sectors of the field – with variations according to Napoleon's grand tactical plan and of course the nature of the local terrain. Such relentless pressure had brought victory to the French Eagles on many important battlefields since 1800; but at Borodino the story was to prove somewhat different.

At first all seemed to be going well for the French. Eugène reported that he had taken possession of Borodino village on the left, Davout was making ground in the centre, and Poniatowski made himself master of Utitsa on the French right. By 7 am, however, a premature attempt by part of IV Corps to push over the Kalatsha River towards the Great Redoubt had been defeated with heavy loss, while on the opposite flank V Corps became pinned down by Russian marksmen tenaciously holding the neighbouring woodland. Eugène reacted on the left by deploying two-thirds of his corps over the Kalatsha, ready to renew the assault on the key to the Russian position. This move did not go unnoticed by Kutusov, who, realising that there was now little likelihood of a major French onslaught over the lower reaches of the Kalatsha, began to draw off formations from this wing and sent them to reinforce the sectors of his centre and left, which were under heavy attack.

The struggle for the *flèches* before Semionovskaya rose to a new intensity as both sides sent in fresh formations. Ney and Friant joined Davout in a renewed attack about 8 am – but Baggavout's Corps arrived simultaneously on the other side to reinforce Raevski and Borozdin, defending the sector. The fortunes of the battle swung this way and that, but the Russians held on to their positions while the French sustained many casualties, including Davout. General Rapp, Napoleon's favourite aide, received his twenty-second wound.

'So it's your turn again. How are things?' inquired Napoleon of Rapp at the dressing-station.

'Sire,' replied Rapp, 'I think you will be forced to send in your Guard.'

'I shall take care not to. I do not want it destroyed. I am certain to win the battle without the Guard becoming involved.'

This sentiment was to be repeated at various times throughout the battle.

Soon, Junot's VIII Corps and part of the cavalry had also been committed to the fighting. For a brief period Eugène's Corps was in possession of the Great Redoubt, but the Russians spared no effort to retake so important a position, the key to their line.

Lieutenant Louis Planat de la Faye described this period as follows: 'The struggle which developed was one of the most murderous I have ever seen... The cannonballs and shells rained down like hail, and the smoke was so thick that only at rare intervals could one make out the enemy masses. The Westphalian Corps [Junot's VIII] was massed in close columns behind the Redoubt and now and then was a target for shells which sent shakos and bayonets flying. Each time one of these shots landed, the poor soldiers fell flat on their faces. Not all of them stood up again.'

This bombardment coincided with the bloody repulse of General Morand's

Division from the Great Redoubt, and soon after, Poniatowski also had to give ground beyond Utitsa. To check this, Napoleon was forced to send forward Friant's Division from reserve. So far the French flanking forces had precious little to show for their efforts; the attritional nature of the battle was clearly established, and almost all Napoleon's reserves — save the Guard — had been sent into action.

Meanwhile, at 10 am, a renewed attack on Semionovskaya by three French corps had begun to make a little ground at the cost of appalling casualties. Three hundred Russian guns opened up against their opponents. 'A formidable array of guns spate forth death,' recalled General Armand de Caulaincourt, Napoleon's Master of the Horse. 'The Great Redoubt belched out a veritable hell on our centre.' Marshal Ney received four wounds at this period, but the Russians suffered a grievous loss when General Bagration was mortally wounded. News of this so dispirited the Russian infantry that they at last gave ground from the *flèches*, and a jubilant Murat hurled his cavalry after them, hoping to turn their retreat into a rout. But once they had reached the Psarevo plateau the Russian *moujiks* turned round, and refused to move back another step.

Nevertheless, it seemed as if the battle was on the point of being won, if only Napoleon would send up the Guard. Repeated appeals for him to do so met with an unwavering response. Earlier years would have found Napoleon close behind the front, inspiring, assessing and giving orders, but at Borodino he remained in the rear near the Schivardino redoubt, listless, ill, querulous, and doubtful of the accuracy of every report brought to him.

By midday, the Russian line had been forced to give ground in the centre. But Kutusov and his generals were afforded time to reinforce their centre yet again with Tolstoy's fresh IV Corps from the disengaged right. The Russians were also in a position to mount a telling diversionary attack. Noting how weakly Eugène had occupied Borodino itself, Kutusov ordered Generals Platov and Uvarov to take the former's 7000 Cossacks and the latter's 5000 cavalry over the Kalatsha and attack the town. This move took the French and Italians completely by surprise, and they were soon contained within the town, sending urgent appeals for aid to Eugène and the Emperor.

Receipt of this disturbing intelligence forced the Emperor to postpone a new all-out attack on the Great Redoubt, while Eugène recrossed the river with Grouchy's cavalry to drive off the newcomers. This done, at about 2 pm the postponed attack went in. While 200 French guns blasted the Redoubt, Eugène's three tiring divisions attacked from the front, and the 2nd Cavalry Corps, commanded by Auguste de Caulaincourt (the Master of the Horse's brother, who had succeeded General Montbrun), prepared to attack the position from the rear. Once again all hell was let loose as the French advanced to the attack in their dense columns, but so preoccupied did the Russian defenders (drawn from part of Raevski's Corps) become with the frontal attack that the French cavalry was able to make a surprise entry into the Redoubt from the rear, led by General Caulaincourt at the head of the 5th Cuirassiers. Although the general was shot down almost at once, this attack proved successful. The four Russian regiments within died to a man, and by 3 am the Great Redoubt was finally in French hands.

This time the French held their ground. The Russian line began grudgingly to recoil. Eugène tried to organise a pursuit with every available horseman, but General Barclay de Tolly with careful timing flung in his remaining cavalry and checked the French some 500 yards beyond the Redoubt. Now it was the Viceroy's turn to implore Napoleon to release the Guard – but he met with no more success than his predecessors. 'I will not demolish my Guard. I am 800 leagues from France and I will not risk my last reserve.' As a result the Russian cavalry was able to cover the ordered withdrawal of their infantry.

Kutusov was not yet ready to admit defeat. Doctorov and the Guard Corps were ordered to prepare a counter-attack towards the village of Semionovskaya. Noting the ominous preparations, Davout pointed out the danger to Napoleon. Although he again refused to use his beloved Guardsmen – who bitterly resented their day of inaction – on the grounds that there might be another battle before Moscow was reached, the Emperor authorised the use of the reserve artillery. These eighty guns were rushed to the threatened sector and brought down so effective a fire that the Russian attack never materialised; which was just as well, considering the exhausted condition of the French infantry and cavalry.

Meanwhile, on the far right of the French line, Poniatowski was making another effort to secure the important knoll beyond Utitsa. This time he succeeded and by 5 pm the French were holding almost the whole of the original Russian line. Yet there was still plenty of fight left in Kutusov's decimated formations. Although the whole Russian line fell back at this juncture, it did so only as far as the next ridge, where to the amazement and perturbation of the French it calmly faced round again and began to re-form a line of battle. 'Far from being in disorder,' Marshal Bessières, commanding the Imperial Guard, noted, 'they had retreated to a second position, where they seemed to be preparing for a fresh attack.'

In fact, neither side was in a condition to renew the battle. The firing slowly died away, and some attention could at last be spared for the thousands of wounded lying in heaps all over the battlefield. The French conveyed as many of their casualties as possible to the neighbouring abbey of Kolotskoye, but the ambulance services, such as they were, proved hopelessly inadequate for the task, and many hundreds had to be left lying on the field to die. To gain a bare mile of ground, the French had suffered well over 30,000 casualties. Included in this number were forty-seven generals, thirty-two staff officers, eighty-six aides-de-camp, and three dozen colonels commanding regiments. For the Russians' part, it is estimated that they lost all of 44,000 killed and wounded.

Napoleon spent the night after the battle in his quarters. His health had deteriorated further. Almost everybody anticipated a renewal of the battle on the morrow. Napoleon justified his repeated refusal to send in the Guard in the following words, addressed – between naps – to General Mathieu Dumas and Count Daru, Secretary of State. 'People will be surprised that I did not commit my reserves in order to obtain greater results, but I had to keep them for striking a decisive blow in the great battle which the enemy will fight in front of Moscow. The success of the day was assured, and I had to consider the success of the campaign as a whole. That is why I keep my reserves in hand.'

Yet had the battle been a real success? The Emperor had prophesied a victory to Caulaincourt before battle was jointed. 'We shall win the battle. The Russians will be crushed, but it will not be conclusive if I do not take prisoners.' What was the record of Borodino in this respect? According to Ségur, 'from 700 to 800 prisoners and twenty broken cannon were all the trophies of this imperfect victory. Many Russians had preferred death to capture.'

To their immense relief, the French learnt that the Russians were retiring from their second position during the night. There was no attempt to speed their departure. The French army had fought itself to a standstill, and deemed itself lucky to be left in possession of the field of battle. To everybody's surprise, Kutusov, after holding a council of war, went against the majority opinion and announced that no further opposition would be offered and that Moscow should be abandoned to the French. Their time would come, he assured his generals, provided they retained the Russian army in being and awaited the right moment. The physical loss of Moscow was a matter of only secondary importance. It was a bold decision – one that might well have cost a less trusted figure his head.

Seventy-five miles and seven days later the leading cavalry of the Grand Army cautiously entered the gates of Moscow. They found it almost deserted. The populace had evacuated their Holy City, and had followed the Russian army to the south and east. 'Napoleon himself hastened up,' recalled Ségur. 'He paused in transport: an exclamation of happiness escaped his lips . . . "There, at last, is that famous city! It is high time!"' The reaction of his men was predictably the same. As the formations breasted the final hill at two o'clock, 'the sun caused this great city to glisten with a thousand colours. Struck with astonishment at the sight, they paused, exclaiming "Moscow! Moscow!" Every one quickened his pace; the troops hurried on in disorder; and the whole army, clapping their hands repeated with joy "Moscow! Moscow!" just as sailors shout "Land! Land!" at the conclusion of a long and toilsome voyage.'

General Miloradovitch, commanding Kutusov's last rearguard, was given permission to retire from the city without undergoing attack. Once this evacuation was completed, a silence settled over the scene. Napoleon moved closer, towards the Dorogomilow Gate. Puzzled by the lack of any sign of life within the city, the Emperor permitted Murat (suitably arrayed in his most flamboyant uniform in honours of the occasion) to enter with the cavalry to summon the *boyars* to make their formal submission. Soon officers returned with the incredible news: 'Moscow is deserted.'

Napoleon was dumbfounded by this evidence that the Russian spirit of resistance had not been broken. He had expected to be greeted by the princes and burgomasters with the keys of the city; he had also anticipated that the defeat of the Russian army and the occupation of his religious capital would bring Tsar Alexander suing for terms. Neither assumption proved correct. The chilling question could not long be ignored: had the great march to Moscow been in vain?

13

RETREAT FROM MOSCOW

*I*t *is quite possible that the French retreat from Moscow is the best-known military disaster in recorded human history. The scale is epic, the suffering incalculable, the outcome catastrophic. All the elements of Greek tragedy are present. Night-filming part of Tolstoy's interpretation of the saga — the cossack raid against an encamped French detachment, the freeing of Pierre Bezhukov and the Russian prisoners, the death of young Petya Rostov — near Novi Sad in a temperature well below zero was an unforgettable experience. It was so cold that even the special video-cameras seized up, and the trade union representative of the film-crew was for ever negotiating higher rates of overtime payment with the producer as the temperature dropped. Everybody was highly uncomfortable despite being wrapped up to the ears — so it was just possible to appreciate to a small extent what it must have been like for the dwindling band of survivors of Napoleon's Grand Army of Russia in the final weeks of 1812, as strategic defeat deepened into near-total human catastrophe — both sides suffering, but the French and their allies the more.*

Despite the many, many accounts and analyses of this mighty tragedy, there is still useful work remaining to be done. Almost all attention has naturally enough been focused on the central sector of the front, where Napoleon's army group shrank by the end from the some 470,000 that entered Russia over the Niemen in June 1812 to the 25,000 or so survivors who staggered out the following January. The flanks, as a result, have tended to be ignored or taken for granted. The defection of the Prussians under General Yorck is well documented, but mainly as a political event rather than as a military one. What else happened to Marshal Macdonald's northern flank which reached Riga near the Baltic coast before being brought to a halt? Conversely, what happened to General Schwarzenberg's Austrian formations that held the extreme southern flank near the Pripet Marshes? The major histories of 1812 touch upon these areas — but because the horrors of the retreat were less extreme on these distant sectors they tend to be (to my mind) inadequately treated. Similarly, the role of the Russian partisans — the 'People's War' that von Clausewitz describes in On War, *which so attracted Soviet military historians down to the near present — not least General Pavel Jiline, who has already been mentioned — probably needs reassessment now that the 'political' approach has become transformed by recent events. There are many biographies devoted to the charismatic Kutusov, and one excellent one by Josselson on Barclay de Tolly, but I do not know of any full treatment of Prince Bagration (mortally wounded at Borodino), or of Platov (commander of the Don Cossacks) or again of Davydov, coordinator of the widespread partisan raids and depredations – at least not in English. Perhaps Russian and Ukrainian historians will be able to supply these wants in the easier political and military conditions now prevalent. Let us hope so. Tarlé's great* Napoleon's Invasion of Russia, 1812 *– published in translation in London in 1942 – needs bringing up to date. So a considerable amount of worthwhile work remains to be done.*

†

Napoleon lingered in Moscow for thirty-five days. The period was not wholly uneventful, for fully two-thirds of the city was destroyed in a vast conflagration (15–17 September), and parties of Russian cavalry and partisans were soon attacking the tenuous communications linking the Grand Army with Smolensk. Otherwise everything was deceptively quiet at the outpost line a few miles beyond the capital. Kutusov deliberately played on the French desire for a negotiated settlement, and Cossack leaders assured Joachim Murat, the commander of the French cavalry, whose flamboyant uniforms and dashing style they regarded with something akin to awe, that the war was as good as over. French emissaries set off for St Petersburg bearing peace overtures.

Alexander, however, under strong pressure from his advisers, proved totally unreceptive to these approaches. His mercurial character contained a strong streak of stubbornness that Napoleon had never managed to fathom. 'This is the moment my campaign begins,' Alexander was heard to remark. Every day the French stayed in Moscow was placing them more surely in the power of the Russians. By now, new Russian forces were on the move, Generals Wittgenstein and Steinheil coming south with 40,000 men from the Army of Finland, Admiral Tshitsagov marching north with the Army of Moldavia to join Tormassov's III Army and bring it up to a strength of 65,000; these forces were far stronger than the much-reduced French units holding the over-extended flanks. For the rest, Kutusov still retained the 110,000 survivors of the I and II Armies to the south of Moscow, facing a French striking-force which now numbered barely 95,000 men. In other words, the initiative was passing into Russian hands, and Napoleon – with over 700 miles of vulnerable communications behind him – was in an impossible military position. Every day he remained in Moscow, moreover, was bringing the dreaded Russian winter closer, but few practical steps were taken to prepare the army for it.

The Emperor slowly began to face up to the realities of his situation, and on 18 October he warned his subordinates to be ready to quit Moscow on the 20th.

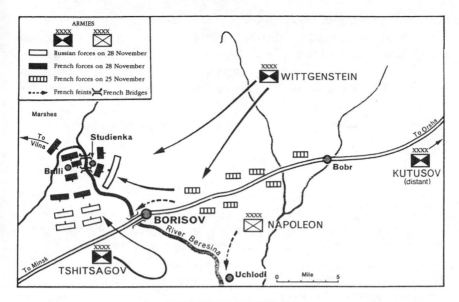

CROSSING THE BERESINA 1812

By a coincidence, however, the 18th witnessed a sudden attack by part of Kutusov's army against the drowsy French outposts near Vinkovo. Only Murat's personal intervention staved off disaster, but news of this surprise induced the Emperor to bring forward the departure date by twenty-four hours.

So it was on 19 October 1812 – only four months after the campaign had begun – that the retreat from Moscow began. Behind Napoleon came 95,000 men, 500 cannon, and many thousand vehicles of all kinds, piled high with loot and supplies, the wounded and camp-followers on the top. 'It looked,' recalled Ségur, 'like a caravan, a wandering nation, or rather one of those armies of Antiquity returning with slaves and spoil after a great devastation.'

Napoleon's immediate aim was to return to Smolensk to make use of the supply arsenals there and to rejoin the 37,000 men of IX Corps. At first he thought to move his Army southwards to Kaluga, brushing Kutusov aside *en route*, before striking west through fertile and unravaged areas. He was soon induced to change his mind. On 23–24 October the advance guard became engaged in a bitter action with a Russian force at a river-crossing near Maloyaroslavets. In the end the French had the better of this, the Russians pulling back, but while Napoleon was reconnoitring the area on the 25th he was almost taken prisoner by a party of Cossacks. This narrow escape induced him to reverse his line of march and move off north-west to rejoin the well-trodden post-roads to Smolensk near Borodino. This was a desperate step. It doomed the army to retraverse ground which had already been laid waste twice that year, first by the Russians and then by the French. It also took the troops across the battlefield of 7 September, past '30,000 corpses half eaten by wolves. The Emperor's troops passed rapidly by, casting shuddering glances at this immense tomb,' recalled Baron Marbot. The only comforting feature was the weather, which remained mild and fine.

Having induced the French to retire along the central corridor, the Russian armies began to move in for the kill. It soon became evident that the long flanks of the French front were caving in under pressure; by early November, which found Napoleon at Viasma with a fifty-mile column straggling behind him, Wittgenstein was reported near Tsashniki and closing fast with the Beresina River line which the French would have to pass, while on the other flank, Tshitsagov appeared to be nearing Slonim, thus threatening French supplies massed at Minsk. As for Kutusov, he was moving parallel to the main French column a little distance to the south. Napoleon's army was soon in difficulty. The few supplies carried from Moscow were consumed, and the devastated countryside held nothing for the footsore columns. More and more men began to abandon their loot, then their weapons, and soon a growing crowd of hungry stragglers began to gather round the rearguard.

Napoleon hurried on for Smolensk, where he hoped to find both men and supplies. Russian attacks on the long column began to be more frequent. On 3 November, I Corps was cut off near Fiodoroivsky, but was rescued by IV Corps, next ahead in the column. The same day the first flurries of snow fell, the first severe frost being encountered on the 9th as the advance guard reached Smolensk. The leading troops rioted, and looted the magazines, wantonly destroying what they could not carry off, leaving little for the men behind. French morale was already reaching breaking-point; a division of fresh reinforcements tamely surrendered to an inferior Russian force; once proud army corps were fast becoming pitiful rabbles.

The Emperor had originally planned to halt at Smolensk to rest his army and take stock of the situation. Now he decided to march for the Beresina without delay. The Russian armies on his flanks were making such progress that both the Dnieper crossings at Orsha and those over the more distant Beresina at Borisov were endangered. So on the 12th the advance guard left Smolensk, but it was not until the 17th that Marshal Ney, commanding the rearguard, was at last clear of the city.

On that day Kutusov – who so far had seemed in little hurry to get to grips with the French – tried to block the column near Krasnyi. He got more than he bargained for; the order 'la Garde au feu' was given, and, according to a Russian onlooker, the French line 'passed through our Cossacks like a hundred-gun ship through a fishing fleet'. Kutusov promptly drew off to lick his wounds, and the retreat went on. By this time there was no sign of, or news from, Ney's rearguard, but Napoleon could not delay. Orsha was safely reached on the 19th, its bridges intact, but Napoleon already knew that Minsk and its 2,000,000 sorely needed rations had fallen into Russian hands – and that it would now be a race against time to forestall Tshitsagov at the crucial Beresina crossings at Borisov. The Emperor accordingly gave orders for the army to destroy all surplus transport – a fate shared by the bridging train. This last measure was almost to prove fatal.

Napoleon was under no illusions about the dangers he faced. 'This is beginning to be very serious,' he confided to Caulaincourt. Leaving Orsha on the 20th, the column staggered on, its discipline almost non-existent. Next day morale was given a fillip by the sensational arrival of Marshal Ney and the survivors of the rearguard, given up for lost four days earlier. After being cut off, Ney had fought a brilliant withdrawal against overwhelming odds and escaped over the frozen Dnieper with 900 men to tell the tale. 'I would sooner have given 300 millions from my Treasury than lose such a man,' Napoleon exclaimed; henceforth Ney was universally known as 'the bravest of the brave'.

On the 22nd, however, the army's morale sank again when long-feared tidings reached headquarters from Oudinot's advance guard. Tshitsagov had won the race for Borisov and destroyed the bridges. Even worse, an unseasonable thaw had set in, turning the Beresina (normally hard-frozen in late November) into a raging torrent. With Wittgenstein (30,000) closing in from the north, Tshitsagov (34,000) holding the crossings to the fore, and Kutusov (80,000) moving up from the rear (albeit at a respectful distance), it seemed that what was left of the French army – deprived of bridging equipment – must be doomed. By this desperate juncture there were only some 49,000 French troops still under arms and perhaps 250 guns, despite the fact that Oudinot's II and Victor's IX Corps (24,000 men between them) had recently joined the main column from the northern flank. Perhaps as many as 40,000 stragglers should also be taken into account, although their military value was nil.

Such was the sorry state the once 460,000-strong Central Army Group of the Grand Army of Russia had been reduced to. The question now was one of stark survival for this remnant of a once-fine army. Could a way be found over or round the Beresina without a bridging train, and could three converging armies be fought off? The odds seemed very long. The Imperial Staff ordered a further reduction of the remaining coaches and wagons. The state papers were burned – a fate shared, according to Ségur, by a large number of regimental *tricolors* which the Emperor was determined should not fall into Russian hands.

In the event, a combination of fortunate circumstances saved what was left of the Grand Army. The first of these was the equivocal attitude of Kutusov. The main Russian army bore the recent scars of Krasnyi, and memories of Borodino were still fresh in many minds. As a result the Russian commander-in-chief showed little eagerness to close with his opponent, but hung off some thirty miles to the rear, preferring to leave the final elimination of the invader to his colleagues and 'General Winter'. This greatly reduced the numbers of troops the French were called upon to face during the next critical days.

Secondly, an act of intelligent disobedience on the part of General Count Jean-Baptiste Éblé made the bridging of the Beresina barely possible. Against orders, he had saved two field-forges, two wagons of charcoal, and six of sapper tools and bridging equipment from the conflagration of the army trains at Orsha. The pontoons themselves had been destroyed, but, provided sufficient timber could be found within range of any proposed bridging site, the building of bridges was still within the bounds of possibility.

Of course any such bridges would be extemporised and therefore liable to be flimsy, so it was very important to find a favourable, shallow site. For some time this seemed an insuperable problem, given the presence of a Russian army on the far bank with detachments guarding all known crossing-places. But then fate intervened for a third time in the person of Brigadier-General Corbineau and a detachment of cavalry. Corbineau had been serving on detachment near Vilna under General Wrede before receiving orders of recall to his parent unit, Marshal Oudinot's II Corps. Approaching the Beresina from the west, he successfully eluded the Russians, and, even more important, found a peasant who revealed the presence of an unmarked ford near the village of Studienka. Braving the cold water and ice-floes, Corbineau crossed the Beresina with no more ado on 23 November and reported his arrival to an astounded Oudinot. The marshal informed the Emperor, who at once saw the opportunity this timely discovery afforded the army.

To cross a river in spate in the proximity of a powerful foe was under any circumstances a hazardous undertaking, but for a while Napoleon regained all his old fire and energy as he tackled the problem. First, it was vital to distract Admiral Tshitsagov's attention from the intended crossing-place. Several feints were put in hand, but the main task of deception was entrusted to Oudinot, who descended to the river-bank near Uchlodi, several miles below Borisov, on the 25th, with a mixed crowd of soldiers and stragglers, and gave every impression of preparing bridges. The Russian commander fell for the bait, and drew his forces off southwards, leaving the Borisov–Studienka stretch of the river virtually unguarded. He did not even take the precaution of destroying the single causeway leading over the marshes towards Vilna from the west bank of the Beresina – another stroke of great good fortune for the French. 'I have outwitted the Admiral!' exulted Napoleon when Rapp brought him the welcome news. 'He thinks I am at the point where I ordered the false attack...'

Immediately a complex plan of operations was put into effect. Count Éblé was to take charge of the engineers and *pontonniers*, demolish the houses of Studienka for the sake of their timber, and with it build two 300-foot bridges over the Beresina, completing them as early as possible on the 26th, covered by a small force commanded by Corbineau that would have crossed the river the preceding night.

As soon as one bridge was completed, Oudinot's II Corps, followed by Ney and III Corps, were to cross the river to create a defensive flank facing towards Borisov, ready to hold up any attack by Tshitsagov once he realised what was afoot. These formations would be followed as fast as possible by Headquarters, the Guard, and Eugène's IV Corps, which would form a fighting reserve near Brilli, leaving Davout's I Corps and Victor's IX Corps to hold the eastern bridgehead against any attack by Wittgenstein's Russians. The I Corps would then file through the intervals between Victor's divisions down to the bridges, and lastly IX Corps would make good its escape before Éblé destroyed the bridges. The whole army would then file off through Brilli towards Vilna and safety. All in all, this represented a good plan. It was marred by only one oversight: no specific provision was made for the crossing of the horde of stragglers. The Emperor assumed they would save themselves during the intervals between the arrival of major formations at the bridges. He estimated that the entire operation would take two to three days.

The first bridge was open at 1 pm on the afternoon of 26 November, thanks to the selfless heroism of Éblé and his men who had toiled through the previous night, often up to their armpits in freezing water, to place the extemporised trestles and planking in place. Oudinot at once led 11,000 men over to form the defensive flank near Stachov, followed by a division of heavy cavalry and two light guns. Half-way through the afternoon the second, larger, bridge was operational, and the artillery was hurried over. So far there had been no sign of Russian reaction on either bank, and the time-table was being followed despite three temporary breaks in the flimsy structures, which Éblé and his devoted engineers again worked all night to repair and strengthen.

By the early afternoon of the 27th, Imperial Headquarters and the Guard were safely across. Then at about 4 pm three trestles on the artillery bridge suddenly collapsed. The hitherto orderly columns immediately became an hysterical mob as each man tried to fight his way to the remaining bridge, which became jammed with frantic men. By the time order had been restored, several hundred unfortunates had been trampled to death or swept into the river to drown. Éblé, after successfully repairing the gap, literally had to carve a path through the corpses and abandoned vehicles at the end of the slighter bridge to make room for IV and I Corps, which safely passed across during the evening.

Two hard battles had meanwhile been raging for most of the day as Tshitsagov (now fully aware of his error) and Wittgenstein (marching in from the north-east) closed with the French bridgeheads from their respective sides. But Oudinot and Victor proved more than a match for their opponents, and the crossings went on unhindered until the breakdown in the afternoon. At dusk the gunfire died away, and a period of peace descended on the bridges. Now would have been the ideal time for the hordes of non-combatants to make their way over to the west bank – as Count Éblé repeatedly implored them to do – but hysteria had given way to complete apathy and the unfortunates chose to huddle together round meagre fires on the eastern side of the river.

On balance, the operation was still going extremely well. During the night of the 27–28 November, however, a setback occurred when General Partonneaux's Division of Victor's Corps lost its way in a snowstorm and marched into the Russian lines, where it was compelled to surrender. This loss severely complicated Victor's rearguard role on the 28th, for it left a large gap on his right flank which time and again the Russians almost turned. About midday they were able to bring guns into action against the bridges, whereupon there was a repetition of the previous day's panic. Enemy bombardment and the volume of traffic caused the artillery bridge to break down again, flinging more desperate men into the icy river. However, concentrated French artillery-fire from the opposite bank forced the Russians to fall back out of range. The withdrawal of the rearguard could now begin, and it was completed by one o'clock the next morning. Fortunately there was still no sign of Kutusov.

The western bank had also been the scene of a dire struggle for much of the 28th as Oudinot and Ney grappled with overwhelming numbers of Tshitsagov's troops. At one stage Oudinot was almost routed, but he personally rallied his men before falling, seriously wounded. Ney at once assumed overall command, and, thanks to the inspired charge by Dumerc's cuirassiers, which caused 2000 Russian casualties, the situation was stabilised once more, Tshitsagov falling back under heavy pressure.

Nightfall again brought a period of peace and quiet. There now only remained the human flotsam of the stragglers to evacuate over the bridges, but once again many of them, suffering probably from battle-neurosis and exposure, refused to budge until morning.

General Éblé was now charged with the final task of destroying the bridges. He delayed the fatal moment until nine o'clock on the 29th in the hope of giving the remaining stragglers and camp-followers a chance to cross, but until the fires were lit they made no move, despite repeated warnings and entreaties. Then, when it was too late, the frightful scenes of the previous days were repeated as they all rushed headlong for the bridges. Some perished in the flames, most fell into the river as the structures subsided with a hissing crash and a shower of sparks. The Beresina was blocked with frozen corpses for weeks to come. The pathetic survivors on the east bank – estimated to number 30,000 – received short shrift from Wittgenstein's Cossacks.

At a cost of some 25,000 combatant and probably 30,000 non-combatant lives, Napoleon had survived the crossing of the Beresina, and was in a position to claim a strategic victory in that he had broken out of the Russian trap. Only twenty-five guns had been lost, and the French had inflicted at least 20,000 casualties on the Russians. The true heroes of the battle had been Éblé and Dumerc, whose gallant *pontonniers* and cuirassiers had alone made the achievement possible.

On paper at least, the problem of the retreat from Moscow to Poland had been solved; no serious obstacle now lay between the French and Vilna, and the Russian forces showed little inclination to seek a further battle. But the human problem of survival was far from won; the worst of the frosts were still to come during the bitter month of December. Napoleon, however, saw fit to leave his army at Smorgoni on the 5th to return to Paris (there to scotch rumours of his own death, which had already occasioned the conspiracy of General Malet some time before, and also to set in train the raising of new armies ready to meet the Russian advance into Germany the following spring). The story of the last stages of the retreat is grim in the extreme, with thousands more men succumbing to disease, starvation, and exposure as the ever-dwindling survivors shuffled westwards.

In the New Year of 1813 a mere 25,000 frost-bitten and emaciated survivors of the Central Army Group came out of Russia, to be joined by perhaps a further 68,000 men from the outlying corps. In seven months, Napoleon had lost 570,000 men and over 1000 cannon. For their part, the Russians had lost at least 150,000 soldiers, besides unknown numbers of civilians; but the survivors could console themselves with the knowledge that the soil of Holy Russia was clear of the invader and that a great strategic victory had been won. No such consolations could be offered the French, as one ally after another (led by Prussia) began to desert them. Napoleon's insatiable ambition and gross miscalculation of the staying-power of the Russian armies and people in general, and of the Tsar's character in particular, had resulted in a terrible catastrophe on a scale almost without precedent in the annals of military history. The French Empire was now ultimately doomed.

14

AN UNDERGROOM AT WAR –
EDWARD HEALEY, 1815

*T*he outcome of Leipzig in October 1813 was the loss of Germany to the French
*Empire. Save only around Hamburg, where the intrepid Davout fought on bravely,
the war moved west of the Rhine and on to French soil. With a massively outnumbered
army largely made up of schoolboys and pensioners, Napoleon proceeded to fight one of the
most brilliant campaigns of his career, although the inevitable outcome rendered it almost
pointless politically. With Wellington's victorious army – despite Soult's valiant attempts
to stem the flood – pouring into southern France, and a new British force landed in
Holland, the Emperor parried, dodged, riposted and thrust again and again with his
small army against the tightening ring, determined to preserve Paris and in the hope that
Allied dissensions would yet save him. At length, the pressures proved too great and the
morale of his key subordinates snapped. At Fontainbleau, on 20 April, following The
Mutiny of the Marshals led by Ney (which forced him to abdicate after Marmont
surrendered Paris with hardly a fight), Napoleon paid an emotional farewell to his Old
Guard and set off for exile on the island of Elba off the Italian coast.*

*But not for long. On 1 March 1815 he landed in the south of France, and on the 21st
was back in Paris, de facto Emperor once more. There followed the so-called Campaign
of the Hundred Days north of the Franco-Belgian frontier. A victory over Blücher
awaited Napoleon at Ligny on 16 June, the same day that Ney fought Wellington to a
draw at neighbouring Quatre Bras, and the Emperor drove on towards Brussels – only to
halt facing the Allied position at Mont-St-Jean, while Grouchy with the right wing of
the Army of the North sought for Blücher's retreating Prussians some miles to the east.
The result was the celebrated double-battle of Waterloo-Wavre on 18 June 1815 – and
Napoleon's utter and final defeat.*

*At the furthest possible point away from the Emperor or the great Duke on the social
scale, a British undergroom aged fourteen years, servant to Lieutenant-Colonel Scovell,
experienced much of the campaign of Waterloo and its aftermath, although not the climacteric battle itself. Years later he wrote down his memories of this dramatic period very
much from 'the worm's eye view'. These papers came to light during the late 1980s, and I
had the privilege to edit them for first publication. As it would take up too much space to*

reprint the complete documents here, I have included only my Introduction and one or two representative passages to give the flavour of Healey's writings.

✝

The annals of the Napoleonic Wars do not lack eye-witness accounts by serving officers, NCOs and men – and not surprisingly, given its fame and notoriety, the campaign of 1815 in Belgium is particularly well provided for in this respect. By the early nineteenth century – thanks to the Sunday School movement and the very first beginnings of army education inspired by the reformers of Shorncliffe camp and other far-sighted soldiers of a liberal persuasion – almost all officers and a higher proportion of other ranks than ever before in the British army were literate men, also endowed in varying degrees with an intellectual curiosity that encouraged them to note down and comment upon the events they were called upon to participate in. It is nevertheless a welcome event to be able to place alongside the well-known military memoirs, the recorded recollections of a servant and groom – namely those of Edward Healey, 'servant to Lt Col Sir George Scovell, KCB, Assistant Quarter Master General to the British Army in the Campaign of 1815', and indeed to place them beside those of the Duke of Wellington's cook, also recently published (amidst some little controversy) in 1985 for the first time. The *Journal of Edward Healey* was brought to my attention in mid-1984. It would appear that this *Journal* had not been published before my edited version published in the summer and autumn numbers of the *SAHR Journal* for 1986.

Who exactly was Edward Healey? Alas, apart from the very little he tells us at the outset of his *Journal* (for example that he was born in 1801 and lived at Canterbury) we know absolutely nothing about him. Research has to date not even revealed whether he was employed by his master after Waterloo, along with his former-batman father; we do not know whether Scovell brought him as a groom or in any other capacity to the Royal Military College, Sandhurst, for part or all of his daunting twenty-seven-year sojourn as first lieutenant-governor and then governor of our famous institution between March 1829 and April 1856. But Healey – if his *Journal* can be deemed reliable evidence and his own work – was a man of some literary ability, certainly more than one might expect from an undergroom of the early nineteenth century.

Scovell goes down into Sandhurst's history only for his passion for shooting rabbits and his draconian (and predictably unsuccessful) edicts designed to deter his enterprising young charges from poaching on what he regarded as his sacred preserves – the College rabbit-warrens. The ex-intellectual veteran otherwise left no mark or memory upon the premier school of military education in

Britain, comments the Sandhurst historian, Hugh Thomas. His medals, swords – and a painting of 'Copenhagen' (Wellington's horse) that he tactfully commissioned – remain on display, however, at Sandhurst today, together with his portrait in Topper's Bar, Old College. The side-chapel also contains a suitable memorial plaque.

Whether Edward Healey spent many a summer's night chasing, and seeking to apprehend on behalf of his master, gentlemen-poachers or bunny-raiders from amongst the 180 Gentlemen Cadets practising unofficial night-patrolling skills over the College's warrens in the hope of supplementing their meagre diets and (no doubt) of infuriating their governor still further – if indeed he remained in Scovell's service at Sandhurst at all after 1815 – we shall probably never know. More to the point, when we come to assess the value of his *Journal* we must first consider its authenticity. One is bound to feel that the original manuscript has been much 'tidied up' and improved by an unknown but scholarly hand at some time in its existence – unless we have in Healey very much of a *rara avis* of his own, or any other time – namely the highly literate stable-lad. That having been said, there is, however, no reason to cast doubt on the genuineness of the main textual content. As will be pointed out below, Healey makes mistakes and misinterpretations which Sir George would never have committed (were he to have wished to conceal himself behind his groom's pen for some utterly unfathomable reason unless it were to avoid the attentions of the DPR [Army] of his day). Similarly, most of the incidents described – with certain exceptions – are fascinating day-to-day trivia so beloved by modern military historians when we can discover them. Except over such points of detail, Healey has little of great importance to add to the well-described events surrounding Waterloo; but what he has to say has a certain freshness and impact which can transfer the reader to the streets of rumour-filled Brussels or (later) of an apprehensive welcoming Paris in a way that few other contemporary accounts can rival.

Strangely, the least valuable part of his writing is the lengthy, inaccurate and highly tedious description of the battle of Waterloo; at which Healey in any case was not present as his narrative makes clear, and which accordingly must be based on hearsay. For the rest, remarkably little had to be added or taken out (in marked contrast with my recent experiences with Private Deane of Queen Anne's Footguards a century earlier I might add) – and I close by wishing the reader an interesting excursion into the campaign of 1815, as seen through the eyes of a very young, highly receptive, junior servant of a distinguished officer on Wellington's staff; 'the worm's-eye point of view' of an author who was – on his own admission – just fourteen years old in 1815.

[31 May]

'... The Downs presented a very beautiful sight, for it was almost impossible to count the number of ships that were there, all with their decks covered with soldiers and I suppose they each would have presented a similar scene to what was going on on board the *Scipio*. It was very tedious lying so long there, and there being above 40 horses below caused it to be extremely hot, and give forth not one of the most odoriferous of scents. Nevertheless some of the men were below playing at cards, others were mixing up dumplings on the boards, some drinking, some smoking and some rolling about like dead men with the sea sickness – altogether presenting a scene not to be met with every day. I was glad that I escaped the sickness for the sick were only knocked about like so much lumber, nobody pitying or caring anything about them. I remained most of the time on deck – though I had to go down occasionally to assist feeding the horses, which was a most unpleasant job, for the horses stood on beach stones at the bottom of the vessel, in two rows, with their hind quarters to the ships sides, and their mangers ran down the middle just under their noses, to which they were tied, and just enough room was left between them to squeeze by to feed them, and soldiers' horses being very wicked, they kept continually snapping at anyone who passed. Several men got bit by them and they kept up a continual row, biting and kicking each other. Each man took his turn 4 hours to watch them, and he was sure to be hoarse before his time was up, for he had to keep continually shouting at them, but I dare say the poor things disliked their situation as much as we did, they sweat very much from the intolerant heat, and there was no means of doing them any good.

We were all much pleased to hear the orders given to set sail in the night of the 31st and I was at a loss to know how they could manage it in the dark in such a great crowd of shipping. . . . Near Ostend we were ordered into the boats, and rowed to shore, at least near to shore, for they made us jump out of the boats into the breakers and get ashore as well as we could so we were all wet through to begin our first night's campaigning. I heartily wished myself at home again, but it was no use, and nothing was more useless than to complain for that only got one laughed at or sworn at. We had scarcely got safe on shore before we saw our horses swinging in the air, so that we were obliged to go again in to the sea up to our middles to catch them as they came on shore. Two sets of slings were kept in use, so that while one horse was swimming between the ship and the boat having the slings taken off, another was swinging over their heads. It made the horses very fresh after such a long confinement ... but such was the quickness of all their proceedings that in less than $1^1/_2$ hours, all was cleared from the ships and they were under sail again for England. People who have not seen such sights must draw them in their own minds, for they are past describing clearly – fancy between 20 and 30 ships discharging a somewhat similar cargo to the *Scipio's*, all on to the beach – the luggage thrown in all directions, numbers of horses running loose – and when we got a little together not knowing where to go, getting a civil answer from no one – and a thousand other disagreeablenesses....

I must now describe our first commencement [establishment] on this campaign. The best charger was saddled for Sir George, and the three others for ourselves, each having a large blanket folded under the saddle. The pony, a sort of Galloway about 14 hands high, and the Spanish mule, a very fine animal nearly 15 hands high, were both saddled with packsaddles for carrying all our luggage. The horse carried a portmanteau on one side, a canteen on the other and a camp bedstead on her back. The mule carried a portmanteau on each side and the camp bed and bedclothes on her back, the rough pace of the horse caused him to be very troublesome as it shook the luggage off so many times, but the mule went along so easy that her load never moved. A large tarpaulin covered each load, so that rain could not hurt it. Having all things ready we started about 8 o'clock. I rode one of the horses, Sir George passed us on the road with my father following him.... I was very much astonished at the sagacity of our mule, she ran loose and would hurry on about a quarter of a mile in front of us and would then graze till we came up, and then she would start off again in the same manner, but if she ever found any confusion on the road, such as coming up with regiments of soldiers and baggage, etc, she would then keep close to our horses. She was an old campaigner, and was taken from the French at the Battle of Vitoria in Spain. She was taken with three others that were drawing a piece of cannon. She was the most useful animal I ever saw...

[15 June]

The town was very gay and bustling, all day long soldiers were parading, music playing and the streets continually full of all sorts of uniforms. There were balls every night and plenty of amusement for those who wanted it. It appeared more like troops assembling to be reviewed than to fight, for no one seemed to think of fighting, though towards the 13th or 14th it was said they were going to prepare for hostilities on the 25th and soldiers were to be seen in various parts with their swords taking to be ground, and linen drapers shops were full of them, purchasing cloth to make themselves bandages, but in a general way things were going on as if nothing was the matter.... In short, everybody in Brussels seemed happy. But a damper was put on all the gaiety on the afternoon of the 15th. Thousands of people assembled on the ramparts nearest to Waterloo, listening to a rumbling noise in the air. Some said it was distant thunder, others said it was cannonading. However, it caused an alarm, and officers were ordered to join their respective regiments and the troops were ordered to be in readiness to turn out, but towards evening the noise died away and seemed to be quite forgotten.

A ball was given by the Duchess of Richmond and the Duke and his staff all attended it, and all was gay as usual, but towards 12 o'clock a little silent sort of confusion began, every one enquiring what was the matter, and beginning to recollect the noise they had heard in the afternoon. I repaired to Sir George's billet and my father to the stable. Sir George arrived in a few minutes, it was now past 12 o'clock. He ordered the black horse to be saddled immediately, that being his best charger...

[16 June]

A scene that baffles all description now began. Drums, trumpets, bugles, all kicking up the finest discord that ever was heard. The inhabitants all rose from their beds, and the soldiers were collecting in the streets, such shouting, swearing, crying, arms rattling, dragoons and officers galloping about, in short I should think the confusion at Babel was a fool to it. The worst part of the business was to see the officers' and soldiers' wives hanging about them, almost brokenhearted and wanting to go with them, but that could not be allowed. Every praise is due to the inhabitants for their kindness, both in assisting the men, and afterwards taking care of their wives. What caused the confusion to be worse than it need have been, was that everybody thought the French were close at the gates. This dreadful state of things continued till about half past one o'clock, and then it was astonishing to see the order at that time as if by magic. All the troops were on the parade and ready to march. The Park was full and all the streets round it, and in a very few minutes the order was given to march, drums and fifes were playing away as merry as possible, and bugles were sounding beautiful ... Daylight was now set in, so that people could see what was going on, and about 4 o'clock the troops began to march through Brussels in an almost unbroken line.

... The ramparts nearest the road the troops were gone were now beginning to be crowded by the people listening anxiously to hear when the troops fell in with the enemy, and the troops having marched so very early it was evident that the French were still at a great distance, as not a sound was heard yet ... Soon after 11 o'clock the cry was given that cannonading could be heard. I ran to the ramparts and could hear it quite distinct. I could feel my heart begin to beat when I first heard it in a dreadful manner, and I have no doubt many a thousand felt as I did. I heartily wished myself back in Canterbury, but that could not be ... Between 12 and 1 o'clock it could plainly be heard they were at it without joking. The noise came through the air like a quantity of heavy muffled balls tumbling down a long wooden stairs – or perhaps more like a rolling ball, and causing it now and then to hop about on the head of a big drum... Nothing was now talked of but plans of self-preservation, and such like, till between 4 and 5 o'clock when the wounded men began to come in from the battle. Thousands rushed to the gates to make enquiries. It was a most dreadful sight to see the poor fellows cut and maimed in the manner they were. They gave a dreadful account of it – said it was a dreadful slaughter.... The place where they fell in with the enemy was called Quarto Bras, about 25 miles from Brussels, and they had to fight very hard, and it was astonishing how well they maintained their ground against such a superior force. The people were now convinced that the noise they heard the day before was cannonading, for we got intelligence of the battle of Ligney on that day between the French and Prussians. It was a most dreadful affair, the Prussians fought like tigers, the village of Ligney was taken and retaken three times till the dead bodies on a bridge were piled higher than the parapet walls. No troops in the world ever fought better than the Prussians on this occasion.

... But to return to Brussels, the wounded were now beginning to be very numerous. A great many went to hospital, and those who had been in Brussels before sent to their old billets, and a great many were taken in by the inhabitants. Great numbers of tradesmen now began to show the most praiseworthy kindness to the wounded, some by taking them voluntarily into their houses, others by slinging a basket of eatables on their back, and a small keg of wine or brandy under each arm and going out on the road to meet the wounded and give them a little comfort in their afflictions. Several hundreds of the tradesmen left Brussels loaded in this manner to assist any poor fellow that came in their way. Every now and then a waggon or farmer's cart would make its appearance full of wounded, and a most shocking spectacle it was. No poor fellow was allowed to ride who could make use of his legs, as there was such difficulty in procuring vehicles. Towards dark the cannonading ceased, but every body was on the tiptoe of enquiry – the poor wounded were pestered to death with enquiries, some crying "Where's the Duke?", others "Have you seen such a regiment?", the women "Have you seen my husband?" but chiefly "How's the battle going on?", to which enquiry the answer generally is "Oh, very bad, worse than anything in Spain", but nothing accurate could be got at. The body of the Duke of Brunswick was brought in in his carriage, he was killed soon after the action began, by a cannon shot. His troops fought most gallantly, they consider they have some private injury to avenge. They say that the Duke's father was taken prisoner by the French somewhere and that he was murdered whilst a prisoner and they have sworn eternal hatred to the French. They carry the black flag with the skull and crossbones, and neither give nor take quarter. They stuck bravely to our men in this day's action. Sir George returned to Brussels about 11 o'clock this evening, he seemed much fresher than we had any reason to expect, but the poor horse was dreadfully knocked up. His landlord had soon prepared a good supper and everything comfortable for him.

He said it would be a dreadful affair before it was over. After his supper he gave orders for his brown mare and his baggage horse to be ready at 2 o'clock. It was now 12 o'clock so he laid down about two hours.

{17 June}

At 2 o'clock he was called, and was soon ready.... After he had gone we were all on the alert again. Troops kept passing through, and the people gathered again on the ramparts to listen to the commencement of the firing, and the least extra noise that was heard, they'd exclaim "It's begun" – but they had not long to listen this morning for it begun very early, but did not seem very distant. The weather was showery and very gloomy at times. The wounded began to arrive early this morning, and before 11 o'clock a many had come in, but not so many as the previous day. They were having a more cool and calculating fight this morning, and the report was circulated that the British were retreating which caused very great alarm, and they were actually retreating, but it was merely to take up their position in front of Waterloo. Towards the evening the cannonading was very loud and we could not help thinking they were getting very close to Brussels, which caused a great fright to a many of the inhabitants. Sir George arrived again between 11 and 12 o'clock, as cool as possible. He was well attended to again. He had not received a scratch, and both horses were quite safe. He said they had retreated to the Duke's favourite position, and that they had lost comparatively but a few men today.... Sir George said "Ah, tomorrow will be a dreadful day, for the Duke is determined to decide the matter on the position he has taken today. Many thousands will fall". He ordered his black horse again to be ready at 2 o'clock to be given to a dragoon to lead. He asked his landlord if he would like to go, but the invitation was politely declined.... A great deal of business was arranged previous to his departure. He made arrangements with the landlord to secrete our heavy luggage in case of a retreat, and wrote directions for us in case he was killed. He enclosed them in his desk with orders to break the desk open if he was killed, and after giving us all strict charge to keep steady, and mind what we were about, he mounted his horse and took leave of us in a very kind manner, expecting never to see us again ... leaving us in a more serious mood than hitherto. We saddled our horses all ready for moving in a moment...

{18 June}

During the morning I went several times towards the park to see all I could, as this was the most public part of the town. It was in a great bustle, but people seemed astonished at not hearing any cannonading, but between 10 and 11 o'clock the thundering commenced, but not very loud at first, yet it did not require to go on the ramparts to hear it for it could be heard any where quite plain. What seemed to astonish people very much was the almost unbroken procession of every description of vehicle loaded with ammunition. These were artillery carts and waggons, the Waggon Train waggons and the country people's carts of every description, and everyone was chalked upon to tell what they contained. The figures and letters on them were large enough to be read for at least a mile distance, some were marked 4 pounders, some 12 pounders, some 18 pounders, but the greatest number were marked 9 pounders. One would have thought there was enough ammunition to fight for seven years. I always thought it a hard case enough to press farmers' waggons and carts to carry baggage, but I thought this much harder to press them to carry ammunition into the field of battle, though I suppose they only went to the rear of the army. They all returned to Brussels laden with wounded.

About 1 o'clock today the roaring of the cannon was tremendous, nearly three hundred pieces of cannon were now dealing out destruction in all directions, and the wounded gave shocking accounts of the severity of the battle. They were now within 10 or 12 miles of the town, and people were in a dreadful state of anxiety, every now and then the noise would appear a little loud and the people would exclaim "Oh they are coming, the English are beaten". The noise of the cannon was about as loud as if you had taken a number of cannon balls and rolled them down a wooden stair case and then heard them at about 20 yards off. Some persons pretended they could hear the musketry, but I think that was impossible, without they were like the Irishman who said he could hear the grass grow.

On account of this last two days' bustle we dare not go for our rations, so that we had now nothing left for the horses. So my father said he would venture as far as the commissaries' stores to fetch some hay and corn; accordingly towards 3 o'clock he mounted me on the mule with the forage lines. . . . I had not gone far before I met about 50 of the Brunswickers coming at full gallop, crying out "Franceuse, Franceuse, the French, the French" [in fact the Cumberland Hussars]. My mule, being a very headstrong animal, immediately turned round and mixed with this flying mass – but she had sense enough to turn from them when we came to the street that turned towards her own stable. I must say now that I was most desperately frightened. Such a scene of confusion had now began as baffles all description. Carriages and horsemen, in trying to pass each other, were all thrown down together, and this happened in many parts of the town. My mule was at full gallop, and nothing could stop her. . . . The people in all directions were closing their doors and windows and pulling down their signs.

When I arrived at our billet the people were endeavouring to close the gates, but a party of the artillery prevented them. These artillerymen had come for rations and would have their meat. The people said "Oh, the French are coming" they replied that they would have their meat "if the French or the Devil himself came". This happened very lucky for me, as I should have been fastened out had it not been for the artillerymen.... For about an hour and half the most dreadful confusion was going on, not one part in ten took things so easy as we did, but we may thank the valet for it. He had seen such things many a score times in Spain and Portugal, and he was therefore quite right in his opinion this time, but had it not been for him we certainly should have mounted and joined the flying masses. Thousands reached Antwerp before the mistake was discovered, and hundreds of officers' servants cut away their baggage and lost the whole of their masters' property. The confusion may better be imagined than described.... At one spot on the road about twenty horses were killed, and of course the men shared the same fate. It is supposed that above a thousand men and horses were killed in this unfortunate affair. The town of Brussels was left in command of the Commandant, I believe his name was Colonel Jones. He knew this was a false alarm and as soon as he could collect a few dragoons they drew their swords and began to scour the streets, striking everybody they saw running, and order was soon restored – but the women as in most cases caused the greater part of the mischief, for scores of them came through Brussels in the morning following their husbands. They were well mounted, riding astride on men's saddles, they had on boots and trousers like dragoons, and wore a gown over all, with small round bonnets on their heads. I think they belonged to the Brunswickers and German Legions – for I saw no caricatures of this sort amongst the British, and these women were amongst the first retreating party who entered Brussels screaming all the way as they came. They rode well, for their horses' feet made the fire fly out of the pavement. I never shall forget them, for they galloped on straight forward and if the D...l had been in the way, they would have went over him, but I'm afraid a many of them must have lost their lives in this very sad affair, may we never see the like again.

... We'll call it now about 6 o'clock. The cannon were roaring most lustily and the rain coming down in torrents. Everybody was at the highest pitch of excitement, the poor inhabitants expecting the French to plunder them and ill use them in their old fashioned way, but not one word was said against the bravery of the British. The people seemed satisfied that the British would struggle well for victory, everything now was wearing a very gloomy aspect. The wounded men who were coming in were giving shocking accounts of the action. The people kept asking them "Are the Prussians come?" to which they shook their heads and said no. Every body knew that the French were much more in number than the English. About 8 o'clock accounts arrived that it was now getting worse than ever, each side was wound up to the highest pitch of desperation, each seeming determined on victory. It was just after this that news came that the Prussians were appearing in sight which cheered up the spirits of the inhabitants and English in Brussels. But by the time we got the news in Brussels the Prussians were already engaged. A great rush was now being made to the gates of the town to see what caused such a confusion in that part, when up comes five or six thousand French prisoners, escorted by some British dragoons. It was now said it must have been these men that caused the false alarm, as they first entered Waterloo, and it very likely was the case. The poor fellows cut a sorry figure, they must have fought gallantly for scarcely one of them had a hat or cap on, and nearly all of them were more or less wounded, principally sabre wounds. They were all drenched to the skin with rain and covered with mud. A few thoughtless people insulted them, with "Where's Boney now?" and such like, but speaking generally they were more pitied than anything else. They marched straight through the town to Antwerp, and were there put on board our ships. It is almost incredible to anyone when told the condition the men were in. Our cavalry, though mounted on such high horses, were so completely plastered with mud that the red of their coats could only be seen in patches. On the sides of the road where they had to ride to escort the prisoners, it was up to the horses' knees every step in mud, worked up so well that it might almost be swam in.

... We'll call it now 9 o'clock, and the roar of the cannon had gradually died away. People were crying "Is it over? Who's won? Are they only stopped on account of darkness, etc, etc.", when all at once the welcome news arrived, that Wellington had gained the day, and the French were flying in all directions. This news dispelled all the gloom, every one was smiling, the wounded were being caressed and the poor women comforted as much as possible. All the past calamities of the day were being made quite light of, and no one looked so proud as the British soldier.

In the afternoon of this day I had been in a public house kept by an Englishman of the name of Lancaster, exactly opposite our billet. One of the 95th Rifles was sitting there. He had just come in from the battle but I don't know on what duty, as he was not wounded, he had had two balls through the legs of his trousers, and whilst we were talking to him he pulled three cartridges out of his pouch, exclaiming, "Well, I did not know I had one left, there's three more Frenchmen standing than there should have been, had I known of these three rounds of ammunition". He said he had been in the Peninsula War, and that he could make every shot tell. A son belonging to the landlord asked him for the cartridges, he said No, I'll make them tell yet if I have an opportunity. We asked him to tell us his opinion of the battle, as it was past 3 o'clock when he left him. "Oh" says he "Its a d...d unfair fight. They are above two to one of us, and Wellington won't let us charge or we'd beat them now, we are obliged to stand still in squares and be mowed down like rotten sheep. They keep looking out for the Prussians, but no Prussians are to be seen. Never mind, we've lost no ground and we'll beat them yet. Lord Wellington don't know how to lose. We had a rare burst with them this morning at a Gentleman's house called Hanjoumont on the right. The devils try'd hard but we got it and kept it. If the Prussians do not come up soon, we shall try what a grand charge of the whole army will do, for I hear that is the order, and the men are very impatient for the time to arrive and I am sure the French will not be able to stand it". During this recital a good quantity of oaths were used, he spoke pretty well the sentiments of the troops for they all appeared to hold the French in utter abhorrence.

. . . We were on a continual look out for Sir George, as we were told that the staff would return to Brussels that night. It was impossible to get any intelligence of him from any of the wounded. They all said he was most likely killed. However about 12 o'clock he arrived on (I think) a troop horse, but a dragoon was following him and took the horse away. His own horse was wounded and left behind. He said that about 4 or 5 o'clock he was passing in front of some French guns and was riding at the time between Sir William Delancy and Lord March, when a cannon shot came, and knocked down Sir William Delancy and Lord March, leaving Sir George alone mounted. Sir G dismounted to assist his unfortunate friends, and went first to Sir William Delancy, but Sir William desired him to assist Lord March for, says he, "I am mortally wounded". However, he had Sir William put away as safe as possible, for the moment, and then attended to Lord March and had him carried to the rear. About this time, that is after Sir George had again mounted, a cannon shot came under his arm. He most fortunately had his hand up to his hat at the moment, to save it falling off. It came through his cloak and carried away a great piece of his coat under his shoulder and under his arm, without in the least injuring him. It likewise shaved the hair off the horse's rump, about the size of the palm of your hand, as clean as if done with a razor, leaving it quite white. Shortly after this a shell burst near Sir George and wounded his horse in five places, leaving him (Sir George) still unhurt. . . .

[19 June]

It was now daybreak on the 19th and we were anxious to know what were the orders, when to our great satisfaction we were told that we were not going to march till next day, as the Prussians were much more afresh than the British and had therefore undertaken the pursuit of the French, a job they were very fond of, as the French had beaten them only three days previous and pursued them, so they were glad of this chance of retaliation . . .

[22 June]

This morning we were ordered to march to Le Cateau, and about 6 o'clock we started. After travelling through dirty lanes and fields for some time, we came into the main road again, and to our great annoyance joined the line of baggage, which reached several miles, but every now and then we travelled in the fields on the road side taking up about 20 yards of ground. The roads were in a horrid state, as the French had thrown trees across, and dug great holes, to stop our progress and blowed up all the bridges. In short, every obstacle they could throw in our way they did. During the morning a dragoon game galloping along, saying the French were going to make a stand, having received reinforcements. It made us feel rather queer as we thought all the fighting was over. In the middle of the day we looked out as usual for a clover field and soon found one. Whilst here some of the heavy dragoons passed, and amongst them the miserable remnant of the Scots Greys – looking about 150 and most of them having two horses. We stayed here about an hour, and then proceeded looking each way if we could see the French, but none could be seen.

About 6 o'clock we entered Le Cateau, a small, shabby looking town, the white flag was flying in all directions, and preparations were being made for an illumination.... We could not think what was up, but on enquiring were told that Louis the 18th and Royal Family were coming in that evening, so we made all haste to see the sights...

[26 June]

We were ordered to march to a place called Roye, at which place we arrived early in the morning, at least before 12 o'clock. We found a great number of Prussians in the place, and a rough lot they were. We were billetted on an inn, a rather comfortable place, and whilst we were at work in the yard, we heard a row in the house. On running to see what was the matter we saw our valet in the kitchen preventing a Prussian soldier from robbing the people. He drew his sword, but one of our men in the yard who was cleaning his things, ran into the house with his drawn sword in his hand and threatened to run the Prussian through, at which the Prussian made a speedy retreat. He had mistaken the valet for the landlord. The people immediately treated us with some wine and praised the English very much. But in the afternoon when we had got pretty comfortable, the orders came to turn out immediately, and we marched several miles farther, and about 6 o'clock arrived at a long straggling village. This was to be headquarters. We were now in the Prussian line of march, and this village was a specimen of what we might expect if we continued to follow the Prussians. Not an inhabitant was to be seen, they had all fled to the woods and the whole of the houses were wide open. Sir George took his billet at a large farm house, the furniture in it was all broken to pieces, the beds all cut open and scattered about in all directions, we were obliged here for the first time to put up Sir George's camp bed, and unpack all our cooking utensils, as nothing was to be got for use in the place. We had not far to go for rations, which made it rather comfortable. Several fresh dragoons had joined us today, as an order was given for three men of every horse regiment to join Sir George for letter parties; three of the 11th had joined us, and three of the 1st Dragoon Guards, one of the 1st Dragoon Guards brought his wife with him, which was a very good job as we were beginning to want a washerwoman. The dragoons littered down the farm yard for their horses, and we made our beds under a gateway. We received orders to march next day to a place called Pont St Maxence....

[28 June]

... One day I got into a scrape whilst staying at St Denis. The German Hussar was lying asleep in the stable and I took a pack saddle and put on him and fastened him to it with the forage lines, and then left him, but just as I had done this the landlord came running to Sir George to tell him that some soldiers were plundering his wine cellar.... We all ran to assist the landlord and surrounded the entrance to the cellar. There was Sir George, the valet, my father and me, and the man of the 1st Dragoons. We had not been there a minute before three men rushed out, knocking nearly the whole of us down, but my father succeeded in capturing one. He belonged to the 27th Foot. He was directly sent to the Provost Guard, where no doubt he received three dozen. In returning to the house we met the Hussar. Sir George says to him, "Where was you that you did not come when called?" He replied in broken English "Me could no come, dam boy make me saddle". Sir George immediately says to me, "You d...d young rascal, what do you mean by making that man saddle, do you think the men and horses are not harassed enough, without you making the man saddle for your amusement". I replied I did not make him saddle, to which the man replied "das ist nix gute" (that's not good) "you did make me saddle". I then explained to Sir George, who told me not to play any more tricks with the men. As soon as Sir George was gone, this Hussar says to me, "Got for dam, what for you make me saddle?" I only laughed but I thought I had better not get in another scrape for such a trifle. During our stay here the weather was beautiful, and we could hear distinctly every now and then the French cannon firing from their heights at Paris on our advanced posts, but they did not damage. We stayed here till the 2nd of July and were all well refreshed, and had become very friendly with the people of the house, who would frequently exclaim "bon English Prussians nix bon", and on the morning of our departure, we took leave like old intimate friends.

[2 July]

The route this morning was for Paris and away we went merry enough thinking to be in Paris before night.... We thought now that the French must mean fighting again. We were not a long time in reaching Neuilly, and here we were billetted again on a beautiful mansion on the border of the Seine, and very near the bridge which is on the direct road from Paris. It was here said again that we were going to stop two or three days, as the Duke would allow the French three days to agree to the terms of capitulation, though Blücher sadly wanted to take Paris by storm, but Wellington had more prudence and discretion.... During our stay here, we went to the river side and washed all our linen, and the soldier's wife washed Sir George's. Soap was plentiful, and we managed very well. We did without using irons, the sides of the river each day was crowded with soldiers, all turned into washerwomen.

[6 July]

... On the 6th we marched between 9 and 10 o'clock, and were very soon at the barriers [gates] of Paris, which were closed. We remained there upwards of half an hour, till the French army had marched out. They marched out with bands playing and colours flying, and having their arms, so they could not grumble on that score. The gates were then thrown open and we marched in with bands playing and colours flying. The place seemed like as if some great festival was going to take place. The shops were all open, and the women, all dressed up at their windows waving white handfs. and crying "Vive Wellington, Vive les Anglais", in all directions. Everything was seemingly forgotten of past grievances. We remained some time in the street, but at last Sir George got his billet on the house of Monsieur de la Marre in the Rue des Capucines, but our horses were billetted on a stable near the Porte (?) St Denis, nearly two miles from Sir George. This was very inconvenient but could not be helped. The British troops were the first to enter Paris, and were the only troops allowed to take up the barracks, or to encampe in the neighbourhood. During the whole of the 6th and 7th, the troops kept coming in, but only to march through. Alexander the First came at the head of the Russians and was received wherever he passed with loud acclamations of "Vive l'Empereur", and it was a good excuse for them, for no doubt many of them meant their own Emperor. The Russians were hours in passing, then came the Austrians with their Emperor, he was received in the same manner. The Austrian army had a very grand appearance nearly all dressed in white, some of their cavalry were splendid regiments, particularly the Hungarian Hussars. Prince Schwartzenberg was their commander-in-chief. He was billetted in the same house as Sir George, he was a fine looking man, but very fat. I should think he was not less than 16 stone. Old Blücher got much cheered at the head of the Prussians, though the French mortally hated him and his army but the French were regular gluttons at this moment, giving vent to their loyal feelings. Louis 18th and suite arrived in the midst of the troops, and was greeted on all sides with "Vive le Roy", their feelings of loyalty were now worked up to the highest pitch, though I dare say many thousands were glad to see him for under Napoleon they had but a miserable and turbulent existence. I suppose the marching of the allied troops through the town was merely to let the people see the immense number of them. They seemed never to finish passing. They were estimated at upwards of 200,000 men. It was a well arranged affair for the whole of the Russian and Austrian army to arrive at Paris at the same time as the English and Prussians . . .

It was decided now for each nation to claim the property that Napoleon had taken from them, and a pretty sacking of the place commenced. The great gallery of the Louvre was stripped of above two thirds of its paintings, and the Austrians claimed the beautiful brass horses and car on the triumphal arch in front of the Palace of the Thuilleries. The feelings of the people were much excited at seeing such devastation taking place, and at times they became so violent that the cavalry on duty were obliged to charge them.

We had not been many days in Paris before Lady Scovell arrived from England. She had been all through Spain and Portugal so this life was nothing new to her, and this was the second time she had been in Paris, for the English army took Paris only the year before this affair. The officers' ladies kept arriving every day, for it was well known all fighting was at an end.'

Shortly after this, Sir George ordered his household to return to England.

15

HOW WARS ARE DECIDED: NAPOLEON – THE FALL OF A GIANT?

A^{t the beginning of this book I addressed the question of how the wars of the} *Revolutionary and Napoleonic period began – suggesting some of the major causes. As we approach the end, it is fitting to examine a few reasons for Napoleon's ultimate failure – as delivered by me in a paper to the British Commission for Military History at Rhodes House, Oxford, in April 1990.*

The BCMH deserves a word or two here. A predecessor had existed in the late 1920s and 1930s, but had to all intents and purposes collapsed at the outbreak of war in 1939. In the post-war period it remained dormant, until by chance Brigadier Peter Young, reader in Military History at Sandhurst from 1959 to 1969, my predecessor-but-one in the (renamed) post I am relinquishing after almost a thirteen-year tenure in mid-January 1994, received an invitation to attend the XIIth International Historical Congress to be held in Vienna in 1964. Not able to accept in person, he passed on the invitation to Dr Christopher Duffy and myself – very much 'Young Turks' in those days (or so we liked to think), and we accepted with alacrity. As no BCMH was in existence, we attended only as observers in the first instance, Dr Duffy contributing a short communication on the state of Military History in Great Britain as he saw it. We found ourselves made most welcome by the International President, General Regele of Austria, and his secretary-general, the Belgian scholar and museum curator, Albert Duchesne. Greatly encouraged by this, we soon fell under the spell of international conferencing, which combines the grave consideration of more or less scholarly papers submitted by many different national commissions (some twenty were then in existence – thirty-five today) with much convivial discussion with scholars and friends between sessions and deep into the night (probably the greatest single value of these meetings). Interleaved with the working days come the occasional visit to palaces, art collections, museums, military displays laid on by the host nation, and other notabilia to add yet another facet to these five-yearly occasions – which see up to 5000 historians of every aspect of this great hydra-headed discipline descend upon a city not unlike a swarm of locusts.

Between quinquennial congresses, individual national commissions take turns to host intermediate colloquies or smaller conferences. It was at the Paris Colloquy of 1969 that we heard the secretary-general regretting the lack of a British Commission per se during the administrative session, and there and then we decided to take the plunge. Discreetly tossing a coin on the distant benches, Dr Duffy emerged as British Secretary-General-elect and I as British President-elect, and to thunderous applause we announced the reconstitution of the British Commission.

For a few years the pair of us in fact constituted the complete British Commission, and as such attended the XIIIth Congress held at Moscow in 1970 mentioned in another Introduction, and then in 1973 the colloquy held in Stockholm which saw the birth of the United States Commission, in which process we played a small but not unimportant part. Ever bolder, we announced our intention (blessed in advance by our Commandant of that time) to hold a British colloquy at the Royal Military Academy Sandhurst in late September 1974 as a continuation of a meeting already planned for Montpellier. The British event proved a notable success despite some unseasonably cold weather, the high-point being the gracious presence of the recently wed HRH Princess Anne and Captain Mark Philips (then on the RMAS military staff) as the guests-of-honour at the farewell dinner. This noticeably impressed the Soviet delegation, as recorded elsewhere.

With the decision of the CIHM that all commissions, no matter how large or small, should be required to pay an identical annual subvention in Swiss francs, my Secretary-General and myself not unnaturally decided that the time had come to throw open the BCMH's doors to British scholars of like mind. Accordingly, we organised a public meeting one Saturday morning at the National Army Museum in London at which we established the principle that the BCMH should be an independent rather than a state-supported organisation. This meeting was surprisingly well attended – and we soon found ourselves with first twenty, then forty-five and ultimately some seventy-eight members (until today the membership stands at over 120), all paying a 'national' or 'international' subscription of (then) £5 or £7.50 a year, and the problem of finding the 200 Swiss francs pa international subscription had been resolved. The BCMH was at last solvent.

From 1975, the BCMH held one or two annual meetings each year at various locations – the first residential conference being held at Winchester in October of that year – to consider a pre-announced theme for which papers were invited. Eventually Dr Duffy – pressed by much scholarly work – relinquished the secretary-generalship to Peter Simkins of the Imperial War Museum, who in his turn gave staunch service before passing on the post to Gary Sheffield of our War Studies Department at Sandhurst. For many years the honorary treasurer was Lieutenant-Colonel (retd.) Alan Shepperd, MBE, succeeded by John Chapman and then John Lee. At length, in 1987, after 19 successive years as President, I decided it was high time for a change in the leadership of the BCMH to take place, and handed the duty on to Professor Brian Bond of King's College London, under whose guidance the BCMH has greatly flourished to the present day.

The handover took place at a residential conference held at Bournemouth on the day after the great British hurricane of that year – but it is doubtful if this was a natural

231

portent marking the change in the BCMH's presidency. Unlike the strange overnight events in the streets of Rome before the Ides of March in 44 BC, or the appearance of Halley's Comet in 1066 – each signifying a dramatic and abrupt change in ruler – no further great upset appears to have been portended, although those who lived through that turbulent October night are likely to remember it for life. Consequently the BCMH goes on from strength to strength, with some half-dozen university professors amongst its membership, and three meetings (one of them residential) each year.

Since 1980 I have been honoured to hold the elected position of an international vice-president (recently renamed un auditeur) *in the Bureau of the CIHM, so my participation at both British and international levels has continued, to my great and lasting pleasure.*

†

The Napoleonic Wars effectively ended at sunrise on Saturday 15 July 1815 when the Emperor Napoleon (known to his contemporary British foes and to certain modern British authors as simply *General Bonaparte*), embarked on the small brig *L'Epervier* at anchor in the Roads of Rochefort harbour, thence to be carried with his suite and baggage to the entry-port of HMS *Bellerophon*, there to be greeted by Captain Maitland RN and an astounded Royal Marine sentry – who was ordered not to present arms as the distinguished visitor came aboard.

Always adept at histrionics, the newcomer paused to declaim: 'I come like Themistocles, to sit at the hearth of the British people', before shaking hands with Maitland while his solemn-faced entourage looked glumly on. But Napoleon was at his most genial and prepossessing – and within half an hour had everyone from the Captain to the last-joined ship's-boy eating out of his hand, metaphorically-speaking. 'Confound the fellow!' expostulated Admiral Lord Keith. 'Give him half an hour with the Prince [Regent] and they will be the best of friends in all Europe.' Napoleon, indeed, had precisely that intention. Hoping that he would be offered exile in England, a fast pacquet boat was on its way bearing a letter addressed to the Prince Regent that is still to be seen on display at the Public Registry Office in Chancery Lane. In translation this runs as follows:

> 'Pursued by the factions which divide my country, and by the hostility of the powers of Europe, I have now finished my political career, and I come, like Themistocles, to sit at the hearth of the British people. I put myself under the protection of the laws which I claim from Your Royal Highness as the most powerful, constant and generous of my enemies.'

As we say in Yorkshire, 'fair words butter no parsnips', and although 'Prinny' must have been highly flattered by the last allusion (and indeed, by 1824, had convinced himself that he had actually taken a dashing part at Waterloo) the British government of Lord Liverpool was taking no more risks where Napoleon's person was concerned. After being transferred aboard HMS *Northumberland* at Torbay without ever setting foot ashore, and after having been made the cynosure of many boatloads of sensation-seeking tourists rowed out in the hope of gaping at 'the Corsican Ogre' in person (although very few could claim to have caught any glimpse as Napoleon had no intention of becoming a circus sideshow), the Emperor found his appeals rejected, and on 7 August HMS *Northumberland* weighed anchor and set sail for the South Atlantic – and the island of St Helena. Interestingly, some of Napoleon's notebooks from *'l'Ecole Militaire'* and even earlier have survived and included in one is the short and trenchant entry: *'Sainte Hélène – petite île.'*

Before he sailed, Napoleon revealed a little of the iron beneath the charming and courteous exterior of the *ci-devant* Emperor, when he spoke as follows to Captain Maitland. He did not consider himself, he began, the prisoner '. . . but the guest of the English. If the government, in ordering the captain of the *Bellerophon* to receive me, as well as my suite, desired only to set a trap, it has forfeited its honour and sullied its flag.'

That Napoleon had been massively defeated at Waterloo by the combined action of Wellington's Allied army and Blücher's Prussians – and then forced into exile on the distant South Atlantic isle of St Helena – there is no doubt. Whether, however, we may claim that Great Britain emerged the winner in psychological terms – then or now – is quite another matter. Let me cite three cases that spring to my mind, two ancient, the third modern. Both involve Frenchmen addicted to what we may term uncritical 'Emperor worship'.

An influential French author of the nineteenth century was the celebrated Honoré de Balzac, novelist, short-story writer and (in part) historian. Commenting upon an edition of *Les Maximes de Napoléon Ier* which he had just completed editing (albeit under a nom-de-plume), Balzac grandiloquently gives forth as follows: The soul of Napoleon passes before us. Wellington was an accident ... France may say with pride that from the depths of his tomb Napoleon still combats England.' Such hyperbolic rubbish deserves little attention, but is indicative of a widely felt Gallic mood.

The great novelist Victor Hugo was similarly ensnared in the myth. In *Les Miserables* for instance, he makes much of a supposedly 'sunken road' into which hundreds of French cuirassiers obligingly fell atop of one another, shouting (of course) *'Vive l'Empereur!'* rather than 'Geronimo!' or the French equivalent of 'Ware Holes!' (which would have been more appropriate under the circumstances) and thus ruined the superb massed cavalry charges' chances of success against Wellington's squares in his right centre. Now there was a sunken stretch of road (now disappeared save for the monument to Colonel Gordon which indicates the original height of the terrain in the vicinity, all the earth having been dug away in the 1820s to build *la Motte du Lion*), but this lay north of La Haie Sainte farmstead on the west side of the Charleroi to Brussels highway – some 400 yards away from where the doomed charges against the squares were taking place. A case of complete and deliberate historical distortion by an author who should have known better, for largely jingoistical reasons – and one that almost every French child has imbibed as 'truth' with his or her mother's milk ever since.

The modern instance of uncritical Gallic worship of Napoleon includes a hearty dislike for all things British as well (including a certain author) but makes my point even more strongly. As a member of the Napoleonic Society of America, I occasionally include an article in its bi-monthly *Bulletin*. In the February 1992 (Number 34) issue the editor included the final chapter of my 1988 book *The Illustrated Napoleon*, which comprises my mature view of the Emperor, entitled 'Napoleon's Legacy'. This – to my mind – very carefully balanced view of Napoleon as man, statesman and soldier drew down upon my head the vituperations of a certain French American who described himself as 'Executive Vice-President of the Union of French in Foreign Countries' and 'General Secretary of the French War Veterans' of a certain large city in California – but who had better remain nameless here. I will cite one or two choice selections. He expressed his discontent with several articles in Number 34 in no uncertain terms, even threatening to resign his membership if the contents did not improve in terms of hagiography of Napoleon. His '... personal preamble' ran in part as follows:

> In 1940 in the French Army I did belong to the 39th Infantry Regiment, formerly 39th of the Line [in Napoleon's time]. Our colors [sic] were carrying some prestigious names: Arcole, Rivoli, Ulm, the battle of the Marne, and Verdun. I had to read your *Bulletin* to learn, for the first time, that Napoleon chastised its members, and learning this from the poisoned pen of a former British officer made it even worse.
>
> After this personal preamble, I am going to try reviewing the contents of your *Bulletin*, which made me wonder if your Society is only a front to better calumny the Emperor under the disguise of promoting a better understanding of his accomplishments...
>
> Page 13 – *Napoleon as a Man and Leader*, by David Chandler (Royal Academy, Sandhurst). A rubbish of English views and insults to the Emperor's memory. Coming from Sandhurst explains, by itself, the reasons.
>
> Page 19 – *Was Napoleon Poisoned? I Certainly Hope So!* by George F. Will, columnist. Another bucket of manure and insults...

and much more in the same vein. Usually, the best policy is to ignore such vituperations, but because he went on in due course to attack Professor Dorothy

Carrington's *Napoleon and his Parents* – 'Another typically British name . . .' I felt as a gentleman bound to leap to this distinguished lady's defence (as well as that of Sandhurst and myself) and give this frog-eating Johnny *crapaud* a line or two in return.

This duly appeared in the next issue, and I think I gave back as good as I had received. After sympathising with him about his regiment's disgrace in 1796, giving chapter and verse for General Bonaparte's rebuke to the 39th and 85th Regiments of the Line on 7 November 1796 (in particular *La Correspondence de Napoléon* Volume Two p. 103, letter No. 1170), I demonstrated that the 39th never had Rivoli upon its colours (citing the French Ministry of War's official lists drawn up in 1900) before proceeding as follows:

> However, whilst I fully subscribe to the great philosopher Voltaire's dictum to the effect that however much he might disagree with a person's views he '. . .*would fight to the death to protect his right to express them* . . .' I would remind the possibly humourless M. — that there is a moment when liberty becomes license, and he would do well to think before he writes on matters that he clearly knows very little about.
>
> Dorothy Carrington, incidentally, who is also accused of writing 'another bucket of manure and insults' is in fact a most distinguished scholar, as *Bulletin No. 34* by a fortunate chance makes perfectly clear to M. —'s presumed discomfiture on p. 31 by reporting her receipt of an honorary doctoral degree from the University of Corsica! Dr. Carrington therefore also deserves a complete public apology from our very 'new' member, as does the Royal Military Academy Sandhurst for the inference in paragraph eight.
>
> If no satisfactory apologies are forthcoming, then Jacques —will no doubt take the only course open to a gentleman. We must wait and see.

Needless to say, and just as I expected from such a strutting Gallic cock, we are still waiting. However, in my *postscriptum* I proceeded to deliver my *coup de grâce*:

> PS. I am . . . always very interested to learn more about foreign Regiments, and I am writing to my friend General Delmas at the French Military Archives at the Château de Vincennes for details of how the 39th performed in the cataclysmic campaign of 1940. Better, I sincerely hope, than their forebears, like it or not, on 4 November, 1796.

My gamble turned up trumps. The French archives duly revealed that in 1940 the three battalions of the modern French 39th Regiment survived the German onslaught just three days before being scattered, and most of them made prisoners of war. I forwarded the document to M. —, but with delicacy forebore to publish it in *Bulletin No. 36*. Enough is enough and I felt I had gained the upper hand in the spirited exchange. But this all goes to show how ill-informed and wholly inaccurate – and indeed extreme – so much 'jingoistic' or hagio-graphic criticism can be.

All the same, to return to the events of July 1815, 'Perfidious Albion' had clearly done it again. Without a doubt, we had won the physical war, but it is still arguable whether we had (or indeed have) won the psychological struggle against Napoleon. Very recently, more hyperbole has been coming out of the Paris ministries to the effect that ratification of the Maastricht Agreement confirms Napoleon's ultimate victory – by setting up the European Community he had dreamt of, but been frustrated from achieving by (of course) British hostility and conspiracy! 'Now [1992], 177 years after Waterloo, l'Empereur has justly triumphed...' and more in the same *genre*. Well, let us wait and see.

Whatever his unquestioning worshippers may aver, Napoleon had been far from popular in the nineteenth century, as this 'Nursery Ballad' (c. 1840) demonstrates:

The Nursemaid's Cautionary Song for Children
Baby, baby, naughty baby,
Hush, you squalling thing, I say;
Hush your squalling, or it may be
Bonaparte may pass this way.

Baby, baby, he's a giant,
Tall and black as Rouen steeple
And he dines and sups, rely on't,
Every day on naughty people.

Baby, baby, he will hear you
As he passes by the house,
And he limb from limb will tear you
Just as pussy tears a mouse.

I feel that the psychological damage these verses inflicted on Victorian children must have been dire indeed. But even in France, 1804, pointed anti-estab-lishment (presumably Bourbonist) verses were in circulation.

I lived very long on borrowing and charity,
Of Barras, vile flatterer, I married the whore;
I strangled Pichegru, assassinated d'Enghien,
And for such noble efforts obtained me a crown.

Napoleon's enforced allies also had a few words to say. In Spain, in 1813, when ordered to cry *'Vive l'Empereur!'*, the Swiss conscripts in fact shouted out something extremely rude in German which sounded much the same. Thus anti-Napoleonic sentiments were not restricted to *'les Roshifs'* of the British Isles – although Gilray and Rowlandson sometimes took matters to extremes in their cartoons, and visitors to Brighton Palace can still inspect the Prince Regent's chamber-pot which has the head of Napoleon standing forlornly as a target in its centre. And, something that particular enraged the distinguished captive of St Helena, the British government with deliberate *lèse majesté* would only refer to him as 'General Bonaparte' until his death in 1821. Thus Britain did not always show a full amount of *politesse* to their enemy.

Napoleon was, of course, by any standard phenomenal in his abilities and, in some cases it must be admitted, their perversions. The true 'first world war' (as the Napoleonic struggle has been dubbed) came to an end in large measure due to certain aspects of his achievements and to certain defects in his personality.

First the sheer statistical evidence of the wars associated with his name is daunting enough. They lasted for almost twenty-two-and-a-half years with one fifteen-month break – the Peace of Amiens. Thus for an entire generation larger or smaller parts of Europe were at war – from 20 April 1792 (when the French Girondin government declared war on the Emperor Francis II in his capacity as King of Bohemia) to 20 November 1815, the date of the signature of the Second Treaty of Paris.

This considerable period of time saw the formation of seven coalitions against France by various combinations of European powers of which Great Britain, followed by Austria, were the most deeply involved. Of these coalitions Napoleon was instrumental in destroying five, succumbing only to the sixth and seventh. In terms of casualties estimates vary from a 'high' of 1,750,000 Frenchmen killed and incapacitatingly wounded to a 'low' of 450,000. The only certain statistic is that of 15,000 French officer casualties between December 1804 and April 1814 – in other words over the life-cycle of the First Empire. Add to these the military and civilian casualties of the other European countries and a figure of between five and six million dead becomes likely. Which brings us to one important point. Why, if Napoleon destroyed five coalitions, was he incapable of securing a lasting peace? Why has he gone down to History only as 'Napoleon', and not, in the style of Alexander, Charlemagne and Frederick II, 'Napoleon the Great'?

Many answers could be suggested – the implacable hostility of Great Britain high amongst them. Between January 1793 and November 1915 Britain was at war for over twenty-one-and-a-half years (the Peace of Amiens excepted), Austria for thirteen-and-a-half years, Spain for eight-and-a-half, Prussia almost six-and-a-half – the same as Tsarist Russia. France herself, of course, was at war with someone (usually a mixed grill of foes) for twenty-two-and-a-half years. Britain's intrepid persistence against the ambitions of Revolutionary France and then 'the Corsican Ogre' was made feasible by one geographical feature – the existence of La Manche or the English Channel, guarded by the Royal Navy which from at least 1805 had no true rival and certainly no equal.

Another suggested partial answer to the question relates to one basic human frailty in Napoleon's personality and nature – namely a complete and devastating lack of tact. He was aware of the quality's importance, particularly when he considered himself to be treated without it by others. 'War, like politics, is a matter of tact' he wrote in May 1796 – challenging the Directory's intention to divide the Italian command between Kellerman the Elder and himself. He won his point – 'One bad commander is better than two good ones; Kellerman will command here as well as I.' In this instance his 'tactfulness' took the form of the dispatch of a large convoy of loot from Italy to Paris.

As an individual Napoleon could be by turns charming, hypnotic and caring, or foul-mouthed, unspeakably rude and even physically violent. Marshal Berthier was once seized by the throat before having his head hammered against a stone wall. The unfortunate Minister Molé was kicked in the crotch for presenting an unpopular set of economic figures. Many a servant (but fewer soldiers) was struck across the face or shoulders with the riding-crop the Emperor habitually carried. He was as abrupt with women as with men at court. 'Madam – they told me you were ugly; they certainly did not exaggerate,' or, again, 'If you appear again in that despicable dress you will be refused entry.'

At the diplomatic level Napoleon could be equally acerbic and brusque. 'What are the lives of a million men to a man such as I?' he asked Prince Metternich at a peace conference in 1813. His description – apparently flattering – of Queen Louisa as 'the only real man in Prussia' was more of a snide comment on the lack of manly characteristics in her decidedly uxorious spouse, Frederick-William III. He became increasingly impressed by her at Tilsit, however.

Napoleon was equally rough in his attitude towards the Papacy. It was truly a bold step to 'restore the altars' in Republican France by the Concordat of July 1801. But by 1804 he was forcefully expressing himself as follows: 'For the Pope, I am Charlemagne . . . I therefore expect to be treated from this point of view. I shall change nothing in appearance if they behave well; otherwise I shall reduce the Pope to merely Bishop of Rome.' One is slightly reminded of Stalin's cynical question: 'How many divisions has the Pope?'

An examination of the terms that Talleyrand and later Clarke exacted from defeated enemies or backsliding allies and even neutrals indicates well enough why it was impossible to convert an ex-foe into a convinced friend. Time and again his extreme demands for territory, money and above all men to swell his armies laid the basis for future revanchism rather than true pacification. Napoleon always had to hand down his terms contemptuously from Mount Olympus to grovelling client-states. He had scant time for compromise – 'all or nothing' could have been his motto. If Europe was to have peace it must be a *Pax Napoleonica*. As Wellington once remarked, 'Boney is not a gentleman.' Nor was he by contemporary standards, although he had both taste and discernment. He always knew how the old monarchical families regarded him. As early as 1801 he declared that '... between old monarchies and a young republic a spirit of hostility must always exist. In the present state of affairs every peace treaty means no more than a brief armistice; and I believe that my destiny will be to fight almost continuously.' In sum he was a fatalist – 'everything that is to happen is written down.'

As mentioned above, his terms of peace were harsh. In July 1806 he compelled the Emperor Francis II of the Holy Roman Empire to lose a number, and become merely the Emperor Francis I of Austria and Hungary. Whole provinces would be torn away – to improve the Empire's strategic position or resources, to reward allies, or simply punish a foe. Thus, on 26 December 1805 (after Austerlitz), three million Austrian subjects (or one fifth of the entire population) found themselves Bavarians, Württembergers or Italians by the terms of the Peace of Pressburg. One-and-a-half years later by the treaties of Tilsit (July, 1807), the Kingdom of Prussia lost all its territories west of the Elbe to create the new Kingdom of Westphalia for Jérôme Bonaparte, while King Louis Bonaparte of Holland absorbed East Frisia and the Grand-Duchy of Berg, and received further large tracts of choice territory – in effect reducing Prussia to merely four provinces. Even then, a huge indemnity was to be paid to France before occupation forces were withdrawn from even those.

On this point it is interesting to note the remarkable resilience of France under similar uncomfortable circumstances after 1815. Part of the Allies' terms included a huge indemnity demanded by Prussia in revenge for that of 1807 imposed by France besides a vast reordering of France's border provinces. Yet it is clear how excellent had been Napoleon's constructive, economic and industrial reconstruction of France by the commercial and other Codes of the period 1801–4 in particular. To everybody's surprise, France had completed all reparation payments in full by late 1818 – several years ahead of schedule – and accordingly was released from military occupation, and a little later (by the Congress of Aix-la-Chapelle) also permitted to join the Holy Alliance. Thus fared the vanquished. As for the main victor – Great Britain – after a short postwar boom of prosperity she was suffering widespread social unrest and agrarian misery by 1819 as a deep recession bit into the economy – the presence of 300,000 demobilised and jobless soldiers and sailors greatly exacerbating the situation. As Sir John Clapham wrote of 1816 in 1920 – 'Great Britain – though victorious, suffered acutely. Mismanagement was largely responsible for her sufferings – mismanagement of demobilisation; mismanagement of taxes; mismanagement of food supplies and so on. But suffering due to international dislocation following war could not have been avoided by management, however good.' Prussia also had internal troubles, as did Austria, Spain and Tsarist Russia. All this misery France in large measure avoided despite the 'White Terror', avoiding mass social agitation of the type gripping Great

Britain at the time of the Cato Conspiracy of 1821 – the plot to assassinate the Cabinet.

Certainly, then, Napoleon cannot be depicted by even his greatest worshippers as any 'dove of peace', although some try to do so. The price of his favours was always too high in terms of men – always men – money and policy (both diplomatic and commercial), as the ultimately fatal attempt to impose the Continental System on an unwilling Europe from December 1806 would demonstrate. As a Minister – M. Mollien – once sagely remarked of Napoleon, '. . . that although his common sense amounted to genius, somehow he never knew when to stop.'

A.J.P. Taylor in *How Wars End* (1985) asserted that it was the corruption of the Marshalate that lay at the root of Napoleon's ultimate failure. Certainly he bound them in a spider's web of privilege and often wealth, determined that they should never be able to break themselves free. This largely cynical policy certainly rebounded upon his head with a terrible vengeance. In 1815 only seven of the twenty-three marshals still alive rallied to his side. Some thirteen, anxious to retain their privileges and survive *à la* Vicar of Bray, rallied to the Bourbons to a greater or lesser extent.

In my view Napoleon himself never fully succumbed to corruption. He was just '. . . a great, bad man' as Clarendon said of Cromwell, who exhausted France just as he had exhausted his marshals. To a large extent he must bear responsibility for the collapse of his Empire. Many, many reasons besides the few treated here could be discussed. The deterioration of his army as it steadily became an international force after 1805; the failure to contain the Royal Navy; the failure – from 1812 – to avoid a war on two fronts separated by 2000 miles, leading inevitably to dislocation and strategic over-stretch or consumption; the ever growing problems of command and control; the improvement in Napoleon's opponents – the Arch-Duke Charles, Kutusov and above all Wellington – whilst his own concepts stagnated: 'I have fought sixty battles, but I know no more now than I knew at the beginning'. All these features – and more – account for the ending of the Napoleonic Wars in 1814 with the postscript of the Hundred Days the following year.

The roots of failure as I hope I have demonstrated were within Napoleon himself. He in fact spoke his own epitaph as early as 1805. Speaking of a failing general of dragoons he said: 'Ordener is worn out. One has only a certain time for war. Another five or six years and even I must call a stop.' Six years from 1805 bring us to the eve of 1812 – and Russia. From that great disaster onwards it was just a question of time.

16

NAPOLEON: CLASSICAL MILITARY THEORY AND THE JOMINIAN LEGACY

A s great a military phenomenon as Napoleon was bound to leave an influential legacy behind him. Since the onset of the age of gunpowder there had been no commander to compare to him, and no system of waging warfare that was so dramatic and drastic at one and the same time.

Two great 'interpreters' of Napoleonic warfare emerged – both of whom had first-hand experience of Napoleonic wars. The first was the Prussian Carl von Clausewitz (1780–1831). The second was the Swiss Antoine Henri Baron Jomini (1779–1869).

Clausewitz was a Prussian junior staff officer who was taken prisoner after the battle of Auerstädt in 1806. Following his release, he served as assistant to General Scharnhorst during the secret reformation of the Prussian army, and served as tutor to the Crown Prince of Prussia. In 1812, he deserted to join the Tsar's army and served at Riga. He was instrumental in helping negotiate the Convention of Taurrogen whereby General Yorck and the entire Prussian corps serving under Marshal Macdonald declared themselves neutral in January 1813 – starting the processes which by March had led the complete kingdom of Prussia to abandon its unwilling alliance with Napoleon and to join the Allied Sixth Coalition. In 1814 he rejoined the Prussian army, and served as chief-of-staff to General Thielmann during the Campaign of the Hundred Days, fighting at both Ligny and Wavre.

Promoted to major-general in 1818, he became director of the Prussian Kriegsa-kademie, and began to undertake the impressive oeuvre of historical writing which included his Campaign of 1812 in Russia (Greenhill Books, 1991) and military philosophy which will for ever be associated with his name. His most influential work, On War, was completed by his wife, for Clausewitz had succumbed to cholera in 1831. His true influence dates from the 1860s, and became increasingly pervasive by the First World War, first in Prussia, then (although often misunderstood in translation) in England, France and the United States, and remains of importance to the present day. He taught of war as a philosophical concept, stressing that it was '... the continuation of policy by other means', that it was subject to many types of 'friction', and that 'the bloody *solution of the crisis' (or the destruction of the enemy's army in a decisive battle and thus of his national will and ability to resist) was the ultimate aim of every campaign.*

Baron Jomini attacked the subject of Napoleonic warfare from a different viewpoint. A volunteer who joined the French-sponsored Swiss army, by 1804 he had written his Treatise on Major Military Operations *which impressed even Napoleon when it was brought to his attention. Despite the early enmity of Napoleon's chief-of-staff, Marshal Berthier, from 1805 Jomini became increasingly associated with the Grand Army, serving as either chief-of-staff to Marshal Ney or on attachment to Imperial Head-quarters. He fought with Ney in Spain and later in Germany, but in late 1813 deserted to the Russian army to escape Berthier's vindictive attentions. After taking part in the Campaign of France in 1814 with the Russian army, he spent the remainder of his life in the Tsar's service. His ideas became influential in the USA before the Civil War (1861–5), as well as in Russia during the earlier Crimean War (1854–5). Today his ideas are re-emerging to attention as they escape from the formerly all-pervading influence of Clausewitz.*

His approach to the phenomenon of Napoleonic Warfare was more pragmatic than Clausewitz's, and is analysed in the chapter that follows. The material formed the basis of a lecture given to the Higher Command and Staff Course at the Staff College, Camberley, in 1987.

†

Coming as I do from an institution where G.F.R. Henderson, the author of *Stonewall Jackson*, served and taught as a member of the faculty, it is only proper that I should preface my reflections by a quotation from the sage colonel. He was no great admirer of 'principles of war' or other abstractions, but argued that detailed military history should speak for itself. In one passage he praises Clausewitz for his emphasis on the importance of moral factors in war, but, he goes on, 'Clausewitz was a genius, and geniuses and clever men have a dis-tressing habit of assuming that everyone understands what is perfectly clear to themselves.' Those who have struggled with the more abstruse passages of *On War* will no doubt know what he meant – but those who have had the privilege to study the words of the Prussian master in the fine modern English translation by Michael Howard and Peter Paret may not be aware of how fortunate they were to have the 1976 Princeton edition available to them. Those of an older, tougher generation – amongst whom I must, alas, include myself – had the more dubious pleasure of being exposed to the three, dread, red-bound volumes of the standard 1908 translation, and will never forget being faced by the phenomenon of whole printed-page single sentences which defied compre-hension by any simple mortal even after four attempted readings.

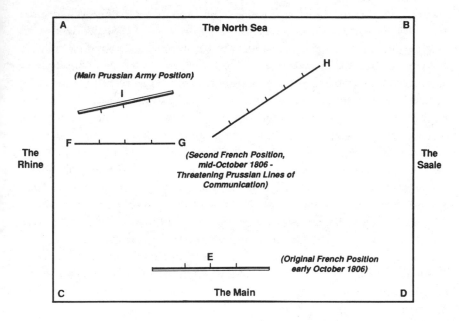

JOMINI'S REPRESENTATION OF THE PRUSSIAN CAMPAIGN OF 1806

However, at Oxford in the 1950s I had the privilege to be tutored by the late C.T. Atkinson of Exeter College, and his approach to military history was far more down-to-earth – I am tempted to say 'Jominian'. He was a strong believer in taking history as you find it, and used hard facts rather than sweeping abstract concepts as the basis of his teaching. Adopting a similar approach, I intend first to consider the supposed phenomenon of Napoleonic Warfare in an attempt to pinpoint its special features which so impressed contemporaries – and indeed posterity down to the present. Second, I shall consider Baron Jomini as the interpreter of Napoleon's art of war and as the father of classical military theory, and the influence he has wielded down to the present day. So, in the words of the Apocrypha, 'Let us now praise famous men and our fathers that begat us' – in this instance those who have conditioned our military thought, and especially Baron Antoine Henri Jomini.

The influence of 'the Little Corporal' on the conduct of land warfare was both dramatic and profound. Distrusting the more traditional features of eighteenth-century positional warfare – which centred around time-consuming sieges – after his experiences in besieging Mantua in North Italy (4 June 1796 to 2 February 1797 – or some eight months) and Acre in what is today Israel (18 March to 20 May 1799 – in this case unsuccessfully), he consistently sought the decisive battle in order to break his opponent's political will, and thus induce the acceptance of a dictated pacification to France's advantage. As we shall see,

Napoleon was not in many ways an innovator – except in one significant respect. This was the all-importance of using mobility as a means of applying remorseless psychological pressure upon his opponents: Napoleon fused marching, fighting and pursuit into a single remorseless process, affording his enemy no time to draw breath. The best example is the campaign against Prussia in 1806: Napoleon pre-empted Berlin's declaration of war by invading Saxony from Bamberg on 8 October, passed the difficult Thuringerwald, changed his line of operations by a swing to the west in order to fight the Prussians at the double-battle of Jena-Auerstädt on the 14th (although neither the form nor the precise locations of those engagements was precisely foreseen), and then unleashed a devastating pursuit to the Baltic coast which the French reached three weeks and 150,000 prisoners-of-war later. A month had sufficed to humiliate and almost destroy supposedly the strongest army in Europe – although not to bring peace. From Bamburg to Lubeck is some 500 km in a direct line.

Although we need to be cautious in matters of comparison and the use of examples, the impact of Napoleonic warfare on his times can be well illustrated by comparing two celebrated marches separated by a century. In 1704, Marlborough won great acclaim by marching an allied army eventually 40,000 strong from Bedburg to the Danube – a distance of some 600 km – in a little over five weeks. In 1805, launching his campaign against the Third Coalition, Napoleon's Grand Army (210,000 strong) covered much the same distance in just eleven days. Admittedly roads had improved considerably over the intervening period, but in other basic respects the two feats are broadly comparable if only to illustrate the dramatic increase in strategic mobility obtainable by the later period.

Of course another underlying factor was the development of the all-arm army corps system – in effect miniature armies capable of marching and indeed fighting alone against superior numbers for up to twenty-four hours if need be before reinforcement: thus Marlborough's 'scarlet caterpillar' had been replaced by a far more flexible and enveloping network of separately but steadily converging, hard-marching, self-contained formations. The French army corps provided Napoleon with his ideal weapon for waging war at the strategic and operational levels.

Napoleon was not, *pace* the legend, a great innovator in terms of either doctrine or military institutions. These he inherited in equal measure from the old Bourbon regime of pre-1789 and the Revolutionary armies of 1792–9. His greatness lay in the total and ruthless execution and exploitation of other men's ideas. He added pace to the conduct of war, and this, allied to his sheer audacity, boundless opportunism, professional mastery and personal, charismatic leadership, made him a devastating opponent and, for a decade, virtually unbeatable. As Abbé Siéyès acutely remarked: 'He knows all; he understands everything; he can achieve anything.'

Although he denied using any 'system of manoeuvre', a close study of his campaigns will reveal two underlying patterns or concepts used, with adaptations on every occasion, time and again, to achieve a favourable battle situation. First there was the method much approved by Jomini, the 'strategy of the central position'. Faced by numerically superior foes, Napoleon often sought to divide them, and then defeat each section in detail in turn, relying on local, rather than overall, superiority.

Using the light cavalry screen to locate the enemy's main formations (and to conceal his own), Napoleon would interpose his army between them so as to gain the advantage of 'interior lines'. Leaving a small part of his force to keep one half of the enemy at bay for up to a day, fighting a spoiling battle against long odds – which only the all-round flexibility of the army corps system made acceptable – Napoleon would mass the remainder of his army against the second opponent, with local superiority of force, and hopefully defeat him heavily on the main battlefield. Having forced this foe to retreat, Napoleon would detach a smaller force to pursue and harass, and at the same time force-march the remainder of his army towards the flank and rear of the secondary opponent, who would then be defeated in turn – this time more decisively. Such a concept underlay his first essay at independent army command – the defeat of Piedmont in April 1796; it also lay at the heart of his last; the attack through Charleroi towards Brussels in June 1815.

This manoeuvre had one drawback in that it permitted one opponent to 'live to fight another day'; it did not offer complete victory in itself. Therefore when conditions made it operable Napoleon's favoured strategy was all-out envelopment – a manoeuvre based upon an initial superiority of strength on the part of the French.

Using part of his army to distract the enemy's attention in an irrelevant direction (and giving him the illusion of enjoying the initiative), Napoleon would launch the remainder in a rapid march to threaten the flank and rear, at the same time cutting the foe's lines of communication and retreat. The result would be a 'reversed front battle' – each adversary facing towards his own base – on ground usually of the French choosing and under conditions of French numerical superiority. If defeated, the enemy had nowhere to go: surrender or annihilation were the sole choices as the main French army was between him and his base, whilst the original pinning force would close in to shut the trap. We find Napoleon employing this general idea time and again: in the post-Piedmont phase of the North Italian campaign of 1796 against Beaulieu (albeit without complete success), and in more refined form in 1800, 1805 and 1806.

To achieve a satisfactory battle situation was one thing: to win the resultant battle was something more again. Napoleon was often completely opportunistic: *'On s'engage, et alors on voit'* he remarked to Montholon at St Helena: 'You engage, and then you wait and see.' On other occasions a more sophisticated idea underlay the battle-plan. 'Sometimes the plan of campaign reveals the plan of battle,' he stated on another occasion. 'Only a superior mind will be able to appreciate this.' Here he was probably thinking of the method he employed in 1796 at Castiglione (with only partial success) and at Bautzen in 1813: what is often called 'the strategic battle'. On these occasions he used part of his army to pin the enemy army, however strong, to a known location, at the same time ordering up neighbouring corps to escalate the frontal battle whilst further formations would be ordered to make a fast, concealed march to threaten the foe's revealed line of communication. Meanwhile the French reserve would mass unseen behind the sector of battlefront nearest to the enemy flank about to be threatened.

Once convinced that all enemy reserves had been drawn into the frontal engagement, the outflanking force would reveal its presence and attack. As the foe switched troops from his front nearest to the new threat, Napoleon would unleash his pre-positioned reserve in the decisive breakthrough attack – and the battle would be won.

There was much more to Napoleonic warfare than this, but this over-simplification illustrates, I feel, the basic methods that Jomini set out to analyse. Obviously the systems were far from foolproof: there were telling ripostes available to a cool opponent who was not psychologically at a disadvantage – in other words when Napoleon became predictable in his methods, which dates certainly from 1812 and probably, to a more limited extent, from 1808. 'I have fought 60 battles and I have learnt nothing I did not know at the beginning,' Napoleon once boasted in a revelatory moment.

As already mentioned, Napoleon was not an innovator – only a superb practitioner. But there, of course, lies the rub. As Clausewitz remarks: 'In war everything is simple; only the simplest thing is very difficult to achieve.' *Tant pis!* After all, in 'classical warfare' there have really only been six possible operational manoeuvres – although the modern development of air warfare, air mobility and revolutionary guerrilla warfare may be adding one or two more. The original six, of course, are all reflected to a greater or lesser extent in Jomini's voluminous writings, although he emphasised some more than others. Just for the record, these are the following, with a representative example of both ancient and modern application – for most of them go back to Alexander the Great:

METHOD	EXAMPLES
Envelopment of a single flank.	Gaugamela, 331 BC; Gazala, 1942
Envelopment of both flanks.	Cannae, 216 BC; Kiev, 1941
Penetration of the centre.	Blenheim, 1704; Alamein, 1942
Attack from a defensive position.	Zama, 202 BC; Imphal-Kohima, 1944
Withdrawing before striking back.	Salamanca, 1812; Msus, 1942
Surprise attack at enemy's rear.	2nd Bull Run, 1862; Burma, 1945

If we add to these 'gambits' a comprehension of what is meant by a 'line of operations' as opposed to a 'line of communication' or a 'line of retreat'; a firm appreciation of the advantages conferred by 'interior over exterior lines'; and – a vital logistical point that Jomini frequently asserts – an understanding of what is meant by 'strategic consumption' or 'the diminishing power of the offensive' – then you have in a nutshell the greater part of the manoeuvres of war that proved so dear to our Swiss *général de brigade* and military theorist of classical warfare. The last point merits slight expansion. Its relevance is ageless, and in many respects it neatly summarises one major difference of outlook between Jomini and Clausewitz. It is self-evident that sound logistics rather than fine heroics underlies the successful fighting of a campaign, other factors being approximately equal. Longfellow's well-known poem about the fatal effects of the loss of a vital message – ultimately involving the collapse of an army, a nation, even an empire, 'all for want of a nail', illustrates one aspect of the concept, however simplistically. An army advancing deep into enemy territory enjoys the Clausewitzian 'moral advantage' of making ground, whilst the Jominian principle of 'strategic consumption' – the developing mathematically calculable exhaustion and breakdown of offensive power through the action of growing distance from the supporting base area – applies the brake. At the same time, however battered the fighting spirit and morale of the retreating force, in physical terms it is often steadily recovering the further it goes back – assimilating reinforcements and its own depots until, at least theoretically, a state of vulnerable equilibrium is obtained, inviting a reversal of roles unless the initial attacking forces' logistical services are capable of making good the effects of wear and tear in terms of fighting men, munitions, stores and equipment.

This is to ask a great deal – highlighting Napoleon's dictums that 'an army marches upon its stomach' and, more significantly, 'space I may recover, time never.' As participants – on opposite sides – both Clausewitz and Jomini were fascinated, and appalled, by the cataclysm of the Russian campaign of 1812. The same factors reappear with regularity: the 'see-saw' nature of the war in the Western Desert 1940–3 (which, incidentally also provides an excellent example of interior versus exterior lines at the strategic level) is one; the survival of Slim's Burcorps at the end of a 1000-mile retreat in 1942 another; the over-extension of the North Korean forces in the first phase of the Korean War in 1950, a third. Of course Clausewitzian moral factors are equally significant: it is vital that the morale of the retreating force should not descend below a certain level or physical reinforcement may have little effect in checking the victorious advance of the aggressor: the total collapse of the Prussian army's morale after 14 October in 1806 is one example of this; the collapse of that of the French army and nation after the events of 15–18 May 1940 another. On the other hand the Soviet Union was able to survive 'Operation Barbarossa's' initial *blitzkrieg* and the loss of 3,000,000 prisoners-of-war between late June and

December 1941, and recover – possibly the most expensive example of 'trading space for time' in all the annals of warfare.

It is now time to consider more specifically the role and influence of Baron Jomini as a founder and disseminator of the classical tradition in military theory. Of course it is dangerous to hang labels on individuals. Jomini was no more the creator of classical military theory than Napoleon, his great exemplar, was a phenomenon using truly novel military methods. Jomini's concepts were founded at base on eighteenth-century rationalism. The prosecution of the art and science of warfare was relatively late in attracting this searching examination seeking basic principles. Much of what Jomini would write was foreshadowed by the Welshman, General Lloyd, in the later 1760s in his *History of the Late War in Germany* (the Seven Years' War) and his later *Military Memoirs* (1781) – sources, together with Bourcet, Frederick the Great and Guibert, ruthlessly plundered of ideas by that voracious reader, young Lieutenant Napoleon Bonaparte at the Artillery School of Auxonne in 1788 on the eve of the Revolution. But Jomini is remembered whilst Bourcet is all but forgotten because the former received something of a 'seal of approval' from Napoleon as early as 1805, and in any case was in a position to use the Emperor's campaigns as the basis for his analysis and inspiration on a basis of personal experience until 1813; when, after a serious tiff with Berthier, he transferred his sword to the Tsar and in consequence experienced the Leipzig campaign and that of France (1814) 'from the other side of the hill'. Further reasons for Jomini's longstanding influence was his literary fecundity and above all his longevity. As late as the Crimean War in the mid-1840s he was still advising the Tsar – and the sometime Swiss bank clerk died only in 1869, aged ninety.

In addition to Lloyd, Jomini was also influenced by the Prussian Heinrich von Bülow. Between them, Lloyd and Bülow provided the basic vocabulary for Jomini's studies of strategy. They contributed the concepts of the central 'line of operations', 'objectives' and 'bases', the importance of geographical factors and the mathematical analysis of war. Jomini was to stress the prosaic approach to warfare – the establishment of principles and formulae – at the expense of what would be Clausewitz's preoccupation – the 'spirit of war', the important moral factors. But Jomini was not exclusivist in his claims: he freely admitted that: 'War, far from being an exact science, is a terrible and impassioned drama, regulated, it is true, by three or four general principles, but also dependent for its results upon a number of moral and physical complications.' What were these 'general principles'?

He first committed them to paper in 1803, basing his ideas on a close study of Frederick the Great's campaigns and Napoleon's First Italian Campaign. According to his four principles, successful warfare consisted:

'In directing the mass of one's forces successively on to the decisive points in the theatre of war – as far as possible against the communications of the enemy without disrupting one's own.' (*flexibility*)

'In manoeuvring so as to engage this concentration of forces only against fractions of the enemy's strength.' (*surprise*)

In, on the battlefield itself, concentrating '... the bulk of one's force at the decisive point, or against the section of the foe's line which one wishes to overwhelm.' (*concentration of force*)

In ensuring not only that one's forces were concentrated at the decisive point '... but also that they were sent forward with vigour and concentration so as to produce a simultaneous result.' (*offensive action*)

A close study of Napoleon's campaigns shows how much insight and clarity Jomini's ideas can claim. These were the methods of the master – time and again – although the detail inevitably varied. How much Jomini actually contributed to the French operations is more debatable. He certainly served in the Austerlitz campaign of 1805, that of Jena-Auerstädt next year, that of Poland in 1807, and went to Spain in 1808. In the process he rose from the lowly status of expatriate supernumerary officer to the rank of general of brigade, ultimately holding the post of chief of staff to Marshal Ney. In Russia, 1812, he was successively military governor of Vilna and Smolensk. His subsequent experiences to 1815 we have already alluded to. We know that he accurately anticipated the French moves in the Marengo campaign of 1800 – and came to Napoleon's attention in 1805 through his first publications – which impressed the Emperor sufficiently for him to demand why they had not been censored as being over-revelatory of his methods – and even more so in 1806 by accurately divining the Emperor's intentions in the war against Prussia. He later claimed that Ney – not only the 'bravest of the brave' but also, possibly, 'the thickest of the thick' – owed much to his assistance, and that the French disasters sprang directly from the ignoring of his principles. However, there is no doubt whatsoever that he was a contentious, intellectually arrogant and uncooperative subordinate (he apparently sent in his resignation on fifteen different occasions) – who tried hard-working, conscientious and down-to-earth Berthier's patience to the limit before the final, fatal altercation of 1813 which led to Jomini's desertion to the Russians. Similarly, during his later years – mostly spent in the Russian service – he was not averse to furthering his reputation, indulging in 'auto-hagiography', as Michael Howard once described it.

Perhaps the gravest criticism of his concepts was his underestimation of the significance of human weakness in war. Restricting most of his comments to the rarefied level of high commanders, he paid too little attention to the effects of administrative hazards, problems caused by inadequate intelligence, the roles of human fear, rivalry and ambition and of institutional inertia – points that Clausewitz made a great deal of in *On War*.

Nevertheless, his writings were widely read. His *Traité des grandes opérations militaires* was published between 1804 and 1810 in eight volumes; his *Histoire critique des guerres de la Révolution* appeared between 1816 and 1824 in all of fifteen volumes; and the epitome of his writings – *Précis de l'Art de la Guerre* – written for the enlightenment of the Tsarevich Alexander, came out in 1837.

And although Clausewitz's views on the 'big battle' and his fuller discussion of 'war as a political art' and greater stress on the significance of will-power in warfare would cause Jomini's work to be somewhat overshadowed by the later years of the nineteenth century, and reach their peak of acceptability between 1914 and 1918, there is no denying that Jomini's influence was very strong through much of the nineteenth century. Reasons for this are not hard to discover. His reputation based on Napoleon's approval has already been mentioned. Then again, Clausewitz's works received scant attention until the 1870s, even in Prussia, whereas Jomini's writings were widely available. Yet again his approach to the study of the mechanics of military operations was methodical and comprehensive as well as comprehensible. His writings were ideally suited for the many staff courses coming into existence – and certainly helped to inspire Hamley's *Operations of War* which became the 'bible' at Camberley. His writings were also well regarded in Russia, France and the USA. Indeed, it has been said that many an American Civil War general went into battle with his sword in one hand and his copy of Jomini's *Summary of the Art of War* in the other.

In John Shy's cogent analysis of Jomini's works – the *Expansion of War* – the author analyses the philosopher's influence on his own and succeeding generations. Much of his *Treatise* was available in German and Russian before 1812; Napoleon on St Helena praised Jomini's work, and whimsically informed Montholon that he would employ Jomini to run France's military education were an opportunity to arise. Even before the publication of his *Summary* in the late 1830s he was receiving glowing encomiums from such influential sources as William Napier – founder of British military history – and his 'Principles' were being taught at West Point over the Atlantic. Prussia's 'discovery' of Clausewitz in the 1860s, and Bismarck's and von Moltke's triumphs over Austria and then France by 1871, caused a strong swing towards the new *guru* at Jomini's expense, for nothing succeeds like success (and had not the humiliatingly defeated Napoleon III's military concepts been Jominian after all?); and the very obscurity of much of Clausewitz's semi-edited works (which Henderson alluded to) – especially in translation – may have further enhanced his popularity in some quarters, at least until 1918, although in the heyday of the

Second Reich there were German military writers such as Boguslawski and Yorck von Wartenburg who continued to advocate a Jominian approach to the study of war. In the USA of the 1890s Mahan deliberately set out to study sea power from the Jominian starting-point of basic 'principles', repeatedly stressing the need for offensive, concentrated naval action as the only way of securing and maintaining 'command of the seas'. And after the holocaust of the First World War there was a decided swing back towards the Jominian approach by Major-General Fuller and Captain Liddell Hart, whose concepts of armoured and mechanised warfare (major foundations for Guderian's concept of *Blitzkrieg*) were attempted formulae for achieving quick, decisive victory in the most economical fashion possible.

The same may be claimed of the majority of writers on the effects of bombing in the 1930s; everyone was seeking a quick, surgical method of resolving any future, large-scale conflict – and in this search there was little room for 'defensive, attritional, protracted and limited, non-Napoleonic, non-Jominian forms of military action', to quote John Shy. The attritional clash of mass armies as foreseen by Clausewitz, the 'Mahdi of Mass' as Liddell Hart dubbed him, was countered by a call for renewed emphasis on mobility, audacity and skill to outmanoeuvre, outwit and outthink the enemy – and above all to attack the nervous and circulatory systems of enemy strength. Do not these ideas ring equally true today? If the modern view of the relationship between war and politics owes more to the Clausewitzian than the Jominian concept, as do ideas on the fighting of nuclear, ultimate total warfare, then at the same time it can be asserted that any understanding of major conventional, sub-nuclear war is greatly aided by reference to the Jominian tradition. It has formed a major basis for much that has been written on warfare, and in my view will continue to do so.

To draw a few threads together, I propose to outline the nub of Jomini's doctrine by means of a quick analysis of the main thrust of his most influential work, *Précis de l'Art de la Guerre*. It begins – believe it or not – with a consideration of war as an instrument of policy – *not* therefore a Clausewitzian monopoly as a subject – examining its various forms: ideological, economic, popular, in aid of allies, in defence of the balance of power, and in order to assert or defend a country's rights. The second part is devoted to '*politique militaire*' – or domestic questions of military policy. In this Jomini tackles such subjects as how to preserve military morale in time of peace, how to ensure sufficient expenditure on defence, problems of recruiting and forming of reserves, of wartime finance, of command in war. On this last consideration Jomini advises against entrusting high command to a monarch (Napoleon III would have done well to heed that suggestion) and suggests that the commander should be '... a man of experience and courage, bold in battle and unshakeable in danger', backed by a chief of staff who should be '... a man of great ability, straightforward and loyal with whom the supreme commander can live in harmony'.

The third section considers the conduct of war. Jomini distinguishes five subject areas, but really confines himself to the study of only three — and one of those is mainly of only historical interest. The five are: *Strategy* — the most important area of his contribution; *Grand Tactics* — the conduct of battles — which being restricted to the consideration of Napoleonic examples is not of great modern relevance; *Logistics* — 'the practical art of moving armies', his second most important subject area; *Engineering* — by which he means 'siege warfare'; and lastly *Minor Tactics*: but in fact he devotes little space to either of these last two.

We need to examine his two main areas in more detail. Under *Logistics*, Jomini includes a discussion of the organisation and tasks of a General Staff: preparations for war, the preparations of alternative plans, the science of moving troops, the procurement of intelligence, the problems of supply and transport, of siting camps, depots and magazines, not to forget matters involving reinforcements, signalling and medical matters. Although he does not use the phrase, his concept of 'logistics' is much to do with the *science of war*. I feel the following quotation makes this clear: 'Napoleonic operations depended on clever strategic calculations, but their execution was indubitably a master-piece of logistics.' Even though Jomini's earlier writings pre-dated the railway era, whose impact on war would become very significant from the mid-nine-teenth century, and an increasing preoccupation for General Staffs (Moltke's Grand General Staff had its famous railway office for example), much of Jomini's analysis remained valid as a basis for staff duties down to 1914.

However, it was in the consideration of *strategy* that Jomini made what remains his most significant contribution — and his most lasting one — to the study of war. It was the main field for the operation of his principles of war. He defined strategy as '... the art of directing the greater part of the forces of an army on to the most important point of a theatre of war, or a zone of opera-tions'. Tactics — by way of contrast — was concerned with physically applying superior forces at the point of the battlefield on which the decisive blow must be delivered. Reverting to strategy, Jomini insists that great care must be exercised in selecting the true decisive point. Then a sound line of operations must be selected leading from the army's base to the selected decisive point or target. 'The great art of choosing these lines of operation,' he wrote, 'consists in making oneself master of the enemy lines of communication without compromising one's own.' This clearly depended on careful consideration of known enemy dispositions as well as geographical factors. But of course he proceeds to make these relatively simple concepts more diffuse by insisting that circumstances will inevitably affect the *type* of line of operations selected — basing them on 'interior', 'exterior', 'concentric' or 'eccentric' lines — and it is here that his love for diagrammatic representation gets the better of him. As for the correct selection of the 'decisive point', he advises that the enemy's flank and rear (or in other words ideally his lines of communication) are the best targets to attack; or – if sufficiently weak – his centre; but Jomini conceives that as a campaign develops these targets may alternate according to actual circumstances – citing the April to May stages of Napoleon's First Italian Campaign in support, where an initial 'break-in' through the Austrian-Piedmontese centre developed into a series of outflanking manoeuvres (some successful, others not) leading to the near-envelopment of the Austrians before the battle of Lodi in the Po valley.

Jomini is insistent that a line of operations must be spread as widely as possible in geographical terms so as to present several possible 'decisive targets' and thus keep the enemy guessing as to the true target for as long as possible. To achieve this Jomini soars off into the abstractions of chessboard warfare, weaving a hopelessly complex pattern of strategic lines, strategic points, objective points, strategic positions, strategic fronts, operational fronts, operational pivots, pivots of manoeuvre, zones of operations – all painstakingly defined and integrated in such a way as to baffle the simple soldier or fascinate, as Michael Howard has described him, 'the worst kind of intellectual soldier', citing the example of General Halleck, Abraham Lincoln's key military adviser for much of the American Civil war.

All this detail provides a huge analytical vocabulary of military terms – many of them still to be found in direct or derivative use to the present day. These are the aspects of Jomini, together with his geometrical obsession, that are seized upon by his critics to challenge his validity. Even worse, they sadly have had the effect of obscuring his important point – possibly the most important – that the *objective* is always the *enemy's army* – and that *battles are vital to the gaining of victory* – this in direct contradiction of certain assertions by Saxe and Lloyd in the mid-eighteenth century and of Russell Weigley in the late twentieth. I commend the further study of the Swiss soldier's, Jomini's, views in relation to its relevance to the study of modern warfare.

EPILOGUE:
NAPOLEON THE MAN

To write concisely on a large subject is no easy matter, as I have already observed. So when in 1987 the president of the *Napoleonic Society of America*, Robert M. Snibbe of Belleair, Florida, challenged his membership to write a description of *Napoleon the Man* in no more than 275 words, I felt compelled to make the attempt, and accordingly entered the competition. After (to that point) some twenty-seven years of intermittent study of that 'great, bad man' (to borrow Lord Clarendon's description of Oliver Cromwell which I still find best sums up my own considered opinion of 'the Man of Destiny' or 'Corsican Ogre' – according to taste), and almost a dozen published books written on the man or aspects of his period – perhaps a million words in all – I felt that such a test of *reductio ad absurdum* would be good for me to attempt. The result of my not inconsiderable labours were the lines that follow – which in due course earned me the 'silver medal award' of the NSA.

In youth he cut an unprepossessing figure – short
In stature, awkward in gait, quaint in speech.
Nicknamed '*paille-au-nez*' at Brienne, a decade
later Parisian *cocottes* dubbed him 'puss-in- boots'.
'How funny he is, this Bonaparte,' opined Josephine.

Yet, as many discovered, his compelling grey-eyed
gaze could put a soul in thrall. Napoleon
was charisma personified. 'So it is that I,'
admitted the embittered, feared, war-hardened General Vandamme,
'who fears neither God nor Devil, trembled like
a child when I approached him.' 'A moment
later he put on his general's hat', recalled
Massena, 'and seemed to have grown two feet.'
In 1815 even the crew of HMS *Northumberland*
succumbed to the stout little Emperor's magnetic appeal:
here was a man of powerful personality indeed.

Feared in war, admired in council, Napoleon was
ever the supreme opportunist. A workaholic, his intellectual
powers knew few limits until, latterly, delusion clouded
reality. Millions died – but there was an outstanding
creative achievement too, in lasting codes of law,
systems of education, and commerce. As Talleyrand observed:
'He knows all; he does all; he can
do anything'. Yet, as Minister Molé perceived: 'Although
Napoleon's common sense amounted to genius, somehow he
never quite knew where the possible left off'.

Napoleon was – with lapses – a loyal husband, an
affectionate step-father and a doting parent to
his infant son, but callous to his staff.
Ruthless and cunning in debate, he waged warfare
pitilessly, yet spoke much of peace, *Pax Napoleonica*.
Was he a good or evil man – or
both – a 'great bad man' as Clarendon said
of Cromwell? Perhaps. But he indelibly marked History.

BIBLIOGRAPHY BY CHAPTER

CHAPTER 1. THE ORIGINS OF THE REVOLUTIONARY AND NAPOLEONIC WARS

This subject has been most comprehensively treated up to the Peace of Amiens in T.C.W. Blanning, *The Origins of the French Revolutionary Wars* (London, 1986), which includes a comprehensive bibliography. A.J.P. Taylor's chapter in *How Wars Begin* (London, 1979) is particularly useful in extending the subject to the Napoleonic Empire period in his first case study. Two older volumes, Sir John Fortescue, *British Statesmen of the Great War* (Oxford, 1911), and R.B. Mowat, *The Diplomacy of Napoleon* (London, 1924) are still useful on their subject areas, as are the more modern treatments of the causation of subsequent wars of the period, especially A.B. Rodger, *The War of the Second Coalition* (Oxford, 1964), and the celebrated trilogy by Piers Macksey: *The Strategy of Overthrow, 1789–99* (London, 1974), *War without Victory, The Downfall of Pitt, 1799–1802* (London 1984) and *The War in the Mediterranean, 1803–10* (London, 1957). On the British view of the wars from the breakdown of the Peace of Amiens to Waterloo, see C.D. Hall's recent study, *British Strategy in the Napoleonic War, 1803–15* (Manchester, 1992), while Albert Sorrel, *L'Europe et la Révolution Française* (Paris, 1913) remains very useful for the French point of view, as does Arthur Lévy, *Napoléon et la Paix* (Paris, 1902); Georges Lefebvre, *Napoleon*, English translation in 2 vols (London, 1969) is also a seminal work. On the whole subject of the causation of wars in general see Geoffrey Blainey, *The Causes of Wars*, (Melbourne, 1977), A.J.P. Taylor, *op. cit.*, and Raymond Aron, *Peace and War* (Princeton, 1966). Particularly full of insights into French politics leading to war in 1792 is H. Michon, *Essai sur l'histoire du parti Feuillant* (Paris, 1924); for the Austrian, German and Prussian views see A.R. von Arneth (ed.) *Joseph II und Leopold von Tuscana; Ihr Briefwechsel von 1781 bis 1790* (Vienna, 1879), L. von Rancke, *Ursprung und Beginn der Revolutionkriege, 1791–2 (Leipzig, 1879), and K. Heidrich, Preussen im Kampfe gegen die französische Revolution bis zur zweiten Teilung Polens* (Stuttgart and Berlin, 1908).

CHAPTER 2. THE RECONQUEST OF EGYPT: THE BRITISH VIEW

The best available British account of Napoleon's conquest of Egypt is still C.J. Herold, *Bonaparte in Egypt* (London, 1963), backed by the relevant chapters in A.B. Rodger, *The War of the Second Coalition* (Oxford, 1964). The most important documentation for the development of British policy is contained in the *Papers of Hendry Dundas* (held at Duke University Library, N.C.) and those of *William Wyndham, Baron Grenville* to be found in *The Dropmore Papers* (British Library, London). The naval operational side is well covered in two Navy Records Society volumes, namely *The Private Papers of Earl Spencer*, four vols, (London 1919–24) and *The Keith Papers*, vol. 2, (London, 1950), together with *The Dispatches and Letters of Lord Nelson*, vol. 3 (London, 1845) for the earlier period (1798 to 1800). For the military side we are still mainly dependent on Sir John Fortescue, *History of the British Army*, vol. 6, (London, 1912). The first two Macksey volumes cited under Chapter 1 above have much of relevance, and may be supplemented by Lord Liverpool, *The Swedish Knight* (London, 1964), a biography of the mercurial and controversial Commodore Sir William Sydney Smith.

CHAPTER 3. THE EGYPTIAN CAMPAIGN OF 1801

Besides the *Dundas* and *Dropmore Papers* cited for Chapter Two above, *The Diaries of Sir John Moore* ed. J.F. Maurice (London, 1904), vol. 1, are of central importance. Carola Oman, *Sir John Moore* (London, 1953) remains the standard biography of the commander of the assault landing. As for the writings of other participants, J. Morier, *Memoir of a Campaign with the Ottoman Army in Egypt*, (London, 1801), Lt. Col. C.G. Gardyne, *The Life of a Regiment* (the Gordon Highlanders), (London, n.d.) and Sir Charles Bunbury, *History of the British Expedition to Egypt* (London, 1854), are still significant, as is James Moore's two-volume *Life* of his brother (London, 1834). *The Keith Papers* vol. 2, (Navy Records Society, London, 1950) are of importance for the light they throw on Army/Navy cooperation, 1800–02, for once successful. Further work on this area is required.

CHAPTER 4. ADJUSTING THE RECORD: NAPOLEON AND MARENGO

The basic French documents are to be found in *La correspondance de Napoléon 1er*, vols 6, 28 and 30 (Paris, 1858–70) and in Capt. J.R.M. de Cugnac, *La Campagne de l'armée de réserve en 1800*, two vols, (Paris, 1900); the latter contains many of the verbal depositions taken by the *Dépôt de la Guerre* and later suppressed on Napoleon's orders for the reasons discussed in this chapter. Of considerable interest (but highly inaccurate), is the 'official' account by Napoleon's Chief of Staff, the *de jure* but not, of course, *de facto* commander of the French Army throughout the 1800 Campaign, Louis Alexandre Berthier, *Rélation de la*

Bataille de Marengo (Paris, 1806). A good overall account of events in Italy, 1800, is Sir John Adye, *The Napoleon of the Snows* (London, 1931). The first full examination of Napoleon's rewritings of the battle record is to be found in Général H. Camon, *Génie et métier chez Napoléon* (Paris, 1930). More work is presently in progress on the Austrian and Italian viewpoints.

CHAPTER 5. THE NAPOLEONIC MARSHALATE

There have been numerous studies of 'the twenty-six' or *les gros bonnets* (the 'big hats') as the subalterns of the French armies dubbed them. The most significant reference works are both by G. Six, his classic *Dictionnaire biographique des généraux et amiraux français de la Révolution et de l'Empire*, two vols (Paris 1934), and his equally important *abrégé* (published after his death) *Les généraux de la Révolution et de l'Empire* (Paris, 1947) which analyses his findings drawn from the earlier work. For a good read (but factually very unreliable) there is A.G. Macdonnell, *Napoleon and his Marshals* (London, 1934); far more reliable is M le Duc de Lévis-Mirepoix (ed.), *Les Maréchaux de France*, (Casablanca, 1960) which places the Napoleonic Marshalate in its overall setting, while R.F. Delderfield, *The March of the Twenty-Six* (London, 1962) and R. Humble, *Napoleon's Peninsular Marshals*, (London, 1973) are both useful. P. Young, *Napoleon's Marshals*, (London, 1973) is a valuable aide-mémoire based upon Six's two-volume work. Also valuable is L. Chardigny, *Les Maréchaux de Napoléon*, (Paris, 1977), as is a series of articles published in the bi-monthly journal *Le Souvenir Napoléonien* during the 1970s. On most of the individual marshals there are many books (details of which can be found in the *Biographical Notes* appended to each chapter in D.G. Chandler (ed.), *Napoleon's Marshals*, (London & New York, 1987). The shadowy Marshal Pérignon still awaits an individual biography. Also to be noticed, and possibly the latest French aide-mémoire on the subject, is Jacques Jourquin, *Dictionnaire des Maréchaux du Premier Empire* (Paris, 1986).

CHAPTER SIX. NAPOLEON'S MASTERPIECE: AUSTERLITZ, 2 DECEMBER 1805

When preparing my own short work on the subject (for the *Osprey Campaign Series*), I found the massive documentation to be found in J. Colin, *La Campagne de 1805 en Allemagne*, five vols, (Paris, 1902–08) of the first importance although, strangely, the coverage ends in mid- November 1805 and thus does not reach the climacteric battle. C. Manceron, *Austerlitz*, (Paris 1962 & 1966) is readable but rather disappointing. Perhaps the best full monograph devoted to both the campaign and battle remains C.J. Duffy, *Austerlitz*, (London, 1977) which benefits from the use of many Russian sources. For the Austrian point of view there is the reprint of General Stutterheim, *A Detailed Account of the Battle of Austerlitz*, (Cambridge, 1985). Probably the best account by a low-ranked participant is *The Note-books of Captain Coignet*, (latest reissue, London, 1986); *Note-book Four* (which includes the coverage of 1805) is included as the 'Campaign Book' in the video *Austerlitz, 1805 – Napoleon's Greatest Triumph* issued by Cromwell Productions, (Stratford-upon-Avon, 1993).

CHAPTER SEVEN. COLUMN VERSUS LINE: THE CASE OF MAIDA, 1806

Central to the study of this subject and to the thrust of this particular lecture are three volumes by, or linked to, the great historian Sir Charles Oman. His original paper, *An Historical Sketch of the Battle of Maida*, given on 28 November 1907, is printed in *The Journal of the Royal Artillery Institution*, vol. 34 (1908). Subsequently, it reappeared in Oman's *Studies in the Napoleonic Wars*, (London, 1929, facsimile reprint 1987). Oman's *Wellington's Army*, 1809–1814 (London, 1913, facsimile reprint 1986) is also relevant as it reflects on the tactical antecedents of the Peninsular Anglo-Portuguese army, including Stuart's short south Italian campaign of 1806, and in a footnote on p. 78 Oman partially retracts his earlier statement that the French fought in column there. This, however, he did not mention in his later *Studies, op. cit.*. Richard Glover, *Peninsular Preparations: the Reform of the British Army, 1795–1809*, (Cambridge, 1963) is most helpful. An important article on Maida by James R. Arnold appeared in *The SAHR Journal* vol. LX, no. 224, (Winter edition, 1982) entitled *A Reappraisal of Column versus Line in the Napoleonic Wars*, which in part reflected and further inspired a controversial and lengthy correspondence in the American journal, *Empires, Eagles and Lions*, particularly in issues nos. 56, 58, 60, 61, 65 and 68.

For the Maida campaign and battle as such, see Sir John Fortescue, *History of the British Army*, vol. 5, (London 1910, and 2nd edn 1921). The British view figures strongly in J. Anderson, *Recollections of a Peninsular Veteran*, (London, 1913), C. Boothby, *Under England's Flag from 1804 to 1809*, (London, 1900) and Sir Henry Bunbury, *Narratives of some Passages in the Great War with France*, (London, 1854). The French experience will be found in Lieutenant Grisois, *Le Combat de Maida*, an article in *Le Spectateur Militaire* (Paris, 1828), and in the unpublished *Correspondance du Général Reynier ... du 11 février 1806 au 29 décembre 1807*, to be found in the *Archives de la Guerre* at Vincennes under *Registre* No. C5/31. J. Rambaud, *Naples sous Joseph Bonaparte*, (Paris, 1911) is also useful, as is the latest work devoted to the subject, namely P.G. Griffith, *Column and Line*, (London, 1981).

CHAPTER EIGHT. THE BATTLE OF SAHAGUN, 1808

Basic reading for this subject is to be found in Sir John Fortescue, *History of the British Army*, vol. 6, (London, 1910) and above all in Sir Charles Oman, *History of the Peninsular War*, vol. 1, (Oxford, 1902), which is fully referenced. Of great importance are two contemporary accounts, H.C. Wylly (ed.), *A Cavalry Officer in the Corunna Campaign, 1808–09: the Journal of Captain Alexander Gordon*, (London, 1913); and Lord Cannock (ed.), *The Diary of the Adjutant of the XVth Hussars*, published by the *SAHR* in 1936 as 'Special Publication no. 4'. Lord Anglesey's biography of his ancestor, *One-Leg*, (London, 1961) is also useful. On cavalry matters in general see J.S. Lawford (ed.), *The Cavalry*, (London, 1976); and, rather dated but still of use, G.T. Denison, *A History of Cavalry*, (London, 1877, reissued 1913). L. Cooper, *British Regular Cavalry*, (London, 1965) provides an excellent overview, as does more recently P. Warner, *The British Cavalry*, (London 1984).

CHAPTER NINE. WELLINGTON IN THE PENINSULA: A REASSESS-MENT

The basic source of information is the vast *Dispatches of Field Marshal the Duke of Wellington,* 13 vols edited by Lt. Col. Gurnwood (London, 1837–39), supported by *The Supplementary Despatches and Memoranda*, 15 vols jointly-edited by the Second Duke of Wellington and Gurnwood, (London, 1857–72). A useful selection from these is A. Brett-James (ed.), *Wellington at War*, (London, 1961). S.G.P. Ward's two books, *Wellington's Headquarters*, (Oxford, 1957) and *Wellington*, (Oxford, 1963) are of central importance to this study. Of more recent biographers of the Duke, see Lady Longford, *Wellington, the Years of the Sword*, (London, 1969) and Lawrence James, *The Iron Duke*, (London, 1992) – the first a very good account, the latter a competent if somewhat conventional retraversal of the Duke's military career. Also important are *The Creevey Papers*, ed. J. Gore, (revised edn London, 1963). For the French point of view, see Comte M. Dumas, *Souvenirs, 1770–1836*, two vols, (Paris, 1839) and Maréchal E. de Castelanne-Novejean, *Memoirs*, two vols, (London, 1950) which are both revealing on the scale of French counter-insurgency operations and the mental strains engendered by the bitter guerrilla war placed atop the conventional struggle against Wellington. A modern, overall French account is to be found in H. Lachouque, Tranie and Carmigniani, *Napoleon's War in Spain*, (English trans., London, 1982). See also bibliography for the following chapter.

CHAPTER TEN. WELLINGTON AND THE GUERRILLAS

Apart from frequent references in Sir Charles Oman, *A History of the Peninsula War*, seven vols (London, 1902–14), the Spanish guerrilla struggle has never been the subject of a monograph. Hopes that the mass of new Wellingtonian papers deposited at Southampton University Library in the 1980s might help supply the deficiency have to date proved in vain. There is a very useful chapter in Jan Read, *War in the Peninsula*, (London, 1977), and a thought-provoking article by Jac Weller in the *Royal United Service Institute Journal*, May 1963 issue, but otherwise the researcher has to rely on small passages here and there. For the French point of view there is no lack of evidence in almost every Peninsular

War memoir. Foremost amongst these are M. Dumas and E. de Castelanne-Novejean (as cited for Chapter Nine above), together with A.J.M. de Rocca, *In the Peninsula with a French Hussar*, (English translation of original title, *Memoirs on the French War in Spain*, London, 1815; reissued under new title in 1991) and Général A. Bigarré, *Mémoires du ... Aide-de-Camp du Roi Joseph*, (Paris, n.d.). A recent view based upon a mass of Spanish sources, championing the claims of the Spanish regular forces is C.J. Esdaile, *The Spanish Army in the Peninsular War*, (Manchester, 1988), and an article qualifying the importance of the guerrillas – 'Heroes or Villains?' – by the same author appeared in *History Today*, April 1988 issue. Much work remains to be done in this area.

CHAPTER ELEVEN. THE RUSSIAN ARMY AT WAR, 1806 AND 1812
Preparing this subject I turned particularly to the published reminiscences of Sir Robert Wilson, that 'very slippery fellow' as Wellington dubbed him, attached as an observer (official or self-appointed) to the Tsar's armies during parts of the wars of the Fourth and Sixth Coalitions against Napoleon. His *Brief Remarks on the Character and Composition of the Russian Army* (London, 1810), and his *Narrative of Events during the Invasion of Russia by Napoleon Bonaparte ...'* (London, 1860), contain many first-hand observations and critiques. A. Brett-James (ed.), *General Wilson's Journal, 1812–14*, (London, 1964), is also of great value. Two rather dated biographies of Wilson are: H. Randolph (ed.), *The Life of General Sir Robert Wilson*, two vols, (London, 1862); and G. Costigan, *Sir Robert Wilson – A Soldier of Fortune in the Napoleonic Wars*, (Madison University Press, 1932). Since my piece was first written in 1970 an important addition to Wilsonian literature has been the biography by M. Glover, *'A Very Slippery Fellow'*, (London, 1977). Further valuable information, (above all, illustrations of Russian soldiers), is to be found in the Osprey *Men-at-Arms* series, nos 185 (1. Russian Infantry) and 189 (2. Russian Cavalry). See also the bibliographies for Chapters Twelve and Thirteen below).

CHAPTER TWELVE. BORODINO: 1812
There is a wealth of treatments on Napoleon's invasion of Russia, starting with C. von Clausewitz, *The Campaign of 1812 in Russia* (reprinted, London, 1992). Général P. de Ségur, *History of the Expedition to Russia*, (latest edition, retitled as *Napoleon's Russian Campaign*, Westport, Conn., 1959) is also useful, but needs using with caution. The most significant treatment is still Général A.A. de Caulaincourt, *Memoirs*, vol. one, (London, 1950) – a true classic which has led to many reconsiderations; while Heinrich Vossler, *With Napoleon in Russia*, (London, 1969) gives a Württemberger's dramatic recollections.

Of secondary works, many documentary sources and tables of information are to be found in G.F. Nafziger, *Napoleon's Invasion of Russia* (Novato, California and London, 1988 & '90), and another recent work is Richard K. Riehn,

1812: Napoleon's Russian Campaign, (New York, 1990). For a good selection of first-hand accounts see A. Brett-James, *1812* (London, 1966), and above all, P. Britten Austin, *1812: The March on Moscow* (London, 1993), a distillation of over 100 memoirs and journals. On the major battle of the campaign see C.J. Duffy, *Borodino: Napoleon against Russia, 1812*, (London, 1972) – which uses many Russian and German sources. A perceptive biography of Barclay de Tolly (the Tsar's minister of war and sometime commander-in-chief before Borodino) is M. & D. Josselson, *The Commander*, (Oxford, 1980). On the campaign the best modern Russian account is P.A. Jiline, *Gibel, Napoleonovskoi Army S Rossy*, (new edition, Moscow, 1974), and the same author's *Kutusov*, (Moscow, 1982), is the standard biography of Kutusov – both works requiring some caution as reflecting some Soviet bias of their era. The best available life in English is R. Parkinson, *The Fox of the North*, (London, 1976). Also consult the bibliography for Chapter Eleven.

CHAPTER THIRTEEN. RETREAT FROM MOSCOW

With the exception of the volume by P. Britten Austin (which only takes the French as far as Moscow), all the works cited for the last chapter above are equally relevant to this chapter; in the cases of Caulaincourt and de Ségur (in the original English edition of 1825) their second volumes refer. Caulaincourt's recollections (recorded each night) of Napoleon's musings during the long journey back to Paris from Smorgoni are especially important. To this must be added *The Memoirs of Sergeant Bourgogne, 1812–1813*, (London, 1979) – particularly important for a survivor's vivid recollections of the long retreat. A selection from these memoirs are included in the video-book package by Cromwell Productions Ltd, *Napoleon – the Road to Moscow*, (1992). Also to be consulted are R.F. Delderfield, *The Retreat from Moscow*, (London, 1967), and N. Nicolson, *Napoleon 1812*, (London, 1986). It is to be hoped that Paul Britten Austin will in due course complete his *magnum opus*, which he accurately terms 'a word-film', with a full treatment of this horrendous retreat.

CHAPTER FOURTEEN. AN UNDERGROOM AT WAR: EDWARD HEALEY, 1815

Edward Healey's recently discovered *Journal* is a first-hand account of a young lad's adventures as a junior servant of Wellington's head of intelligence during the Waterloo campaign, and as such stands by itself. Only a sample of his *Journal* has been included here, but the full edited manuscript – less his highly inaccurate, derivative account of Waterloo itself which is valueless – is to be found in the *Journal of the Society for Army Historical Research*, vol. LXIV, summer and autumn numbers, 1986.

Books on Waterloo itself are, of course, legion. Here I would only mention an almost random selection. A.F. Becke, *Napoleon and Waterloo*, (one-vol. edition, London, 1936, and two-vol. edition, London, 1914), remains amongst the best. For a volume of useful extracts from contemporary accounts (British, French and German) see A. Brett-James, *The Hundred Days*, (London, 1964). French views of the campaign and battle are to be found in H. Houssaye, *1815 – Waterloo*, (Paris, 1898) and H. Lachouque, *Waterloo* (Eng. edn, London, 1975). E. Kaulbach has provided a Prussian view in Lord Chalfont (ed.), *Waterloo, Battle of Three Armies*, (London, 1979), but P. Hofschröer's forthcoming book, *Waterloo – a German Victory* will indubitably supplement this. Jac Weller's analysis, *Wellington at Waterloo*, (London, 1967, reissued 1992) is most thought-provoking. The most recent books are G. Wootten, *Waterloo, 1815*, (no. 15 in Osprey's *Campaign Series*, London 1991) a very useful retraversal of the subject, and in A. Schom, *One Hundred Days – Napoleon's Road to Waterloo*, (New York, 1992), particularly useful for the political background.

Still of use, although inaccurate in detail, is W. Siborne, *The Waterloo Campaign, 1815*, (two vols 1844, one vol. 1848, 1900 and reissued 1990); this leads to his son's volume, H.T. Siborne (ed.), *The Waterloo Letters* (London, 1891, reissued 1983 and 1993), a selection of the first-hand accounts used by his father in the preparation of both his celebrated models of the battle – presently to be seen at the National Army Museum, Chelsea, and (the smaller one) at Dover Castle – and his monograph. It should be noted that Siborne *père's* validity on many points of detail has recently been challenged by D.C. Hamilton-Williams in his *Waterloo – New Perspectives – the Great Battle Reappraised* (London, 1993). Two volumes of essays are P. Griffith (ed.), *Wellington Commander: the Iron Duke's Generalship*, (Chichester, 1984), and A.J. Guy (ed.), *The Road to Waterloo* (Alan Sutton, Stroud – for National Army Museum – 1990). Cromwell Productions Ltd have produced the book and video pack entitled *Waterloo*, based on Cavalié Mercer's *Journal of the Waterloo Campaign* (London, 1927 edn). See my *Waterloo – The Hundred Days* (London, 1980).

CHAPTER FIFTEEN. HOW WARS ARE DECIDED: NAPOLEON – THE FALL OF A GIANT?

A.J.P. Taylor, *How Wars End*, (London, 1985) gives as usual a spirited and controversial analysis and very personal point of view. Raymond Aron, *Peace and War* (Princeton, 1970) has a very philosophical approach which merits close consideration, although he is not the easiest of authors to follow. T.N. Dupuy, *Understanding Defeat*, (New York, 1990) has a far more pragmatic approach to the subject. A.B. Rodger, *op. cit.* bibliography for Chapter One, has a valuable final chapter on the making of the Peace of Amiens (written by Dr C.J. Duffy to complete the work after its author's death). R.F. Delderfield, *Imperial Sunset* (London, 1968) traces the fall of Napoleon through the War of German Liberation (1813) and the short but brilliant Campaign of France (1814), so well portrayed by Henri Houssaye, in his *1814*, (Paris, 1888). Caulaincourt (as cited in the bibliography to Chapter Thirteen above), vol. 3, is of the greatest importance – revealing for the first time Napoleon's attempted suicide at Fontainebleau at the time of his first abdication. The French view of Napoleon's last weeks in France and then last years on St. Helena has been faithfully portrayed by Gilbert Martineau in (to cite the English translations) *Napoleon Surrenders*, (London, 1970), *Napoleon's Last Journey*, (London, 1972) and *Napoleon's St. Helena*, (London, 1967).

Posterity's verdict on the Emperor has been mixed. A superb survey, taking the subject down to 1945, is Pieter Geyl, *Napoleon, For and Against*, (London, 1948, reissued in paperback, 1987). The subject is also extensively treated in Jean Tulard's *Napoleon – the Myth of the Saviour*, (Paris, 1977), which has an extensive bibliography and a useful discussion of on-going debates and areas needing further attention. The same author has also contributed *Napoléon à Sainte-Hélène*, (Paris, 1981) and many other works on the Emperor and his times, and is today's best-known and most influential – if slightly controversial – French scholar in the field.

CHAPTER SIXTEEN. NAPOLEON, CLASSICAL MILITARY THEORY AND THE JOMINIAN LEGACY

The debate concerning the relative status of Clausewitz and Jomini as interpreters of Napoleon's achievements in war has recently been reopened, largely due to Russell Weigley's *The Age of Battles*, (Indiana, 1991), which seriously queries the real value of what Clausewitz termed '*the bloody solution of the {political} crisis*'; and also to a lesser extent in John Keegan, *A History of Warfare* (London, 1993). The definitive edition of Clausewitz's great classic, *On War* is that jointly-edited by M.E. Howard and P. Paret (Princeton, 1976) – the first and most welcome re-translation of the German first edition published in 1832. A useful introduction to the prolific Prussian military *guru* is Michael Howard, *Clausewitz* (Oxford, 1983). A similarly helpful introduction to the almost equally fecund Baron Jomini is Xavier de Courville's short biography of that title (Lausanne, 1981), although one drawback is that it lacks a full bibliography. Antoine Henri Jomini's probably most influential work, *The Art of War*, was recently republished with a perceptive introduction by Charles Messenger (London, 1992). See also Michael Howard's analysis in *The Theory and Practice of War: Essays Presented to Captain B.H. Liddell Hart* (London, 1965), and John Shy's relevant chapter in the new edition by Peter Paret of *Makers of Modern Strategy* (Princeton, 1986). Russell F. Weigley's volume, *The Age of Battles* (Indiana, 1991), also repays careful study.

As to which interpreter of the Napoleonic wars will emerge the more favoured, only time will tell. For, as Professor Geyl stated in 1946, '... History is an argument without end'.

DAVID G. CHANDLER, D. LITT.

Qualifications and Academic Honours

Bachelor of Arts – Honours School of Modern History, Oxford University (1955)
Certificate of Education (towards Diploma) – Oxford University Department of
   Education (1956)
Master of Arts, Oxon (1960)
Doctor of Letters, Oxon (1991)
President, British Commission for Military History (1968–88)
President of Honour, BCMH (1988–   )
International Vice President, International Commission for Comparative Military
   History (1975–   )
Fellowships: Fellow of the Royal Historical Society (1966)
                     Fellow of the Royal Geographic Society (1968)
Awards: Gold Cross of Merit, awarded by the Polish Government in Exile 'For Services
               to Military History'
             National Service Medal, awarded by the British Legion 'For Crown and
               Country'

Teaching Positions

1960–61   Lecturer, Department of Modern Subjects, Royal Military Academy,
           Sandhurst
1961–69   Lecturer (1961–64), Senior Lecturer (1964–69), Department of Military
           History, Sandhurst
1969–80   Deputy Head of Department of War Studies, Sandhurst
1969–70   Mershon Visiting Professor in Military History, Ohio State University,
           USA
1980–94   Head of Department of War Studies, Sandhurst
1988   Mary Ann Northen Chair in Humanities, The Virginia Military Institute,
           USA
1991   Chair in Military Studies, USMC University, Quantico, Virginia, USA

Audio Visual Credits

1971–73   Military Adviser to BBC TV, *War and Peace*
1980   Historical Adviser to the Commonwealth War Graves Commission
1981–83   Military History Adviser to the Services Sound and Vision Corporation,
           Remagen, 1945 (1981) and *Battle of the Reichwald* (1983)

1992–   Military History Adviser to Cromwell Productions Ltd, *Campaigns in History* series

1992–93   Military Consultant to Seventh Art Productions (for Channel 4), *Great Military Leaders*

1993   Military History Consultant to BBC World Service, *From Hoplite to Harrier: a Radio History of Warfare*

AUTHOR'S PUBLICATIONS

A Traveller's Guide to the Battlefields of Europe (Editor)
UK: Hugh Evelyn, 1965; USA: Chilton, 1966; UK: Patrick Stephens, 1988, Thorson, 1990
The Campaigns of Napoleon
USA: Macmillan, 1967; UK: Weidenfeld & Nicholson, 1967
Robert Parker and Comte de Mérode-Westerloo: The Marlborough Wars
UK: Longmans, 1968; USA: Archon Books, 1968
Napoleon
UK: Weidenfeld & Nicholson, 1973; USA: Saturday Review Press, 1973
Marlborough as Military Commander
UK: Batsford, 1973; USA: Scribner, 1973
The Art of Warfare on Land
UK and USA: Hamlyn, 1974
The Art of Warfare in the Age of Marlborough
UK: Batsford, 1976; USA: Hippocrene, 1976; UK: Spellmount, 1990
A Dictionary of the Napoleonic Wars
USA: Macmillan, 1979; UK: Arms & Armour Press, 1979; USA: Simon & Schuster, 1993; UK: Greenhill, 1993
Waterloo: The Hundred Days
UK: Osprey, 1980; USA: Macmillan, 1980
An Atlas of Military Strategy (1618–1878)
UK: Arms & Armour Press, 1980; USA: Free Press, 1980
The Journal of John Marshall Deane
UK: Society for Army Historical Research, 1984
Sedgemoor 1685: An Account and an Anthology
UK: Mott, 1985; USA: St Martins Press, 1985
Napoleon's Marshals (Editor)
USA: Macmillan, 1987; UK: Weidenfeld & Nicholson, 1987
The Military Maxims of Napoleon (Editor)
UK: Greenhill, 1987; USA: Macmillan, 1987
The Dictionary of Battles (Editor)
UK: Ebury Press, 1987; USA: Holt, 1987
Battles and Battle-scenes of World War II
UK: Arms & Armour Press, 1989; USA: Macmillan, 1989
Land Battles of the Second World War (Editor)
UK: Colour Library Books, 1990
Austerlitz 1805
UK: Osprey, 1990

World War II on Land
UK: Mallard, 1990
The Illustrated Napoleon
USA: Holt, 1990; UK: Greenhill, 1991
Great Battles of the British Army as Commemorated in the Sandhurst Companies (Editor)
UK: Arms & Armour Press, 1991; USA: South Carolina University Press
Sandhurst: The Royal Military Academy – 250 Years
USA: Harmony House, 1991
Jena 1806
UK: Osprey, 1993
D-Day Encyclopaedia
(Editor, with Brig Gen J.L. Collins)
USA: Simon & Schuster, 1993; UK: Helicon Press, 1994
On the Napoleonic Wars
UK: Greenhill, 1994
The Oxford Illustrated History of the British Army (Edited, with Ian Beckett)
UK: Oxford University Press, 1994
'Flanderkin Serjeant': The Journal of John Wilson, 15th Foot (Editor)
UK: The Army Records Society, 1995

PUBLISHED CHAPTERS

'Blenheim, 1704' and 'The Development of Fortification', in *Great Military Battles*, ed. Cpt Cyril Falls. UK: Weidenfeld & Nicolson, 1964.

'The Campaign in Abyssinia, 1869', in *Victorian Military Campaigns*, ed. B.J. Bond. UK: Hutchinson, 1967; Tom Donovan, 1993.

'Marlborough's Army', in *A History of the British Army*, eds. P. Young and J.P. Lawford. UK: Arthur Barker, 1970.

'The Art of War on Land', in *The New Cambridge Modern History Vol VI*, UK: Cambridge University Press, 1970.

'Chronology of the English Civil Wars', in *The English Civil Wars – A Military Handbook*, eds. J. Tucker and L.S. Winstock. UK: Arms and Armour Press, 1972.

'Blenheim, 1704' and 'Austerlitz, 1805', in *The War Game: Ten Great Battles Recreated from History*, ed. Peter Young. With a Preface by Aram Bakshian. USA: Crescent Books, 1973.

'Abyssinian Adventure', in *The British Empire*, Part 44. UK: Time-Life Books, 1972.

'The Art of War', in *Readers Digest History of Man: The Last Two Million Years*. Readers Digest Association. USA: Readers Digest Association, 1973.

'The Cavalry of the Sun King', in *Cavalry*, ed. J.P. Lawford. UK: Sampson Low, 1976; Bobbs Merill, 1976.

'The Battle of Gazala, 1942', in *Great Battles of the Twentieth Century*. UK: Hamlyn, 1977.

'Capt. William Siborne and his Waterloo Models', in *The Road to Waterloo: The British Army and the Struggle Against Revolutionary France: 1793–1815*, ed. Alan J. Guy. UK: Alan Sutton, 1990; National Army Museum, 1990.

PUBLISHED ARTICLES

'The Egyptian Campaign of 1801', part I. *History Today*, vol. 12 (February 1962).

'The Egyptian Campaign of 1801', part II. *History Today*, vol. 12 (March 1962).

'The Campaign of 1704, 1, The March to the Danube'. *History Today*, vol. 12 (December 1962).

'The Campaign of 1704, 2, Operations Leading to the Battle of Blenheim'. *History Today*, vol. 13 (January 1963).

'From the Other Side of the Hill: Blenheim, 1704'. *Society for Army Historical Research Journal*, vol. 41 (June 1963).

'Napoleon's Battle System – An Examination of Napoleonic Strategy during the "golden years" of the First Empire'. *History Today*, vol. 15 (February 1965).

'Adjusting the Record: Napoleon and Marengo', part I. *History Today* vol. 17 (May 1967).

'Adjusting the Record: Napoleon and Marengo', part II. *History Today*, vol. 17 (June 1967).

'The Fight at Gazala, 1942'. *Purnell History of the Second World War*, vol. 3, no. 5 (1967).

'The Siege of Alicante: An Heroic Episode during the War of the Spanish Succession'. *History Today*, vol. 19 (July 1969).

'Borodino'. *History Makers* (1969).

'West Africa, Seizing the German Colonies'. *Purnell History of the First World War*, vol. 1, no. 13 (1969).

'Bombardment of the East Coast, 1914'. *Purnell History of the First World War*, vol. 2 (1969).

'The Russian Army at War, 1807 and 1812'. *History Today*, vol. 20 (December 1970).

'The Retreat from Moscow'. *History Makers*, (1970).

'The End in the Cameroons'. *Purnell History of the First World War*, vol. 3, no. 15.

'Cambrai, 1917'. *Purnell History of the First World War, vol. 6 (1971).*

'The National Army Museum'. *History Today*, vol. 22 (September 1972).

'Marlborough, Genius of Blenheim'. *The Observer Magazine* (1972).

'The Battle of Cambrai'. *The Observer Magazine* (1973).

'Marlborough as a Military Commander'. *Royal United Services Institute for Defence Studies Journal*, vol. 118, no. 3 (September 1973).

'With the Napiers in the Field'. *The Folio Magazine* (1973).

'Marlborough'. *British History Illustrated*, vol. 1, no. 1 (1974).

'The Battle of Sahagun, 1808'. *History Today*, vol. 24 (November 1974).

'Blenheim and the Campaign of 1704'. *British History Illustrated*, vol. 1, no. 5 (1974).

'Haunted Acres'. *History Today*, vol. 26 (November 1976).

'Salamanca, 1812'. *British History Illustrated*, vol. 2, no. 7 (1976).

'Siege Warfare in the Peninsula'. *Hinchcliffe-Hunt Journal* (1977).

'Aspern-Essling, 1809'. *War Monthly*, issue 43 (1977).

'Drill Books and Tactics'. *History Today*, vol. 31 (March 1981).

'Reenacting the Military Past'. *History Today*, vol. 31 (July 1981).

'The Historian and the Media'. *History Today*, vol. 31 (August 1981).

'Fluctuations in Strength of Forces in English Pay sent to Flanders during the Nine Years' War, 1688–1697'. *War and Society 1* (September 1983).

'Two Invasions That Never Came'. *Military History* (1983).

'The Fight at Gazala'. *Purnell History of the Second World War*, vol. 9, New Monthly Edition (1984).

'The Re-enactment Scene in England'. *Living History*, (1984).

'What is Military History?' *History Today*, vol. 34 (December 1985).

'The Secretary-at-War, 1689–97: His Position and Influence during the Campaigns of William III in Flanders'. *War and Society*, vol. 1, no. 5 (September 1987).

'The Battle of Sahagun, 1808'. *David Chandler's Age of Napoleon*, 1 (October 1987).

'The Emperor Napoleon's Brush with Cossacks'. *David Chandler's Age of Napoleon*, 1 (April 1988).

'The British Army in Egypt: March to September, 1801'. *David Chandler's Age of Napoleon*, 1 (August 1988).

'The Battle of Corunna'. *David Chandler's Age of Napoleon*, 1 (August 1988).

'England's Greatest Soldier'. *MHQ: The Quarterly Journal of Military History*, vol. 3, no. 1 (Fall 1990).

'Austerlitz'. *MHQ: The Quarterly Journal of Military History*, vol. 5, no. 2 (Winter 1992).

'L'Angleterre et la conquête de la Méditerranée'. *Samothrace*, no. 2 (Spring 1993).